JÄMAICA GENESIS

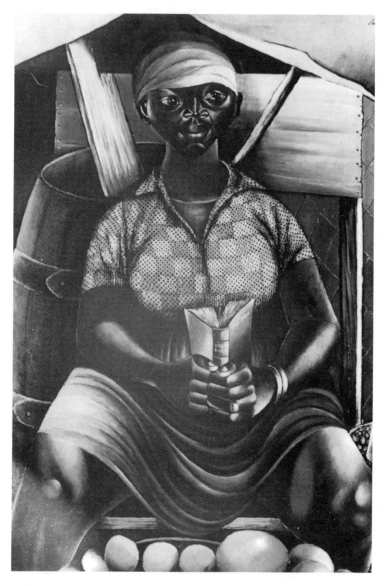

Osmond Watson, *The Laud Is My Shepherd.* Courtesy of the artist and the National Gallery of Jamaica, Kingston.

Diane J. Austin-Broos

JAMAICA GENESIS

— — — —

RELIGION AND THE POLITICS OF MORAL ORDERS

THE UNIVERSITY OF CHICAGO PRESS

CHICAGO AND LONDON

Diane J. Austin-Broos holds the Radcliffe-Brown Chair of Anthropology at the University of Sydney. Among her previous books is *Urban Life in Kingston, Jamaica,* (1984).

BR
1644.5
.J25
A97
1997

The University of Chicago Press, Chicago 60637
The University of Chicago Press, Ltd., London
© 1997 by The University of Chicago
All rights reserved. Published 1997
Printed in the United States of America
06 05 04 03 02 01 00 99 98 97   1 2 3 4 5

ISBN: 0-226-03284-1 (cloth)
        0-226-03286-8 (paper)

Library of Congress Cataloging-in-Publication Data

Austin-Broos, Diane J.
    Jamaica genesis : religion and the politics of moral orders /
Diane J. Austin-Broos.
        p.   cm.
    Includes bibliographical references and index.
    ISBN 0-226-03284-1 (alk. paper).—ISBN 0-226-03286-8 (pbk. :
alk. paper)
    1. Pentecostal churches—Jamaica.   2. Sociology, Christian—
Jamaica.   3. Jamaica—Church history—20th century.   4. Jamaica—
Religious life and customs.   I. Title.
BR1644.5.J25A97   1997
289.9′4′097292—dc21   96-39540
                                                                    CIP

For my mother

Won't you help to sing
another song of freedom,
It's all I ever had,
Redemption Songs,
Redemption Songs.
                    Bob Marley

. . . it is impossible in my experience to understand black
culture and black civilization in the New World without
understanding the cultural role of religion . . .
                    Stuart Hall

CONTENTS

◆ ILLUSTRATIONS

FOREWORD

Diane Austin-Broos needs no introduction to specialist students of the Caribbean. Through a long series of publications firmly grounded in intensive field research, beginning in 1971 and continuing to the present, Professor Austin-Broos has enriched our knowledge of Jamaican society and culture through her deeply considered, and relentlessly probing, analyses. The present work is of wide general interest, bringing her study of Jamaican Pentecostalism to a point where it forces a reconsideration of Jamaican history and culture, but also suggests new ways of approaching the study of religious movements in the world of late twentieth-century transnationalism and raises provocative questions about politics in that milieu. It is deliberately situated in relation to the extensive body of work on religious movements in sub-Saharan Africa and invites consideration of Pentecostalism as a global phenomenon.

As Austin-Broos is the first to recognize, her analysis is both a culmination and a beginning—the culmination of a long process of personal discovery, and the beginning of an even longer process of comparative and historical research that will be suggested, even required, by this book.

One major theme around which her analysis is constructed is, at first glance, deceptively simple. Enslaved Africans, transported to Jamaica to labor on the sugar plantations, brought with them a meaningful set of beliefs and cultural practices that sustained them through the merciless regime of slavery and plantation society. Like others before her, Austin-Broos has attempted to capture the central elements of that cultural system, characterizing it as an ontology focused upon an ethic of eudemonism and healing and incorporating a process of magical rite that she, following authors such as Stanley Diamond and Roger Abrahams, refers to as "trick." This complex was profoundly modified by the experience of Jamaican slavery and by the cultural domination inherent in British colonialism, but it was sufficiently vibrant to present a challenge to the Christian missionary movement that emerged from the antislavery agitation of the late eighteenth century, to con-

tinue past emancipation itself in 1938, and to linger on into the later nineteenth century. The core denominations of the missionary movement all
came out of pietistic Protestantism—principally Methodists, Baptists, and
Congregationalists—and therefore out of a European tradition of radical individualism and uncompromising concepts of sin and responsibility that were
the very opposite of eudemonism, as Weber so graphically showed. An ontology very different from that encompassed by slave practices of African
origin.

Numerous scholars have dealt with this engagement of African and European culture, progressing from the fragmentation of trait analysis proposed
by Herskovits (1966) to the closely related notions of survivals and to speculative historical reconstruction of one kind or another. Only occasionally, as
in Edward Brathwaite's book *The Development of Creole Society in Jamaica, 1770–1820* (1971), has careful attention been paid to the dynamic of
creation of a specifically creole, or local, culture (Brathwaite 1971). The
strength of Austin-Broos's work is that her point of departure is detailed
ethnography—not speculative history—and a profound appreciation of the
complexity of the processes of cultural creation in the contexts of peripheral
capitalist societies. In a book entitled *Jamaica Genesis* there is bound to be a
certain amount of speculation and schematic rendering of historical events,
but that is clearly recognized. A full history of the struggle of nonconformist
missionaries has yet to be written; their struggle not only against the hostility
of planters reluctant to see their slaves emancipated in any sense of the term,
but also against the habits and customs of a people who had endured coer-
cion without losing a sense of the meaning and even the joy of life. The same
struggle was engaged in Britain, of course, for the ethic of methodical existence coupled with the repudiation of pleasures of the flesh was not eagerly,
or widely, embraced by a majority of ordinary people. Be that as it may,
Professor Austin-Broos is wholly convincing in her analysis of the way in
which a Jamaican creole religious discourse was created out of the confrontation of radically distinct cosmologies through practices intimately related
to the circumstances, the ecology, of the practitioners. And what makes her
analysis convincing is the fact that her starting point is the most detailed
account of Jamaican Pentecostalism yet to appear. As she puts it herself:

> The initial engagement between Africa and Europe in the domain of ritual
> practice I typify through a reading from within Pentecostalism. I look back
> from the vantage of Pentecostal practice, and the features of its Jamaican
> style, to discern the discourse that shaped that style. My method entails
> the view that this is not *the* history of Jamaican religion but, rather, a his-
> tory that can give an account, adequate in the domain of meaning, of how
> Pentecostalism became Jamaican (pp. 5–6).

The flavor of Weberian language and methodology is palpable and highly effective. The exploration of the second confrontation, between early Jamaican creole religious discourse in the form of Revival Zion, and the Pentecostalism that came from an increasing involvement with the United States reveals the social contexts into which that religious discourse flowed and to which it conformed. In the process, Austin-Broos raises a number of extremely important issues.

First is an issue long neglected in the analysis of Jamaican society: the crucial importance of north American influence in the shaping of Jamaican and, indeed, West Indian society. Those of us who worked in the West Indies during the formative period of Caribbean studies were preoccupied with the legacy of, and the struggle against, European colonialisms. Although the influence of North America upon Cuba and Puerto Rico was obvious enough, its impact on other territories was not given due weight, partly because of the fixation upon formal social structures and a failure to examine the overseas experience of ordinary West Indians, especially Jamaicans, caught up in the powerful currents of labor migration in the late nineteenth and early twentieth centuries. Austin-Broos skillfully documents that experience and its reverberations among the displaced within Jamaica itself, shifting the focus from some vague notion of "cultural influence" to very specific contexts of experience. And it is here that, in the past, she took up another theme that is of the greatest significance for the present analysis (see Austin-Broos 1991–92).

In 1938, riots and disturbances broke out in widely separated parts of the British West Indies. Generally interpreted as responses to the deteriorating economic conditions that radiated out from the industrialized centers affected by the Great Depression, these disturbances sparked hope that a revolutionary consciousness had finally emerged among the West Indian working class. However, building upon the work of Ken Post (1969), and others, Austin-Broos observes that Jamaica has never developed an effective class-based politics, even in the wake of the popular uprising of 1938. Departing significantly from Post's notion of the displacement and refocusing of consciousness on Africa, she suggests that it is a mistake to concentrate solely on the indeterminancy of class relations and the consequent failure of revolutionary class politics. Instead, one must examine other significant social movements that emerged or strengthened during this period, two of which endured beyond 1945.

Marcus Garvey's United Negro Improvement Association was in a terminal decline by the end of World War II. The back-to-Africa aspect of his movement, however, became an integral part of a small cult known as Rastafarianism, which developed an Old Testament explanation of the divinity

of the newly anointed emperor of Ethiopia, while Garvey's Black Nationalism became the common currency of West Indian nationalist movements.
The other major development during this period was the penetration into
Jamaica of North American Pentecostalism, which found its main appeal
among the urban poor and displaced rural migrants. Rastafarianism and Pentecostalism, for all their profound differences, are both deeply rooted in fundamentalist biblical Christianity, and both have had enormous influence in
Jamaica and beyond, even though they have not been embedded in formal
political movements. In his first work on the rebellion of 1938, *Arise Ye
Starvelings,* Post dismisses Rastafarianism as retreatism and fantasy even
though it addressed the racism of Jamaica's colonial social order. He also
ignores its religious dimension except as one form of the "Ethiopianism" that
appears in various forms throughout the history of African American society
(Post 1978). In a subsequent work, *Strike the Iron* (1981), he gives much
more recognition to Rastafarianism as an important part of the Black Nationalist consciousness of the Jamaican working classes, paying attention to both
its internal divisions and its relation to the dying embers of Garveyism. Pentecostalism is completely passed over by students of revolutionary politics
although it is "the largest social movement in Jamaica" with at least 60,000
active adherents and "its nominal adherents constitute a quarter of the population" (Austin-Broos 1991–92, p. 300; see also Appendix 1 of the present
work). However, Austin-Broos's argument is much more complex than a
mere headcount would suggest.

Skillfully drawing out the differences between Rastafarianism and Pentecostalism in terms of their gender significance, Austin-Broos points up the
manner in which women's participation in the labor force has been consistently underrecognized. While the role of women during the slave regime
has come to be appreciated, the fact that women constitute almost half of
the modern Jamaican laborforce and a third of household heads is curiously
neglected. As Austin-Broos says, "By and large these women are not union-
ized although they vote. If they have an organization, it is Pentecostalism.
But do they have a politics?" (Austin-Broos 1991–92, p. 302).

Rastafarianism, for all its prominent publicity, is a small, male-dominated
movement in which women are few in number and definitely subordinate.
With its militant rejection of participation in state politics (except for a small
and spectacularly unsuccessful faction), defiant behavior in dress, use of marijuana, and deification of the Emperor Haile Selassie, it has enjoyed symbolic but not numerical importance. Pentecostalism, on the other hand, as
this book shows in graphic detail, is overwhelmingly a women's organization
in spite of the formal leadership role of male deacons, pastors, and bishops.
The rhetorical question of whether Pentecostal women have a politics is an-

swered in the affirmative, of course, though Austin-Broos must concede that for all the joy and satisfaction it affords Pentecostal women, it is a politics of local significance only, with minimal impact on state politics, and empowerment of its adherents is largely countered by the wider context of racism in which it must exist.

Pentecostalism afforded a means for Jamaicans to step outside the constraints of the colonial hierarchy, with its stress upon conformity to "respectable" (that is, English) norms of marriage, family life, language, and dress. Through the north American connection it even afforded some measure of upward social mobility, especially for male pastors who were sponsored for training in the United States. Ironically, the larger regional system in which the United States is dominant turns out to be equally racist and equally confining. Discussing these issues in detail, Austin-Broos tries to show that the popular concept of resistance is hardly adequate to an understanding of the politics of this kind of religious expression. In spite of the sense of moral superiority that comes from the experience of being a Pentecostal Saint, and even because of the profound joy that is achieved during Pentecostal worship, the potential for social—as opposed to personal—transformation inherent in these movements seems to be small.

Pentecostalism is the most rapidly growing religious movement in Latin America and in other parts of the world where it similarly flourishes among populations displaced and marginalized by economic change. Whether it can be understood in the terms laid out here remains to be seen, but certainly this book invites comparative analysis along a number of dimensions. Especially valuable is the depth of the sympathetic understanding presented here, without which comparison remains vacuous. This book is about *Jamaican* Pentecostalism in all the social, economic and historical particularity from which comparison must proceed. It is tempting to the religiously "unmusical" (as Max Weber put it) like myself to suppose that the small Jamaican Pentecostal churches will follow a path similar to that taken by many small churches in the poor areas of the urban United States. That is, either they emerge, flourish for a while, and then disintegrate, or they become bigger and more prosperous as their congregations become upwardly mobile socially. In the latter case there is a marked tendency for the eudemonism described by Austin-Broos to become muted; excessive bodily motion is discouraged, glossolalia is more sedate, and political potential is merged into wider racial consciousness and movements. It is difficult to see such a development taking place within Jamaica itself, though there are indications in the book of similar attempts to modify forms of worship in churches with upwardly mobile congregations.

As long ago as 1965, Philip Mason, in a foreword to a book on Pentecos-

talism among West Indians in Britain (Calley 1965), warned against interpreting Pentecostalism either as compensation for poverty and marginality
or as resistance against oppression. He pointed out the many positive aspects
of Pentecostal community life and the fact that church members are frequently among the more prosperous of Jamaican migrants in Britain, not the
poorest. These positive aspects are certainly stressed here by Austin-Broos,
who moves away decisively from simple deterministic explanations in terms
of political economy. In that respect her work challenges some broader interpretations that see evangelical Christianity as a continuing projection of
the Puritan revolution, destined to accompany economic modernization and
eventual secularization. As David Martin has noted in his comprehensive
study of Pentecostalism in Latin America, Protestantism had traditionally
lacked the capacity to "go native." Until, that is, Pentecostalism brought "together the ancient layers of spiritism, in black Africa and indeed almost everywhere, with a modern sense of the union of psyche and soma. It brings
together the ancient notion of illness as located in the community with the
modern concept of community medicine. . . . Pentecostalism retains the participation found in the fiesta and unites that to a spiritual version of the contemporary encounter group" (Martin 1990, pp. 282–83). In this way Pentecostalism reverses the process of secularization and achieves what Martin
calls "The Latin Americanization of American Religion?" The question mark
is crucial, of course, but the observation fits well with Diane Austin-Broos's
analysis of Jamaican Pentecostalism.

Finally, the demonstrated correspondence between gender relations in
Pentecostal practice and the forms those relations take in the kinship system
throws new light on West Indian kinship. From a feminist point of view it is
as difficult to understand why Pentecostal women choose to exercise their
influence and power in nominal subservience to male pastors as it is to understand why the women who assume such a burden of responsibility for
keeping families together should defer to men as much as they do. This book
goes a considerable way toward rendering those gender relations intelligible
by showing exactly how they are mutually defining and mutually sustaining,
given the profoundly anti-egalitarian legacy of Jamaican history and the patriarchal features of biblical Christianity.

Jamaica Genesis demonstrates the power of ethnographic research combined with philosophical and theoretical understanding. Sustained and pene-
trating study of a limited but carefully chosen range of situations has enabled
Austin-Broos to explore the rich texture of lives that often seem cramped to
the casual observer. She discovers complex meanings and satisfactions that
have enabled many Jamaicans to endure much and to face an equally difficult
future with more confidence than material circumstances suggest. In refus-

ing to dismiss this confidence and endurance as mere political passivity, Austin-Broos has contributed to the empowerment of her informants and to the discernment of her readers.

Raymond T. Smith

University of Chicago
Autumn 1996

PREFACE

As I began to learn about Jamaican Pentecostals in the 1980s, my curiosity was heightened by two particular texts. These were Joseph Moore's 1953 doctoral dissertation on *The Religion of Jamaican Negroes* and George Simpson's 1956 monograph on "Jamaican Revivalist Cults." Both these accounts recorded the well-established presence of Pentecostalism in Jamaica's religious spectrum and presented data indicating that at least some Zion Revival groups had been influenced by elements of Pentecostalism. Both texts suggested a continuous world of revival religion that presented no absolute break between Zion Revival and Pentecostalism as they were practiced in Jamaica. On the other hand, as William Wedenoja (1978) indicates, it is true that the ritual styles of the two religions are different. In Zion Revival, possession rite in a major band presents an image of an elaborate cosmology in which each participant represents a part. Pentecostal possession rite involves forms that suggest a series of dyadic relationships between each individuated saint and the One God and his Holy Spirit. While the difference between Jamaican Pentecostal practice and its American counterparts should be acknowledged and addressed, it is also true that this religion signifies a further step away from a nineteenth-century embodiment of what it was to be West African in Jamaica. Zion Revival, or Revival, is significantly different from Pentecostalism, though both fall within the larger genre of New World revival religion.

These divergent aspects of Pentecostalism could be seen to present a puzzle unless it is understood that cultures both change themselves and also assimilate other forms of practice to their own continuing logics. Some Jamaicans with whom I spoke were antagonistic to the Pentecostal presence, while many others did not distinguish Pentecostals from other revivalists. These differing attitudes reflect the complexity of the cultural process involved. They are integral to the environment in which I worked with Jamaican Pentecostals, perhaps the ones least concerned by these forms of dilemma. For myself, the issue always has been to understand why so many

Jamaicans have been drawn to Pentecostalism and to understand this in a manner that addresses the dynamics of Jamaican culture, its power to interpret and assimilate new forms even when those forms are hedged about with regional power and influence. Other missionary churches of the early twentieth century, including the very successful Seventh Day Adventists, still have been markedly less successful than Pentecostalism in Jamaica. Others again, such as the Church of Christ, have remained minority churches. These variations suggest that something other than regional hegemony has been at work in the rise of Pentecostalism. Possibly, I postulated as I worked, Pentecostalism has carried with it meanings and forms of rite able to engage with a Jamaican world. Conversely, I also would learn that Jamaican religious have taken Pentecostalism in and re-rendered it for their environment. These considerations propelled me to an interest in the history of Pentecostalism in Jamaica and to an interest in Jamaican meanings in Pentecostal rite. These two concerns have remained the prominent ones in this book.

I sought to trace as much as I could of Pentecostal history in Jamaica in order to establish that this religion was not simply a product of the 1950s but had much deeper roots in Jamaica. That the Jamaican Pentecostal evangelist George White could fill Kingston's Ward Theater at the beginning of the 1930s, and have a photograph of the occasion published in the *Jamaica Daily Gleaner*, seemed something important to convey if Pentecostalism were to be addressed as a genre integral to twentieth-century Jamaican popular culture. I came to see that this event was made possible not only by Pentecostalism but also by a more diffuse revival culture and its religious discourse and poetics. Most of the historical work that I did was in the form of oral histories and collecting local published works from among the various churches. In addition to my field records of rite and other practice, these oral histories and the discussions I had with saints about Pentecostalism comprise the data on which my account is based. I cite sections of these interviews and records as data in the text. Elizabeth Pigou from the Department of History at the University of the West Indies in Mona helped me with newspaper research focused mainly through these oral histories. I owe her an enormous debt, as I do the Pentecostals, Holiness pastors, and Revivalists who assisted me: Dr. Joseph Byrd (in Cleveland, Tennessee), Reverend Milton Davidson (Kingston), Reverend Morris Golder (South Bend, Indiana), Bishop Lesmon Graham (Kingston) and his father, Percival "Pappi" Graham (Clarendon), Leader Henry Linton (St. Ann), Bishop Guy Notice (Kingston), Bishop D. B. O'Hare (St. Ann), Sister Russell, Jr. (Kingston), Reverend Adrian Varlack, Sr. (Cleveland, Tennessee), and numerous other Pentecostals in Kingston and the Clarendon hills especially.

The second major task was to typify, from an anthropological perspective, Jamaican meanings of Pentecostal rite. This was a complicated task, for the perspective of an outside observer engaged in cultural anthropology and not a Pentecostalist herself was always going to be at a tangent from the perspective of practitioners. Nonetheless, I hope that in the following text I have captured some Pentecostal meanings that are significant for all those involved. Certainly, I am extremely grateful to the many Pentecostalists who talked with me about their world and the meaning of their rite. In addition to those mentioned above, I wish to thank, in this particular respect, Bishop Ronald Blair of the New Testament Church (Kingston), and especially Reverends Carmen Stewart (Kingston), Verty Thompson (Clarendon), Herbert Malcolm (St. Ann), and Sister Sarah Rowe (St. Thomas), who assisted me beyond measure. I am acutely aware that Pentecostalists will not agree with all my conclusions. Yet I trust that the real respect and affection in which I hold their world are evident throughout the book.

Charles V. Carnegie and Connie Sutton read an earlier version of the manuscript and gave me very constructive advice as I began to refine the final work. Over the years, I have sustained a dialogue on Jamaican religion with Barry Chevannes that surfaces in my conclusion. Closer to home, I would like to thank John Cook and Ben Phillips for some very useful discussion in areas that pertain to this research. Jeannie Ellard read most of this work and gave me extremely helpful comment. Of course, notwithstanding this help, I bear full responsibility for the data presented here, and their interpretation.

David Brent at the University of Chicago Press has given me encouragement, and I am grateful to him. Various people have given me assistance in the course of research and in production of the manuscript. These include Frances Errington (in Cleveland, Tennessee), Judy Grant, Anne Robertson, and Robyn Wood. Maisie Staveley helped with photographs and maps, for which I am very grateful indeed. In addition to this Sydney support, I also thank Wendy Warren Keebler and Matthew Howard of the University of Chicago Press.

My final thanks go to Frank and Harry Broos, who have witnessed this particular labor with a certain phlegmatic tolerance which is possibly the best demeanor to assume with an academic in the house. Over the years that it has taken to put the book together, they have not complained although they might have, many times. To Nadine Isaacs—who would greet me at Kingston's Norman Manley Airport with the comment, "Oh, Di, back to go to church again!"—I give the thanks that is due to a very good friend.

Diane J. Austin-Broos

Sydney, 1996

INTRODUCTION

What was captured from the captor was his God . . .
—Derek Walcott, 1974

[Colonized people have] often *made of* the rituals, representations, and laws imposed on them something quite
different from what their conquerors had in mind; they
subverted them not by rejecting or altering them, but by
using them with respect to ends and references foreign to
the system they had no choice but to accept. They were
other within the very colonization that outwardly assimilated them; their use of the dominant social order deflected its power, which they lacked the means to challenge; they escaped it without leaving it.
—Michel de Certeau, 1984

Enter Pentecostalism

How to figure an American-derived religion that has captured a quarter of
Jamaica's population?[1] That is the conundrum that shaped this book. Ranged
beside Rastafarianism, Jamaica's cosmopolitan and critical religion, or the
local Zion Revival, Pentecostalism commonly is seen as the regional hegemony, an exogenous force antagonistic to the island's Caribbean culture.[2] Yet if
this alone is said of Pentecostal practice in Jamaica, it also should be said of
Jamaica's entire Christian world. Jamaica has a religious discourse defined
extensively by Christian lore. In fact, Jamaican culture as a whole is infused
with ideas of redemptionism derived from a Christian source. This source
was once external to Jamaica, or at least to the African cultures of the slaves.
It was introduced into Jamaica first by Spanish Roman Catholics and then by
the established Church of England. They were followed by sectarian missionaries, among them Americans of African descent.[3] If Pentecostalism is
simply hegemonic, so, too, were the early years of the larger discourse of
which it is a part.

But there is more to be said of both the present and the past. It is easy to
see that the early Jamaicans of African descent took Christianity and interpreted it, not dispelling its hegemonic aspects but muting, deflecting, and
redefining them in ways that created a Jamaican world. In the words of Dick
Hebdige (1979, 19), Christianity in Jamaica is a history of "struggle for possession of the sign." Or, again in the words of de Certeau, "use" changed

1

Christianity's meanings. The Jamaican practice of Pentecostalism conformed to a similar course soon after the religion was introduced in the second decade of the twentieth century (cf. Glazier 1980; Smith 1978; Wedenoja 1978, 1980). This process has diverged from the initial interpretations of Christianity. It is a different age, and Jamaicans today are a different people from the slaves of the early nineteenth century. In addition, Jamaicans through this century have been linked to the United States and Britain by extensive systems of communication that work against the constitution of a purely local knowledge. Near the end of the twentieth century, the process of indigenization is invariably a more muted affair than it was in the early nineteenth century. Nonetheless, Pentecostalism, like its Christian predecessors, has been interpreted in Jamaica and has become an extremely powerful nexus of Jamaican and Caribbean meaning.

I came to an interest in Pentecostalism and what it might mean to call it "Jamaican" through the practice of fieldwork. Preparing for the field, I took an interest in Jamaican religion, though not in Pentecostalism. In fact, I remained unaware of the Pentecostal presence in Jamaica. In the lower-class area of Kingston where I worked, there were no Rastafarian communes and just one Zion Revival band, which stayed for only a couple of years.[4] All over the neighborhood, however, there were large and small Pentecostal churches. They debated assiduously with one another and sometimes formed co-operating networks linked by the work of lower-class women, often guided by lower-class men. This complex of religious organizations became part of my field experience and drew me in through a mixture of interest, enjoyment, and disdain for its seeming intolerance. Having to buy myself a hat and strip myself of jewelry and cosmetics in order to go to church to listen to powerful sermons on sin was one aspect of my engagement. Another was the enjoyment involved in the music of this Pentecostalism, joyful choruses sung with verve that seemed part of the "nation language."[5] Close to the heart of my experience was meeting a number of women, women who maintained admirable lives despite their many adversities. On my first Christmas in Jamaica, I remember being hugged by such women, big, sturdy women in white who knew I was away from home. They sought to comfort me because their pastor had reminded them of those who were distant "from family and friends."[6]

Against a background of other such encounters and systematic fieldwork on religion, I was not surprised when a Jamaican friend converted to Pentecostalism. In fact, her progress into the church seemed to trace an exemplary path. I had met Winifred in 1972 when she was pregnant with her fifth child at the mere age of twenty-four. I was seeking neighborhood residents for a range of interviews. She told me with a smile, and with her large belly protruding, that I might as well interview her, because "me here, me not goin' anywhere, jus' livin' the sweetheart life." She and her common-law husband lived in a small apartment with their children. He worked in a mechanic's yard in a neighboring area. In subsequent years, Winifred bore two more children, changed her residence to a housing estate, obtained a loan, and bought a house with the help of the wages from her husband's new job. He had gained employment at a bauxite works near the inland town of Mandeville. Although she appeared to be in a good position, life became increasingly difficult for Winifred as her children grew. The children could not find work, and her eldest girl began having children of her own. Winifred's husband, she suspected, had started another household in Mandeville. He still returned to see the children, but his money was no longer shared around, and he was angry when she asked for it. She took in washing to make some money. By the time she was thirty years old, her elbows were grossly swollen with arthritis. She was thin and probably anaemic as well.

When her fifth child, a son, was born, she had asked me to be godmother and, perhaps in honor of my persona, chose a baptism in an Anglican church. We arrived, with neighborhood and family friends, all dressed in our very best. The child was duly baptized with names celebrating sports heroes. There was a crowd of mothers with babies to christen, and after the ceremony the rector picked out some mothers and asked them to sit at the front of the church. Winnie began to giggle and whispered to me words to the effect that the "preaching" was about to begin. The rector came and addressed the women on the desirability of marriage and the transgressions of Christian practice involved in the "sweetheart" or "concubinage" life. The young women sat there like schoolgirls and waited for the rector to finish. Winifred did eventually marry her common-law husband in order, she proposed, to help with the housing loan. They opened a joint account. Marriage secured a certain respectability which at first she expressed at the new estate by attending a conservative Brethren church. As life became more difficult, however, and as disappointment with her husband heightened, she increasingly complained of the "strict an' stern" Brethren. On a return visit in 1983, I found that Winifred had become a Pentecostal saint.[7] Rather than seeing her as having been defeated by events, I regarded this as, culturally, a natural course for a Jamaican woman of her circumstance.[8] Later, she went to New York to work in a domestic position secured through church associates. Marlene, her eldest daughter, was left in charge of the other children. Sometime thereafter, she secured residence and took most of her children to the United States. I tried to contact her in New York without success and also tried to trace her through relatives and friends. We did speak once by telephone, but I have not seen Winifred or my godson again, and I miss their company in Jamaica. Her life is the life of a Jamaican woman, and her religion is an integral part of it.

Creole Culture and Religious Discourse

This book is a study of the emergence of a Jamaican religious discourse of which Pentecostalism became a part during the twentieth century. In order to understand this process, I wish first to rehearse an argument proposed by Edward Kamau Brathwaite (1971) in his account of "creole society." That argument sees Jamaican culture as the product of "two cultures of people, having to adapt themselves to a new environment and to each other" (Brathwaite 1971, 307; cf. Bolland 1992). Brathwaite underlines that the "friction" between the initial cultures was not only "cruel" but also "creative." It generated a larger "continuum" of culture that would come to define a Jamaican world (cf. Smith 1967; Mintz and Price 1976). This continuum, with its referencing to Europe (and the United States today), leads some among the powerful and the weak to overlook the culture's creativity, to be "mimic men" of a foreign norm even while there unfolds in Jamaica a "rich folk culture" of enormous power (Brathwaite 1971). The juxtaposition of Africa and Europe, rather than of the Caribbean and both, has been a result of this oversight. Keen to establish African roots, scholars and laymen alike sometimes have overlooked the cultural creativity that finds its home in Jamaica itself.

By cultural creativity here, I do not mean always autonomous or even conscious creation but, rather, the re-contextualizing and new use of practices and knowledge that might be read as merely hegemonic. The construction of a pantheon for the early Zion Revival in which the spaces once reserved for African ancestors were taken over by Bible figures is one example of change through use. These biblical figures acquired new meanings while indisputably coming from the Book (cf. Wedenoja 1978). Another example of change through use is the interpretation of water baptism, and especially baptism by complete immersion. Rendered as a form of healing in early Jamaican Christianity, this rite had meanings more akin to an African tradition than to the intent of missionaries. The role of music as an embodiment of worship rather than as a frame for worship is a third example of ways in which use subverts the ostensible meaning of the sign and allows symbolic mediations unintended by the hegemonic force. Geertz, more than other anthropologists, has discussed the significance of use in meaning, the underlying Wittgensteinian point that meaning comes through the logic of practice (Geertz 1973a; Wittgenstein 1968). Geertz's object was to re-position the study of meaning in observable practice rather than solely in the categories of speech. De Certeau opens up a further concern when he observes that the significance of major symbolic representations can be assessed only when "we gauge the difference or similarity between the production of the image and the secondary production hidden in the process of utilization" (de Certeau 1984, xiii). The definitional power of meaning is mediated by its use both at different points in a milieu and across different times and social groups.

In his critique of de Saussurian accounts of meaning, Bourdieu takes up this issue of practice to show how it articulates with issues of power and status. The apparent universality of a language or religion rests on a social polysemy in which "the ideological effect of the *unification of opposites* or denial of divisions" comes at "the cost of *reinterpretations*" of a common discourse that harbors "different intentions and interests," interests that will be ranked nonetheless and invested with degrees of legitimacy by different orders of society (Bourdieu 1991, 40; see also 1984). Practice here also pertains to the incipient hierarchy of plantation society wherein, as Raymond Smith (1967) has observed, phenomena designated as "European" or "African" were ranked and attributed relative status within a larger system. Part of the meaning of such phenomena has involved their use as indices of positive or negative status, even when the status was contested or the practice— for instance, Zion possession—was attributed important and mysterious power. These acts become distinctions that through use have made them something Caribbean or creole rather than simply African (cf. Bourdieu 1984). Similarly, the act of mimicry in the colonial and neo-colonial context must rapidly become another act as it operates not merely to imitate but also to secure prestige (or unintended denigration) from within a local system of meaning (cf. Brathwaite 1971, 307; Taussig 1987a, 134).

Jack Alexander (1977, 432) underlines that a characteristic of Jamaican culture is not so much that the culture is simply Africa and Europe mixed but rather that some Jamaicans describe their culture in this way (see also Smith 1995). So, in the arena of religion, Christianity creates a dilemma within a Jamaican cultural frame. Clearly European-derived, can it ever be Jamaican if "Europe" is opposed to "Africa"? An account of meaning as use or practice softens the edge of this dilemma and offers a constructive way to consider a domain that is central to Jamaican life. Christianity *becomes* Jamaican while bearing as part of its Jamaicanness ranked folk renderings of its origins and its attendant meanings and power. Throughout the discussion at hand, I will refer often to a "creole" discourse, meaning by this a genuinely indigenous Jamaican discourse negotiated through the powers of the region as they are encountered in Jamaica. Jamaican Pentecostalism and the discourse that has encompassed it are sites of mimicry, positioned use, and self-conscious creation. All these practices involve the positioning and repositioning of symbols brought to this domain by both the powerful and the weak. While Christianity always has been in some degree hegemonic, it also has been a genuine site of Jamaican cultural creativity.

I demonstrate this fundamental point by means of an interpretive reading of Jamaica's religious discourse. The initial engagement between Africa and

Europe in the domain of ritual practice I typify through a reading from within Pentecostalism. I look back from the vantage point of Pentecostal practice, and the features of its Jamaican style, to discern the discourse that shaped that style. My method entails the view that this is not *the* history of Jamaican religion but, rather, a history that can give an account, adequate in the domain of meaning, of how Pentecostalism became Jamaican (cf. Thornton 1992). By describing my account in this way, I propose to set it apart both from political economy and from histories of "Africa" or "Europe" as they appear in the Caribbean. The analysis pursues a dynamic of meaning that is specifying for Pentecostalism in its Jamaican environment.[9]

Cosmology, Ontology, and Moral Order

The larger discourse that I explore involved a confrontation between cosmologies in the eighteenth and early nineteenth centuries (cf. Comaroff and Comaroff 1991 and Horton 1971, 1975). Sectarian missionaries to Jamaica brought a sense of Christian redemption from the perennial state of sin. This was a sense of sin located in the person and addressed through moral discipline that allowed transcendence only in death. The Christian cosmology, anchored in God, presented an ontology in which evil was located in the person and addressed by moral discipline and rite (see Geisler and Amanu 1988; Ricoeur 1967, 1986a). Especially among the British Baptists, the sectarians most successful in conversion, the address to sin was through moral discipline even more than through rite. Among Jamaicans with an African past, this encounter with sin was shaped by another practice antagonistic to the disciplined subject of Christian moral ontology.[10] Caribbean ideas of "foolishness" and "play," the aura of the trickster persona, were antipathetic to the Christian self (cf. Manning 1973, 1980; Abrahams 1983, 50–53, 186). Studied renovation of the subject was leavened by the innovation of the trick. Likewise in African curing, the address to biomoral malaise and the disordered world of which it was a part came through ritual acts rather than ethical rationalism.[11] The religions of West Africa brought a cosmology in which a multiplicity of spiritual forces, including ancestral living-dead, pervaded and defined the world.[12] Their very presence in daily life brought different notions of good and evil which were not assigned to separate spheres but allowed to reside as ambivalent companions in the world. This was a circumstance expressed in African trickster myth that presented the subject as involved in countervailing tendencies. Stanley Diamond has proposed that entertaining the trickster's ambivalence allowed a capacity to laugh at the self, to engage in a eudemonic present (Diamond 1971, xii, see also Beidelman 1986). By contrast, morality of the Christian type presented heaven as a positive "double" of a negative earth, and joy as reified beyond the world (cf. Fernandez 1982, 309–11).[13]

I noted in Jamaican Pentecostalism a marked tension between moral discipline and ritual eudemonic as they are practiced in the church, between a strong emphasis on guilt and sin and the joyous celebration of healing rite. I interpreted this as part of a discourse in which that original confrontation juxtaposed sin and moral discipline with healing rite and a eudemonic present.[14] Jamaicans would accept sin and a transcendent God. Their address to sin, however, was still an address through healing rite directed to biomoral malaise. And with further intersections from North America, the notion of Christian transcendence would become immanent and embodied in the person, not a heaven inverting the world but a eudemonic Pentecostal saint on earth.

The Politics of Moral Orders

These remarks sketch momentous transformations in the culture of the slaves whose descendants became Pentecostalists. Yet such changes were propelled not simply by abstracted logics but, rather, as I have proposed, through the use and the practices of people who commanded different interests and statuses.

Understanding and relating this process involve two levels of analysis: one is to locate the substantive arenas in which negotiation took place; the other is to capture the dynamic of practice in a theoretical mode. To the first task I have responded by tracing various permutations in a politics of moral orders that began when missionaries confronted the slaves. Missionaries perceived the slaves as fallen beings whose conduct in domestic affairs and in presentations of the person was not only "African" and immoral but also made worse by slavery. James Phillippo's famous remark about the plantations, "every female a prostitute and every man a libertine," was a dramatic statement of the conflict of moral orders that occurred in the midst of the slave regime.

The struggle that ensued between proselytizers and proselytized concerned, on the one hand, the need to be moral in a European way, as a religious task, and, on the other, the equally felt imperative of many Afro-Jamaicans to heal both themselves and the landscape from an evident malaise. In this latter task, Jamaicans were eager to use Christian rite where appropriate, but in so doing they also began to re-interpret Christianity's tasks. And as the nineteenth century proceeded, they became increasingly Christian, but not in ways that the missionaries could always recognize or endorse. This was the beginning of a struggle neither especially conscious on the part of Jamaicans nor precisely articulated. It was, rather, a negotiation of meaning, practices, symbols, and powers through which people sought to address, control, and understand their environment, both in slavery and in the post-emancipation period.

By the beginning of the twentieth century, this politics of moral orders between different cultures had been transposed into a politics of the moral order that informed Jamaica's socioracial hierarchy.[15] Religion had become an integral part of Jamaica's color class stratification. The practice of the black lower classes was typified by middle-class observers as both superstitious and immoral—superstitious for its healing lore and immoral for its enthusiasm and lack of a marriage rite. It was to this milieu of the early twentieth century that Pentecostalism was introduced from the United States. It was used as a vehicle by Jamaicans to circumvent aspects of the British order. Black lower-class Jamaicans could, through Pentecostalism, credential themselves to perform the marriage rite. At the same time, America's powerful revivalism legitimized enthusiasm and spirit possession as well.

The hegemonic aspect of this process is present in Pentecostalism today, not only in the broad racial order that impinges on the Pentecostal world but also, in Jamaica, by a further transposing of Jamaica's politics of moral order. Evident in Pentecostal rite is an intense and gendered negotiation concerning the locus of human sin and especially the sin of "fornication." From within the Pentecostal church, Jamaicans engage in debate concerning proper morality. They present another aspect of the politics that began with the initial missionary moment. Connections made between the "sweetheart life," concubinage, and the myth of the Fall make this ritual debate an eminently Jamaican one that involves both women and men.

Yet in my account, the politics of moral orders is not only a substantive theme. It is also a perspective from which to explore the dynamics of practice in religion. As a category in religious discourse, "the moral" in a Jamaican milieu refers to particular practices involved mainly with marriage and rite. These are foci for debates that concern notions of religious being. But the idea of a "moral order," as the order of values and meanings through which subjects are defined within a cultural milieu, is also a broader field reinvigorated in recent years by new views of the person and the politics of the subject. My account of Pentecostal practice, and its discursive environment, is linked with an interest in the subject and the ways in which subjects act to redefine their being. This focus on the relation between religion and the constitution of persons has grown out of other, earlier accounts of religion as ideology. These accounts acknowledge that religion is negotiated, mediated through power relations. Accounts of religion in terms of ideology also suggest, however, forms of homogeneous experience, either domination or resistance. For the Jamaican case, and especially for Pentecostalism, I was looking for a way to address a more highly nuanced experience. Otherwise, a large portion of Jamaican practice in the domain of religious life might have had to be dismissed simply as domination. My field engagement with Pentecostals, and especially Pentecostal women, suggested a different view of Jamaicans re-valuing for their own use the teaching of past religionists.

In her account of Tshidi religion, Jean Comaroff makes a useful distinction between "ideology" as lived experience and "ideology" as explicit discourse (1985, 4–5). I interpret the term *"ideology"* in a broad Dumontian sense (Dumont 1970, 263 n. 1) to mean simply "systems of ideas and values," the social positioning of which has been debated by numerous writers including Marx (1972a), Engels (1972), Althusser (1969; and Balibar 1970), Dumont (1970), and Bourdieu (1977). Ideology as lived experience for Comaroff involves "the coercive dimension of society and culture, the medium through which particular relations of domination become inscribed in the taken-for-granted shape of the world" (1985, 5). Explicit discourse, on the other hand, Comaroff describes after Raymond Williams as "belief" or "conscious imagination" that seeks to construe the world. Jean Comaroff and John Comaroff (1991, 24) elsewhere describe this ideology as generally the "possession" of particular groups, "susceptible" to apprehension as a matter of "interest and therefore open to contestation."[16]

Yet Comaroff also suggests that this process of contestation can involve "symbolic mediation," a process mainly of "signifying practice" only "partially subject to explicit reflection" (1985, 5–6). In other words, this is a process of contestation that is not a distinct and conscious engagement between forms of explicit discourse but rather a negotiation of continuing practice itself. Ideology as "lived experience" need not be merely coercive or inscribed. Through use it is negotiated, and on a daily basis. This form of negotiation is mediated by the polysemic capacity of signs which often acquire new meanings through the process of everyday use. Comaroff comments that where the South African Tshidi's responses to the mission were concerned, "the polysemic metaphors of the Old and New Testaments offered a haven for the critical imagination" (1985, 2). Derek Walcott makes a similar point when he observes that "the subject African" of the New World "understood too quickly the Christian rituals of a whipped, tortured, and murdered redeemer" (1974, 11; cf. Austin-Broos 1992). The rich text of the Bible symbolically can mediate established orders and become a vehicle for the articulation of felt conflicts and contradictions that issue in new uses of the text and divergent genres of Christian practice. As Jean Comaroff observes, this process is often only partly explicit.

To describe one dimension of this practice as a politics of moral orders, rather than simply as "symbolic mediation," confirms that this process can define a subject and a milieu. It involves negotiation of the values by which people live their lives, the implicit priorities of action that constitute their being (Foucault 1986; cf. Parsons et al. 1962). In the domain of Jamaican religion, part of this negotiation has been to affirm through dance and song that joy is a part of Christian rite (Hopkin 1978, 25–26; and see chapters 3 and 7, below). This negotiation has involved Jamaicans giving various emphases to ritual transformation and moral practice in their status as believers in Christ. Intense debate around the status of marriage belies this broader concern with rite, itself connected with competing notions of sin. Understanding sin as biomoral malaise to be healed rather than disciplined is an issue of representation but also of the moral ontology of persons constituted through practices (see Mauss 1985; Taylor 1985; Taylor 1989, 8–9; Fortes 1987; Foucault 1985, 1986). It proposes a trajectory for the person that is different from inevitable sin. It reaches back to West African practice, and also toward the perfectionism that is part of American revival culture, to generate a distinctive version of the Christian persona. Such a practice has been sustained within Jamaican Pentecostalism.

This constitution of subjects has consequences for the social field they articulate with their consociates (Geertz 1973b, 365; cf. Schutz 1962–66). Jamaican Pentecostals are particular Christians and also particular Jamaicans. They cluster residentially in neighborhoods and spend a large part of their non-working time in activities related to the church (cf. Csordas 1987). At the workplace, they tend to cleave to those of a similar persuasion and, where possible, assist in the employment of other Pentecostalists (cf. Asad 1983). The social field thus defined cuts across major spheres of structuration in their lives (cf. Giddens 1979). Pentecostals do not thereby escape the "coercive dimensions of society" or even, in a bodily sense, the inscriptions of the dominant order. Yet the genres of practice in which they are involved allow them to explore possibilities within this larger frame. They are able to generate distinctive modes of identity. Possibilities for practice in the world are defined through these group dynamics and bring particular inflections to practice that can alter the salience of other domains, especially institutional politics. When, for instance, Pentecostals juxtapose religious rite with the political act, find a rendering of Jamaican history in their reading of the Bible, or celebrate high-density living as a way of bringing community, they thereby distance themselves from institutional politics (see also Austin-Broos 1996). In fact, their practices carry the potential to criticize or to reinforce the established orders of governance, and some Pentecostal leaders have exploited one or the other course.

Still, practiced re-valuation of being as opposed to a perennial but fleeting eudemonic, or an enduring but utopic critique (see Ricouer 1986b), depends on sustaining the practice that provides the "conditions of truth" for a world (Asad 1983, 243; Berger 1969, 45–51; Austin 1981; cf. Geertz 1973c, Turner 1969). Jamaican Pentecostals sustain themselves as saints on earth and present a particular Christian persona articulated through a discourse that is part of a Jamaican milieu. Yet, within a larger regional order dominated by the United States, they are less able to sustain a subject in opposition to a racialized world that, from time to time, has pronounced on their moral being. As a consequence, Pentecostal saints can be both "saints on earth" and also Jamaicans who experience the racialism of their region. Saints respond to this circumstance in different ways, and in differing degrees, deploying their practice to create a world that is negotiated continually.

The "politics" of moral orders therefore refers to the fact that there is always a negotiation of the meanings and values that define a subject, an "ethics" of practice and being (cf. Foucault 1986). These negotiations concern the power not only to image or represent but also to valorize subjectsthrough desirable practices.[17] Such a negotiation of power has revolved around the issue of marriage not only in religious life but in Jamaican society at large. Marriage and the sanctification of sexuality have been a touchstone of the politics of moral orders that consumed the early missionaries and led many in the colonial middle class to see in Zion Revivalists merely an echo of the missionaries' "African immoralist." As the anthropology of Raymond Smith has shown, "marriage" takes on a meaning in Jamaica that is intimately implicated in hierarchy, that belies the distinction between public and private life and articulates aspects of the socioracial order (Smith 1987, 1988). The ability to be marriage celebrants that American Pentecostalism brought to its many pastors was symbolically potent and practically effective in building Pentecostalism's church organizations. It helped to construct a bridge between folk practice and institutionalized religion as important as the early finances that came from the United States. It was integral to defining enthusiastic religion as "moral" and thereby instrumental in transgressing a central Jamaican symbolic representation of being black and lower-class, the representation of being confined to concubinage (cf. Smith 1987, 1988). That this negotiation of the subject retains a hegemonic dimension can be seen in the meanings of Pentecostal rite that in different modalities alternately figure women, men, or both as the protagonists of fornication who should be saved by the church.

Discussions of society in terms of moral order were a major feature of Durkheimian sociology applied to stateless societies or small-scale social groups (see also Myers 1986). This sociology has been linked intimately with the Maussian-inspired concern to look at different constructions of the person in different societies (e.g., Mauss 1985; Fortes 1987; Carrithers, Collins, and Lukes 1985). Indeed, it is through varieties of moral order that different persons are defined. This anthropological focus has intersected with more contemporary concerns with the "subject" and the politics of identity (e.g., Faubion 1995; Turner 1994; see also Foucault 1980, 1985, 1986; Taylor 1985, 1989, 1991, 1994; Rosaldo 1989; Sider 1993; Nettleford 1970; Brathwaite 1984; cf. Ashcroft, Griffiths, and Tiffin 1995). This intersection has underlined that contemporary societies often harbor a multiplicity of subjects brought together by colonial conquest, the constitution of ethnic groups, or that of gendered or class collectivities. The politics of identity associated with large-scale ethnic groups gains its specificity from the marked emphasis in that politics on the objectification of essential identity (cf. Comaroff and Comaroff 1992; Smith 1995; Turner 1994). Other like forms of politics are not necessarily so engaged with this type of representation. They proceed as negotiations of value that become a politics of defining the person or, as I would propose, a politics of the moral orders in which subjects sustain themselves through modes of representation and practice that can mediate, criticize, or reinforce the larger orders of governance.[18] This focus on moral order as well as symbolic mediation carries with it the post-structuralist insight, though one foreshadowed by Weber, that subjectivity is not merely inscribed or created at will but rather is the product of intersubjective experience that carries with it negotiations of values, practice, and the authority of symbols (Weber 1968, 4; cf. Faubion 1995, 10). To talk of the "politics" of moral orders is to acknowledge that anthropology's "person" is constituted through a field of intersubjectivity that also can exhibit a wide range of modalities of power.

I have found these foci useful in exploring certain commonalities in the politics of Jamaica's religious discourse that span the arenas of race and social class as well as gender relations. To speak of the politics of moral orders through which people seek to define and value their being allows an address to the politics of a daily lived experience. It allows an account of the intersections of meaning and power in religion without reducing religion to one or another group interest. The account can demonstrate cultural process without reifying religious practice as a univocal force in a predetermined politics. This is not to say that Pentecostal practice in Jamaica is not politically "relevant," it is. But it may not be the intention of all religious, or even most religious, to engage with major structures of governance. Their concerns, informed by issues of race, social class, and gender relations, may be expressed in more intimate ways that also shape Jamaican culture (Weber 1968, 306, 937; Bourdieu 1991, 163–251; Smith 1988, 26–28).

Notwithstanding these observations, Pentecostalism is important for Jamaica as a vehicle for American influence in the region, and, in part, this book is about America's influence on Jamaica; that great regional "sea-change" whereby the United States rather than Europe became the dominant power. This change, which has gathered pace through the course of the twentieth century, has emerged at the century's end as a major trans-nationalism that calls into question the very conditions of viability for a local knowledge (cf. Basch, Schiller, and Blanc 1994). This context makes all the greater the challenge to demonstrate that Pentecostal practice in Jamaica has become Jamaican practice rather than a mere hegemony derived from a foreign source.[19] In demonstrating this particular point, I trust that the following account opens a new and thought-provoking window on Jamaica's trans-nationalism. The impact of this circumstance has not been simply to bring unmediated foreign cultural forms to Jamaica. Rather, from the very beginnings of Jamaican culture, these inputs, often uninvited, have been interpreted, and the process of this interpretation has shaped not only society and culture but Jamaican moral ontology as well, the very senses of what it is to be a Jamaican person.

In pursuing this argument, the following study underlines that all realities are constituted culturally and in terms of specifying meaning articulated through practices. Even in the Caribbean, with its history of incorporation into a Western economic order, the logic of political economy alone is quite unable to reveal the significance of local practice for a people. In this endeavor, I have been influenced by a number of anthropologists working in the field of colonial engagement and post-colonial culture who, in the last decade or so, have sought to generate culturally informed accounts of some of the significant transitions of history in the non-Western world (see Comaroff 1985; Comaroff and Comaroff 1991; Kelly 1991; Povinelli 1993; Price 1990; Sahlins 1985, 1995; Smith 1988; Taussig 1987a). Notwithstanding its early incorporation in elements of a Western order, Jamaica's transitions in religion, now more than ever before, should be engaged in dialogue with these other milieus not least because Caribbean renderings of Christianity are one of the great examples of the politics of poetics in the modern world (cf. Walcott 1974). The moral and the imaginary of this biblical poetics have been negotiated in equal degree.

PART ONE
THE MAKING

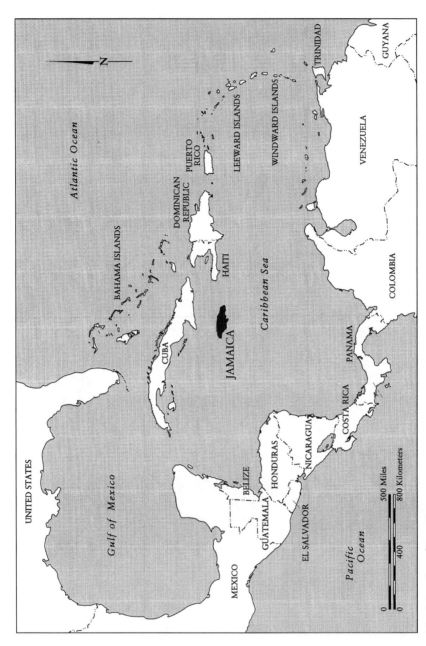

Map 1. Jamaica and its region

1   Cast into a Tumultuous World

> Hungry men and women and children have a right to call
> attention to their condition.
> —Alexander Bustamante, 1935

> The Kingdom of God is at hand for Jamaica. To God be
> the Glory. Jamaica woman, Praise!
> —George White, circa 1927[1]

Pentecostal religion in Jamaica is a genre of revival religion with intimate links to the island's past. It is also a major aspect of American influence in the region. Yet to capture Jamaica's Pentecostalism, to grasp its significance for those involved, is also to understand that for many Jamaicans a Christian cosmos is their bracketing of the world, the major lens through which they perceive the events that shape their lives. While some Jamaicans live with a strong sense of the secular state, others, and perhaps a majority, live in a world informed by God. His aspects in the Holy Spirit and Jesus are the protagonists in this milieu. For some, they promote personal transformation rather than "social change." They stand as alternative or supplements to the parties, unions, and social institutions designed to address the people's needs, and they furnish Jamaica with a biblical poetics that is close to the heart of experience.

Jamaican Pentecostalism

The world of Jamaica's Pentecostalism is divided between trinitarians and unitarians.[2] The latter maintain that the apostolic church preached only "in Jesus' name," for Jesus, they believe, was the living God. The "oneness" doctrine is ritually expressed by baptizing only in the name of Jesus and not in the name of "the Father, Son, and Holy Ghost." Jamaican trinitarians reject the idea that theirs is a faith in "three different persons." They emphasize the notion of a triune God—the God of creation is the Trinity—that they share with many other Christian churches. Notwithstanding this doctrinal division, all Pentecostal religion in Jamaica is strongly Jesu-centric. Even trinitarians address Jesus as much as, if not more than, the being of God-the-Father. As American Oneness churches were a further revelation from the trinitarians, the similarity is not surprising. The personalism of Pentecostal rite tends to focus attention on Jesus (Anderson 1979, 176–88; Synan 1971).

17

Among New World Africans, however, engagement with Jesus reflects something more: a dwelling on Jesus Christ the Redeemer, the savior from "Babylon," and a lesser concern with the remote and omniscient God. In Jamaica's Christian tradition, this mode of interpreting the faith was there among earlier groups including Revivalists and Garveyites. It continues with the Pentecostals today.[3]

Jamaican Pentecostals generally believe that above and beyond conversion to the Word of God, there is a process of sanctification whereby a believer is rendered morally pure and capable of leading a "holy" or sinless life. Some church leaders regard sanctification simply as an empowerment to pursue the holiness state which will be established gradually over many years. Among rank-and-file believers, however, and many of their local pastors, the idea that sanctification is a completed work is very prevalent and seen to bear an intrinsic relation to the status of being a saint. This is the case especially among older Pentecostals who cherish the idea of moral perfection.[4] In the trinitarian churches, the initial conversion and this second stage of spiritual empowering are referred to as "justification" and "sanctification" (see Stone 1977, 234–35). Where water is the baptismal medium that justifies people in faith, the Holy Spirit is the baptismal medium that sanctifies people for holiness. Pentecostals so sanctified refer to themselves as "saints." A process of "tarrying," or seeking for the Spirit through constant prayer and supplication, often conjoins the two ritual stages (Stone 1977, 234–35; cf. Anderson 1979, 180).

For all Pentecostal churches, sanctification or Spirit baptism is and can only be confirmed through "speaking in tongues." This is also the specific phrase employed by Jamaicans to describe the ecstatic experience. They mean by it, sometimes, "glossolalia" or a language unintelligible to humans that is conferred by God so that saints can address him. They also can mean "xenoglossy," or the instantaneous mastery of foreign tongues for the purpose of evangelism (Anderson 1979, 16–19). It is more usual in Jamaica for "tongues" to be understood as glossolalia.[5]

In Jamaica, it is common for Pentecostal women to dress in white for communion services. Some churches have their women dress in white every Sunday. This use of white garb to signify purity is shared with practitioners of Zion Revival, Jamaica's older revival religion dating from the Great Revival of 1860–61 (Chevannes 1971a, 1971b; Curtin 1970; Hogg 1964; Simpson 1956). Unlike Revivalists, the Pentecostal women do not wear turban wraps to cover their heads. Nevertheless, the emphasis on white, in conjunction with ecstatic services that proceed for many hours, leads many Jamaicans to assume that Pentecostal practitioners have very close relationships with Revival religion. They are grouped by observers as "clap-clap" churches, the churches of the poor and "ignorant." This view also is confirmed by the fact that both religious forms sustain vocal male pastors with large female follow-ings (cf. Hollenweger 1972; Austin-Broos 1987b; Cucchiari 1990; Gill 1990). The motif of a male religious leader with a large female band juxtaposes for Jamaicans ideas of holiness and "rudeness" that inform the humor of every-day life.[6] For the purveyors of this humor, Revival and Pentecostal modes are one.

Within their own world, however, the two groups are quite antagonistic. Pentecostals view Revivalists as trucking in magic, the work of the devil, in their practice of curing techniques related to folk healing.[7] Healing is a cen-tral component of Pentecostal practice, but this is a healing from the Holy Spirit. Pentecostal healing is more often rendered as a cleansing that makes the body a vehicle for Spirit. A clean body signifies a thoroughly cleansed soul. Revival healing, on the other hand, can be realized on Revivalists and non-Revivalists alike. It signifies more the power of the healer than the purity of the person healed. Revival also can address forces of evil beyond the per-son, including the forces of obeah or witchcraft. These different interpreta-tions of healing reflect more or less emphasis given to sin in renderings of Christian cosmology. From the Pentecostal point of view, Revivalists, like all other Christian groups, lack the revelation of speaking in tongues. They are therefore debarred from the cleansing from sin signified by Holy Ghost pos-session. Revivalists see Pentecostals as part of the growing "church business," as part of a commodified religious world issuing from America. They point to Pentecostalism's relations with the metropolis but also to the emphasis on tithing in the churches that forms the basis of institutional funding.[8]

Notwithstanding these points of conflict, the popular view of these churches as related is in fact quite correct. Both of their respective entries into Jamaica have been indicative of major moments in the development of revival reli-gion in the metropolitan world.[9] If their attitudes toward sin and healing vary, in both groups there is a focus on redemption. Believers try to "get right" with God through the ministry of Jesus Christ (see also Dayton 1980). Along with the considerable influence of Adventist Christianity, these groups pur-vey throughout Jamaica a climate of eudemonic hope in the present and mil-lennial expectation for the future.

In Jamaica, the two major types of Pentecostal churches are often distin-guished by the styles of their names. The unitarian churches generally have "Apostolic" as part of their designation. The term simply emphasizes that a congregation seeks to maintain the church in the mode of Jesus' apostles. The most prominent among the unitarian churches is not distinguished in this way, however. The United Pentecostal Church (UPC) is a branch of the U.S. church founded in St. Louis in 1945 (Reynolds n.d., 33). The UPC en-tered Jamaica in 1947 and thereafter grew rapidly in major urban centers (Russell 1986, 9–10). It has been a relatively wealthy church, and its well-furnished temples draw very large crowds, especially in Kingston, Ocho Rios, and Mandeville. The trinitarian churches are most commonly known as "churches of God" because of the theocratic origins of this Pentecostal organization. The Church of God in Cleveland, Tennessee, was founded in 1904 by A. J. Tomlinson. He became the general overseer of a rapidly expanding organization that accepted the Pentecostal doctrine around 1908 (Phillips 1986, 5–14, 31; Conn 1955). Tomlinson split from the main church in 1923 when his personal guardianship of the church was challenged. This challenge reflected a move away from an organization based on inspirational theocracy and toward a more routinized form of government (Stone 1977). The Jamaican New Testament Church of God is aligned with the founding Church of God in Cleveland. The Church of God of Prophecy was the name adopted by Milton Tomlinson, a son of A. J. Tomlinson, for one of the two break-away groups that were a product of the 1923 split.

These two churches have been notable for their penetration of Jamaica's population. They established themselves as part of the Church of God's initial outreach to Jamaica beginning in 1924. In the 1910s, there had been other initiatives in the Bahamas, Cuba, Barbados, the Virgin Islands, and Argentina (Conn 1959, 293). Among these endeavors, the Jamaican initiative had been the church's notable success. In America itself, the Church of God has predominated in the east-central and southern states from Tennessee and Kentucky through the Carolinas to Florida. Although the church is a very clear second to the California-based Assemblies of God, America's largest Pentecostal church, its geographic position has been strategic for its Caribbean initiatives (Anderson 1979, 114–36). The Assemblies of God came to Jamaica only in 1941 and has not been able to equal the growth of the churches of God.[10]

Other major trinitarian Pentecostal groups in Jamaica include the International Foursquare Gospel Church that Aimee Semple Macpherson established in 1923 as a breakaway group from the American Assemblies of God (Anderson 1979). A more modest group of Elim churches is loosely affiliated with the English Elim that separated from England's Apostolic Church in 1921 (Gee 1949; Calley 1965, 150–58). There is also a vast variety of indigenous Pentecostal churches, both trinitarian and unitarian. Among the more interesting of these are the Kingston City Mission, a trinitarian church that has proselytized widely in both England and North America, and two unitarian churches, Rehobath Church of God in Christ Jesus, Apostolic Inc., and Shiloah Apostolic Church of Jamaica, Inc., both of which grew out of the first and now defunct Pentecostal Union in Jamaica.[11] A third prominent unitarian church is the Pentecostal Gospel Temple, an indigenous break-away group from the United Pentecostal Church that came to prominence in the 1970s through the work of its female pastor. Another trinitarian church, with a television ministry developed in the 1980s, is the Deliverance Center based in West Kingston. Notwithstanding this indigenous dynamic, the three churches that probably have had the greatest impact on Jamaica are the New Testament Church of God, the Church of God of Prophecy, and the UPC.

By the 1980s, Pentecostalism had become the espoused faith of roughly half a million Jamaicans in a population of around 2.3 million (see appendix I, below). Two Jamaican census categories, "Church of God" and "Pentecostal," address the Pentecostal world. The relative sizes of these categories suggest that Pentecostal trinitarian churches of God have become the most common religious organizations in Jamaica, the predominant folk church of a people that once defined its religious commitment in terms of an Orthodox Baptist faith and its unorthodox companion, Zion Revival.[12] Pentecostals of one variety or another constitute a quarter of the entire census count and roughly one-third of those with an expressed religious affiliation. Does this mean that a quarter of Jamaica's population is Pentecostal? As regular church attenders and full church members are very much smaller proportions of the population than the census categories, which reflect, after all, only nominal affiliation, these census categories, particularly "Church of God," might be read in another way: that where once a Baptist affiliation was the standard nominal religious affiliation in Jamaica, that standard is now Church of God. This phenomenon reflects regional changes in the Caribbean that have proceeded throughout the century. The legacies of Britain's colonialism have been gradually eroded as American influence has become more expansive. The divergent ideas about sin and healing among Revivalists and Pentecostals also reflect, however, Jamaican negotiations of rite that have an integrity of their own.

Pentecostalism took root in Jamaica in the 1920s and 1930s after tentative beginnings in the 1910s. The period was one in which a range of social movements became established: Rastafarianism emerged as a distinctive doctrine, and Jamaica's nationalism and unionism came to their fruition from disparate beginnings at the turn of the century. These movements were the forerunners not only of contemporary nationalism but also of Jamaica's current gamut of nation-state politics, and certainly that politics has been influential for many. In the 1982 census, some fifty years after Pentecostalism emerged, more than six hundred thousand Jamaicans declared no religious affiliation at all. Yet twentieth-century life in Jamaica has not been an inexorable march toward secularization. Nor have political reactions been the only reactions to the regional milieu. Pentecostalism takes its place alongside these other movements as a major response to the environment that emerged in the early twentieth century. This was a religious response in which Jamaicans interpreted events from within a specifically Christian cosmos rather than a secular one. And these were Jamaican people largely uninvolved in unionism or in the labor experience that sustained other types of movements. Many of these Jamaicans were women.

Pentecostalism also signals a circumstance in which Jamaican people reoriented themselves from a purely British colonial world to one in which the United States would play a central part in their lives. The movement represents a step beyond earlier revivalisms to a twentieth-century genre of religion with extensive American connections. The movement has thus been a complex phenomenon, fueled by a creole logic of Afro-Christian responses to the world and by a regional dynamic of American domination in the region. The period in which Pentecostalism emerged as a Jamaican movement was one in which these trajectories met.

The Reconfiguration of a Regional Environment

The milieu of Jamaica's new religious movement had its beginnings in the last three decades of the nineteenth century. A new tropical crop, bananas, became the leading industry and the major vehicle for the impact of American capital on the island. The United States had begun a period of economic recovery following the Civil War and was looking once again for opportunities to expand its overseas trade. Tropical fruit and sugar would prove to be, for a while, a highly favored venue. It would not be long before this economic interest was followed by military and political excursions in the region. Following the Spanish-American War of 1898, America made its commitment to the Caribbean and rapidly became dominant over the declining power of the European nations. This was so notwithstanding the latter's continuing political presence in the region. In Jamaica, profits from bananas were used to revitalize sugar. The fillip for this development came not so much from America but from a European demand for sugar during the First World War (Austin-Broos 1988). The American interest in Jamaican bananas, like the dearth of sugar beet in Europe, would prove to be a passing phenomenon. Nonetheless, it produced significant social change in Jamaica. A newly prosperous export economy was socially manifest in the growth of Jamaica's middle class (cf. Bryan 1991). This class defined its ethos of quiet respectability in terms of a British protestant culture handed down from sectarian missionaries (Henriques 1968, 152; Smith 1965a, 164–66). As the middle class grew, it created a demand for a range of services that expanded its own professional ranks and also the ranks of the urban lower class. The children of prosperous farmers moved into the professions or else into the middle ranks of the colonial civil service (Post 1978, 77–113). Lower-class people, particularly women, expanded their involvement in domestic, personal, and petty commercial service (Higman 1983). With opportunities expanding in Jamaica's urban areas, as well as overseas, the steady trail of people from the land grew rapidly in the first three decades of the twentieth century. Migration, which had been mainly circular migration to the banana parishes and Panama in the late nineteenth century, became a one-way movement away from the land in the course of the twentieth century (Roberts 1957, 133–64). The period marked the decline of Jamaica's small farmer class.

The development of a banana industry brought prosperity to some Jamaicans but also heralded a more difficult life for many. The cultivation of bananas in Costa Rica began in 1871, and by 1891, Central and South America were supplying the Boston Fruit Company, forerunner of United Fruit, with two-thirds of its merchandise. Between 1903 and 1921, Jamaica was hit by five hurricanes, and although the industry recovered, it was thereafter beset by difficulties of intense South American competition, recurrent plant disease, and the monopolistic tendencies of the American companies (Hall 1964, 75–79; Olivier 1910, 1936; Marshall 1982, 8). The inability of the Jamaican producers to penetrate the American market and find a stable niche there was indicative of a more general situation in which Jamaican labor and commodity production were increasingly subject to shifts in American capital. This process was to cast Jamaica in a particular role. The island society would not again be the hub of a larger trading system as it had been in the days of the British "triangular trade."[13] Rather, Jamaica was pushed to the periphery of this new American system which concentrated its economic and strategic focus on Central America and Cuba.

Some Jamaicans, responding to this process, traveled to Panama to work on the canal, while others went to banana plantations in Costa Rica. Still others relocated in Cuba to work in an expanding sugar industry. These migrations, extending from the 1880s to the 1920s, stimulated further movement at home (Roberts 1957, 133–41). In Jamaica, a regional market economy spread to previously remote rural areas, and even more workers were drawn to service the middle class, which itself would have a limited role in the larger regional system (see Lobdell 1988).

Concurrent with these reconfigurations in economic life, there was further dramatic change in the lives of Jamaicans. The period that followed the emancipation had involved a decline in external trade and a localization of rural life (Eisner 1960, 318–45). The rapid withdrawal of British economic interest had been both a cause and a consequence of the emancipation (Curtin 1970, 3–23; Green 1976, 35–64). This was the context in which Jamaica's early Revival religion took root. Its animated universe of spirits and ghosts and its biblical pantheon of prophets were consistent with a highly localized environment. This rural environment and, with it, Revival religion, was nevertheless to be overtaken.[14] Jamaica's roughly forty years of relative isolation from the metropolitan world was sustained only by North America's self-absorption in the Civil War. Not long after the United States began its reconstruction, it also began to draw Jamaica into its sphere of cultural influence. Bananas were important not only as an industry but also for the communications the industry established. During the 1880s and 1890s, at least eight different trading companies secured themselves in ports along Jamaica's northern shore. In the same period, the number of steamship lines out of Jamaica expanded from one to seventeen. Among other ports, these lines sailed to New York, New Orleans, Philadelphia, and Boston (Hall 1964, 72–73). In the first twenty years of the twentieth century, these developments allowed relatively free passage of people, goods, and information between the United States, Jamaica, and the larger Caribbean. This traffic was influential beyond the domain of commerce and manifest itself in political and religious life. It was to promote a sense of popular organization and would facilitate the formation of unions in Jamaica. It was to augment ideas about nationalism and freedom from racial prejudice with themes culled from the Harlem Renaissance.[15] It was also to bring to Jamaica a repertoire of revival and fundamentalist religion, movements that had found fertile soil in a post-bellum America and were now reaching out to the people of Jamaica.

Social Movements in a Changing World

The Jamaicans who left the land temporarily or permanently in the years between 1880 and the 1930s were confronted with enduring features of a regional system. Men experienced the dislocation of demanding itinerant labor on a scale that far exceeded the intra- and inter-parish migrations of the emancipation period. They increased their earnings in Panama and Cuba, but in alienating and insecure positions. For women who remained on the land, the period presented the vagaries of a regional economy, exacerbated by a gender stratification within the labor force. Women moved from agriculture to service occupations at the turn of the century in the face of stagnation in the rural sector. In the 1910s, particularly in parishes that combined sugar cane and peasant cultivation, women moved back to the land to replace migrating men. From the 1920s and into the 1930s, as men returned to resume their places in agriculture, women moved en masse into service (Lobdell 1988; Higman 1983). We can surmise in some degree the sense that these Jamaicans had of their position, though recorded recollections are fairly scarce. Written reports of the times, including those of Marcus Garvey, generally come from the more educated (see also Brodber 1980, 1984).

Awareness of possibilities within the region was almost certainly matched by fears and misgivings. Laborers traveling overseas saw the chance for alliance with other New World Africans, but also the systemic nature of their shared condition. This process, which occurred at the sites of mass labor and also in capitals such as Havana and New York, would have profound effects on Jamaican ideas. Where men faced the hierarchy of regional labor, women involved in service in the houses of the middle class faced a domesticated form of stratification. These women now confronted, after sixty years of freedom, employers who extensively controlled their position. In both cases, Jamaicans faced a heightened experience of subordination that collapsed the issues of race and class into a sense of heritable condition (cf. Austin 1979; Austin-Broos 1994). As some Jamaicans moved to distance themselves from forms of servitude remembered from the past, others would connect the past with the present in a view that because they were African, they were continually assigned to menial positions. To be black, poor, and landless, or cultivating at a near subsistence level, became historically marked and valued in relation to those who were now middle-class. The poor and the black, specifically, were identified as "African," as those who had not developed from their initial position in the stratified societies of the Caribbean (Lewis 1987; Carnegie 1973). The impact of these encounters with socioracial hierarchy, informed by values and images from the past, has been documented for a male arena of nascent state politics but conceptualized less for Jamaica's women (cf. Brodber 1984). Where nationalism and Rastafarianism have been associated with the responses of men, Pentecostalism was used especially by women to address the moral politics of their position. This is not to suggest that Pentecostalism was their only response (see French and Ford-Smith n.d.). It was, however, a prominent one that would shape the feminine culture of Jamaica's lower classes and leave its imprint on the whole society.

The impact of the labor migrations was marked. For men, the Panama experience stands as the centerpiece of the period. Although Jamaicans were earning more in Panama than they could in Jamaica, labor conditions at the canal were deplorable. Mortality rates among workers were high. Prior to effective action against mosquitoes in 1904, many suffered the ravages of malaria as well as cholera and yellow fever. Pneumonia was also a hazard in the rainy season. Early on, workers were housed in poorly ventilated barracks with bunks stacked one on top of the other. The men were governed by authoritarian rules with fines and physical punishment for absconding or acts of aggression. Under the American Isthmian Canal Commission, a color bar was imposed. Black laborers lived separately from all other white employees and, along with immigrant labor from southern Europe, were paid in Colombian silver while white Americans were paid in gold. "Gold" and "silver" were the euphemisms used to refer to white and non-white domestic, recreational, commercial, and industrial facilities. As many of the overseers were Southern whites still smarting from the Civil War, it was perhaps inevitable that race relations would be strained, even bitter (Newton 1984, 132; Senior 1978, 62–69; Langley 1980, 76). At the same time, the labor migrations gave workers ample opportunity to place Jamaica in a larger frame of reference. They learned in Cuba and Central America of the fragility of political regimes and of the possibility of competing strategies for social change (Iglesias Garcia 1985, Knight 1985). They met white members of a regional proletariat and thereby came to question the extraordinary status attached to whites within Jamaica. Migratory labor in Panama, and elsewhere in the region, completed the introduction of Jamaicans to wage labor and gave a sense of political organization beyond the rural village. It also gave them grounds to forge new initiatives that might secure their status as "full free" beings.

Although the successful "Colon Man" was celebrated in Jamaican song, the euphemism "a silver man" recalled the experience of segregation in an impersonal labor market dominated by America and condoned by the British regime. Predictably, it was this Panamanian arena that constituted a shared experience for a number of Jamaicans who became leaders of popular movements within Jamaica itself. Amy Jacques Garvey maintains that her husband's travels through Costa Rica, Panama, and Ecuador radicalized his view of the black man in the New World: "he saw the awful conditions under which they labored—no protection from the British Consul and no efforts for their welfare" (Garvey 1970, 7; Hill 1983–85; cf. Lewis 1987, 57–65). Alexander Bedward, the early religious radical, was a returnee from Central America, as was each of the founders of Rastafarianism (Smith, Augier, and Nettleford 1960, 6–9; Hill 1983, 39). Bedward is known for his announcement of the imminent destruction of the white populace and the firing of Kingston as the "black wall" of his followers confronted the "white wall" (Chevannes 1971a, 49). It was this sense of being encapsulated in a white world, of being confronted by a white wall, that gave an impetus to both Garvey's United Negro Improvement Association (UNIA) and the Rastafarian movement, with their shared emphasis on a return to Africa away from life in the New World. Doctrines of the Ethiopian type had been common in Jamaica since the turn of the century (Post 1969; 1978, 160–72; Hill 1983). It was in this particular context of migratory labor, however, that these utopian critiques came to the fore (cf. Ricouer 1986b). Rather than see Rastafarianism and Garveyism as the tail end of colonial politics, it is more illuminating to see them as modern forms of redemptionism responding to pervasive hierarchy (Austin-Broos 1988; cf. Bakan 1990).

Events that began in the 1880s with the labor migrations and the clear delineation of a wage labor force reached a culmination in 1938 with Jamaica's labor rebellion. The circumstances that fostered this rebellion were fed in significant part by the repatriation of labor from Cuba and other locations at the onset of the depression. Conditions in Jamaica were exacerbated by the restrictive immigration policies operative after 1924 in the United States.

These regional factors combined with the steady depopulation of the countryside to generate high unemployment, low wages, and enormous frustration among labor. The rebellion gave a fillip to union organization in Jamaica and brought to early prominence Bustamante's Industrial Trade Union.[16]

Bustamante himself had traveled extensively in the region and spent many years working in Cuba, Panama, and New York City (Eaton 1975, 13–15). Unionism for Bustamante meant popular mobilization, not to bring down capitalism but rather to present a united front to employers and governments alike. Bustamante appreciated both the wealth of the larger system into which Jamaicans were drawn and its power. His strategy was to temper that power through collective bargaining and to harness the wealth, as far as possible, for the benefit of the people. In order to operate freely within this new system, Jamaica had to overcome the arbitrary political barriers of the remnant British regime (Hill 1976). In this view, Bustamante was joined by nationalists of much longer standing who had been involved since the turn of the century with a series of small associations advocating greater rights for black Jamaicans. These associations included the Jamaican Pan-African Association, the National Club, the Jamaica League, the Reform Club, Progressive League, and the National Reform Association (Carnegie 1973). These groups preceded the People's National Party which would bring together, for a very short time, the populist, Bustamante and the nationalists' champion, Norman Washington Manley.[17]

Bustamante grasped the mood of the nation and was ultimately successful in his quest, becoming Jamaica's first prime minister elected by universal suffrage. Yet by underlining possibilities in the regional system, Bustamante glossed over its many constraints. These constraints were embodied in the racialism of the United States and in the stratification of labor that continued, under that racialism's influence, throughout the Caribbean. The recognition of a Caribbean hierarchy was embodied in a succession of other popular movements. Garveyism and Rastafarianism, less compromised than Bustamante by aspirations to state power, acknowledged and opposed the racial principle.

Notwithstanding these initiatives in Pan-African politics, unions had become by the later 1930s the principal form of popular organization. This process occurred at a time when women were leaving a rural workforce finally subject to some unionization (Phelps 1960; Post 1978, 238–61; French 1986). The women who became vendors were yet to organize, and for the women moving into domestic service, there were no unions available. Whether they were men or women, the small farmers who stayed on the land still had only limited representation. These Jamaicans faced events that involved the emergence of nation-state structures but structures to which they had limited access and also gave only limited salience. Their view of the world at the turn of the century was at once local, magical, and infused with a creole cosmology. Religious rite was a response to suffering and also a means to a better life. In addition, these people's experience of racialism was local and domestic rather than regional and proletarianized. The "Back-to-Africa" movements relied for their appeal on a sense of a regional industrial order infused with racial prejudice. They did not address immediately the more subtle stratifications involved in a maid's encounter with her mistress, or even the hierarchy of rural village life. The situation of those who sustained this position between a local, rural, and ritual world and a secular political one is epitomized by women entering domestic service in the first three decades of the twentieth century.

As domestics, women received average money wages of less than forty pounds a year, which was well below wages for comparable work in both Britain and the United States (Higman 1983, 129–30). Their material situation was a little better than those involved in rural labor, for in addition to money wages, they received accommodation and some payment in kind. They experienced, however, strong symbolic statements of their subordinate position. Servant accommodation was often in rude huts separate from the employer's house, and even when incorporated within the house, seldom was there direct access from these quarters to the main living area. Servants were separated and kept in their position even in the modest houses of clerks and shop assistants. For these women and a number of their menfolk, the world of labor and associated movements was still a distant one.

A sense of these women's lives is gained from Herbert G. de Lisser's account of their position. De Lisser was a leading advocate for Jamaica's banana industry, editor of the *Jamaica Daily Gleaner*, for a time co-leader of the conservative Jamaica Imperial Association, and a publicist for Jamaica who sought closer relations with the United States. He was among Jamaica's conservatives, a politically prominent spokesman for the planter class. Yet as a young man, he had Fabian sympathies and wrote as a novelist-observer of local life (Carnegie 1973, 162–77). In the first decade of the century, he already was writing about Jamaica's new army of female employees. In his novel *Jane's Career*, he made justly famous the social personality of a young rural woman who became a domestic servant in Kingston. In 1913, de Lisser made the following comment on Jamaican society:

> It will be apparent that if out of a population of less than nine hundred thousand, most of whom serve themselves, the number of domestics is forty thousand, almost everybody who has the slightest pretensions to be considered anybody employs a servant. In fact you are not respectable if you have not a servant. (de Lisser 1913, 97)

This affirmation of the status concerns of the newly confident middle class underlines one important cause of the dramatic re-structuring of female labor that occurred in the course of the early twentieth century. De Lisser moves on to describe the progress of young country girls into service:

> in some parts of the island field-work is almost the only form of employ-
> ment open to women. But most of the girls dislike it, and public sentiment
> revolts at the idea of girls of tender age working along with boys and
> men. . . . The aim and ambition of every decent countrywoman, therefore,
> is to secure for her girls good places as domestic servants. (de Lisser
> 1913, 98)

De Lisser comments elsewhere (1913, 96) on the rigors of small farm cultivation. It is likely that the very physicality of the work turned women to
thoughts of domestic service as much as the moral sensibilities of their mothers and menfolk. His account, moreover, naturalizes the preference for domestic service in a period when the limits of the rural economy were gradually reached. De Lisser sketches the conditions of young domestic workers
"placed" as unpaid labor in the homes of the middle class:

> More often than not they sleep on a bundle of rags on the floor; but this
> they take to be no hardship. They are fed coarse food: rice, yams, sweet
> potatoes, bread, saltfish and split-peas . . . with meat very occasionally. But
> for fresh meat most of them never develop a liking, not having become
> accustomed to it in their youth. Their passion is for pretty clothing, and
> this taste is gratified to a limited extent by wise mistresses.
>
> Thus their life may pass from year to year until they are eighteen. They
> are not unlike serfs, but decidedly they are not unhappy. (de Lisser
> 1913, 100)

De Lisser's account conveys not only the girls' material conditions but also
a sense of intimate hierarchy. In the closest physical contact with their employers, their circumstances were perceived to be nothing but appropriate.
These serf-like "schoolgirls," as they were known, were inclined to leave this
situation around the age of eighteen (cf. Henriques 1968, 151). Often a
woman would leave at the behest of a lover by whom she would later bear a
child. These events in time would lead the woman back into service of a more
responsible kind. She would then reside either at the yard of her employer
or more probably in a yard with others of her class. De Lisser describes a
possible life cycle for the domestic:

> the possession of . . . children may compel her to give up a comfortable
> room in a big and fairly sanitary yard, and may oblige her to rent a little
> place in an insanitary yard, paying the rent out of the scanty wages she
> receives. . . .
>
> Periodically she comes into possession of a "friend," and then, for the
> time, her burden may be lightened. But as her family grows, grows also the
> necessity for her to work harder and more steadily. Then someday her el-
> dest girl goes off to "look a living" for herself, or her biggest boy departs to

carve out an independent career. . . . If she lives to be old, she will probably become a regular member of a church, and her children will see that
she and their father do not starve. (de Lisser 1913, 104–5)

There is no reason to believe that these conditions changed very much in the
following thirty years. Edith Clarke's (1966, 93–96) account of the economic
situation of women moving into sugar towns in the 1930s is equally austere.
Clarke's account, like de Lisser's, points to the economizing of sentiment that
was involved in a woman's attempts to acquire a male earner for her household. And yet this was not the mere economizing of sentiment. Notwithstanding their economic position, women often endorse the "sweetheart
life." Reflecting on her life in service, a Kingston woman once remarked to
me, "Me have four or five children den, han' I'm livin', they call it 'sweetheart
life,' not livin' wid my husband, jus' free han' quiet." Being "free han' quiet"
signified a release from a troubled domestic environment in which a husband, himself beset by unemployment, proved unreliable and at times aggressive. Even when it is initially sought by women, marriage is not always a
condition happily sustained in a lower-class milieu (cf. Sobo 1993, 190–96).[18]
The consequences are readily recognized, however: "Say I goin' te church.
They don' accept me as much as they would accept you that have six, seven
children han' married." This conjuncture of public and private conditions in
the early years of the century, and even now, has allowed ample scope for the
respectable to denigrate the lives and morals of their servants and legitimize
their own position through appeals to Christian piety.[19] Churches, as de Lisser observes, have been institutional mainstays for lower-class women and
their immediate kin. Yet churches also have been a major voice condemning
them for their life's condition. The ritual resolution of this dilemma is present
in Pentecostalism, a Christian practice that would circumvent the denigration of orthodox religion.

   The spate of reports and commissions that followed the labor rebellion of
1938 reflects the moralization of women's position. A strong focus on land
settlement schemes and extension services for farmers addressed the interests of the rural men. The male landless would be catered for through the
further development of trade unions. Where women were concerned, however, there was little discussion of their work and extensive comment on welfare measures to improve their homemaking skills (Moyne 1945, 220–21).
The only measure proposed to address the situation of Jamaica's domestics
was the construction of hostels in major towns to accommodate working
women. This proposal, however, was never acted upon (French 1986, 13).
Instead, the wife of the governor, Lady Huggins, launched a Mass Wedding Movement in 1944–45 in order to regularize the families of Jamaican
workers. After some early impact, this initiative proved largely unsuccessful
(Smith 1966, iv–v).[20]

The report of the Moyne Commission was particularly adamant concerning the need to constitute proper families in Jamaica with a male income earner at the head. These recommendations were made as part of aspirations to protect the economically vulnerable: lowly paid women and their dependent children. There was little attempt, however, to see these women as a significant component of Jamaica's labor force. Rather, the presence in the workforce of women with children was seen as an inadvertent outcome of profligacy. Even the policy adviser T. S. Simey, who was careful to caution against coercive moral measures to cope with the "economic evils of promiscuity," remained within the bounds of these conventional understandings (Simey 1946, 182–91, 224–26).

During the slavery period and throughout the nineteenth century, there is little evidence of gender being used as a criterion to debar women from agriculture or from other forms of physical work. There was an evident stratification in relation to trade and field occupations, but certainly women were judged to be fully part of the manual labor force (Higman 1976, 187–201). Within the peasant milieu of the post-emancipation, the position of women planters was equally established. The expansion of the middle class at the end of the century, however, promoted the idea that women should not work "out." This was but one moment in the ideological delineation of classes according to levels of education, mores, color, and social style (Norris 1962; de Lisser 1913). The fact of women working "out" became representative of a moral failing in the women, in their class, and in their cultural tradition. Hence the focus on "promiscuity" as a serious social issue.

Concurrent with these developments, illegitimacy became an increasingly prominent concern. Marriage as an institution had been discouraged among the slaves. It remained thereafter the sacrament most problematic in religious practice even when Jamaicans accepted Christianity (Henriques 1968; Smith 1988, 82–89). It would become in Pentecostal practice a central sign of holiness with meanings closely related to Jamaica's racial and social class order. A concern with marriage on the people's behalf was confined at first to the sectarian missionaries. As the nineteenth century proceeded, however, sectarian Christianity became a status marker of the rural middle class, and, along with this development, marriage itself became an index of civilization, of movement from a state of slavery and from an African permissiveness. In 1885, the Jamaican governor had received petitions concerning the issue of illegitimacy. Bishop Nuttall, head of the Anglican Church in Jamaica, and on many issues an enlightened man, issued a pamphlet concerning the "Public Morality" (Smith 1988, 104–5; also see Bryan 1985). This pamphlet was produced after his own petition, like others, had failed to move the governor to action. Although Nuttall rued the immorality of profligate sexuality, he was careful to indicate that the immorality extended through the whole society. Some of his middle-class supporters had a different view. Middle-class women in particular took marriage and a commitment to orthodox religion as major marks of their status and used this characteristic to differentiate themselves from "native Africans" (Smith 1987, 187; cf. Smith 1965a, 164). Some fifty years later, in 1941, the bishop of Jamaica chaired a new Committee on Illegitimacy and Concubinage. Again recommendations were made for militant action by the government and the churches against the illegitimates (French 1986, 16). Following the unsuccessful mass wedding program, the 1950s saw a spate of social science studies providing analysis and explanation for Jamaica's irregular families. Science now assumed the responsibilities of religion (Kerr 1952; Henriques 1968; Blake 1961; Clarke 1966).

In the 1930s and 1940s, women and men who remained on the land or migrated into towns were progressively encompassed in a larger nexus of market relations and regional patterns of race and class. Concurrently they were subject to the local moralizing of their position. And to this particular Jamaican discourse they brought the practice of a rural creole people. Their experience of a moralized hierarchy they interpreted in a religious mode that made their suffering and circumstance an index of their capacity for holiness. Pentecostalism, a popular religion opposed to the ecclesiastical mores of the middle class and endorsed by representatives of a powerful white America, became a vehicle for women and politically peripheral men to valorize their experience. To these Jamaicans, it presented a model of moral perfection that they could make their own in opposition to the more established churches. Pentecostalism addressed the Jamaican experience of hierarchy through a ritual transformation of the person. The Pentecostal saint, saved and cleansed, received power through the Holy Ghost and wisdom from direct engagement with God that was evidenced by speaking in tongues. Pentecostalism represented a response to change in Jamaica as significant as unionism and Rastafarianism. It was nevertheless a faith that endorsed the status quo and proposed a transformation of the inner person. Where Rastafarianism cast Jamaicans as the victims of history who should be its heroes, Pentecostalism made Jamaicans responsible for their being and proposed a strategy of moral redemption through transforming Christian rite.

The political and religious movements of the early twentieth century formed a fabric of related response to Jamaica's colonial hierarchy. This hierarchy was increasingly questioned through the expansion of regional experience which brought migration, new engagements with race and social class, and new mediums of practice. As they moved toward a more urbanized and metropolitan life, the culture of the rural classes was rapidly transformed. This situation underpinned the complex mix of politics and religious modes that characterized Jamaica's popular response. Cast into a tumultuous world, Jamaicans sought to articulate a range of values through the new social movements. As they pursued these projects, regional and local forces met. Pentecostalism would articulate one moment in a regional engagement. Yet regional and American forces were not alone in propelling Pentecostalism forward. Alone they cannot account for the complex and continuing struggle that absorbed its Jamaican interpreters. This struggle reached back much farther into the nineteenth century to the period of the emancipation and the free village system.

2 A Certain Moral Inheritance

The love of freedom is naturally so strong in man, that, when once he has grown accustomed to freedom, he will sacrifice everything for its sake. For this reason discipline must be brought into play very early; for when this has not been done, it is difficult to alter character later in life. . . .

We see this also among savage nations who . . . can never become accustomed to European manners.

—Immanuel Kant, 1960 (1899)

to be for the black man . . . is to be for ancient, abhorrent and unEnglish practices. It is to be for that *bête noire*, indiscipline.

—Anthony Winkler, 1995

Pentecostalism is striking in Jamaica for the manner in which it juxtaposes the moralism of a Protestant tradition with an emphasis on the power of rite to heal and create a saint. Although Jamaican Pentecostals must strive through daily practice to be holy, it is magical possession by the Holy Ghost that actually makes a believer a saint, one who can aspire to a sinless life.[1] Also striking is the manner in which a very strict moral code still allows for eudemonic fervor. When Jamaicans go to church, they go "to have a good time today," to revel in a musical performance entirely debarred in its secular form (see Hopkin 1978). The dancing, singing, and celebrating saints are forbidden in their daily lives to dance, sing, or utter the asides of a "sweetheart" or "freeness" life. Yet some of these forms, transformed and sanctified, have been incorporated in the church.

This tension between an ethical rationalism and the practice of rite and eudemonic is not peculiar to Jamaican Pentecostals. The transforming rite of Holy Ghost possession is common to all Pentecostal practitioners, and certainly in many, if not all, Pentecostalisms, a sense of eudemonic accompanies rite. All Pentecostals also endorse extensive social constraints on the person as required signs of moral worth. Jamaican Pentecostalism shares these forms. Yet in a Jamaican milieu, these features have been interpreted through a religious discourse bequeathed by the emancipation, so that the tension has a meaning that has become specifically Jamaican. Exploring this particular discourse and its impact on a culture means returning to the beginnings of Jamaica's Christianity.

It was around the time of the emancipation that an African sense of affliction and rite quite different from the Christian complex confronted a Calvinist rationalism with an enduring redemptive theme. The ethical rationalism
that the Baptists brought was also a rationalism infused with white European
moral practice assumed as the measure of civilization and of Christian spiritual worth. At the heart of this complex was the ordering and sanctification
of life through the practice of Christian marriage and Christian forms of
sexual restraint. These mores would become in Jamaica not only marks of
civilization but also marks of assimilation to an orthodox Christian faith. This
idiom of religious practice was different from a West African one in which
moral disorder required, first, divination and a healing rite. That rite re-
ordered a suffering body disturbed by spiritual forces in the world that were
themselves brought into play by witchcraft or cosmological breach. Rites
devoted to healing the body also addressed a disordered world, and healing of the body, not discipline of the body, was the African path to renewed
moral order.

Another major divergence marked this engagement of cultures. The Christian joy in the "kingdom come" that Baptists and Methodists share with Pentecostalists was different from the West African view of a living fulfillment in
the present (cf. Sobel 1988, 20).[2] Christian joy is premised on redeeming the
sinner from an evil world to a world of transcendent good associated with
the One God. The West African sense of ritual practice has been based on
the expectation that rite can address evil in the world and allow a present joy
in life.[3] African experience proposed an ambivalent world in which there
would be a passage back and forth between moral states. This passage was
an integral part of a cosmology in which a multiplicity of spiritual forces
pervaded and defined the earth. Felicitous West African life was perhaps a
changing state but required no ultimate transcendence. Transcendence of
a flawed human present, which would always be a flawed present, was central
to European Christian practice (cf. Genovese 1976, 212).

This confrontation of religious milieus was reflected in the dialogue between ethically rational Christian churches deriving from a missionary practice and the Jamaican Zion Revival which accepted aspects of Christian faith
but maintained both a concern with healing and an aesthetics of joy in life, a
eudemonic embrace of rite. The tension for African peoples among rite, eudemonic, and an alien moral code became the source of an enduring discourse that has shaped both Zion Revival and Pentecostalism. Each religion
has had in Jamaica major external stimuli reflecting both political change and
forms of European Christian revival (cf. Beidelman 1982). Each, however,
also reflects a dynamic process of cultural transformation set in train within
Jamaica through the engagement of Africa with Europe.

Ethical Rationalism and the Mission's Christian Black

The moderately Calvinist Particular Baptists supported by the Baptist Missionary Society[4] were among the first of the major Protestant groups to embrace the cause of foreign evangelism as one that should address the "whole human race."[5] Along with the Methodists and Moravians,[6] they would bring to Jamaica a form of Christianity that de-emphasized the liturgy and placed the focus on ethical acts based in a rationally conceived moral code. Baptist and even Methodist enthusiasm was subordinated in everyday practice to the concern with moral being. This was a legacy of the post-Enlightenment in which behavior itself became a sign of grace in the face of a remote and judging God (Brown 1985, 58–67; Weber 1958, 95–154; Tawney 1926, 234; de Certeau 1988). In the introduction to his account of Baptist evangelism in Jamaica, Phillippo makes reference to the sense of a worldwide moral task:

> Revelation looks with the same benign aspect on the sun-burnt negro as
> on the inhabitant of a more temperate clime—to the bond as to the free—
> to the savage as to the philosopher; all are alike the offspring of the same
> common parent, involved in the consequences of the same apostasy, heirs
> of the same immortal destiny and alike capable of being restored to the
> happiness and prerogatives of their exalted nature. (Phillippo 1970, 1)

To be restored from the apostasy, the fallen state, was to lead a properly Christian life. In their quest, Phillippo and his kind did not especially discriminate between the apostasy of the white and the black.[7] Missionaries preached equality in the sense of equal capacity and need to be saved. Yet the egalitarianism of the missionaries was ambiguous. It promoted a view of Africans as intellectually equal to Europeans and equally adept at practical skills. In time, it also would establish that the enslavers required redemption no less than the enslaved. Yet the dispositional changes involved in African redemption were considerably more intrusive than those required for a European. Not only was plantation slavery a sinful regime, but so, too, was the condition of being an African. As Horace Russell (1983, 53) has observed, the missionaries were driven by a desire "to reinstate the African into the human race." They sought to vindicate a European morality besmirched by more than a century of slavery. They thus thrust upon Jamaicans and other descendants of slavery "the awesome responsibility of being the moral conscience of the world," of righting for the reputation of Europe the wrongs of the slavery epoch. In the process, European ethical rationalism would confront forms of cultural innovation derived not only from West Africa but also from Jamaica itself. The outcome would not be simply another "white" regime. This process would produce in time a new creole religious form.

The missionaries viewed the emancipated slaves in positive as well as negative ways. To propose that the slaves were part of the apostasy was also to propose that they were capable of redemption and not entirely beyond God's kingdom. The systematizing of religion as ethics would teach that all human beings could be moral depending on their circumstance, and the process of being moral embodied the process of being saved. In order to establish that they might be saved, the Africans who had been enslaved were redefined as historically corrupt rather than inherently depraved (cf. Russell 1983, Lewis 1983; see also Jordan 1969, Davis 1966, Henriques 1974). The source of their corrupted lives was seen to lie in their ignorance as Africans, exacerbated by their enslavement. Once the slaves had gained their freedom, their ignorance could be addressed. The emphasis was shifted from a peculiar African nature to the historical influence of a New World environment (see Austin-Broos 1992).[8]

Even the ameliorists and defenders of slavery were frequently in agreement with missionaries over the environmental influence of slavery on moral disposition. John Stewart (1823, 205), a contemporary observer, noted in his chronicle that "there is in the very nature of slavery, in its mildest form, something unfavourable to the cultivation of moral feeling." Among those missionaries who came to support the anti-slavery cause, this view was elaborated. One of its most self-confident expressions comes in a post-emancipation publication from the Religious Tract Society (RTS): "The demoralizing influence of slavery might have been easily foreseen by every right mind, because the system carried on its very front a direct violation of three great moral precepts; that which regards the security of every kind of property, in saying 'Thou shalt not steal'; that which gives a special recognition to the Divine presence among us, by enjoining a hallowed observance of the sabbath; and that which has a bearing upon all the virtues of social life, by honouring all the rights and relationships of marriage" (1842, 117).[9]

Integral to the revaluation of the African as a redeemable soul was the need to pose, in opposition to the planters, the vision of a form of social life separate and alternative to the plantation. If environment impeded the redemption of the African, then a more appropriate context had to be evolved. Such an environment is described, implicitly, in the missionary comment cited above. Baptist missionary William Knibb, in an address to the slaves just before emancipation, was even more explicit: "To be free you must be independent. Receive your money for your work; come to market with money; purchase from whom you please; and be accountable to no one but the Being above, whom I trust will watch over you and protect you" (quoted in Hinton 1847, 289). Knibb emphasizes that the emancipated slave must become a viable, independent economic unit within a cash economy. The RTS statement stipulates further that this must be a system in which property, including the property of the person, is respected, in which temporal life makes room for the sabbath, and in which the missionary model of the family, with Christian marriage at its base, is the dominant social form. And for Knibb, this milieu would involve especially the creation of respectable homes. He observed in England in 1845, "everyone who has seen as I have the wretched cottages in which the peasants were obliged to live, knows perfectly well that it was impossible to instil the finer virtues of Christianity, which glow amidst the amiabilities of social life, unless a comfortable home could be provided" (quoted in Hinton 1847, 486–87).

The Baptist free village system was the concrete embodiment of this alternative social environment that would realize a moral and religious vision (Paget n.d.; Mintz 1974b). It would coalesce in a remarkable fashion with the skills and aspirations to small-scale farming developed by the slaves within the plantation regime (Mintz 1974a). To a form of organization based on agricultural tasks would be added an ideology of the mission. At least in the missionary's imagination, Jamaicans would redeem themselves to God as they engaged the yeoman life.[10] In the process, a new persona emerged for the emancipated. The sober and industrious "Christian black" replaced "Quashie," the devious trickster slave (Russell 1983; Patterson 1967, 174). For more than a century within Jamaica, this missionary image of village life posed a moral alternative to plantation slavery. The ideas of property, family, and religion that were secured in this initial rural context would continue to inform the images of life even of a twentieth-century middle class (see Austin 1979; 1984a, 149–209; Austin-Broos 1988; cf. Olwig 1993, 69–89).

In addition to the social and moral strictures that sectarians would impose upon the emancipated came a distinctive aesthetic presented by the sectarians as a norm of proper Christian life. During the years of slavery, New World Africans had limited opportunity to engage in the plastic arts of West Africa. Their modes of representation were attached almost exclusively to the abilities of the person. They were manifest in speech, dance, other forms of bodily movement, masquerade, and the carnival celebrations of the Christian calendar. That calendar had been muted and transformed through its interpretation in the Book of Common Prayer. This episode of interpretation stripped the planters' religion of its magic, if not of its engagement with the rounds of nature. West African ritual invention coalesced with this inheritance, along with the imperatives of tropical plantation life. Christmas, Easter, and the period of the harvest were celebrated with vigor, while the Sabbath as such had only a modest significance (Long 1774, vol. 2, 424–25; Beckford 1790, vol. 1, 386–90; Lewis 1969, 50–59). To these festivals, which became in time all-island affairs, the slaves added their own informal entertainments as well as mortuary observances. The totality presented an extravagant affirmation of life associated with the planters' casual Christianity. Typical of this process of cultural transformation was the Christmas parade called John Canoe, a wonderful flowering over the years of African and European masquerade in concert (Ryman 1984).[11] Christian ritual observance, such as it was, had become a medium for display and artistic innovation in which the planters became observers of the Africans at play.[12]

Throughout her diary for the years 1801 to 1805, Maria Nugent, the governor's wife, registered distress at Jamaica's style of Christian observance (Wright 1966). The sectarians' judgment on the process whereby religious festival had become a major vehicle of Jamaican artistic forms was even more severe. Not only did they bring to the New World the puritan rejection of religious iconography, but they also sought to make of each person an anti-icon of the self. They proposed that the body be extensively clothed and confined in its movements to utilitarian forms. The very conduct of the person should represent the empowerment of God conceived in ethically rational terms. In 1825, the Anglican Reverend R. Bickell observed with some satisfaction that slaves who became Christian were "ashamed" to join the John Canoe (see Cassidy 1971, 260; cf. Phillippo 1970, 242–43). The Baptists would demand even more: that all hint of revelry be expunged from Jamaican life.

In the 1830s and 1840s, Jamaicans who aspired to become Christian blacks were therefore faced with an acute dilemma. Those who supported their freedom from slavery were also engaged in a different project to reconstruct their selves. The missionaries placed upon the emancipated slaves a broad and rigorous ethical program that inevitably staunched the eudemonic of freedom. The religious sects and movements that follow in a chain from the emancipation chart Jamaican attempts to supersede the persona of the Christian black. And the tension evident in Pentecostalism today among rite, eudemonic, and ethical rationalism remains a continuing statement of the tensions that informed this initial engagement. The dynamism of these later transformations, of which Pentecostalism is one major form, is properly counterposed to the austere moralism of James Phillippo's mission ideals.

The Missionary View

In his account of the slavery system, Phillippo constantly emphasizes its capacity to dehumanize the slave and thereby confer on Africans in the New World a status "not distinguishable from that of passive brutes." The slaves' daily routine, Phillippo observes, was in other countries "performed by horses, oxen and machinery." Consistent with this assimilation of the slaves to beings beyond society, their legal rights were hopelessly curtailed, and they were denied "all opportunities of Divine worship" (1970, 158–61).

The tenor of Phillippo's view is revealed more accurately, however, when his withering opinion of slavery is placed alongside his opinion of Africans.

Phillippo makes some adverse comments on the ideas of African inferiority sustained by Montesquieu and Long, the Jamaican historian.[13] He nonetheless notes the inability of the African to read, to calculate time, and to arrive at properly rational decisions (189–92). He comments of Africans under slavery, "Enthralled and bowed down by a system that returned them to the level of the brute . . . they were altogether destitute of taste and genius . . . the dwarfs of the rational world, their intellect rising only to a confused notion and imperfect idea of the general objects of human knowledge" (191). Added to this was a debased moral state maintained through ignorance and superstition. Phillippo cites with approval the opinion that the "aggregate character" of the various African peoples "amalgamated into one society under the influence of slavery" was "irascible, conceited, proud, indolent, lascivious, credulous and very artful," a "general disposition" that "may safely be asserted to be thieving, lazy and dissimulating" (240).[14] Here was the image of Quashie the slave that Christianity would transform through a process of moral redemption (see also Stewart 1992, 90, 93).

With regard to elements of slave religion, Phillippo was consistently unsympathetic. He parodied the attempts by slaves to placate the spirit of a dead relative, to ensure its welfare in the afterlife while simultaneously protecting the living from its desires and griefs (144–45; cf. Hogg 1964, 61–63). He also discarded as superstition the complex of myal and obeah beliefs whereby slaves embraced a world in which human and spiritual forces interact (247–48; cf. Hogg 1964, 65). Animated ideas of good and evil embodied in a natural-social environment made little sense to the Christian concerned with the internalized evil of sin. Clear moral evidence that all these beliefs were simply debasing superstition—and not an alternative religious form— was found in the fact that the slaves, without the benefit of Christianity, were unable to maintain the cleanliness of their persons or the sanctity of their sexual lives. In fact, Phillippo observes, the African ridiculed the "sacred institute" of marriage, polygamy was common, and women were especially debased (218–19). In Phillippo's view, there was no order to slave domestic life: "Licentiousness the most degraded and unrestrained was the order of the day. Every estate on the island—every negro hut was a common brothel: every female a prostitute and every man a libertine" (218; see also Knibb 1842, 27).

Not only did Phillippo presume the moral depravity of a religion and culture that remained opaque to him, but his description of dancing indicates the sectarian's total lack of rapport with any element of West African aesthetics:

> On some occasions the dance consisted of stamping feet, accompanied
> by various contortions of the body, with strange and indecent attitudes:

on others . . . the lower extremities being held firm, the whole person
was moved without raising the feet from the ground. Making the head and
limbs fixed points, they writhed and turned the body upon its own axis. . . .
Their approaches to each other, and the attitudes and inflexions in which
they were made, were highly indecent, the performers being nearly naked.
(241–42)

The Strategy for Change

All this could begin to change only following the emancipation, when the
Baptists in particular sought, through the free village system, to construct
a new environment for the emancipated slaves (Phillippo 1970, 289–90;
cf. Gardner 1873, 458–63). The elements in the construction of a New
World Christian were industry promoted through private property, education, and conversion. And with Christian conversion would come a different
aesthetic of life.

Phillippo notes confidently of the post-emancipation experience that "the
term indolent can only be applied to the black population in the absence
of remunerating employment" (234). Under the new regime, the villages,
which maintained their own cultivations and also provided the workforce for
nearby plantations, presented a hive of industry:

> On returning from their daily labour the men almost uniformly employ
> themselves in cultivating their own grounds or in improving their own little
> freeholds, and the women in culinary and in other domestic purposes until
> driven to their frugal repast and to repose by darkness and fatigue. (235)

Phillippo cautioned against the introduction of more immigrant labor into
Jamaica as a threat to the livelihood of those already resident on the island
(94–98). Nonetheless, his account of rural life ignores not only the extensive
vagrancy and squatting created by landlessness and unemployment but also
the fact that women retained and expanded their participation in agriculture
(see Cumper 1958; Hall 1959; Eisner 1960; Olivier 1936).

Phillippo finds the product of the freemen's industry in neatly organized
villages and furnished cottages that "are in all respects equal, and some of
them superior, to the tenancies of labourers in rural districts of England"
(220–21). In this setting, which could allow a generalized self-esteem, education was pursued with alacrity. Phillippo estimates that in 1841, there were
approximately one hundred eighty-six day schools, one hundred Sabbath
schools, and thirty evening schools throughout the island. These schools had
an estimated attendance of around thirty thousand. Children, he reported,
studied assiduously, and, as a result, the range of occupational skills had expanded rapidly to equal that available in England.[15] Phillippo concludes:

the black skin and woolly hair constitute the only difference which now exists between multitudes of the emancipated peasantry of Jamaica and the tradesmen and agriculturalists of England.

Nor are the intellectual faculties of this calumniated and oppressed people in any respect inferior to the rest of the species; *they have simply been suspended from inaction, and the absence of those influences which were necessary to their development.* (201; emphasis added)

With these comments, Phillippo confirms his environmental rendering of the African's moral corruption under slavery. He expresses complacent faith in the strategy to produce a Christian black by replicating a European yeoman.

Addressing the project of conversion, Phillippo cites the enthusiasm with which schoolchildren would memorize large tracts of the Bible (197). He recounts a village congregation gathering at the call "Come to prayers" and families after the Sunday service sitting by their cottage trees engaged in reading scriptures and singing hymns (224, 233). This Jamaican pastorale was made possible, in Phillippo's view, by the spread of Christian marriage. In December 1840, the celebration of marriage by missionaries was legalized. As a consequence, Phillippo suggests, marriage came to be associated by Jamaicans "with everything virtuous and honourable in human conduct" (232). Phillippo also reports triumphantly that funerals proceeded "nearly in accordance with civilized custom" and notes how attendance on the deceased had been modified to conform with Christian mores (260–62). The Sabbath was now observed, and the "frantic orgies" of Christmas and other holidays had been dispelled (260). Moreover, "attendance at dances, merry-makings of any description as well as at horse-races, are all sins which are visited with excision in all the Jamaica churches with which the author is acquainted" (334). Bible study, observation of the Sabbath, Christian marriage, and a puritan aesthetic complete the model of tutelage involved in redeeming the African soul.

Phillippo's account of Jamaica some five years after the emancipation is not so much a description as a blueprint for the Christian black. It envisages a transformation that is startling not only for its divergence from the previous slave regime but even more for its stifling of the culture of the slaves embedded in a Caribbean life (cf. Green 1976, 352). The missionaries assumed that their ethical rationalism was a mode of life accessible to all. Creole ideas of illness or affliction reflecting obeah or spiritual disorder were understood by the missionaries only as corrupting superstition. Their practice of ethical rationalism with its disciplines of the body not only repudiated the world of play and its carnivalesque aesthetic, it also sought to stifle in Jamaica an intense eudemonic of freedom which both transformed and re-embodied an African sense of joy in the world.

West African Religion and the Creole

Accounts of the West African religion brought to Jamaica have emphasized rites performed for the dead, belief in spirits both benign and malign that could have a propensity for possessing the living, and the secretive practice of witchcraft, or obeah, once combated by myal rites and now combated by the rites of Revival churches and Pentecostalists (Hogg 1964, 61–63; Patterson 1967, 182–207; Turner 1982, 52–54; Schuler 1980, 33–37; cf. Bastide 1978 and Simpson 1978). Patterson also adds belief "in a supreme being too remote to be active in the ordinary affairs of men" and "belief in and use of charms and fetishes" (cf. Rattray 1923, 141).[16] Extrapolating from twentieth-century sources, it is also likely that in West Africa these ritual practices and associated ideas were supported by cults, sometimes clan-based and sometimes extra-clan concerns that varied in their complexity from region to region (Patterson 1967, 183; cf. Ellis 1890, Forde 1954, Fortes 1945, Herskovits 1938, Horton 1964, Parrinder 1961, Rattray 1923).

In Jamaica, where clan organization fell away and undermined belief in ancestral living-dead, concern with the ancestors became family-based and, later, transformed in more radical ways (Gardner 1873, 184–87). By the late nineteenth century, biblical prophets rather than ancestors cohabited at a distance the world of the living. They secured Jamaican Revivalists through their presence and empowering possession.[17] In time, this empowering possession was associated with the practice of healing as healing became a central motif in Jamaican Christian practice. The common West African concern for the dead changed and diffused in other ways: into Jamaican duppy or ghost beliefs that in turn helped construct Jamaican obeah (cf. Hogg 1964, 60–61).

"*Obeah,*" the word for witchcraft practice, possibly derives from the Twi meaning "witch" or "witchcraft person," though even this practice, as Fortes observes, was unevenly spread within West Africa (Cassidy 1971, 241; Fortes 1987). And in Jamaica, obeah deployed wandering ghosts of Jamaican construction and elicited its own ritual response. Jamaican "*myal*" evolved over time to combat the effects of obeah. This was a different complex again, and the word's derivation, possibly Hausa, remains obscure. The practices the word described, however, were certainly influenced by Christianity (Gardner 1873, 191; Long 1774, 77–81; Schuler 1980, 41–43). The logic of Jamaican obeah, with its various techniques to "put on spirits" and the myal rites to take them off, therefore is seen more properly as a Jamaican phenomenon shaped by a Christian presence. The emphasis on possessing spirits, so evident in Jamaica today, is there but less prominent in African rite. The stable complex is divination, either to discern witchcraft practice or else to recommend rites of immolation to appease an ancestor or another form of spirit (cf. Bascom 1969). Parrinder describes types of mediumship associated with Yoruba divination that did involve spirit possession; and Drewal has re-affirmed more recently the role of women in Yoruba possession (Parrinder 1961, 78; Drewal 1992, 182–86; cf. Beattie and Middleton 1969, Lewis 1971, Nadel 1946).

These comments of a general nature indicate the aporias involved in writing about African religion in Jamaica. The African heritage has become creole as well as the heritage of Christian Europe. And if Christianity's hand seems to rest more heavily, this fact should fuel a search not only for African connections but also for the uses and forms that have become creole (see also Mintz and Price 1976). The African-cum-Jamaican focus on healing rather than a disembodied ethic is one such central and enduring form with which the missionaries would continually grapple. Healing often came in conjunction with possession, and this further use of embodied rite was seen as "heathen" in Jamaica until the advent of Christian revival began to redefine its practice.

Ripostes to the Christian Black:
Healing and the Trickster Eudemonic

In a range of West African religions, one role of ancestors, ghosts, and nature spirits was to map out interdiction in the world, and breach of interdiction often was evidenced by the experience of malaise.[18] Behavior displeasing to ancestor spirits, neglect of important ritual occasions, and vengeance wrought by a haunting ghost or by an offended nature spirit were forms of breach in which moral wrong would intersect with physical malaise (Rattray 1927, 147–48; Herskovits 1938, 194; Bascom 1969; Goody 1962). Repair of the breach and the affliction very often proceeded through divination, appropriate sacrifice, and sometimes the transfer of a felicitous spiritual empowerment from the diviner to the patient. These possessions could involve shaking bodies, transformed voice, and forms of vision.[19] Wrongful acts incurring affliction might be willed and deliberately performed. They also could occur accidentally or by mere oversight. Yet whether the breach was intentional or the product of accident, its redress was always a general concern.

Just as interdiction mapped the world, so the rites to restore its breach secured the world and sustained the domain of clan concerns. As a consequence, in West African healing, finding a remedy for the patient was as much a concern of the kinship group as it was of the individual person. And occasionally this shared involvement could result in the possession of a relative of the patient (Herskovits 1938, 238; Bascom 1969). The affliction caused by breach of interdiction was a real index of disorder in the world.

Re-ordering the body to re-order the world was an immediate, real, and corporate concern at the heart of moral order in an African world. As both Richards (1970) and Horton (1967) indicate, the diviner's task was a complex one. Some illnesses could be dealt with herbally, and some that proved intractable to herbs were related to cosmic forces of the ancestral type. Other forms of malaise, however, reflected powers deployed by a witch. The diviner's role was always to determine the specific genre of the malaise as well as recommend a healing course.

These ritual acts to regulate relations between the human and cosmic world were matched by the practice and combating of witchcraft in the context of human social relations (Ellis 1890, 102–3). Witchcraft concerned the manipulation of souls by malignant women and men. Generally, the sufferer was not involved in a breach of interdiction. Rather, the unfortunate victim had become the object of a human aggression, also expressed through conferral of malaise. Witchcraft itself often was regarded as a form of moral malaise based in a particular physical state, and this was a state of which the witch might be more or less aware. Notwithstanding the vulnerability of witches and the controlling fear of witchcraft accusation, the harm done by witches was physical and real within West African ontology.

Discussions of West African witchcraft generally underline the relatively close relations that pertained between witches and those they might afflict. The suspicion, accusation, and perpetration of witchcraft frequently involved people standing in kin relations that were prone to conflict (Rattray 1927, 148; Field 1937; Nadel 1970; Tait 1967; Wilson 1970). In Jamaica, these became not kin relations but rather relations of proximity. In obeah, the source of affliction often would be a disgruntled associate of the victim, who would travel to a neighboring plantation or village in order to recruit a practitioner. This pattern inevitably made the treatment of affliction more diffuse than its counterpart in Africa, for the initiator and the perpetrator were not always identical or locally based. Nonetheless, responses to obeah after emancipation seem very similar to the East African witchcraft movements associated with colonialism (see chapter 3, below). Marwick comments of two such movements that they "both aimed at the complete removal of witchcraft from the country by the systematic destruction or reform of witches and by the protection of their potential victims" (1970, 82). This was the object of myal practitioners in post-emancipation Jamaica, and they drew the practice of Christian rite into the perpetration of their fight.

A restored body in African cultures also has connoted a restored world in which fulfilment was part of the present (cf. Comaroff 1985). The cosmological rendering of moral order in terms of affliction and its healing precluded in African cultures the view that a joy in human fulfillment could come only through transcendence. African "spirit" or "soul" was not a locus of moral order answerable only to God but rather a seat of vitality engaged with the world of the living.[20] African cultures thereby sustained a real sense of eudemonic that embraced felicitous life in the present. Joy could be taken in the world and in its moral ambivalence, which was finessed by the West African tricksters rather than resolved through moral rules conferred by God and aimed at transcendence.

Beyond the domain of healing rite but associated with it in cosmological terms was the Afro-Caribbean aesthetic of play exemplified by Anansi the trickster. Each of these major concerns in turn rebuffed the ethical rationalism of the mission: one through interpretations of the moral in terms of malaise and embodied rite, the other through the interpretation of joy as a this-worldly human and sensuous concern. This connection of Anansi to the practice of healing—as routes to a world of human fulfillment—was amplified in another way. As healing rejected a disembodied ethic, Anansi and the world of play opposed the mission's endorsement of work as an essential dimension of moral redemption. These themes come together in Jamaican Christian rite, which is eudemonic rather than contrite, and in ironic views of the pastor that see him as an ambivalent figure, more often related to Anansi the trickster than to Phillippo's Christian black.

Anansi, the spider trickster, is prominent in the folklore of the Akan group of Twi-speaking people of whom the Ashanti are among the best known. For a significant part of the eighteenth century, from 1730 to 1790, Akan peoples were in the majority of those imported as slaves to Jamaica (Patterson 1967, 137–39; Curtin 1969, 220–30). Their Twi language had an enduring impact on Jamaican creole, and it is not surprising that their trickster tales, rather than others of the West African coast, became ensconced within Jamaica (Cassidy 1971, 10–25). *Anansesem* among the Ashanti included not only spider trickster tales but also a wide range of other folk and "just so" stories describing familiar facts of the social and natural world. In Jamaica, the position has been much the same. Five collections of Jamaican *anansesem* from the 1830s to the 1980s contain, along with spider tales, a range of other stories and songs (Lewis 1969, 253–59; Milne-Home 1890; Jekyll 1907; Beckwith 1924; Tanna 1984). Yet Anansi is the most important figure, who makes a statement about the world and the role in it of the human beings whom he so clearly represents.

Pelton (1980) has described the Ashanti Anansi tales as tales of the "liminal" state (see also Finnegan 1970).[21] He uses the term in the sense developed by Victor Turner commenting on the work of van Gennep (van Gennep 1960; Turner 1967, 93–111; 1969, 94–130). The liminal phase of ritual transition is one in which "persons elude or slip through the network of classifications that normally locate states and positions in cultural space" (Turner 1969, 95). Pelton proposes Anansi's liminal state not as a phase in a ritual transition but as a permanent possibility in social life, a "source of recreative power" in the ability to "breach or invert social rules" (Pelton 1980, 35; see also Beidelman 1982). In Pelton's description of Anansi's liminality, two aspects are especially important: the idea of liminality as a total state and the idea of liminality as an idiom of performance.

Ashanti cosmology conceives of the world as situated between the poles of the sky god Nyame and the earth goddess Asase Yaa, as situated between a reliance on agriculture and on a trade dominated by women. Anansi plays with and between these poles of sky and earth, male and female, production and commerce, intelligence and appetite. In particular, the tales demonstrate the inexorable play of intellect and appetite, of spiritual aspiration and sensuousness that inevitably creates an openness in life, a liminal beyond controlling norm (cf. Pelton 1980, 63–67). Ashanti *anansesem* also exhibit liminality in their actual performance. Rattray has observed that Anansi tales are often crude and in marked contrast to the practice of a people in other respects "most civil and well bred" (Rattray 1969, ix–x). The explanation for this apparent anomaly lies in the particular role allotted to the tales. Clues to this role are found in the fact that the tales are told only at night, and in the fact that the teller speaks a truth disclaimer at the outset: "We do not really mean, we do not really mean [that what we are going to say is true]." And in the tales, topics generally regarded as sacred, including the sky god, ancestors, and sexuality, are treated as though they were profane (Rattray 1969, x–xi). As a genre of performance, Ashanti Anansi tales represent the liminal role of humor in turning the given world upside down and allowing people to step outside their everyday existence to give full vent to the irony and even the ridiculous in life.

Jamaican Anansi tales are both strikingly similar to and different from their Ashanti counterparts. Anansi is the same ambiguous personality of prodigious appetites and exceptional cleverness. He lacks, however, his regular intercourse with Nyame and has taken up instead an intermittent engagement in co-operation and trickery with the figure of Tiger or sometimes Lion (cf. Milne-Home 1890). In the Jamaican Anansi, the trickster negotiates earthly hierarchies without the help or the hindrance of God, but in constant engagement with other mundane figures such as Dog, Rat, John-Crow, and Crab. The Christian God is irremediably remote, and his being is beyond manipulation. When Jamaican Anansi tales address Christianity, it is the pastor's practice and, less commonly, Jesus' that are reinterpreted in terms of the trick. The Christian God's transcendent being places him beyond the ambiguous, and thus the ambiguity of authority and power is inserted within a social hierarchy.

Consistent with the situating of Anansi within an earthly stratification, he assumes the parodied features of a Jamaican peasant. This is represented most vividly in Anansi's style of speech, described by Jekyll as "Bungo talk" (1907, 12–13). This Jekyll describes as speaking "very rapidly" through the nose, using "the most countrified form of dialect" (2; Cassidy 1971, 41–42). "Bungo" may derive from a similar Hausa term meaning a "nincompoop" or "country bumpkin," but also with connotations of an inferior ethnic heritage (Cassidy and LePage 1967, 80; Tanna 1984, 79–80). Cassidy and LePage in their *Dictionary of Jamaican English* define *"bungo"* as "an insulting term meaning very black, ugly; stupid; a country bumpkin"; and "African in the sense of a descendant of slaves whose civility is minimally mediated by European mores" (1967, 80). Tanna observes that Anansi in Jamaica thus has two identities: "the comical and often lovable trickster underdog" and also "the ghost of an African slave past," represented in the poor and uneducated peasant (Tanna 1984, 80).

Anansi in Jamaica is dominated by the search for meat far more than is his counterpart among the Ashanti. His sexual aspirations, on the other hand, are real but more modest and humorous (cf. Rattray 1969, 128–37; Jekyll 1907, 11–13). Tanna suggests that in the modern period, sexuality has been largely confined to another genre, "Big Bwoy" stories. Whether or not this was always the case, it is clear that Jamaican Anansi has been modified significantly under Christianity. In 1890, Milne-Home remarked on the reluctance of Jamaicans to tell Anansi stories to Europeans:

> Whether it is that the great spread of education causes them to fear ridicule on the part of white questioners, or that the systematic discouragement of the clergy of all sects is beginning to take effect at last, certain it is that any one seeking to take down tales from the lips of a negro will have to spend much time, patience, and persuasion ere the narrator will cease to say, "Dat foolishness; wonder Missis car to har dat." (Milne-Home 1890, 2)

Yet if sexuality within Anansi has been modified to a degree and if the tales became situated in Jamaica as a parody of African being, their creole reconstruction has been not merely through a European hegemony but also through an Afro-Jamaican rendering of ontology and moral order. Jamaican Anansi tales, unlike their Ashanti counterparts, are filled with the magical power of music. Anansi fiddles; he sings and provokes others to sing. Music helps to realize the trick and also can celebrate the trick's success. Music becomes part of the magic of the trick. Events are seduced into life by the eudemonic of song rather than realized in utilitarian acts.

Anansi does not question God as such but rather his role in the Christian cosmos as the moral nexus for the world of work. He does this not through studied resistance but rather through the enigma of play. Making labor peripheral to life, Anansi questions in laconic style the logic of a moral dis-

cipline applied to the notion of a laboring self. In this, he resurrects sensuousness and the fallibility of a rational world. As the following two tales relate, this can be a world in which even "de Saviour" and his pastors come to
act like the spider trickster.

> A man called Robin Mice-rat went to his uncle's house where the uncle
> live entirely in the dark. When Robin was leaving, he took a stick and hit
> his uncle. Robin went to "de Saviour" and asked Him how he might be-
> come a big man. Saviour replied that he should kill his oldest uncle. Robin
> returned to his uncle, pretending to be another nephew, and the uncle
> tole him how Robin had "lick" him in the wrong place: "if *heah* . . . him
> ketch me, de fellow would a got me." Robin Mice-rat hit his uncle in the
> appropriate place on the forehead. The uncle was killed. Robin went back
> to the Saviour so that he might become a big man. Saviour said, "You little
> bit of man go kill you oldest uncle, den if me let you turn bigger you would
> do worse!" So from dat day das de reason let you see mice don't bigger to
> dis day. (Beckwith 1924, 59–60)

Another tale recorded by Jekyll shows that "parsons" in a Jamaican environment learn the same tricks as their savior:[22]

> Pastor Puss persuades his congregation member Toad to marry his lady
> friend. Invitations are sent out and preparations made. But Toad also in-
> vites Parson Dog who "come with his gown was to take away the business
> from Parson Puss." Toad expresses his preference for Parson Puss and
> Parson Dog, despite his chagrin, is lured away momentarily to lick the
> blood of a slaughtered hog. Parson Puss marries the couple and Parson
> Dog returns to hear the song:
>
> "When you see a hugly man, When you see a hugly man,
> "When you see a hugly man, Never make him marry you.
> "Parson Dog won't marry me, Parson Dog won't marry me,
> "Parson Dog won't marry me, Cut your eye an' pass him."
>
> Parson Puss is dancing with some of the women who begin to laugh at
> Parson Dog goading him for his ugliness. Dog, in turn, "run in the ring
> an' palm Puss an' begin to fight him." Puss escapes up a tree, but "Dog
> an' Puss can't 'gree until now." (Jekyll 1907, 913)

The rite of healing as moral restitution, with its concomitant experience
of possession, and the eudemonic of play and performance disturbed the
course of ethical rationalism within the Jamaican Christian milieu. The realm
of obeah and the myalist was a moral world of order and disorder that the
missionaries would accept only when the practice of healing through possession became in time the healing of sin. As a consequence, the chronicles
of missionaries are replete with concern that Jamaicans should be weaned
from myal into a properly Christian world. No less a central concern of

the missionaries was the idea of marriage, work, and a sober life as integral to Christian being. The remarks of clergy and state officials on the unruliness of peasant life, on its affinity with sensuous play, and on the flouting of Christian marriage were equal to the obeah fright. One clergyman, as described below, criticized Jamaicans for their "levity" and pronounced that this levity would preclude superior spiritual achievement. The Jamaican novelist Claude McKay captures well this particular milieu in his work *Banana Bottom* (1933). The young heroine, Bita Plant, pursues her vivid country life between the sober influence of the mission and the *jouissance* of rural life. She deploys the "freeness" of her chosen associates to temper the moralism of the mission, which McKay shows in this and other works was especially constraining for Jamaican women.[23] In this milieu portrayed by McKay, women would find in the Pentecostals an enthusiastic healing from sin that would elevate them to the status of saints.

Many Jamaicans would become Christian blacks, and many would be influenced by free village life (cf. Mintz 1974a, 1974b). But the Christian forms that both would choose brought healing with possession, and a eudemonic, into the precinct of the church. Jamaicans used Christianity in ways that were foreign to the missionaries. In so doing, they deflected the path of a Christian hegemony and set in train a moral politics concerning the construction of a Christian subject. Most dramatically represented in this initial confrontation of European and African worlds, this politics would become more intricate as a creole religion unfolded and as Africa and Europe were changed.

Pentecostalism in Jamaica was partly the product of a regional shift in Jamaican and Caribbean social orders. America entered the Caribbean and magnified forms of regional migration that brought internal change to Jamaica. Even those who remained on the island began to embrace a larger world, and some of these embraced that world through the medium of religious forms. These changing styles of Christian practice were not simply exogenous, however, or merely hegemonic in Jamaica. Revival religion and Pentecostalism both have embodied negotiations embedded in a discourse of creole religion that began when missionaries engaged the slaves. The next chapter explores this discourse as it took shape through the nineteenth century and especially during the time known as the Great Revival.

3 Revival and the Healing of Sin

> ... this Meeting views with alarm the distressed condition
> of nearly all classes of the people of this Colony ... [but]
> would also, with deep humility, acknowledge the Divine
> hand. They desire to express the fear that the afflictive
> dealings with which the land has been visited have not
> been sanctified.
>
> —From the resolutions of a Spanish Town
> Public Meeting, May 16, 1865

> [Revivalists] claim to be taught of the Spirit; and their
> influence ... is due to the general belief of our people
> that the Spirit of God works supernaturally and power-
> fully for the salvation of the world.
>
> —George Henderson, 1931

In his account of Jamaica published in 1850, the Reverend David King, a Presbyterian sojourner to the island,
described the sorry state of Jamaican Christianity. Though he noted that the
"negroes" were less irascible than the Irish, he nevertheless listed their numerous "vices": licentiousness, indifference to medical aid, theft, duplicity,
greed, "incapacity to rule," and, finally, levity (King 1850, 46–77). The British Baptists, King was to note, "subsist only by taking charge of more stations
than they can ... superintend" (107). As a consequence, Native Baptists,
"unable to write or even to read," flourished in Kingston and the countryside
(108–9).[1] Moreover, "Obeahism and Miallism," once thought to be declining, were "even now recovering their influence" (112). King's list of "negro
vices" includes at least three vices not previously emphasized in "Quashie"
constructions: lack of interest in medical care, failure in superintendence,
and levity. All three are indicative of the cultural milieu of Jamaicans following the emancipation.[2] They capture both some ingredients of the revival
tradition and, equally important, attitudes toward that tradition from within
Jamaica's hierarchy.

Myalists and the Healing of Affliction

The reluctance to pay for the services of a European physician reflected not
simply the poverty of Jamaicans or even the deterioration of services on the
island. It was also indicative of the people's engagement with an embodied

51

system of malaise that was different from European practice. To those who believed that affliction might be caused by witchcraft, troublesome ghosts of the dead, or a Christian oversight, the treatment of a European practitioner would have seemed both expensive and inappropriate. Restitution would come through an integrated practice that was alien to the European practitioner, a practice of herbal and spiritual craft that might involve immersion to address both moral and physical being.[3] The expectation that pastors also should be healers is dotted throughout the missionary records, notably in the conflict between Reverend Clark of Brown's Town and his assistant, Mr. Johnston, who presented himself as "doctor and minister without charge" to the people; and in the diary of Father James Splaine, who observed that "the anointing with special oils of the seriously ill . . . accompanied by special prayers, was a powerful attraction to the people" (Henderson 1931, 115–20; cited in Stewart 1983, 184).

Even in Phillippo's account of the evolution of "Myalmen" prior to and following the emancipation, there is an emphasis on the manner in which Jamaicans would align Christian rite with the practice of healing. The men often spoke in tongues, offered prophecy on the basis of dreams, sustained penitential devotions to bring on possession by an "angel," and cured the sick by anointing with oil (Phillippo 1970, 270–72):

> the Myalmen, having most of them been employed in attendance on the
> sick in the hospitals of estates, and thereby acquired some knowledge of
> medicine, have, since the abolition of slavery, set up as medical men; and,
> in order to increase their influence, and consequently, their gains, have
> called to their aid the mysteries of this abominable superstition. . . . The
> more effectually to delude the multitude, the priests of this deadly art,
> now that religion has become general, have incorporated with it a religious
> phraseology, together with some of the religious observances of the most
> popular denominations.(263)

Phillippo's judgment would have been endorsed by the Presbyterian Hope Waddell. In his recollections for 1838, Waddell related the story of one of his congregation. Suffering bad health, she was made "a drink of herbs, which, in the middle of the night, caused her to sneeze violently, and cast out of her nostrils two pieces of bottle glass" (Waddell 1970, 136). The curer was a "Myal woman" whose "system was to extract from the diseased body the vitiating substances, which some unknown enemy had, by magic acts, imbedded there. By sucking, or sneezing, or retching, she caused the pins, glass or nails to be extracted from the sufferers' flesh" (137).[4] Waddell would emphasize that myal was perceived by Jamaicans as a curing cult that was "wholly opposed" to obeah: "It affected to cure the sicknesses and remove other evils which the Obea produced. The Myal practitioners counted themselves angels of light, and called those of the opposite craft angels of darkness" (137).

Europeans themselves could only reinforce this association of rites to cure affliction with notions of Christian spiritual power (but cf. Price 1990, 117–44). In his journal for 1816, the planter Monk Lewis reported a disagreement over a woman between two of his slaves, Pickle and Edward. Pickle became convinced, having won the woman, that Edward had worked obeah upon him in revenge. Lewis ridiculed Pickle's fears but nonetheless "offered to christen him, and expel black Obeah by white, but in vain; the fellow persisted in saying that 'he had a pain in his side and, therefore, Edward must have given it to him'" (Lewis 1969, 134–35). The notion here of moral malignancy manifest in physical malaise is clear, as is Lewis's helpful if unheeded proposal that a Christian force could combat the pain. Waddell, too, related a case of a young woman fearful that her shadow or soul had been captured by a malignant "Myal man." He offered his Christianity to relieve her concerns which he identified as a manifestation of evil. Like Pickle, however, the woman remained unconvinced of Christianity's power (1970, 138).

If these two Europeans, layman and cleric, enthusiastically offered the power of Christianity in the curing of affliction wrought by witchcraft without convincing the recipients of its power, others registered greater success. Gardner, recollecting the days of the Great Revival, would note that by that time, "a reputed Obeah man" had added to his repertoire of fetish objects—fowls' feet, fish bones, feathers, and the teeth of various species—"a bell used to summon a sort of familiar spirit," a pack of cards, and "a number of class tickets" from erstwhile Baptist days. When these fetishes were deployed to affect a victim, the fear of them caused sickening and even death (Gardner 1873, 188–89). At the time of the Great Revival, however, and under the influence of "strong, though ill-directed religious feeling," Christian women, Gardner remarked, were fearless before the objects of the obeah's art:

> [The] women who captured [the] old man did not hesitate to handle these
> articles, taking them out one by one, and explaining their nature to the
> writer: all fear was gone. Yet when a few years before [the writer] had ob-
> tained possession of a parcel of Obeah trash, a promise of money to any lad
> in a large school who would step over it when laid on the floor, failed to
> secure more than one volunteer. (188, n. 2)

Gardner recognized, as other writers did not, that this engagement between affliction and Christianity involved not simply a "mixing" of elements but rather a redefinition of the form of Christianity that the missionaries had brought to Jamaica. Limited literacy made it difficult for missionaries to purvey a text-centered Christianity that focused on moral rules, and the cultural differences between the missionaries and their followers meant that their ethical rationalism would have had a limited meaning for Afro-Jamaicans. As the spark of emancipation passed, the freemen's failures to maintain a commitment to marriage, to "clean cottages," and to literacy were failures to connect these practices with forms of empowering significant to them. And so the vice of levity, to which the Reverend King referred, concerned above all the Jamaicans' "inability to grieve for wrong" and the lack of a "profound sorrow for sin." These inabilities, King observed, were "especially unfavourable to that moral greatness which genuine religion demands" (1850, 69–70). The "levity" ascribed to Jamaicans by King, their embrace of a Jamaican eudemonic, was indicative of their rejection of Europe's ethical rationalism.

The complex called "myal" by missionary observers was not simply a nativistic movement or even a consistent millennialism (cf. Hogg 1964, 73; Schuler 1980, 41–44). It was rather a complex of rite and belief that sought to sustain the logic of affliction by assimilating elements of Christianity to it. The Jamaican concern with duppies or ghosts of the dead may well have increased, as Hogg (1964) has argued, in the course of the emancipation. Both physical suffering and social confusion would have encouraged an expansion of witchcraft (cf. Turner 1968). The Holy Spirit, in the form of a dove, and the angels, prophets, and evangelists were summoned by water, prayer, and dance to empower Jamaicans against these misfortunes. Christian teaching on the Second Coming doubtless added a millennial dimension to this complex. The complex nonetheless remained one in which forces constructed from a Christian world were deployed in a West African way to maintain a benign environment. Schuler describes bands in St. James and Trelawny parishes driving out the evil of obeah. Christian formularies were used to combat evil embedded in a place or a person through the use of fetish objects (Schuler 1980, 41–43; cf. Waddell 1970, 187–92; Carlile 1884, 27–28; Stewart 1983, 318–19; Marwick 1970). These enthusiastic cleansings of persons and the landscape in preparation for the Second Coming were one manifestation of a larger complex: Jamaica's rendering of a Christian order in terms that retained a sense of affliction.

It is not surprising, then, that Gardner described the Native Baptists as those who "mingled the belief and even practice of Mialism with religious observance," meaning by "religious" Christianity (Gardner 1873, 357). In his sympathetic account of the original Native Baptists Liele and Baker, Gardner noted that Liele's Christianity was fairly orthodox but for "the washing of feet and anointing [of] the sick" (344). Other Native Baptist preachers, however, relied on dreams and the experience of "convince," a state of swooning away accompanied by visions, as the evidence of Christian conversion. They also adopted "superstitious" practices that could raise up followers who had swooned away. Replete with this power, Gardner emphasized the "overbearing, tyrannical, and lascivious" behavior of the Native Baptist leaders, among whom "sensuality was almost . . . unrestrained" (357). Remarkably, in these very brief comments, Gardner foreshadows fundamental elements of Jamaica's revival complex as it would be manifest in both Zion Revival and Pentecostalism: conversion through the spiritual empowering of possession, healing as central in the fight against sin, foot washing as a rite of cleansing and humility that sustains the cleansing of baptismal immersion, and strong, charismatic leaders from the people constructed by observers as African proponents of sensuality.

It was in this context that Reverend King would list the "incapacity to rule" as a further "negro vice" (1850, 57). King argued that there were indeed leaders of note among Jamaica's "mulattoes," but this was not the case among the "negroes," who, at the slightest elevation in their station, became "vain, irascible, capricious" or else "[failed] in the more important province of moral principle" (58). King identified among such leaders the native teachers and deacons who might take over classes when a European missionary relinquished his post (108). In all, King was responding to a religious complex that had diverged significantly from the sectarian mission.

Revival and the Affliction of Sin

Jamaica's Great Revival began as an extension of the revivals that occurred in America in 1858 and 1859 and in Britain in 1859. These revivals, with their source in America's eastern states, were indicative of major theological developments in America that would see the triumph of Arminianism over Calvinism in the English-speaking world and then the emergence of the Methodist-inspired Holiness movement with its teaching of Christian perfectionism.[5] From these developments would flow Pentecostalism, with its additional practice of miraculous curing and speaking in tongues, forms that Jamaicans would adopt with ease. American Pentecostalism flowered in the first decade of the twentieth century and spread to Jamaica in the second decade. Yet, even by 1858, Jamaica had received representatives from the American Church of Christ, an early product of American revivalism. In 1894, Jamaica would see a Seventh Day Adventist Church established in Kingston and, in 1907, a Holiness Church of God. In the interim, Jamaica would have its own Great Revival in 1860 and 1861. And in December 1887, representatives of the Salvation Army, itself a product of the 1859 English revival, would arrive on the island.[6] These contacts with metropolitan revivalists would inspire Jamaica's own evangelistic movements, including Raglan Phillips's Light Brigade and Alexander Bedward's Bedwardism. The impact of these sallies would move the novelist Claude McKay to write the presence of foreign evangelists into the milieu of turn-of-the-century rural Jamaica. And as these extensions of metropolitan revival began to finger at Jamaica's shores, the churches within Jamaica itself would be influenced by the theological ideas developing in America and England.

This second missionary wave involved a certain displacement of ethical rationalism. Moral discipline came to rest on the prior rite of being "born again." Enthusiastic forms of revival were turned to address the issue of sin.

And as the Baptists moved away from their neo-Calvinism, African affliction and Christian sin became more easily assimilable.

America's mid-nineteenth-century revivalism was associated with the Presbyterian Charles Finney, who would later leave his church and, as professor of theology at Oberlin College, espouse the doctrine known as "Oberlin Perfectionism."[7] Another leading figure was Phoebe Palmer, a Methodist evangelist based in New York, who gathered an extensive circle around her. These two placed an emphasis on willed redemption and perfection of the moral person initiated through revival (McLoughlin 1960, xi, xxvi).[8] Yet, prior to Finney's rise in revivalism, it was "ignorant Methodist and Baptist exhorters" who sustained enthusiastic religion (McLoughlin 1960, xvi). The not-so-ignorant Henry Clay Fish, a Baptist pastor from Newark, New Jersey, published his *Primitive Piety Revived* in 1857. It called for a major revival in America, "the descent of the Holy Ghost upon the churches" (cited in Smith 1957, 49). The book became a major reference for the 1858–59 revival and paved the way for other prominent Baptists, including John Quincy Adams (Smith 1957, 138–39). It is therefore not surprising that although Arminianism and the development of perfectionism is closely associated with American Methodism, Baptists were at the forefront of revival. In 1859, both Charles Finney and Phoebe Palmer traveled to England. The revival's most prominent Baptist supporter in London was C. H. Spurgeon, also a friend of the Jamaica mission. In 1859, he preached enthusiastically of revival in Exeter Hall and claimed that the Baptists had been in revival for the past ten years (Orr 1949, 190–92; Whitely 1932, 79). The English revival was well established when, in 1859, the reverends Edward Bean Underhill and J. T. Brown sailed to Jamaica as delegates of the Baptist Missionary Society (BMS). Despite Phillippo's early optimistic projections, financial difficulties and diminishing converts had led the BMS to support a survey of Jamaica's mission (Underhill 1862, 1879).[9]

Underhill told Phillippo to begin revival meetings immediately. And in June 1860, Phillippo wrote to Underhill:

> I have carried [meetings] on from the last Sabbath in April to the present time throughout the extended district in which my stations are scattered. In the chapels at my different stations, in the class-houses, and in private houses, both in town and country, prayer-meetings have been held, in most cases morning and evening, I going first to one and then to another, to encourage the masses attending them. (cited in Underhill 1881, 304)

The Presbyterian Carlile also wrote of

> regular meetings every morning to pray for the outpouring of the Spirit of God, which we had been led to expect from what we see He has been doing in many Churches in America and Europe. (Carlile 1884, 114–15)

When the revival came, it began in the Moravian churches of Manchester parish and spread to Clarendon and then on to Spanish Town. Further awakenings were reported from Savannah-la-Mar stretching across the southern coastal regions, and also in Bethel Town in the north, to Montego Bay and on to St. Ann (Underhill 1881, 306). Owing to the longevity of the Moravians in Jamaica and the modest scope of their mission enterprise, Gardner could describe the Moravian stations in Manchester, St. Elizabeth, Westmoreland, and St. James as "compact and well-appointed," sustaining "a completeness that only in a limited degree belongs to [others]" (Gardner 1873, 341). It was in this well-established Christian mission environment that the Great Revival began.

Phillippo and Carlile both reported that the revival witnessed various forms of excess (Underhill 1881, 306; Carlile 1884, 126–27). The statement of this excess best known in the literature, however, is that from Gardner who was moved to observe:

> Like a mountain stream, clear and transparent as it springs from the rock, but which becomes foul and repulsive as impurities are mingled with it in its onward course, so with this most extraordinary movement. In many of the central districts of the island the hearts of thoughtful and good men were gladdened by what they witnessed in the changed lives and characters of the people for whom they long seem to have laboured in vain; but in too many districts there was much of wild extravagance and almost blasphemous fanaticism. This was especially the case where the native Baptists had any considerable influence. Among these, the manifestations occasioned by the influence of the Myalmen . . . were very common. To the present time, what are called revival meetings are common among these people. (Gardner 1873, 465; cited in Curtin 1970, 171, and in Simpson 1956, 336)

Yet Gardner immediately went on to remark that "apart from these accessories, the movement effected an immense amount of good." He listed "many thousands of marriages," "evil habits abandoned," and "rum shops . . . forsaken." All of these were signs from an ethically rational point of view that sin was being more properly controlled (Gardner 1873, 465–66).

The forms of enthusiasm for cleansing sin that missionaries were happy to endorse were nothing short of the "screaming, laughing . . . visions and convulsions" that a century earlier observers had identified with Methodism (Latourette 1975, 906). Carlile wrote of the Great Revival:

> Multitudes were falling on every side, uttering the most piercing screams. A gentleman present said he counted thirteen prostrated in one corner of the church at one time. The sword of the Spirit had penetrated a multitude of souls, convinced them of sin, and forced them to cry for mercy. . . .

> Sometimes their attendants would say, pointing to the breast of the suf-
> ferer, There is malice there, or there is uncleanness; and often they would
> acknowledge the truth of it, and cry for forgiveness. (Carlile 1884, 116)

Even Phillippo, the moral disciplinarian, described with satisfaction the following scene:

> The building was filled from top to bottom, and soon after the service
> commenced the greatest excitement prevailed. In one direction were poor
> unlettered Africans pouring out their supplications in some such language
> as this, and in the words of one of them with the utmost earnestness, his
> voice heard above the tumult; ". . . Lord, save me—me a sinner—me a
> drunkard, me a tief, me de Sabbat-broker. Forgive me for mercy-sake. O
> Jesus, save me by dy precious blood." . . .
>   Heaven, hell, Christ, salvation were now no longer uninteresting, un-
> meaning words and notions, but living, substantial realities, which rang in
> the ears and burned in the hearts of the people. (cited in Underhill 1881,
> 309–10)

And G. E. Henderson of Brown's Town, St. Ann, described the revival he had
witnessed as a child in the following terms:

> Men and women of reckless lives were actually stricken down while work-
> ing in their homes or fields in the week days; and would run to their minis-
> ter, as soon as they could, overwhelmed with grief, ejaculating the one
> word, "Sin! Sin" repeatedly, as the prelude to some confessions of disgrace-
> ful conduct. (Henderson 1931, 104)

Henderson observed that from these events sprang the bands of Revivalists
that he would witness throughout his own pastoral career. While some Revivalists were "immoral" and "blasphemous," others "[believed] they [were]
called by God to proclaim a truth largely neglected by Churches that claim
to be orthodox" (105).

Carlile and Phillippo also noted that youth were prominent in the revival.
Phillippo observed of these young people, "some of them prayed with an
eloquence and earnestness I never heard excelled" (cited in Underhill 1881,
118). And Carlile wrote, "Conversions do not in general take place from the
public preaching of the Gospel, but rather from the incessant entreaties of
young converts" (Carlile 1884, 118).

By 1860, an entire generation of Afro-Jamaicans had grown to adulthood
as emancipated people. As Phillippo would observe, "all opposition on the
part of planters and others against the progress of the Gospel [had] ceased"
(cited in Underhill 1881, 305). Released to freedom, the emancipated slaves
were still continually subject to a discourse of moral order sustained by the
churches in concert. And owing to their prominent role in the course of
the emancipation, sectarian churches in particular had influence among the

people. Though the fluctuations in mission numbers indicate intense negotiation, disengagement, skepticism, disaffection, and economic stress, nonetheless, by the 1860s, the fact of appeals to Christian empowerment had
become a part of Jamaican life, an accepted aspect of cosmology and rite to
which the young would have resort. The revival, if it did not secure a stable
increase in numbers for the missionaries, nevertheless acted to secure Christian meanings at the center of ritual life.

This was marked by a renewed interest in the Christian text as an object
to be owned and, where possible, read. Gardner writes of thirty-seven thousand copies of the Bible sold in Jamaica in eighteen months (Gardner 1873,
466). Carlile referred to the increasing labor involved in teaching people to
read the Bible (Carlile 1884, 322). And Phillippo described "an anxious, earnest desire . . . everywhere expressed for the possession of religious books
and tracts, but especially to read, understand and possess the Book of God"
(cited in Underhill 1881, 312). These events secured in Jamaica the salience
of local Christian forms. Thereafter, for many Jamaicans, the Bible would be
a textbook of life, and Christian practice, whatever its form, would be the
bracketing experience of being.

The Baptists and the Morant Bay Rebellion

E. B. Underhill's visit to Jamaica in 1859 had made him familiar not only with
the Baptist churches there but also with the social conditions of the island.
This was evident in the report of his visit published in 1862. In the years that
followed the Great Revival, the rural prosperity of the late 1850s was re-
versed by falling sugar prices (Hall 1959, 240). There was flood and consequent crop damage in 1864, followed by a drought that extended into 1865
(Hall 1959, 242; Underhill 1867, 11). In 1865, as a consequence, Jamaica's
population was acutely distressed, and the churches were battling to retain
their numbers notwithstanding the gains of the revival years. It was in these
circumstances that Underhill, having returned to England, wrote a letter to
Edward Cardwell, secretary of state for the colonies. His letter concerned
the very poor conditions of life in Jamaica. Underhill noted especially the
increase in predial larceny that was consequent on impoverishment. This
impoverishment resulted from the fact that there was insufficient employment for the people who were forced to rely on their cultivations. Yet the tax
regime of the island discouraged them from export agriculture that might
have increased the "flow" of "silver." As a consequence, the people were not
only hungry but "ragged and near naked" (Underhill 1867, 11–15).

There was no particular reason for Underhill's letter to have become public in Jamaica. Cardwell, however, sent a copy to Governor Eyre. Eyre cir-
culated the letter to the custodes of parishes, to judges and magistrates, and
to the island's clergy, asking for responses. This action and the discussion that

ensued engendered a number of public meetings known as "Underhill's Meetings." In the midst of these meetings, freeholders and their representatives petitioned the British government and even the queen. In reply to such a petition from "poor people" in the parish of St. Ann was sent a letter, "The Queen's Advice," written on behalf of the queen by the Colonial Office. Eyre, to counter the unintended influence of Underhill's letter, ordered that copies of the "Queen's Advice" be read both to church congregations and in the schools (Knox 1976). Some Baptist pastors refused to read the "Advice," and this in conjunction with Underhill's letter was sufficient for Eyre roundly to condemn the Orthodox Baptists when the Morant Bay Rebellion occurred (Campbell 1976, 333; Underhill 1867, 3–4; Stewart 1983, 380–94).[10]

The rebellion was led by a cultivator, Paul Bogle, who had a close association with George William Gordon, a Jamaican mulatto and notable. Both men were known for their independent Baptist convictions. Bogle's conviction was an initial calling from his St. Thomas rural milieu, and Gordon's came out of an alignment with the Presbyterians and the Orthodox Baptists following a childhood in the Church of England (Black 1965, 171–74). Unhappy with these alternatives, Gordon established his own chapel in Kingston, where he was influenced by the Great Revival (Fletcher 1867, 68–69). Though he was never formally ordained, Gordon appointed a number of deacons, among them Paul Bogle of Stony Gut in St. Thomas-in-the-East. Bogle, in turn, registered voters for Gordon when Gordon moved his electorate from Kingston to St. Thomas in 1863 (Stewart 1983, 330–32; Black 1965, 173–75). The attack on the Morant Bay courthouse that Bogle led in protest against a ruling on a freeholder claim was attributed by Governor Eyre to the influence of Gordon. Gordon had criticized Eyre in the Jamaican Assembly (Black 1965, 174–75; Campbell 1976, 317–25). He also had presided over a meeting in Morant Bay that sent a deputation on conditions in St. Thomas to the governor in Spanish Town. Eyre refused to see the group led by Bogle. Soon after, a magistrate's ruling sparked the Morant Bay Rebellion, which found Bogle at its head (Campbell 1976, 334–35; Black 1965, 178–79).

After the rebellion, Gordon was hanged for treason, notwithstanding, at the end, his expressed "regret" at Bogle's actions. Bogle also was hanged, along with his "chief colleagues," Bowrie and Craddock (Campbell 1976, 340–41). British militia took vengeance not only on the activists in Morant Bay itself but also on the residents of Stony Gut. According to official reports, 439 people were killed, hundreds were whipped, and a thousand houses were burned (Holt 1991, 302; Heumann 1981a, 1981b).

The Morant Bay Rebellion and its aftermath condensed a range of issues that demonstrated both the strengths and also the limitations of the Orthodox Baptists in Jamaica. Through Underhill, the Baptists voiced the agonies of a social order that precipitated the rebellion in the east. Yet, as a man engaged with the people, Gordon had to move beyond Orthodox Baptist practice in order to sustain his social and religious concerns. His integration of the social and the religious is reflected very clearly in that part of the Royal Commission report on the rebellion that deals with Gordon and Bogle:

> If a man like Paul Bogle was in the habit of hearing such expressions as those contained in Gordon's letters, as that the reign of their oppressors would be short, and that the Lord was about to destroy them, it would not take much to convince him that he might be the appointed instrument in the Lord's hand for effecting the end; and it is clear that this was Bogle's belief, as we find that after the part he had taken in the massacre at Morant Bay, he, in his Chapel at Stony Gut, returned thanks to God that "he had gone to do that work, and that God had prospered him in his work." (cited in Stewart 1983, 389)

In their fight to sustain free villages and generate their own moral order, the Baptists themselves had defined the state as a moral and spiritual regime as much as a structure of politics. Yet they, like the Jamaican government, could not accept the Gordon-Bogle view of a world constituted through God in which politics and morality merged (cf. Robotham 1981, 91; Holt 1991, 299; Campbell 1976, 335).

Their repudiation was reflected in the line now drawn between Native Baptists and Orthodox Baptists, between the creole interpreters of Baptist faith and the British Baptists themselves. Underhill claimed, in response to Eyre, that Bogle and Gordon were Native Baptists, a group entirely separate from the British Baptist missionaries (Underhill 1867, 8). And this distinction had been foreshadowed in a pastors' submission to Eyre. The pastors observed:

> The masses of the people have not yet advanced far in civilization. Their artificial wants are few, whilst the climate is such as to induce habits of indolence. As long as the people could obtain certain comforts without extraordinary labour, they sought after them, . . . but now they cannot be obtained without an amount of energy and labour foreign to their habits. . . . Thus multitudes are now content to dwell in huts which a few years ago they would have been ashamed to occupy. . . . Under similar influences, self-respect being lowered, marriage contracts are neglected, and an amount of immorality is spreading over the land most fearful to contemplate. (Henderson et al. in Underhill 1867, 35)

The pastors' emphasis on the intimate relation among an English idea of ordered domesticity, work, morality, and Christianity was echoed in a similar statement by Eyre himself:

> I believe that civilization must go hand in hand with Christianity, and that until the peasantry of the country can be induced to erect better dwell-

ings, and thereby obtain the means of adopting social habits more in accordance with decency and propriety, there can be little hope that the teaching of the Minister or Schoolmaster will be able to withstand the corrupting influence of evil at home. (cited in Stewart 1983, 380)

The Baptists, descendants of the English Dissenters, institutionally and organizationally could separate themselves from the alliance between church and state embodied in the established Church of England. However, they could not detach themselves from the notions of moral order that they shared with the British establishment.[11]

Jamaican Christians fell away from the missionaries' ethical rationalism, which relied on a constant discipline rather than a healing rite. They did not repudiate central elements of a Christian faith, however. The Native Baptists, now called "Zion Revivalists," adopted notions of spiritual enthusiasm and forms of healing practice that, though abhorrent to the missionaries, still engaged with a Christian world. Many Jamaicans deployed these practices in secret and in concert with orthodox religion (Beckwith 1929, 160–63; Simpson 1956, 366–67).[12] This was possible because Zion Revival acknowledged a Christian cosmos as the encompassing one (Moore 1953, 107–8; Simpson 1956, 371–76; Seaga 1969, 9–10). Central to this creole cosmos was the notion of personal sin as a source of physical affliction and widespread suffering in the world. Jamaicans turned to cure this sin and make a process of spiritual healing the precondition of moral practice.

Zion Revival and the Eudemonic

The Zion Revival pantheon is one in which God presides over all and yet barely engages the Christian believer.[13] God is evoked as the authority on sin but not as the authority who can deal with healing. This role is reserved for Jesus, to whom the Revivalist prays and sings, and for the spiritually active Holy Ghost, who mediates between heaven and earth (cf. Wedenoja 1978, 92–98). It is the Holy Ghost who first enters a believer, often traveling down a wooden conductor attached to the roof of a prayer house or booth, into the ground, and up the believer's legs, or else directly from the conductor through the believer's head. The young practitioner will be thrown to the ground and lie there insensible for at least an hour, sometimes many hours. The Holy Ghost is represented by a dove, drawings of which are scattered around Revivalist churches. A "wheeler," especially adept at bringing down the Spirit, will move in spinning circles around a group of worshiping Revivalists. With arms outstretched, wheelers flutter their hands with delicate and artful movements of the fingers, imitating the wings of a dove. A young Revivalist who has "labored in the Spirit" by "trumping" and "sounding" will then be taken in hand by a senior "mother," who will encourage the novice to pursue further possessions in order to secure his or her own prophet or evangelist, generally one of the Old Testament figures including Amos, Moses, Joshua, Miriam, Jeremiah, or Elijah, or any of the various apostles except the infamous Judas Iscariot.[14] An experienced practitioner may become a vehicle for one of the archangels, Michael, Gabriel, or Raphael. These angels, prophets, and evangelists, in addition to the Holy Ghost, are the principal spirit world with which the Revivalists engage. While the Holy Spirit cleanses and redeems the believer, an act later celebrated by a baptismal rite, the angels and evangelists empower and protect in the subsequent life of Revivalists. The more vigorous the possessions of a revival band, the more successful will be its healing practice (Barrett 1976, 57). In all of this, it is central to Zion Revival to bring spirits down to earth, and a major component of Revival aesthetics involves the aspects of human performance, and of Revival iconography, effective in attracting the Spirit. Ideas of vital nature, music, light, and literacy inform Revival iconography. They are deployed to realize the empowering possession that can heal the practitioners and others.

During the 1980s, "Leader Wally"[15] was a popular healer who maintained a balm yard next to his church not far from the road leading out of Kingston to St. Thomas parish.[16] His healing practice was a source of income and supported his evangelism. While his practice specialized in herbal libations for anyone prepared to wait and pay the fee, he nevertheless constantly observed to his clients that a "finish cure rest on repentance." His balm yard had one large, deep pool with four changing booths close to it. People could take an herbal bath, previously sponged over with an herbal mixture by the pastor's "sister" or "brother" helpers. After the bath, the pastor would "read" the patient's malaise or simply address the malaise without a bath. The patient sat in front of him, between them a table covered in red cloth with multi-colored corn kernels scattered over it. A Bible lay on this table, along with a fully opened ackee fruit, a lighted candle, a number of empty bottles, and a decorative cut-glass stand. The pastor said that his table "catch" the Holy Spirit—the Holy Spirit's color is red—and gave a light to the patient's face that helped him to discern the illness. The kernels and the ackee in turn represented "ripeness" or fulfillment. The consultations I saw were for "belly pain" and "misery" and involved the prescription of different herbal teas along with injunctions to come to "service." Among the herbs the pastor mentioned for these teas were bitter-weed, button-weed, and sweetsop leaf in the first case, and man-of-life, strong-back, and sweet-cup in the second (cf. Long 1973; Laguerre 1987).

The pastor emphasized that although he was wealthy, his was not a "church business," for he only took money for "true true" cures and not for people simply going to church. His ability to heal came from Jesus, however, who alone made teas "work good." This was why people should come to service prior to "bath" or "consultation." Pastor Wally's church had three massive murals, one of John the Baptist with a large black cross cradling Jesus by a river and two with archangels observing Jesus on the cross and emerging from the tomb. This church and acceptance of its power stood as a gateway to the herbal cures, so that Pastor Wally could always require that patients seek redemption as the ultimate cure. The course of redemption through possession by a prophet is not only a healing process, however. It also embodies a joyful performance distinctively Revivalist.

Leader Papa Linton of the Watt Town seal in St. Ann made the following comment in 1986 in his small apartment next to the "Schoolhouse":[17]

> To deal with de sin, you have to live to make it a complete sacrifice. A man who live with vanity cyan dead to sin. We don' rely on other church. Have to lean on de Spirit. We rest on de Spirit. A person don' believe the Spirit, the water not goin' te cure dat man. Dat is why de people come te [Sister Eva] fe cure. Dey come to de seal here, feel de Holy Spirit, and we lend dem de power to cure de baady. Everyone called 'cording to ability. Some are convinced quick and filled wid de Spirit. Many called with affliction, and when dey filled, prophet come to protect 'im. De prophets are de elected servant of God. Dem lookin' after we, care for de people.

To be convinced, with a stress on the second syllable, was the state Baptist missionaries strove to create when they instructed their neophytes. To be convinced with a stress on the word's first syllable is to be transformed by the Spirit of the Lord through an experience of possession. Like many other Zion Revival churches, the Watt Town Revival seal, known as the Schoolhouse, had deep pools situated next to the church. There believers could avail themselves of "holy" baths in consecrated water (cf. Long 1973). These baths were reserved for major ailments including tuberculosis, menstrual disorders, apparent schizophrenia, or other forms of "madness." Tuberculosis, identified as a physical ailment, was treated mainly by herbal baths. The other disorders were all defined as moral disorders requiring spiritual cure with prayer, exhortation, and holy water. Papa Linton kept a large enamel cup of consecrated water on a table directly in front of his lectern. Alongside the cup was a smaller glass and a small china bowl containing more water. On the other side of this table was a very large old Bible, which Leader Linton touched as an icon more than he took it up to read. A kerosene lamp, sometimes lit for worship, stood between the Bible and the water. It was in the proximity of these three objects, often touching the Bible, offering a glass of water, or dipping his hand into the large enamel cup, that Leader Linton laid on hands to pray and elicit lesser cures for recurring headaches, twinges, and pains during the course of divine worship.

According to Papa Linton, the Schoolhouse is one of the two oldest existing Revivalist centers in Jamaica. Its most famous patriarch, William Wallace,

Figure 1. Vital nature and the Holy Spirit (decoration on the walls of the Watt Town Schoolhouse)

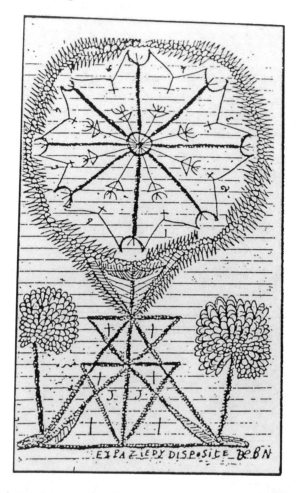

Figure 2. Early Rastafarian diagram with representations of vital nature similar to Revival diagrams (from Hill 1983)

was twenty-two years old in 1860, and although he was not the founder of the band, he was principally responsible for erecting the church.[18] He lived to the age of 103 and, with his daughter, Mother Downer, trained Papa Linton. The church perches on a small hillock in a very remote part of St. Ann, made less remote in recent years by bauxite mining in the parish. One slips and slides along a path of stones and red mud past a tiny shop to reach the site. Beyond the track, the church looms, a very old wooden structure with its floor half concrete and half wood, looking more like a schoolhouse than a church, until one enters through a door at the rear. Then the visitor is bombarded with an overwhelming visual pastiche of Revival icons designed to draw spirits down to empower and heal the living.

Upon entering the church from the rear, one is confronted with a banner hanging from the ceiling:

REPENT
AND BE BAPTIZED
FOR THE COMING OF THE
LORD IS AT HAND

As the eyes travel farther along the ceiling of the church toward the table and the lectern of the leader, three pieces of wood, fashioned partly like arrows and partly like hooks, jut down from the cross-beams. These, I was told, were conductors of the Spirit, shaped to assist its entry into the church. These conductors were described as "workings" of the Spirit, put there at the Holy Ghost's direction. Moving into the church and looking around, one's eye is caught by a number of large wall plaques and pictorial representations etched straight onto the walls. One plaque has a verse from Jeremiah written in black on a white background, the letters A to F printed neatly below it and the figures 1 to 6 below the letters. At the bottom of the plaque are drawn two crosses, colored red with white dots in the centers outlined in green.

JEREMIAH 51 V. 10
THE LORD HATH BROUGHT
FORTH OUR RIGHTEOUSNESS COME, AND LET
US DECLARE IN ZION
THE WORK OF THE LORD
OUR GOD
A   B   C   D   E   F
1   2   3   4   5   6

A plaque on the other wall is a large piece of paper in a photograph frame. It enjoins the believer:

Pray for another, Lord, you said "Bear ye one another's burdens and so fulfil the law of Christ." You also said "Pray one for another that ye may be healed." So right now Lord I pray for the needs of my loved ones, my friends, my neighbours and those who don't even know me.

I bring you the needs of my fellowmen. You know the heart that is broken, the mind that is confused, the soul that is in despair, and the body that is afflicted.

I reach out my heart and touch those in need now I release my faith. For the healing of angry minds, bitter spirits, sinful souls and sick bodies. May all be more whole, use me today to bring healing to one of these. And I will praise you for it. Amen.

Around these and other plaques at various intervals are complex representations of the figure of the dove juxtaposed with dotted drawings of living
flora. Some of these diagrams contain representations of vital nature, the
cross, and the dove in an integrated pattern, sometimes with magical numbers as well. And these diagrams also are interspersed with more modest
drawings and plaques: a diagram of the eye of God and a small plaque simply
of the alphabet, the words "GOD" and "LORD" and the numbers 1 to 10.

```
A   B   C   D
E   F   G   H
I   J   K   L
M   N   O   P
Q   R   S   T
U   V   W   X
Y   Z
GOD
LORD
1  2  3   4   5   6   7   8   9   10
```

As one proceeds from the back to the front of the church, the eye surveys
the table with Bible, light, and water and then the lectern standing immediately behind the table. The lectern is similar in style to those found in many
older Baptist churches, with simple carved panels of highly polished wood.
Papa Linton's lectern is covered with a large yellow cloth, yellow being the
color of "crowned shepherds," the father-leaders of Revival bands. On the
cloth rests another old leather-bound Bible. Beside the Bible on either side
are vases of local bushes and curing herbs, including local mint, breadfruit
leaves, and leaf-of-life. In front of the lectern hangs a faded red banner. Red,
the color of the Holy Spirit, also stands for the powerful archangels. The
banner has two white appliqués, one of a dove and the other a vital plant,
sewed onto its center. Above the appliqués is written "PEACE AND LOVE"
and below them "LET US LOVE FOR GOD IS LOVE," followed by a small
representation of a cross. On either side of the lectern hang American flags.
The juxtaposition in particular of the dove, water, and vital flora reflects the
integration of African and European ideas of media for healing the person.
Looking at the table with the lectern behind it, one is presented with a col-
lage of icons to entice spiritual power and heal the self: Bibles, light, water,
vital flora, the dove, spirit colors, and American flags. Behind all this, pinned
to the wall at the back of the church, is a large glossy picture of Jesus Christ
of the Sacred Heart. The total effect of the church in its modest complexity
is extremely beautiful: a folk creation over one hundred and twenty years of
the efforts of generations to cure the awful affliction of sin by invoking the
icons of a creole world.

At the divine worship services that I attended, the order was nearly always the same: choruses and hymns began the gathering, followed by a reading from the psalms, then prayers and a reading from the gospels, healing through water sprinkling and laying on of hands, a sermon and collection hymn, after which would come further choruses and the possession of band members by their prophets or evangelists, followed by laboring in the spirit, and, finally, prayers and dispersal of the band. Papa Linton held neither communion services, for which he said he was "not licensed," nor thanksgiving tables, which he identified with the blood sacrifice of an animal (cf. Seaga 1969). "Me don' keep tables," he said. "Blood is in Jesus, not outside. We don' need any further sacrifice." He would bury the dead, he said, but was not licensed to perform a marriage. The forms of possession of Schoolhouse believers were also singularly beautiful.

The following account is of a small segment of a Thursday service beginning at around eleven in the morning. Some of the fourteen people attending had come straight from their cultivations to the Schoolhouse. Others had come from home. As the men entered, they placed their hats on pegs driven into the window frames. Some women came wearing white head wraps signifying their purified state, while others wore the color of their prophet or evangelist. A number had pencils stuck in their head wraps, and a few carried battered exercise books in which would be scrawled a chorus or some prayers. The pews of the Schoolhouse were arranged around the walls, leaving the center of the church as open space. The band sang and listened to the readings and sermon standing in a semi-circle in front of the pews. Papa Linton had laid on hands and prayed for a woman suffering with an aching head. He had sprinkled her face and neck with consecrated water and placed his finger dipped in water on her tongue. After the healing, he had preached a sermon mainly with reference to the gospel of Luke 9:1–6, emphasizing the duty of Christians to be filled with the Spirit and to move about healing the people. Following the sermon, the band moved serenely into possession.

The brother with the red shirt and long white wrap around his waist danced, with slow, considered, loping steps, up to Sister Millie, who was slowly moving her head from side to side. The drumming had stopped, and the Schoolhouse was silent but for the breathing and murmuring of the band. He took her hand and held it high above their heads, whereupon he slowly turned her and then allowed her to turn him in turn. Having thereby both entered the Spirit world, the realm in which heaven joins with earth, they offered each other deep, low bows, whereupon Millie swooned to the ground in a quiet, heavily breathing convince. Her partner quietly danced back to his place with slow jogging motions, pushing out his breath with an "Ush . . . ush . . ." sound that gradually grew louder. At that moment, Sister Marlene began to march from the back of the church, stamping down each foot on the spot and chopping her hands, up and down, up and down, in alternate motions of extraordinary force. She was dressed in a light blue skirt, a white shirt, red jacket, and red head wrap. As she marched down the church, her pencil threatened to fall. Sister Marlene continued to march up and down the church throughout this period of the service. In the meantime, Brother David, wearing his blue head wrap, stepped out and first crossed his arms in front of him. Then he began to wheel his arms, crossing them in front of him and then behind him, as he slowly and gracefully turned around the church. As he proceeded, he bowed very deeply to a number of other brothers and sisters, turning one or two as he proceeded. Then he turned a final sister, who stepped from the ring and interposed her own wheeling arms with his, as they circled in almost complete silence faster and faster up and down the church. As they wheeled and circled, the rest of the band, except Sister Millie, who was still in convince, broke into the chorus, "Stand up, stand up for Jesus, ye soldiers of the cross." Following another three choruses, the little band gradually moved stamping and breathing into a circle. Then, humming and murmuring, with a soft "Ush . . . ush . . ." coming from the chest, they began to labor in the Spirit: stamping with one foot, stepping lighter with the other, and breathing out with the "Ush . . . ush . . ." sound. They continued in this way for possibly thirty minutes, always with Papa Linton, or one of the mothers, in the center of the circle. Gradually the laboring became less intense, and finally Papa Linton closed the service with a blessing. Some of the saints had experienced their particular guardians and become, momentarily, cosmic figures of pervasive power and enduring beauty. All of the band had then formed a circle and labored with motions that evoked cultivation to bring the Holy Spirit among them. The echoing hollow noise of the "Ush . . . ush . . ." sound rising gradually in a crescendo was evidence that the Holy Ghost was there. Afterward, band members sauntered away, picking their way down the slippery path back to their individual concerns.

Sister Millie in the spirit was Miriam. Sister Marlene was the Archangel Gabriel. Brother David was Joshua. I was told that his partner was Matthew, the apostle.

The activities and emblems of the Schoolhouse mimic a colonial culture. The representations of literacy and numeracy, an archangel marching like a British soldier, believers with head wraps like those of indentured laborers and with corded waists like those of Jesus' apostles, not to mention women walking to "school" equipped with pencil and exercise book, all speak to metonymic efforts to grasp at the power of other cultures and the various domains under their control. They reflect the influence of literacy that steadily increased in Jamaica to release, in the twentieth century, a form of text-based Christian practice that also retained the practice of healing.[19] To this complex, the Schoolhouse adds a lovely eudemonic of possession that the missionaries could not staunch. Jamaican Revival brought into the church not only the practice of healing affliction but also the grace and the joy of peasant celebrations of freedom. As a consequence, dance and oral culture became integral to Christian performance. A comment from an orthodox pastor tells how the eudemonic was sanctified:

> The people, in the past years, provided their own social entertainment and social outlets such as "tea meeting." A woman was chosen as the veiled queen. . . . The people also had folk story contests and dancing competitions staged in bough booths. These simple festivities were gradually ridiculed, and . . . disappeared. The same sort of people who enjoyed them are now found in the . . . revival meetings [which give] excitement and emotional release [that] the older churches do not provide. (cited in Davis 1942, 43–44)

The orthodox missions' regime sought to use moral discipline as their means to articulate a world. Their project was undermined by continuing cultural differences between Europeans and those of African descent. Their efforts also were undermined by social and political events in which missionaries displayed a failure of will to realize an alternative order. The culmination of this process came in the Morant Bay Rebellion. These events discredited orthodox religion and allowed the expansion of an Afro-Christian rite that treated biomoral malaise through healing practice and possession. Yet, even prior to the Great Revival, this practice employed Christian icons, and with the advent of the revival, the logic of malaise and healing was imbued with Christian ideas of sin. In the complex that came to include orthodox religion and Zion Revival, there was, then, no clear division between the European and the African (cf. Curtin 1970, 171). If the ethical rationalism of the missionaries had been checked by healing and an African aesthetic that transformed Christian rite, that rite and its moral rationale came to inform creole religion. Who in this complex was truly moral—which cultures or classes, which men or women—would be issues integral to the discourse that ushered in twentieth-century life.

PART TWO
THE ADVENT

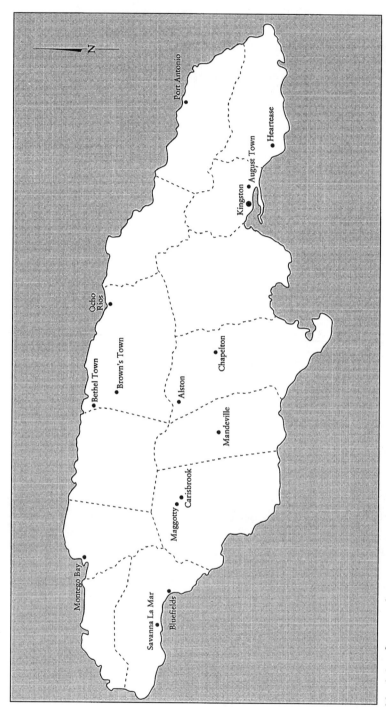

Map 2. Significant sites for Jamaican Revival, 1860– circa 1945

4 Hierarchy and Revival Culture: Precursors to Pentecostalism

> Proximity to America makes the little island the happy
> hunting ground of . . . queer denominations. Seventh Day
> Adventists, Millenial Darwinists, Seven Keys, Pentecostal
> Holiness Missions and other strange inventions are wel-
> comed by groups of unbalanced and disgruntled people.
> —E. P. Price, principal of Calabar College, 1930

B y the early twentieth century, the Orthodox Baptists
had secured themselves in respectable society. They
remained a popular church of the people and yet gave tempered approval to
the state (see especially Bryan 1991; cf. Williams 1991). Their incorporation
in the status quo is indicated by the following comment in a 1929 *Jamaica
Baptist Reporter* editorial. Discussing the merits of empire, the editorial was
keen to observe that "the British Throne perhaps symbolises the greatest
secular influence for Peace and Unity the world has ever known and the
secret lies in the fact that in it the secular includes the spiritual."[1] Paul
Bogle's interpretation of the "Throne" had been as a violent source of affliction. Jamaicans both before and after Morant Bay would seek a healing for
that affliction located beyond the secular order. Only some of them would
concur with the view that the throne includes the spiritual domain.

Hierarchy and Jamaican Religion

Although the church had endorsed the Great Revival, many of the new generation of Baptists looked askance at the American revivals that were spreading to Jamaica as the century began. And within the Baptist organization,
there were moves toward centralization and an emphasis on orthodoxy.[2] As a
consequence, in the late 1920s, there were extensive debates in the Baptist
Union concerning revisions to the constitution.[3] During the course of this
unrest, some pastors wrote to the *Jamaica Baptist Reporter* regarding procedures in the church:

> The things we wish to deal with have nothing to do with anything which
> would run counter to commands of Christ or the Truths He taught. They
> have to do with human business methods, with obligations to each other,
> with our duties in regard to properties entrusted to us by Christian people,

with the creation of a "tone" in regard to Church methods both Godward and manward.[4]

The signatories called for a central salary fund, but also for "mutual council in matters of order and dignity in Church worship and life"; for "the creation of consciousness and pride" within the church. These views reflected the concerns of "younger pastors" regarding ministers in the countryside. Though some Baptists were friends of revival, the Christian practice of the church and especially of its Kingston headquarters was increasingly responsive to the orthodox denominations, including the Methodists and Anglicans. This practice emphasized a moral life as indicative of engagement with God. It also embraced properly British procedures as indicative of encultured religion. The most prominent indices for this practice were, first, a tempered and law-like worship that largely eschewed healing and possession and, second, the embrace of marriage and legitimate issue as a central sign of Christian moral worth. These indices were used in turn to construct lower-class revivalism as superstitious for its healing and possession and immoral for its lack of a marriage rite.

Although views were changing in revival circles, at the turn of the century, Jamaica's status quo still designated enthusiasm, including possession, as "African" and therefore uncivilized. This view with its colonial connotations was itself part of Jamaica's construction of difference. It took the transformations of African and European practice that comprised a creole religion and designated it as inferior and "African" in relation to the rite of the respectable middle class.[5] In the period at the turn of the century, the consolidation of Zion Revival encouraged a spate of "travelers' tales" that further constructed Jamaican folk religion as both nativized—the indigenous practices of the folk—and exotic to a metropolitan world. The writings of Bell (1893), Banbury (1894), Spinner (1896), and Emerick (1915) all carry with them a sense of voyeuristic titillation appropriate to the contemplation of "native" culture. The complex of affliction, healing, and possession that recognized the existence of sin but also recognized other forces for evil including obeah and malignant ghosts was denied an integrity of its own. Observers divided Jamaican religion into real religion from a European source and the confusions created by "superstition" (cf. Bryan 1991, 38–41). The elements of "real" religion were taken for granted, while "superstition" elicited continual comment. Emerick cites Herbert de Lisser as an authority on the issue and demonstrates the interaction between Jamaica's British-oriented elite and representatives of the metropolitan world as they co-operated in the construction of their own orthodoxy in the face of the queer and inferior other (Emerick 1915, 39). Emerick's words are typical of the genre and manage to invoke not only antipathy to African immoralism but also a certain orientalism:

> To attempt to describe Jamaica Mialism, a superstition imported from Africa, is like trying to describe the intricacies of the most cunningly devised Chinese puzzle. Mialism is so mixed up with Obeahism and Duppyism and other cults of African warp, together with whatever in Protestantism and Catholic ritual that may appeal to the bizarre African imagination, that it is hard to tell which is which and what is what. But for all that it is a most interesting study for the student of folk-lore. The interest becomes greater when we find this pagan wolf frisking about in the Christian pasture, among the true sheep. (1915, 39)

Later and more professional observers, including Beckwith (1924, 1929) and Williams (1934), contributed to this construction. Beckwith did this by accepting the construction of lower-class religion as unorthodox and simply "other." As a consequence, she assured her readers that most Revivalists also attended the Baptist church, thereby proving they were truly religious. Williams, on the other hand, sought to dignify this "other" by providing it with a spurious African unity (Beckwith 1929, 161–63; Williams 1934, 50–108).[6]

To this construction and situating of the Zion Revivalist complex within Jamaica's socioracial hierarchy was added the construction of the folk as immoralists barely deserving of a "Christian" designation. The document that best summarizes these latter turn-of-the-century concerns is Anglican Bishop Enos Nuttall's "Letter to Professing Persons," read in all the Anglican congregations on September 13, 1896. Nuttall had come to Jamaica in 1862 as a Methodist lay preacher. He had been ordained later in the Church of England and had proved a dynamic factor in spreading an Anglican influence among the people. No stranger himself to Jamaican revival, he was not entirely antagonistic to the people's revival spirit. He counseled his colleagues to remember its prevalence in Europe and to be judicious in its management (Bryan 1985). Yet Nuttall remained entirely uncompromising on the universal morality he identified with Christians (cf. Bryan 1991, 50–52; Smith 1976; Smith 1988, 104–5). His letter involved a list of "immoralities" that included petty theft, lying and false-swearing in court, "profane swearing in ordinary conversation," "superstition," the breaching of the Sabbath, drunkenness, gambling, and, finally, the "Sin of Sexual Immorality." Nuttall focused particular attention on the last of these immoralities and wrote of it in part:

> [Sexual immorality] is a sin marked in the word of God as specially odious, dishonouring to man's body and soul, and the God who made them. It destroys that true family life which is at the foundation of all social and na-

tional progress. It often causes terrible disease to those who are guilty of it, and it entails both physical evil and social disgrace on their children. (Nuttall 1896, 3)

This sin bringing personal affliction and national malaise required special measures in Nuttall's view. Dwellings should be improved so that boys and girls might be segregated at night. Parents should be ever watchful of "indecent language," and the fathers of illegitimate children should be required by law to support them. On these issues of immorality, Nuttall expressed the solidarity of all the orthodox churches:

> We desire to emphasize our counsels on these moral questions, by pointing
> out that whatever differences of opinion and conviction there may be
> among Christians on certain points of doctrine and Church organization,
> we are entirely agreed on these questions of Christian morality and duty.
> There is no doubt or uncertainty as to what is required of us in these mat-
> ters. He who transgresses in these things must open his eyes to the fact
> that he is breaking the clear law of God, and failing in the plain duty of a
> Christian. (4)

Through Phillippo, Knibb, Underhill, Eyre, and Nuttall can be traced an enduring English concern with the sexual immorality of the people that might be mitigated by improvements in housing. That this was a concern of equal importance to "superstition" and "enthusiasm" is evidenced by the fact that Nuttall, like the religious before him, saw family as the site where religion intersected with the building of a nation. That civility that fostered religion and citizenship alike found its source in a proper family life. In their view, it was as central to being a Christian as any aspect of doctrine or rite. And while Jamaica's many Revivalists sustained their own cosmology and rite with its own sense of moral order, they would not be acknowledged by the churches as truly qualified ministers of Christ.

These issues of enthusiastic healing and morals deployed in the construction of hierarchical difference are central to an explanation of why a movement from North America, which continued that society's own revivalism, would become so popular in Jamaica. The legacy of Morant Bay was one in which Jamaicans in the lower classes were bereft of a powerful religious organization that would promote the re-valuation of their lives. The Pentecostal missionaries would play this role in the wake of the Baptists' withdrawal from the field and the limited success of other missions, including Adventists and Salvationists, who were less responsive to Jamaican culture. In turning to an American source, Jamaicans turned to a two-edged sword. As these American evangelists seemed to legitimate a creole practice, they would modernize and transform it as well. As they seemed to eschew a politics of state, they would introduce new subordinations involved with a trans-national order. Nonetheless, for a period, connection with America would allow many Jamaican religious to circumvent or at least reconstrue the power of the state and its socioracial order. The enduring power of this order, however, is reflected in the fact that the ethical rationalism of Jamaican religion was transformed rather than simply eschewed. Despite the vibrance of creole religion, its proponents and its sometime allies were not immune to constructions of their practice as morally inferior and racially based. The ritual tensions of Pentecostalism, which involve a highly gendered logic, are indicative of these cultural conflicts created by a socioracial order in which religion had assumed a central role.

Revival Negotiates Its Environment

The Revivalists' practice of Christianity placed them beyond established religion and also beyond the legitimation that would allow them to build large popular churches. As literacy spread in Jamaica, it facilitated not only a text-based religion but also greater organizational capacity for black lower-class religious leaders.[7] When new revival sects from America also made healing central to their practice, literacy provided a milieu in which the curing practice of Jamaica's religionists could be redefined and ideologically transformed. Far from being African superstition, new modes of healing through faith in the Spirit could be portrayed as a biblical practice eschewed by the older churches. Some Jamaicans would adopt progressively a fundamentalist rhetoric from America that distinguished between the Bible-based churches and churches that followed "man-made" rules. The assumption of literacy and a new sense of the power of the text made this fundamentalist rhetoric especially appealing. And one central tenet of this Bible-based practice was implicit faith in the healing power of God. An elderly Pentecostalist in northern Clarendon had this to say of Pentecostalism's appeal as it expanded in the 1920s:

> why the people flowing to the New Testament Church of God the more, it was divine healing. Anywhere we went and preached, that brought people that was sick and we prayed for them, and they got healing you see. Then the people them, believe the church for the healing more, even more than the preacher. That goes a lot to the physical, you know, because many of the people them, want that power. Yes man, when the Spirit preaches you feel it, you feel it all over your body. The body feel good. I mean, if you go in the church and the Spirit of God is not in the church, you cyan operate. You just sit down listening, but when the Spirit of God come in, you can turn the body in the Spirit.

To "turn the body in the Spirit" here means not only, as in Zion Revival, to enter that world where heaven and earth conjoin but also to transform the body so that it becomes a vessel of the Spirit. This process would become the cure of sin, confirmed by a baptismal immersion. Healing, faith, and total immersion obviated the need for herbal curings and aromatic baths of consecrated water. The total faith that transformed a person was also a faith that realized healing; one would be a sign for the other in the new Pentecostalism.

The central motif of healing the moral malaise of the body is present in the rise of Alexander Bedward's Bedwardites, in Raglan Phillips's Light Brigade, and in Pentecostalism itself. That Pentecostalism emphasized healing more than the British Salvation Army, the Seventh Day Adventists, and the Holiness Church of God was significant for its greater success. Moreover, the indigenous healing movements that preceded Pentecostalism also indicate a move away from balm-yard baths and herbal curings to modes of healing that increasingly focus simply on the power of the Holy Ghost. Bedward's stress on fasting and consecrated water and Phillips's distribution of blessed "handkerchiefs" were indicative of a re-orientation away from the engagement of vital nature with active Spirit and toward a focus on the Spirit alone. These were changes that also accompanied the progressive estrangement from a natural world that Jamaicans would experience with increasing literacy, urbanization, and regional migration (see chapter 1, above).

As they were prized from agriculture and further individuated in cities and towns, the Pentecostals also engaged a modernity with its own constructions of righteous joy. Along with Pentecostal healing practice, the aesthetic of a modern eudemonic appealed to Jamaican people. It led them to make an intimate connection between the eudemonic practice of Pentecostal rite and their own creole tradition. Another Pentecostal elder observed:

> The Pentecostal churches gave more freedom to the individual to be identified in the worship, while the other, what we say "established churches," it was just a pastor, the pastor, the preacher that did the preaching. The Baptist churches had a certain amount of life in it, in their songs, and some of them would even offer a little shout—an "amen" or a "hallelujah"—in their service, but normally the churches were sort of straight, you know, just regimented. No way in the Pentecostal. It was all expression. Maybe, too, with our African background and our emotional response, we would have more tendency to go towards the Spirit, to receive the Holy Spirit.

These new movements also addressed the moralism of the social order. Many leaders in the new religions desired recognition by the state. In part, this was because of the criminal status allotted those convicted of obeah and the fear among poorer Jamaicans that such a fate awaited other leaders pronounced as unorthodox. This was not an unfounded fear and pointed to the sensitivity of the colonial state as it faced critique of its own moral order. In part, the desire for recognition also involved an aspiration to perform Christian rites, especially marriage and holy communion, which were seen to be the province of "qualified" pastors. Marriage was also a rite for which payment was received. But desire for marriage celebrant status was grounded in reasons well beyond the pecuniary. In the discourse of Jamaican religion, marriage celebrant status was a central sign of legitimacy, of being a practitioner of religion both approved and protected by the state.

Revivalists today often describe themselves as shepherds of the people who are not marriage celebrants. This by no means involves, however, an absence of rhetoric against "fornication" and the "sweetheart" or "freeness" life. Papa Linton and Leader Wally both stressed faithfulness in sexual matters. Their position is summarized by another Revivalist:

> I tell young people to take one person and make yourself comfortable. When you find perfection, that is, one who is satisfactory, marry if you can afford it or live holy with that one person. Don't take two or more at one time. Marrying and having one direct person to overlook your condition is better than to live a whoredom life. (cited in Simpson 1956, 347)

"Whoredom" refers especially to women actively engaged in the sweetheart life. This particular association of freeness with women on the part of male leaders registers a gender politics more fully developed in Pentecostalism. As healing became more concerned with sin, so the notion of healing from fornication became more central to ritual practice. Even for Revivalists, however, who were frequently men ministering to women, these issues were already prominent. Assuming the status of compleat Christian and avoiding the charge of African immoralism involved pastors in preaching the virtue of marriage to women cast in the role of Eve, as inadvert tempters of men.[8]

The anomaly for these pastors, however, was that leadership assumed through revelation rather than accreditation meant that the state, both colonial and post-colonial, denied the status of marriage celebrant to Zion Revivalists. This position left their followers dependent on established clerics, often also of superior social status, if they chose to marry. It also fueled the rhetoric of the orthodox churches concerning licentiousness among Revivalists. Thus, leaders of revival religion have sought accreditation for reasons of religious and moral recognition. And the status of accredited marriage celebrant has been a cutting edge of these negotiations. Alexander Bedward, for example, petitioned the government a number of times for the recognition of his pastors as marriage celebrants (Beckwith 1929, 169). In northern Clarendon, early Pentecostals whose leaders were qualified through revelation went to the Holiness Church of God, an accredited organization within Jamaica, in order to have their marriages confirmed. This was the case even though these Pentecostals did not regard the Holiness group as truly Christian and were forced to employ wedding rings, a form of symbolization eschewed by their doctrine at the time.[9]

As the Orthodox Baptists became distant from revival procedures, a status impasse was thus created for Revivalists who aspired to build enduring Jamaican churches. Able to command considerable followings and generate numerous bands or churches, they were yet unrecognized by the state. It was therefore significant that some of America's Pentecostal organizations were prepared to accredit Jamaican preachers who remained unrecognized in Jamaica. In 1920, for example, a credential that contained the following statement was issued by G. T. Hayward, the black American secretary of the Indiana-based Pentecostal Assemblies of the World:

> This is to Certify that the bearer here of . . . has been called by the Holy Ghost as a Minister of the Word, working in conjunction with The Pentecostal Assemblies of the World, and as recommended to the saints as an ordained MINISTER AND PASTOR in good standing.
>   We recommend him/her to perform all the functions of the Christian Ministry in accordance with the State, Provincial and International Law.
> (Golder 1973, 46)

The document was signed by the organization's executive chairman and the secretary. The normal designation for women so accredited was "missionary" or "evangelist." It was said that "women workers are permitted to officiate in Marriage, Funeral, Baptismal Services and Lord's Supper in cases of emergency" (Golder 1973, 46). Documents like these from America allowed popular Jamaican religious leaders, including the equivalent of Revivalist mothers, to obtain accreditation for the full repertoire of Christian rite. This was a privilege denied them in Jamaica because of either their engagement with revival religion or their lack of education, or a combination of both these factors. As Pentecostal evangelism spread in Jamaica and as American missionaries became more common, Jamaicans attached themselves to missionaries either as exhorters or as evangelists as a first step in the accreditation process. In this way, Jamaica's transition from Zion Revivalism to a major engagement with Pentecostalism marked a circumvention of the colonial state and the status order that was integral to it. It foreshadowed in one small cultural moment the eclipse of Britain's imperial order by the rising star of American regionalism.

The advent of accredited and literate pastors who sustained communications with America and the ability to construct permanent churches in both towns and rural areas allowed Jamaica's enthusiastic healing to be brought "inside" Jamaican churches.[10] The churches would remain, at the outset, the low-status churches of the poor, but they would command a legitimacy in the eyes of the state that was always denied to Zion Revival. The careers of two Jamaican prophets, Alexander Bedward and Raglan Phillips, demonstrate the forms of discourse that informed Pentecostalism's development. Both prophets sustained healing ministries that overlapped the beginnings of Pentecostalism. Bedward was a Revivalist whose travels to Colon gave him the distance from his society to criticize its moral order. Yet his yearning for Christian legitimacy produced an ambivalent religious practice infused with elements of hegemony. Raglan Phillips devised a healing message in association with the Salvation Army and later with the Jamaica Baptist Union. His whiteness and relations with established churches allowed him protections that Bedward lacked. After Phillips's death, the mission he established would become an indigenous Pentecostal church. His career in conjunction with Bedward's demonstrates the cultural and institutional context in which a Pentecostalism from America was rapidly adopted by Jamaicans to become their most populous church.

Alexander Bedward's Martyrdom

The only detailed contemporary record of Alexander Bedward has been provided by a follower, A. A. Brooks (1917), who reported that the movement later known as Bedwardism was begun by an American, H. E. S. Wood, also known to followers as "Shakespeare" (Brooks 1917, 5). In 1876, Woods, who was resident in Spanish Town, was called by God to begin a movement. He worked at August Town above Kingston, where he consecrated a "large jar of water from the Mona River" and named twelve men and twelve women to be the "Elders" in his church. He entrusted two men, Robert Raderford and Joseph Waters, a Baptist and a Methodist, respectively, with maintaining monthly fasts as a preparation for immersion and healing. Prior to his death in 1901, Woods designated Alexander Bedward as his successor (7–8).

Bedward was born in 1859. He came from a poor cultivator's family and in 1883 traveled to Colon as a laborer. Prior to his departure from Jamaica, he had been ill for many years, and when he returned in 1885, he was ill again. Driven by illness out of Jamaica and back to Colon, he had a vision directing him to return to Jamaica in order to save himself and "many others" (10). Bedward had other visions enjoining his return and finally came back to Jamaica later in 1885. He commenced baptismal instruction with Raderford and was baptized on the second Sunday in January 1886 (11). He then worked on the Mona estate for five years before commencing his "public ministry." Brooks recounts:

> On the 22nd December, 1891, A. Bedward made his first public performance at the Mona River, dispensing the water as medicine and baptising. . . .
> [On that] occasion of his first Fast . . . there were about two hundred sick persons, of whom however only seven would take the water as medicine, and they were immediately cured. They thenceforward devoted themselves to the tri-weekly Fast in [Bedward's] Church. (12)

Bedward's ministry involved the practice of fasting in conjunction with healing. Mondays, Wednesdays, and Fridays were fast days and involved a "tea

Figure 3. Alexander Bedward (from Beckwith 1929)

ceremony" for breaking the fast in a style curiously mimetic of European procedures that also evokes the Watt Town dancing:

> Long rows of tables are covered with white cloths, upon which each puts his or her cup (and saucer) in a row on each side of the table. At the head is placed the elements bread and the medicinal water. The tables are seated

by persons clad only in white. Those who are clad otherwise seat themselves elsewhere. All however partake alike. The Minister at the head presides. The Service is opened by singing a hymn, followed by reading of the Word of God with exhortation. Another hymn is sung and prayer offered.

On rising from their knees, each one turns up his or her cup, and while standing, the blessing is pronounced by the Minister. The congregation is then seated while the elements are served. Then all stand with their cups in their hands, when the Minister asks "Are all in peace?" Answer, "Yes." The Grace is said, and each one lifts his or her cup, and breaks their fast. When all have partaken of the elements freely, the rows of cups and saucers are drawn to the centre of the tables and the cloths turned over them. A hymn is sung while the offering is taken up. A prayer follows, arising from which the cups are again uncovered and drawn to their former places. A Grace . . . is sung, and the Meeting closed with the New Testament Benediction. (26–27)

Like the more established Revival tables, this tea ceremony suggests the Anglican holy communion in which the cup and the host or bread are uncovered and then covered again once the sacrificial feast is complete. Yet both phenomena also evoke images of British colonial commensality albeit from rather different periods. Bedward's tea ceremonies were austere affairs in comparison with the Revival tables also often held at the breaking of a fast. These tables might mark the completion of a fast in association with baptism, a mourning period, or an act of cleansing and contrition.

One such table, in its modern garb, was dressed by a lace-edged tablecloth reaching down to the floor of Leader Wally's church. At the front of the table facing the congregation was a three-pronged candlestick holding a red, a yellow, and a blue-green candle. The red candle was representative of love, the yellow was for peace, and the blue-green stood for "forest or wilderness." To their left stood a single candlestick with a black candle representing the mourning that had just been completed. The table was laid with fruits including papaya, mangoes, oranges, sweet-sop, and watermelon. A large iced cake stood in the middle of the table, surrounded by shaped loaves of hard dough bread including two loaves in the shape of doves. There were other white candles scattered across the table, all standing for the purity of the Revivalists, numerous colorful bottles of aerated water, and a few empty Wray and Nephew white rum flasks interspersed with glasses of water. The scene was bound together by lovely vases of flowers and leaves, the predominant color of the flowers being red. At the moment in the service when the table was "broken" by the lighting of the candles and consuming of the goods, the table looked like a princely feast suitable for an early-nineteenth-century governor. Bedward's followers, taking bread and water in the form of tea sipped sedately on a white tablecloth, enacted a representation of another colonial period as British imperial life entered the twentieth century.

Like the Watt Town dancing in the remote Schoolhouse, these aestheticized renderings of felicitous life sought to secure health and well-being through creole renderings of Christian rite.

The massing of people in August Town led "civil authorities" to test the Mona water, which was found to be rich in mineral compounds (Brooks 1917, 12–13). On January 21, 1895, Bedward was arrested nonetheless and charged with "seditious speech and discourse" (Chevannes 1971a, 48–49; cf. Elkins 1975). The *Jamaica Post* of April 30, 1895, reported the offending speech:

> Brethren, the Bible is difficult to understand. Thanks to Jesus I am able to understand it, and I, servant of Jesus, will tell you. The Pharisees and Sadducees are the white men, and we are the true people. . . .
> The fire of hell will be your portion if you do not rise and crush the white people. The only thing to cure all diseases is this Mona water blessed by me first. The Governor can't stop me, the police are here and I defy them to arrest me. (cited in Chevannes 1971a, 49)

Bedward was acquitted of sedition charges and assigned instead to the insane asylum. He later continued his ministry for a period of twenty-five years. When he pronounced his own divinity and ascension day and some months later marched on Kingston, he was declared insane and assigned once more to the asylum, where he died. Notwithstanding this tragic end, Bedward was an effective Revivalist. His followers' bands stretched across the island, and devotees even came from Colon to partake of his healing Mona waters (Beckwith 1929, 169). At least for the first few decades of the century, "Bedwardite" became a census category of the Jamaican government and numbered in 1921 almost as many affiliates as the category "Church of God."

Bedward's practice is striking for its ambivalence toward the colonial order. His labor experience in Colon seemed to make him bold before Jamaican officials in a way that foreshadowed the early Rastafarians (Hill 1983). And, like Paul Bogle, he interpreted the colonial order within his own cosmology and generated a religious response, one for which he was promptly punished, not through death as Bogle was but by a more subtle form of discipline. Yet Bedward also sought to realize the power of whites through mastering their forms of order. This was demonstrated not only in his tea ceremonial but also in the explanation of fasting that he gave to Martha Beckwith. Like clothes, he proposed, the soul was to be tended in its purification: "a day for washing, a day for drying and starching, a day for ironing; so the heart is made clean by the fasts" (Beckwith 1929, 170). Beckwith also reports Bedward's frustration at the state's refusal to register his pastors. Marriage celebrant status had "been definitely denied him, and he had accordingly decided to bring the world to an end. He showed me his black hands," Beckwith writes, "and told me how in the new heaven and the new earth they would be as white as my own" (1929, 169–70). Bedward the shepherd, who sought to resist the colonial order, also sought to discipline the self through a fasting that would cleanse and whiten the heart.

Some fifteen years after Bedward, Rastafarians would develop anew Bedward's Christian critique of the colonial moral order (cf. Chevannes 1971b, 1989). Their critical perspective on that order was shaped in addition by Garveyism, which conjoined in the person of Marcus Garvey both his initial Jamaican experience and the experience of a New World region that stretched from Costa Rica to New York. Rastafarians cut Bedward's Gordian knot by declaring that God was black and that whites were in fact the source of evil. Rastafarians would turn from rites to cure the affliction of sin to exhibitions of empowering knowledge as the means to confront colonialism.

Raglan Phillips and the City Mission

The other potentiality in Bedwardism, the revival culture of curing sin, would engage with Pentecostalism. In this new religious movement, Bedward's figuring of himself as Christ would be routinized and democratized through the community of saints.

This potentiality was pressed steadily forward by one of Bedward's contemporaries whose movement, the Light Brigade, would become a Jamaican Pentecostal church. William Raglan Phillips was an Englishman born in Bristol in 1854. He traveled to Jamaica at the age of seventeen to become a bookkeeper in Westmoreland parish. He subsequently became an attorney's clerk and later publisher of the *Westmoreland Telegraph* in the parish's main town, Savannah-la-Mar (Dorsey 1974; Hobbs 1986, 2). In 1885, Phillips sought to join the Baptist Union as a pastor. Although he was rejected, he maintained cordial relations with Baptists, especially in northern Clarendon. He was listed as an evangelist at the northern Clarendon James Hill church between 1883 and 1892. He pastored the Thompson Town church in 1924 (Clarke 1986, 12, 34; Calley 1965, 159; Dorsey 1974).

Shortly after his initial application to the Baptists, Phillips became a Salvationist (Hobbs 1986, 2–3). With his wife, he began to evangelize in the Bluefields area of Westmoreland. Supported first by General William Booth for his work in Jamaica, Phillips's attachment to healing rites in time brought charges of unorthodoxy.[11] Major James Cooke, an Irishman, was sent by Booth to supervise the Jamaican work (Hobbs 1986, 19–21). Thereafter Phillips's association with the Salvation Army gradually lapsed as he strengthened his ties with rural Baptists again.

In 1906–7, Phillips presided over a revival at James Hill in Clarendon. The revival spread through the Baptist congregations of upper Clarendon and was marked by enthusiasm and spiritual healing. A committee of Baptists was convened at the time to consider "features of his work that seemed to need adjustment." He was endorsed as an evangelist nonetheless, reaching "the masses of the people who are beyond the pale of the churches."[12] Faith healing had been conspicuous in this revival and also, some claim, speaking in tongues (Calley 1965, 159). Phillips remained in Clarendon, working in association with the Baptist church. Eight years later, he began another revival that spread from Thompson Town throughout northern Clarendon to Kingston and to Westmoreland and Hanover.

In August 1924, he had traveled to Kingston to hold meetings in Rockford and Orange Street. A *Jamaica Daily Gleaner* editorial started a debate, which raged through August and September of that year, when it reported that Phillips at these meetings sold handkerchiefs blessed by him and dipped in cotton oil. He claimed that the handkerchiefs had the power to heal through casting out devils. On each was stamped a Bible passage that referred to the apostles healing and casting out devils by anointing with oil (see Mark 6:13). In a letter to the *Daily Gleaner*, a Phillips enthusiast gave this account of one such healing:

> [A woman] had worms in her face. She was anointed as well as prayed
> over. She used also the anointed handkerchief and these [worms] worked
> [their] way down to her legs and then came out.[13]

The *Gleaner* editorial, however, warned against encouragement of superstition and, like Emerick at the turn of the century, evoked a certain orientalism:

> People here are prone to put faith in the wildest impossibilities. The obeah-
> man flourishes, ordinary ailments are frequently attributed to the action
> and agency of ghosts. In such circumstances we should want the people to
> take a rational view of physical diseases, and not wish them to see in these
> the activity of devils. In the East in former days, and even to-day, devils are
> believed to exercise a direct influence on human health. When they are cast
> out, the victim recovers. Thousands of people in Jamaica believe much the
> same thing; only, instead of devils they speak of ghosts—wicked ghosts—
> who are not to be differentiated from devils. Encourage this superstition
> and where shall we be?[14]

The flurry of letters to the editor also revolved around the biblical precedent for Phillips's method stated in the Book of Acts (19:11–12):

> And God wrought special miracles by the hands of Paul: So that from his
> body were brought unto the sick handkerchiefs or aprons, and the diseases
> departed from them, and the evil spirits went out of them.

One letter to the editor observed that notwithstanding this passage, there was no Christian imprimatur for Phillips's practice:

> There is not the least hint that these handkerchiefs or aprons [brought from Paul] had been anointed with oil. This practice is also without divine authority. These articles were carried to the sick from Paul's body, and God honoured the Apostle to the Gentiles by working special miracles by this means.
>
> But we do not read that Paul exacted a certain amount from the sick to whom these handkerchiefs were carried. If any man is so divinely endowed with the gift of healing that articles carried from his body may bring health and cure to the sick, I have no objections to offer. . . . But when one starts up a business of anointing handkerchiefs and retailing them at a shilling or sixpence each, it seems more a money speculation than anything else.[15]

Debate also revolved around whether or not Phillips himself was merely misguided or a charlatan. On this issue, he was defended by the respected George Henderson, the Baptist from St. Ann, who endorsed Phillips's work while eschewing his particular method. Henderson observed:

> Physical healing, by faith in an omnipotent Lord, who is still ready to say "The Lord for the body!" to any who are ready to say "The body for the Lord!" is no new doctrine in the church. . . .
>
> With the sending out of Handkerchiefs . . . Mr. Phillips knows I have but little sympathy. But I want simply to say that I esteem Mr. Raglan Phillips as a devout Christian brother . . . doing a work . . . of going into the highways and compelling the multitudes who are outside the churches to hear the Gospel of the grace of God.
>
> The fact that he "casts out devils" is of far more importance than that "he follows not us."[16]

This debate, by contesting Phillips's methods in terms of biblical precedent, further secured within Jamaica the acceptance of affliction as indicative of sin and the notion of sin as the principal affliction to be addressed by rite and moral discipline. Henderson, the seasoned Baptist rural pastor, acknowledged in his support of Phillips that the people of the "highways and the byways" would engage with rite before ethical rationalism.

In the course of his evangelism, and possibly on a visit to Henderson, Phillips met a young woman called Mary Coore in Browns Town, St. Ann. She was the devout daughter of a respected family and aspired to be engaged in evangelism. Coore and Phillips became a "team," for "she was more easily understood by the people in the interior parts of the island," many of whom were "suspicious" of the Englishman Phillips (Dorsey 1974; see also Chevannes 1989, 135). Phillips's movement was known first as the "Light Bri-

Figure 4. "The Ark" (original church of the Kingston City Mission)

gade," a Caribbean play, it seems, on imperial exploits well beyond the British Salvation Army. Out of their Kingston crusades of 1924 and 1925 developed a new organization, the City Mission Church. When Phillips died in 1930, Coore became his successor. Later, Coore was joined by Delrose Walters, a woman of considerable education, and the two became the founding bishops of the Kingston City Mission. The Mission evolved into one of Jamaica's more prominent indigenous Pentecostal churches, with a religious profile similar to the Churches of God save for the use of uniforms and a set of spiritual ranks still modeled on the Salvation Army. With more than thirty churches in Jamaica and numerous branches in England, Canada, the United States, Belize, and the Bahamas, the church today also reflects the regional migrations of Jamaicans in the twentieth century.

The status of Phillips and his associates ensured the Mission's acceptance in Jamaica. The very respectability of these leaders allowed association with the Orthodox Baptists. Notwithstanding, the Mission's emphasis on healing remained, including the practice of selling cloths. At Kingston City Mission services today, a bowl filled with consecrated bandages, with the same scripture verse marked in red, is carried about the church. The cloths are for sale at a modest price.

The impact of Raglan Phillips was registered in another way when, with a mild poetic license, Claude McKay made him the model for his "Big Revival" in the novel *Banana Bottom*.[17] McKay's passages summarize well the moral dimension of the revivals that would intersect with Pentecostalism:

> Among the masses the [extended drought] was accepted as a visitation from God and because of their sins. Native prophets sprang up everywhere predicting worse times. The religious feeling attained its zenith and it was taken at its tide by a saver of souls, a Briton named Evan Vaughan, and turned into a mighty movement. . . .
>
> He started his Big Revival at one coastal end of the island and carried it triumphantly across the plains and mountains to the other. The majority of the nonconformist preachers competed with one another to invite and surrender their churches to him. The colourful soothsayers and magicians were scattered in confusion before the power of the white prophet of God.
>
> Yet the secret of his power was not easily discernible. He was a very small man, almost dwarflike, meagre, with the face of a cat or an old doll, not lighted by any kind of colour. His ordinary voice remained always on the same dead monotonous level. . . . Yet that voice was able to shake hundreds of hefty peasant men and women and bring them trembling and weeping to confess their sins at the Penitents' Form. . . .
>
> From Jubilee the Revival came over the mountains to Banana Bottom. Eagerly the Reverend Lambert put his church at the disposal of Evan Vaughan. And he was the first with his family to go down to the Penitents' Form. . . .
>
> The young village abandoned its tea-meetings, dances and picnics for the salvation meetings. Couples who had been living in concubinage for years, some having even grandchildren of the free union, now became ashamed and miserable sinners and voluntarily separated until they should be married. So numerous were the "Revival" marriages that the church kept a stock of dollar rings on hand for them. (McKay 1933, 230–33)

In the first three decades of the twentieth century, Jamaicans registered the continuing influence of foreign revivalism and situated their healing concerns within it. The process transformed Jamaican rite, now urban-oriented and lacking the pantheons of Zion Revival. Leaders who lacked accreditation or at least support from an established church were vulnerable to charges of unorthodox practice. Some, in addition, were harassed by colonial police because they interspersed a racial anti-colonial message with their Christian evangelical message. Nonetheless, they registered sin as a central concern for their followers and interpreted the disordered world in terms of the need to heal sin. This legacy from the Great Revival set the scene for Pentecostalism. Brought by mainly white Americans but taken up by black Jamaicans, Pentecostalism gave Jamaican preachers accreditation. It also would accommodate Jamaica's healing rite even as it transformed its mode. Healing would be the healing of sin, and in this the sin of fornication would become a central concern.

5 Preachers and Pentecostalism

The Presbyterians, Methodists and Anglicans are
Churches of the Classes. The Baptists, who . . . cham-
pioned the slaves, the Moravians, the Brethren, and the
Disciples of Christ are the Churches of Masses, but their
leadership and public worship is solidly upper class. The
churches of God, Adventists, Pentecostals and Churches
of Christ are Churches of the Masses, with leadership
largely from the masses. Overlapping occurs quite
widely . . . [but] fourteen out of fifteen adults of the
masses are actively out of the old-line Churches.
—D. MacGavran, 1962

Who were the Jamaican Pentecostalists? In one of
her letters of 1919, the American evangelist Nina
Stapleton observed, "we are working right in the slums among the poorest, and lowest classes" of Kingston.[1] She also foreshadowed the opening
of a mission in Spanish Town, where "many poor people . . . are getting
saved. Some are needing clothing and we help them all we can." The areas
of Jamaica that witnessed early rapid expansions of Pentecostalism were
Kingston-St. Andrew and also the area of northern Clarendon that Raglan
Phillips had made his base. Typifying the original Kingston followers is made
difficult today by the sheer size and fluidity of the city and its extraordinary
proliferation of Pentecostal groups, many of which have not sustained sufficient continuities of membership or written records to allow easy analysis.
Northern Clarendon, which had become an outstanding stronghold of Holiness and Pentecostal Churches of God by the census year of 1943, is easier
to typify, and illuminating as well, because some of Pentecostalism's early
Jamaican leaders were drawn from the area.

The Clarendon of Pentecostalism

The northern Clarendon region constituted the hinterland for some of Jamaica's earliest cultivations, which were located around the Rio Minho on
the coastal plains of the parish. By the early 1600s, a track led from these
southern settlements through Clarendon's Mocho range, via the place now
called Kellits, to the north coast Spanish town of Seville Nueva (Taylor 1976,
15; Robotham 1969, 31). The English settled in the foothills of the Mocho
range, improved the track north, and began to cultivate along the northwest

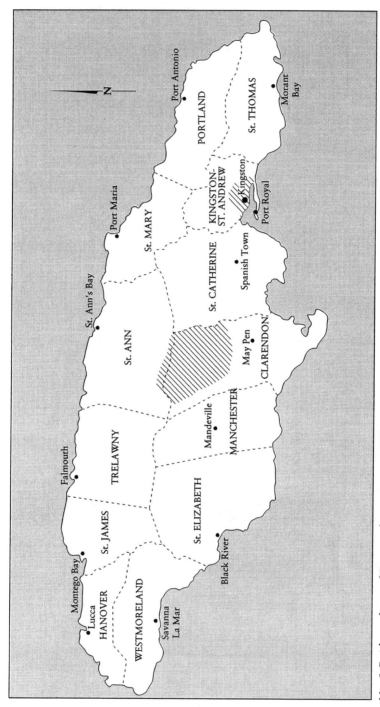

Map 3. Parishes and areas of Pentecostal expansion, circa 1932

section of the Rio Minho. In 1666, the Anglican church constructed a "chapel of ease," St. Paul's, at the place now called Chapelton, and the lands south and east of Chapelton became a principal site of Jamaica's plantocratic class. Around the year 1823, the two hundred and thirty planters of Clarendon owned an average of more than one hundred slaves each, the highest average of any parish in the island (Jacobs 1953, 17). Following emancipation, upper Clarendon became a densely populated area of small farmers and modest plantations. Emancipated slaves settled and often squatted above Chapelton on the northern slopes of the Mocho range and the southern slopes of the Bull Head mountains (Taylor 1976, 38). They planted subsistence crops, raised domestic livestock, and produced "wet sugar," which they sold not only in Chapelton but also in the surrounding market towns of St. Catherine, St. Ann, and Manchester parishes. Farmers also produced coffee and cocoa, and later logwood and sisal as cash crops. They nevertheless were reliant on plantation labor for a portion of their cash. The sugar reversal of the 1840s and the steady decline in sugar prices from the 1870s to the early 1900s had a major impact on the farmers (Taylor 1976, 7). With freeholders under economic pressure, the hillsides were often stripped of their forest and eroded as a result of over-cultivation. As a consequence, the area became subject to flash flooding, which progressively carried away even more topsoil (Taylor 1976, 39–40).

In 1870, a bridge over the Rio Minho was built at May Pen in the foothills of the Mocho range. It was one of the first public works completed by the new Crown Colony government and heralded a rapid improvement in local communications. In 1885, the railway was extended through May Pen to Porus, and May Pen gradually grew more important than Chapelton as a center for the parish. In the early years of the twentieth century, tobacco and banana production expanded in northern Clarendon. To facilitate the transport of rural produce, the railway line was extended first to Chapelton and then, in 1925, to Frankfield in the heart of upper Clarendon. In the 1920s, the American United Fruit Company would establish a flourishing citrus industry in the area.

By the early decades of the twentieth century, British mores and American investment both were influencing local life. Northern Clarendon was a busy freehold and commercial farming zone no stranger to rural recession and poverty. It was a region that had harbored independent small farmers living, nonetheless, in the shadow of a marked sociORacial order. The atmosphere of the area is captured well in a 1910 report on Chapelton and Frankfield:

> Chapelton is a town of considerable commercial importance and a trade in coffee is carried on there, during the coffee season. A few years ago large quantities of sugar, cultivated by small settlers, cured in barrels, used to be sold in Chapelton, but that trade considerably declined during the recent

years of depression in the sugar market. On better prices being obtained, however, the peasantry immediately resumed the use of the small sugar mills. . . . Altogether there are about 800 small sugar mills in Clarendon, of which over 600 are in the Upper District.

Chapelton contains [a number of churches]; a court house, . . . constabulary barracks, and Inspector's quarters, a public general hospital, public works office and store, a large covered market, post and telegraph office, and several large stores. The population of Chapelton is about 900. It stands on a small hill which is naturally drained on every side, and is remarkably healthy, as indeed are undoubtedly the whole of Upper Clarendon and the Clarendon mountains. . . .

Frankfield is an important village 12 miles to the north-west of Chapelton on a good driving road, and is the centre of a large and flourishing agricultural district. In the village are a church, a post office, a dispensary regularly attended by the District Medical Officer from Chapelton and several shops. (Jamaica 1910, 347)

In 1849, the historian G. W. Gardner arrived to pastor a Congregational mission at Chapelton—the mission had been established in 1839 (Gardner 1873, vii). A little less than a century after Gardner's arrival, in 1945, the Congregationalists opened a high school in the area. Baptist chapels were opened at James Hill in 1838 and, in 1839, at Crofts Hill near Kellits and at Thompson Town in the west of upper Clarendon. Phillippo had established the first Baptist church on the plains at Hayes in 1829, a church that was destroyed in the Baptist War and rebuilt in 1837 (Clarke 1986, 12–14; Anonymous 1968, 15; and Turner 1982). Each of these churches, and others as well, spawned clusters of congregations. The Baptists supplemented a considerable Anglican presence throughout the parish, and the two remained, until the advent of the Churches of God, the major Clarendon churches, with a lesser presence provided by the Congregationalists and Methodists. Upper Clarendon has been a particularly well-churched area of Jamaica, a district in which "marriage has the sanction of respectability" and operates as a "hall mark of status," notwithstanding the fact that common-law unions are still very common (Clarke 1966, 82). Also the site of Raglan Phillips's revivalism, the milieu of upper Clarendon shaped Claude McKay's portrait of the gradual demise of mission influence but also the rise, in its wake, of the new American revivalisms.

In the early decades of the century, Clarendon had a consistently high level of male participation in small farming. The period also saw, however, an influx of women into cultivation in the second decade of the twentieth century, when there was emigration of male workers to St. Mary and Portland and to sources of employment overseas (Roberts 1957, 141; Lobdell 1988, 230–33). As Chapelton, Frankfield, and May Pen expanded in the wake of developments in bananas and citrus, the structure of the female workforce changed again. By the census year of 1943, personal and especially domestic service rivaled agriculture as the principal source of female employment. In 1943, some 68 percent of women in the Clarendon workforce were distributed almost evenly between these two categories (Jamaica 1943, 164–65). This redistribution of the female labor force also reflected the return of men from overseas (cf. Roberts 1957, 141). From the 1920s on, Clarendon experienced regular in-and-out migration as men and women moved from more distant parishes through Clarendon toward the urban center of Kingston (Roberts 1957, 155, 159). The migration of women domestics to rural centers and Kingston was integral to this larger movement. And in Clarendon, the expansion of May Pen in particular was marked more by the expansion of service occupations than by the expansion of manufacturing and construction (Jamaica 1943, 161–65).

As the new religious forms from America took hold, northern Clarendon remained a rural milieu experiencing the impact of urbanization, labor migration, and a sense of the modern but not the mass labor of proletarianization. Similarly, for the residents of Kingston-St. Andrew who were drawn to preach and follow Pentecostalism, verbal accounts consistently suggest that Pentecostalism drew the lower classes, and especially women, engaged in modest service occupations. What the city shared with upper Clarendon was the sense of a society beginning to open its doors to the possibilities of the region and especially to America (de Lisser 1913, 80; Austin-Broos 1995).

In the 1920s and 1930s, northern Clarendon was a site of significant social change and re-organization of rural life. It was marked, as H. P. Jacobs wrote, by "the uncertainty of the small proprietors and the growing educated class which was dissatisfied with [Crown Colony rule]" (1953, 17). This sense of uncertainty, produced by change and a certain degree of hope that yet seemed to leave Jamaica's status order untouched, was indicative of a people in transition. The mood also permeated religious life, which local Pentecostals often describe as oppressively ordered under the old colonial regime. Subjected to a subdued liturgy and the moral rigors of a religion integrated with the colonial order, the enthusiasm of Phillips and others was welcomed. This was the Clarendon parish to which George Olson came. Olson, an evangelist for the Holiness Church of God and predecessor to Jamaican Pentecostalism, arrived in Clarendon in 1908.

Jamaican Pentecostalism Begins

Like the Pentecostal movement in America, the Jamaican movement was heralded by a theological forerunner: a Holiness church that preached sanctification or "holiness" through the in-filling of the Holy Spirit. For the Holiness church, this in-filling would be manifest in a generalized capacity to abstain from sin, rather than specifically in healing and the display of glossolalia. And in Jamaica, followers of the Holiness doctrine would emphasize a quiet receipt of the Holy Ghost, described by one practitioner as an "intellectual" experience, rather than the receipt of redeeming Spirit that came through the practice of enthusiastic rite. The Holiness doctrine was first preached systematically in Jamaica by George and Nellie Olson, Americans of Swedish descent who were born in Lake City, Minnesota. In 1907, Isaac Delevante sent a letter describing Jamaica's earthquake to the Holiness Church of God in Anderson, Indiana. He appealed to the church to send missionaries to the island. As a result of this communication, the Olsons traveled to the island, where they met Delevante, who helped them to establish a modest church in Kingston. Indicative of the period, the Olsons sailed on the United Fruit Company's vessel *Captain Baker* and arrived in Kingston via the banana town of Port Antonio on July 30, 1907 (Graham n.d., 1–12).

George Olson was an extremely active evangelist and traveled mainly in the parishes of St. Mary and Clarendon, facilitated by rail links between these areas and his base in Kingston.[2] It is difficult to assess Olson's early success, for the Jamaican census has never differentiated between Holiness and Pentecostal Churches of God. The 1921 census, in which the category "Church of God" first appeared, registered a following of 1,774. It is likely that this figure reflected affiliates mainly of the Holiness church. Although there is evidence that Pentecostal evangelizers had entered Jamaica prior to 1921, Pentecostalism still was not especially prominent. Active Christian evangelists at the time, including Raglan Phillips and George Olson, used the pages of the *Jamaica Daily Gleaner* to advertise their activities in Kingston and the parishes. Pentecostal involvement in this practice only blossomed in the mid-1920s, which suggests that prior to this time, particularly in the second decade of the new century, the doctrine still was finding its feet on the island. By 1920, the Holiness Church of God, on the other hand, had regular notices placed in the *Daily Gleaner* similar in style to those of the established churches.

The work of the Holiness Church of God in St. Mary and Clarendon was pushed forward in both instances by Jamaican converts. These were teachers and modest public servants, for the church appealed mainly to the lower middle class.[3] An elderly member of a Clarendon church, converted by Olson, gave this account of the latter's progress in rural Jamaica:

> Once Brother Olson was traveling back to Kingston . . . and while he was walking he would preach the gospel. He had a terrible boil and he was suffering, but he had to go because he had the call to go. And while he was walking, a dray—a mule cart, you know—must have been carrying bananas and wood and so, come along and saw the man struggling. He offered him a ride . . . and he was so glad he jump up on this cart. And there was a bunch of bananas stacked there, that was the only cushion, and he

fell on it and he lay down and in a few minutes he was gone asleep. And the owner and driver of that cart look around and look on that man sleeping. He was like Jesus in figure. He was just like his portrait and all the paintings we have of Jesus. And when that man look at him and reason how far he came from, not looking money, looking souls of men, and how he had suffered and sacrificed everything and the very innocence of his face, the very humility causing him so to be resembling his Jesus Christ, his Master, that man bowed there. That was the only gospel that was preached that morning, and he got converted.

This story of proselytization lingers on the theme of a savior ministering to the gentiles, to those who remained beyond the ken. It also involves a white savior ministering to the black. The account inscribes a biblical imagery onto the landscape: the ambulatory evangelist, who possibly traveled more often by train, is represented as ministering in a wilderness that is nonetheless a place where bananas are cultivated. Pentecostalism proper in Jamaica would partly eschew these images of the white ministering to the black by rapidly producing a large group of Jamaican evangelists. Yet Pentecostalism would share with the Holiness group the experience of Jamaica as a biblical order to be sustained through the confession of sin and the spiritual transformation of the self, a transformation embodied in healing.

In America, a number of the early trinitarian Pentecostal churches began as Holiness churches in the late nineteenth century, and only in the first decade of the twentieth century did they make the transition to Pentecostalism. This transition was encouraged by two major moments of Pentecostal revival, one at Topeka, Kansas, in 1901 and the other at Azusa Street in Los Angeles in 1906. For New World Africans, the Azusa Street in-filling was especially significant, for it has been said to have involved two Afro-Americans, William Joseph Seymour and his future wife, Jennie Moore, ministering to a white couple, Brother and Sister G. W. Evans (cf. Anderson 1979, 70; Lincoln and Mamiya 1990, 79). This event has become a charter myth for black Pentecostals, who deploy it as a statement of the spiritual ascendancy over whites that they propose for New World Africans.

Followers of the new Pentecostal practice that embraced not only holiness but healing and glossolalia as initial signs of redemption indicated their doctrinal allegiance by inserting "Pentecostal" or "Apostolic" into a previously established church title. As leadership was often revelatory, churches developed and declined quite rapidly, passing through processes of fission and fusion. The designation "Church of God," Paul's term of address to Christian communities, is, like "Apostolic," simply a signifier of biblical orthodoxy rather than a differentiating title. These characteristics carried over to Jamaica, where there has been in the course of the twentieth century an extraordinary proliferation of Pentecostal churches bearing as part of their title

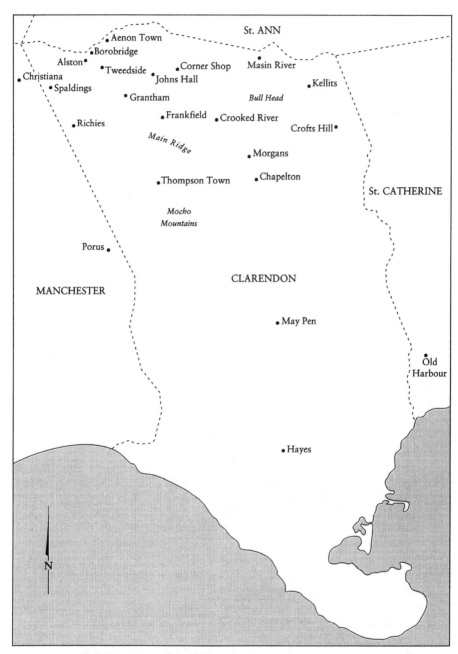

Map 4. Major Pentecostal sites in North Clarendon

"Church of God," "Pentecostal," or "Apostolic." It would be a complex task to tell the full history of Jamaica's Pentecostalism. Central elements of the meaning of the movement can be gleaned, however, from some characteristics of its early expansion and of its Jamaican proponents.

An Early Pentecostal Initiative

In 1922, the *Jamaica Daily Gleaner* published the following notice concerning the Apostolic Church of God, later to be known as the Pentecostal Holiness Church of God, located in Wild Street, Passmore Town, an inner neighborhood of Kingston:

> Notwithstanding the recent shark scare, a largely attended baptism by immersion in the sea took place at Rae Town [Kingston] on a recent Sunday morning. Fully five hundred people must have been present, and the number of candidates was said to be forty-eight. The baptism was in connection with the Apostolic Church of God at Passmore Town of which Elder Harper, from the United States, is the minister. While the baptism was taking place, a line of canoes with spectators joined in a curve to keep off any harbour sharks.[4]

This vivid image of crowds of people massing to observe a collective immersion captures one dimension of early Pentecostalism in Jamaica. Evangelists, who often declared unusual experiences of healing, proceeded by baptizing followers who had been "felled" or "struck down" in the Spirit, often undergoing healing as well. They were heralded thereby as transformed and elevated moral beings joining a community of saints, a community that professed to situate itself both above and beyond Jamaica's socioracial order. The constantly emphasized plurality of baptisms, the liberal "outpouring" of beneficent Spirit, built a sense of alternative community available to the penitent. Regular notices for the Pentecostal Holiness Church of God continued throughout 1922 and indeed throughout the decade.[5]

Another church, in Allman Town, also figured prominently in *Daily Gleaner* notices of the mid-1920s. This was the Pentecostal Church of God in Christ, a missionary outreach of C. H. Mason's Mississippi-based Church of God in Christ.[6] The American church was founded in 1897 and became Pentecostal in 1907. It was a black southern organization and grew in time to become a church with branches in all fifty American states and twelve other countries (Mason 1985; Lincoln and Mamiya 1990, 76–91). The church had considerable success in Jamaica, with early major branches at Mt. Ogle, St. Andrew, and Heart Ease, St. Thomas. It persists in Jamaica to the present day under a changed name and as an independent church. Notices for these two churches during 1924 and 1925 are interspersed with notices for the ministry of Raglan Phillips and also for the Pentecostal Assemblies of the World designated briefly during 1925 as the Apostolic Faith Mission but consistently under the guidance of a Jamaican, George White.[7]

There had been, however, at least one previous major Pentecostal initiative in Jamaica. In 1917, J. Wilson Bell had written to the *Church of God Evangel*, organ of the Pentecostal Church of God in Cleveland, Tennessee. He had sought affiliation with the church and his appeal was described by its leader, A. J. Tomlinson, as "a plaintive Macedonian cry from . . . Jamaica."[8] Tomlinson responded by sending an American evangelist, J. S. Llewellyn, to Jamaica in April 1918 (Conn 1959, 62). There followed a pastor, J. M. Parkinson, and his sister Nina Stapleton, who set up a number of preaching stations on various Kingston intersections, the most popular at Cross Roads just north of the city center. Nina Stapleton was known as an outstanding evangelist and converted a number of prominent Jamaican Pentecostalists. One of these was Rudolph C. Smith, who would return to Mainridge, Clarendon, and there baptize Henry Hudson. Smith and Hudson became, respectively, the first Jamaican overseers of the Church of God of Prophecy in Jamaica and the New Testament Church of God.

Various events intervened, however, both in Jamaica and in America, to make this process a complicated one. A coroner's inquest was held in Kingston on March 26, 1918, concerning the death of a small girl, Victoria Wilson Bell. The child, along with one of her brothers, had become ill on February 11 after eating unripe ackee.[9] The brother and two others had survived, but Victoria died. The *Daily Gleaner* report stated:

> The father of the children was the Rev. Wilson Bell, a minister of the Apostolic Faith, and the tenets of this religious body were against the use of medicine. Accordingly, when the child became ill, the father and mother neglected to consult a doctor.[10]

As a result of this inquest, Bell was committed for trial on the charge of manslaughter, and the case came to the Kingston Circuit Court on May 3, 1918. Solidarity had been expressed already back in Cleveland, Tennessee, where Bell's situation was addressed along with the struggles of saints in Barbados:

> Our friends on the Islands are having some troubles. J. Wilson Bell, of Jamaica, has lost one of his little children. Four of them were poisoned severely by eating some unripe fruit. God healed three of them and one died. Because Brother Bell would not resort to remedies and physicians they have him in the toils of the law. We do not know the outcome yet. He needs our prayers.
>
> On the island of Barbados they are threatened with prosecution if they have a prayer of any kind or a funeral service over a child that has not been

"Christened" by the minister of the English church. . . . Some of our people in [Barbados] are having some trouble about vaccination. Their children are shut out of school unless they are vaccinated. . . .

　　The last days are upon us and we must stick together and pray for each other and help each other all we can.[11]

This commitment to the healing power of God in opposition to the colonial order, and in the shadow of the millennium, was the form of solidarity that American Pentecostals offered to Jamaican people.

　　Bell was acquitted of the manslaughter charge, but not without a warning from Jamaica's chief justice that "if the defendant failed in the future to summon medical aid and did anything to accelerate the death of a member of his family, he would be held responsible." The judge observed that the case should "serve as a warning to those in the community who might hold similar views."[12] The early Pentecostals here emerge as part of the same revival tradition that involved Bedward and Phillips. The Jamaican middle class looked on them with similar concern and characterized them as similarly ignorant (see also Arscott 1971). Yet their association with established American churches protected them from the state's excess, an excess modified by its own commitment to Christian doctrine, which offered annoying legitimation for this most recent round of superstition.

　　Following the trial, Wilson Bell left the Church of God and struck out as an independent evangelist frequently critical of colonialism. He appears in 1919 representing the Pentecostal Mission of America and in this role held a gathering at the Kingston Queen's Hotel, then a hostel for disabled ex-servicemen. Some years later, in 1925, as Bell continued his unorthodox career, he was involved in the founding of the Black Christian House of Athlyi along with Mrs. G. J. Garrison of New Jersey and S. A. Jones, president of Garvey's United Negro Improvement Association (see also Hill 1983, 27).[13] The House of Athlyi, a forerunner of the Rastafarian movement, was infused with the ethos of revival religion. Garrison is described in the *Daily Gleaner* report as "the lady representative [from America] and a woman who received the Holy Ghost at . . . fifteen."[14]

The Church of God Evangelists

Notwithstanding the loss of Bell, Church of God evangelism continued through Rudolph Smith. Smith was the son of a prosperous small farmer; he resided in Alston at the northernmost tip of Clarendon. He had traveled to Kingston in search of work and was there converted by Nina Stapleton. He returned to Alston in 1921 and subsequently became an itinerant evangelist in the north Clarendon area. In 1922, he organized his first permanent church at Mainridge, south of Alston but still within the north Clarendon region. A 1922 letter to Tomlinson printed in the *Church of God Evangel* summons a continuous Pentecostal world that bridged Jamaica and America. Smith reported:

> One woman called us up and gave a piece of land to build a place of worship on. She was willing to dig up cocoanut trees, banana trees and coffee trees which bear quite heavily. This struck the hearts of many who were against us and they confessed that it is truly the power of God. Eight souls have received the Holy Ghost, speaking in other tongues according to Acts 2:4. There were devils cast out of many who were healed.[15]

This account of a Jamaican small farmer exchange—"cocoanut," banana, and coffee for the Holy Ghost—may have passed unremarked in the metropolitan world. In Jamaica, however, it would have had a considerable impact. Smith underlines the fact that people were prepared to exchange significant value in the cultivator's world for the promotion of spiritual work, and especially for healing from forms of malaise incurred by "devils."

In this same letter, Smith announced the saving of Henry Hudson and of numerous others in the Mainridge area. He also observed to the saints in America that notwithstanding the gift of land, "we need help to even half finish [the church]" and thereby avoid the loss of further souls. Another of Smith's early converts was "Pappi" Percival Graham, like Hudson the son of a north Clarendon farmer. Graham remained with the Mainridge church and ultimately established a new church at nearby Pennants in 1948. Hudson, however, proved the more vigorous preacher, and during the years 1922 to 1924 he established three churches at Morgans, Borobridge, and James Hall. From Borobridge on the northern border of Clarendon, members of the church carried the Pentecostal message to Aenon Town and on into the parish of St. Ann.

During this period, converts in the region subscribed to the *Church of God Evangel* and wrote letters to its editor, A. J. Tomlinson. The *Evangel's* printed material became an important legitimation of the Pentecostal message among the people, tangible evidence that the proponents of Pentecostalism were engaged with a larger and more powerful world. This deployment of a newly prevalent literacy went hand in hand with more traditional practices. With Pentecostalists being opposed in the north Clarendon region by Baptists, Congregationalists, and the Holiness church for their "dancing, leaping and shouting" in the Spirit, subscription to the magazine was important evidence of attachment to "the true Church of God."[16]

Following the debacle of Wilson Bell, the Church of God missionary effort received a further setback when the Cleveland church divided in 1923 (see chapter 1, above). The American evangelists in Jamaica were recalled, and both Hudson and Smith were forced to continue independently. Hudson

Figure 5. First-generation Pentecostals from the Clarendon Hills

expanded his work in Clarendon and established numerous congregations (Conn 1959, 65). An elderly Pentecostal woman in northern Clarendon recalled her healing and the making of a church:

> I was sick in 1919 comin' up 1930. After dat, in 1930, I wus sitting down inside de house here one day, and I heard a voice talkin' but I look up and don' see anybody. So I call m'husband outside, and he say, "Send by de

> elders of de church." I begin to send to de churches dat is in de district . . .
> Baptist church, Congregational church, Holiness people, all de meeting
> churches dat was here. . . . and I cyan get any healing. Dey come and pray
> but I cyan get healed. So I read about one church; it's at Mt. Providence.
> Me sister married to a man livin' dere. Dey pray for me and I feel better.
> But me don' join; me not goin' join 'cause me don' like dem. [I say to me-
> self,] "I will stay at de Congregational church. Dey're nice." But after dey
> prayed, after dey laid hands on me and prayed for me and I find I was
> really healed, den I went with de [Pentecostal] church. And de minister,
> Minister Hudson, preaching said de text: "Moses my servant is dead; now
> derefore arise, go over dis Jordan thou, and all dis people unto de land
> which I do give to dem." (Joshua 1:2)"

In this account, the sister commended the power of Pentecostal practice
over other churches unable to address her malaise. The length of her illness,
like Alexander Bedward's, signified that healing made her anew, not just the
healing of a passing illness but a transformation of body and soul. Her first
inclination was to remain with the more socially accepted Congregational
church, but when she was "really healed" or transformed, she determined to
become a Pentecostalist. Hudson's preaching convinced her, moreover, that
she should return to her father's cultivation across the Rio Minho and there
begin a church.

She began by holding cottage meetings at her parents' house:

> Me sister comin' all de way from Mt. Providence now. Dey heard about
> what was happened. . . . My sister say dat de Lord said dat she mus' come
> to de inhabitants of [de area] and preach. And de church start and after-
> ward de crowd was too big. Dat place out dere [in me father's yard] cyan
> hold dem. We went away and buy a piece of land down the road.
>
> So one morning, when I was comin' up [to cultivate], goin' down de eve-
> ning, [in] de night I dreamt a little, I couldn't describe it, look like an ark.
> I only see de little t'ing drivin', comin' to me and as I was goin' down de
> driver say, "Where you goin'?" and I say, "Me goin' move, move de church."
> Den he say, "You goin' down, church goin' down and de ark is goin' up."

As in Rudolph Smith's account, this one also presents the fact that a follower
gave arable land to a church as evidence of the manner in which a life was
transformed. Through her account of her dream, the sister rendered the
building of a church as a biblical event:

> Yu remember de Philistine and remember de ark? Yu remember de Israel-
> ites dem? When de Philistines fought against de Israelites and win de
> battle dey took over de ark. Yu remember de time dat de ark return, re-
> turning back an' it was donkey cart dat drive de ark? It's in de Old Testa-
> ment. So he say, "De ark is goin' up an' de church is goin' down."

The allusion was to the first book of Samuel, where in fact two cows were chosen by the Philistines to pull a cart carrying the ark of the God of Israel away from Ashdod. The presence of the captive ark at Ashdod had caused the destruction of the people. The ark, along with gifts of recompense from the Philistines, was directed "up" and "along the highway" until it stood in the field of an Israelite, Joshua of Beth-shemesh. The Pentecostal sister cited Samuel's comment on the saga:

> If yu do return unto de Lord wid all yu hearts, den put away strange
> gods . . . and prepare yu hearts unto de Lord, and serve him only; and he
> will deliver yu out of de hand of de Philistines. (1 Samuel 7:3)

The sister interpreted the donkey cart loaded with sugar that she saw in her dream as representative of the ark. In her dream, the driver of the cart had given her a piece of sugar cane and told her to carry it "up" to where the church should be:

> Han' he pushes inside de ark like dis, and took out a head of sugar 'bout
> dis length and said, "Take dis to de holy place." He give it to me and say I
> mus' take it till I come up.

As a result of her prophetic dream, the sister did not locate the church on the original site but rather on a hill above it. There a church was built that protected the followers of Henry Hudson from the Philistines of the local area, the practitioners of orthodox religion. This account of a Jamaican battle against the Philistines retains an echo of the revival theme that the moral disorder of Jamaica's world inheres within the colonial regime. Yet in this sister's Pentecostal account, the healing of self is privileged as the principal means of addressing disorder.

Through this and other like events, the influence of the Church of God spread rapidly. In recognition for his services, Henry Hudson was appointed overseer of the church in 1935. Thereafter, Hudson moved to Kingston, where he remained for the duration of his term as overseer (Conn 1959, 65).

A. J. Tomlinson re-organized his followers in Cleveland, Tennessee, and proceeded independently of the Church of God. He observed in 1929:

> We could have a dozen churches on [Jamaica] . . . in three or four months
> with the proper skilled workmen that know the people and the methods to
> use to gather them into the fold.
>
> I do not advise that any of our people from the States go to these Is-
> lands. The natives can do much better than we can and at less expense.
> They understand their people and the natives understand them. Their
> need is means to help with their expenses.[17]

Figure 6. Church of God of Prophecy in Pennants, Clarendon

In the event, Tomlinson sent a missionary couple, the Kinders, who established a relationship with Rudolph Smith. After the 1923 recall of American evangelists, Smith had joined O. G. Harper's church in Passmore Town. He became a prominent Kingston evangelist and, when the Kinders approached him, agreed to rejoin Tomlinson's church. In time, this organization became the Church of God of Prophecy, though it was known at the outset as the Bible Church of God.

Smith was ordained in Cleveland, Tennessee, as a minister late in the year of 1935 and was soon thereafter appointed as overseer of the church in Jamaica. He remained in that position until his death in 1974. Smith was reportedly a dynamic organizer, a man of great charm, and a profoundly persuasive preacher. He is portrayed as one who "traveled thousands of miles on foot over the island to preach the Word and the Message of the Church of God." He reputedly established ninety-six churches in the first twenty years of his ministry, an extraordinary feat for a man who shied away from public promotion.[18] Hudson, a man of similarly impressive personality, nevertheless remained as church overseer for a mere five years. He was forced to resign in the face of charges of immorality, a fate that had befallen T. A. Sears, the black American overseer, in 1925 (Conn 1959, 64–65). Jamaica's Church of God would remain thereafter a church of black pastors led by white American overseers who maintained the mission link with Tennessee. The New Testament Church of God was formally incorporated in 1949, and the Church of God of Prophecy was incorporated under its present title in 1964.[19] Consistent with their standings in America, the New Testament church has the larger following, though the two remain today Jamaica's largest trinitarian Pentecostal churches.

The "Oneness" or Unitarian Evangelists

George White was born in the parish of St. Elizabeth and came to Kingston as a young man. In the early 1920s, he delivered bread for the Huntington Bakery and had become associated with the Pentecostal Church of God in Christ based in Allman Town. His future wife was the maidservant of a light-skinned woman, J. R. Russell (née Price), later to be known as Mother Russell. In 1919, following a Pentecostal experience, Russell had returned to the family's home at Brown's Town. With the help of two Pentecostal preachers, Arthur Watson and H. Lee, she instigated a revival that spread to a number of towns throughout St. Ann's parish. Her maid, Melvina Needham, was one of the early converts.[20] White and Needham were married in Kingston in 1924. The *Daily Gleaner* notice of the wedding and of related activities suggests that Watson, Lee, and White already were engaged in the systematic building of a church:

> An interesting wedding will take place at "Oakland," Penrith Road, Cross Roads. Wednesday 19 inst., 10 a.m. Evangelist George White and sister Melvina Needham will be united in marriage. The ceremony will be conducted by the District Elder, Arthur Watson. Evangelist George White is the minister at present in charge of the Pentecostal Mission at Carisbrook, a few miles from Maggotty, St. Elizabeth, where a splendid work is in progress. Another special baptismal service will be held 6 a.m., December 14th in the river running through the village of Maggotty. Between 50 and 60 new converts will be added to the church by baptism. With favourable weather there should be a record crowd of witnesses on this occasion.
>
> Evangelist H. Lee and workers will come from Brown's Town, St. Ann's to assist in and share the blessings anticipated. From this place Elder Arthur Watson will visit Brown's Town, St. Ann's to conduct a series of meetings with the people of that town and district. Christianity with Holy Spirit energy, will be the theme in these services.[21]

Figure 7. George White (*Minute Book of the First Convention of the Jamaican Union of Apostolic Churches*, 1941)

By mid-1926, George White's churches at Carisbrook and South Parade in Kingston were consistently described as branches of the American Pentecostal Assemblies of the World (PAW), a "Oneness" group first organized in Portland, Oregon, in 1912. This American group was joined by the larger General Assembly of the Apostolic Assemblies in 1918. In 1924, there was a fission in the movement along racial lines, with the whites forming themselves into a Pentecostal Ministerial Alliance (Golder 1973, 138). The PAW continued as a mainly black Oneness organization, and this was the group with which George and Melvina White became affiliated as minister and evangelist in turn.

George and Melvina White visited PAW headquarters in early 1927. Their good standing with this organization was confirmed by a *Daily Gleaner* no-

Figure 8. Melvina White and Pentecostal Evangelists (*Minute Book of the First Convention of the Jamaican Union of Apostolic Churches*, 1941)

tice in April 1927. White, described by some as the "St. Paul of Jamaica," was clearly invoking the aura of an earlier revivalism even as he received accreditation from America:

> *Pentecostal Assemblies of the World*: Missionary Branch of PAW, USA at 22 Bond St. Service will begin at 3 a.m. on Sunday, then at 5 o'clock all will be conveyed by "private cars" to Hope, where 22 or more candidates will be baptized in the Hope River. Two couples of this said assembly will be united in holy matrimony next Sunday morning, under Pentecostal ceremonies by the pastor Elder Geo. A. White.[22]

The formal recognition as minister of religion and marriage celebrant that had eluded the leaders of Zion Revival was realized by Hudson, Smith, and White. White displayed the achievement proudly and with a degree of Jamaican verve that cast him and his contemporaries as serious religionists who

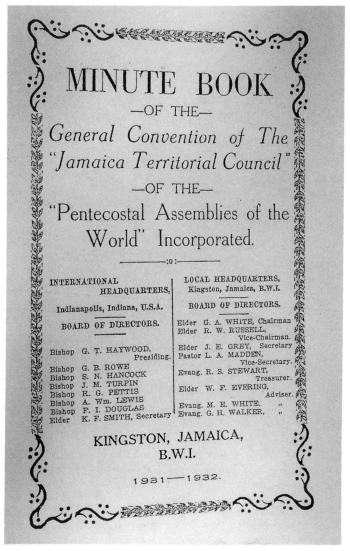

Figure 9. Title page, George White's convention book, 1931–32

also played trickster to the state. They circumvented the government's restrictions by association with American churches.

Notices show White engaged in the full repertoire of Pentecostal activities: foot washing, the laying on of hands for healing, baptism, marriage, and communion. In 1928, others joined the field of Oneness preachers. J. S. Maxwell and Elder D. H. Georges, a Jamaican who had become a Oneness evangelist in the United States, also began activity in Manchester parish under the title "Pentecostal Apostolic Faith Mission."[23] In September 1929, White opened a new church, the Emmanuel Apostolic Tabernacle, at the corner of King and Beeston streets. The notice for the event observed:

> For several years past the Penticostal [sic] Assemblies of the World have had missionaries in the field whose work have met with gratifying results, and many have joined the ranks of Christianity. Their phenomenal growth has necessitated the erection of this building.[24]

It is this locale that many early Kingston followers of George White's church remember, where nights were spent in rowdy evangelistic meetings while children slept on wooden benches or on the floor. Emmanuel Apostolic Tabernacle became a community and a world for West Kingston Pentecostalists. It would have a continuous history under George and then Melvina White, who delivered its congregation as one of the largest in Kingston today.

In June 1930, the first Pentecostal convention in Jamaica was sponsored by the PAW at Kingston's Ward Theater. The second convention in 1931 produced a Minute Book, which showed White, as chairman of the convention, at the head of a considerable religious movement and, probably because of the strategic advantage of an initial base in Kingston, more influential than either Hudson or Smith.[25] The Minute Book also reflects something of the politics of White's position. Applications for pastors to be credentialed with the PAW were channeled through him. White used the occasion, for example, to challenge the PAW credentials of Elder D. H. Georges and call him to account before the convention.[26]

In 1931, the PAW in America merged with the Apostolic Church of Jesus Christ to become the Pentecostal Assemblies of Jesus Christ (Golder 1973, 139). In 1932, White himself, now designated as "Bishop," appears presiding at Emmanuel Tabernacle and leading a considerable church with branches listed in thirteen locales.[27] White's engagement with black nationalist Christian concerns was indicated in September 1932, when he invited the Reverend J. Daley of the African Methodist Episcopal Church to speak at Emmanuel Tabernacle on "A Trip through West Africa."[28] In the following year, White opened a new church building at Spanish Town for a group pastored by Mrs. M. G. Weekes, who was in fact White's sister.[29]

White reached the pinnacle of his power in the early 1930s, and the subsequent years were ones of confusion leading to tragedy. In 1933, the white Pentecostal Ministerial Alliance, forerunner to the United Pentecostal Church, opened a church in Jamaica at Constant Spring just north of Kingston. White's relations with the churches associated with the Alliance were ambiguous, close association without any move to joint affiliation.[30] In the

1930s, White traveled regularly to conferences in America held by the Assemblies of Jesus Christ. He was provided with a secretary by the American organization, which now also had become dominated by a white bishopric (Golder 1973, 138). By June 1936, White, retaining the title "Bishop," had determined on an independent path and established the Jamaica Union of Apostolic Churches.[31] In this, he anticipated black bishops in America who split from the Assemblies of Jesus Christ to reform the PAW in 1937. Early in 1937, however, and before White's initiative came to fruition, White was expelled from Emmanuel Tabernacle on a charge of immorality involving, legend has it, his white American secretary. White subsequently traveled to the United States and England, returning briefly to Jamaica during the early 1940s. He would never again be involved in Pentecostal evangelism within Jamaica.[32]

Melvina White carried on her husband's work and, in 1941, organized the first convention of the Jamaica Union of Apostolic Churches with Elder Penman of Emmanuel Tabernacle in the chair.[33] However, divorced from George White's charismatic leadership and American financial support, the Union splintered during the 1940s. Some churches remained with the PAW, while some embarked on an independent course.[34] Melvina White pastored the Emmanual Apostolic Tabernacle until her death in 1978. She saw it grow to a congregation that numbered more than a thousand.

In America in 1945, the United Pentecostal Church emerged out of three previous "Oneness" organizations. Mother J. C. Russell, along with her husband, made contact with the new body in St. Louis, Missouri. Mother Russell had been active throughout the 1930s, holding prayer meetings in Goodwin Park and Rockford in Kingston. She and her husband rented a property in Wildman Street, Kingston, which remained thereafter a center for Oneness worship. In 1947, at the Russells' invitation, Pastor V. Reynolds and his wife arrived in Kingston to establish a branch of the UPC at Wildman Street. The church subsequently expanded with further large branches in Mandeville and Ocho Rios.

Race and Morality in the Pentecostal Movement

There is now considerable tension between some followers of the churches that were once part of George White's Apostolic Union and representatives of the United Pentecostal Church. This tension was exacerbated in 1986, when Mother Russell published a "brief history" of unitarian evangelism in Jamaica that made no mention of the Apostolic Union (Russell 1986). The United Pentecostal Church in America is described as racially biased by many Jamaican unitarians. Some also have proposed that in spite of good academic records, black theological students are not always welcomed by the

American church. One man observed that after an initial acceptance by the church, his application to study was rejected, it seemed, on the receipt of his photograph showing him to be a dark-skinned man. Some believe that this bias has extended into Jamaica itself, where George White has been denied proper recognition for his work.

Similar concerns are sometimes expressed in discussions with trinitarians. It is commonly proposed that after experience with Tennessee segregation in the 1930s, Rudolph Smith was unwilling to travel to America and remained mainly in Jamaica. His death was caused, a story has it, when a black colleague in the Bahamas was deprived of the position of overseer for his church. "They have taken away his work," said Smith, and was taken mortally ill with a stroke.[35] The story proposes that for Rudolph Smith, racism in the church was an appalling intrusion of "man-made" practices.

The Church of God of Prophecy has remained smaller than the New Testament church despite vigorous evangelism. Like the indigenous unitarian churches, it also has remained until recently mainly a church of the lower classes, while the New Testament church for some time has spanned the lower classes and the lower middle class. This, too, is attributed by some trinitarians to the fact that Henry Hudson's fall conferred a white governance, with its additional resources, on the New Testament church in Jamaica for a period of around fifty years.[36] Jamaican Pentecostals often complain of the insensitivity of white Americans, as in the comment from an independent unitarian bishop that Americans "insisted that the choirs be robed and that everything be done in an American way. The attitude was different in Jamaica, because even if a person came in barefoot to the church and received the Holy Spirit, Jamaicans would praise the Lord for him." The bishop offered the further reflection that "Jamaicans accepted Pentecostalism because they already lived in a spirit-filled world. They were Africans themselves. . . . The whole world of Jamaica was busy with spirits, so the message of the Holy Spirit was welcome. Americans didn't need to tell Jamaicans that" (see also Austin-Broos 1996).

The bishop's resentment of white superintendence, like that of Rudolph Smith's, reflects a common view among Pentecostals that the American movement is racially biased, and also biased within Jamaica. Jamaican Pentecostals who parry these claims often point to the "falls" in which both George White and Henry Hudson were involved. The observation often is made that one or the other preacher lost control of his movement through "foolishness," or profligacy. Whether or not these events are linked explicitly with the reassertion of white superintendence, accounts of Pentecostal history in Jamaica often linger on one or the other preacher's transgression as indicative of a Jamaican milieu. The events are related in a humorous tone, but not without an air of regret. These accounts are thereby part of the dispart of the discourse established through the nineteenth century that characterized Jamaican revival in terms of "failure in superintendence" and in the "province of moral principle," proposed a essentially a white domain. Jamaican Pentecostals have been better able than Revivalists to contest this hegemony because they can be marriage celebrants and live now in an independent nation. Nonetheless, the intimate relationship between Jamaican Pentecostals and their counterparts in the United States, where many preachers are now trained, also makes this racialized discourse harder to confront in a definitive way. This can be seen in the very strong focus on "fornication" and the "fall" that is present in Jamaican churches today.

Carrying these many implications, a modern Pentecostalism emerged through the work of black Jamaicans. The movement has been the product of an intersection of three dynamics: a discourse of creole religion that was shaped through the nineteenth century, a new American evangelism that was part of a larger regional shift, and the uses to which Jamaicans would put this new form of revivalism in the midst of their socioracial order. The initial milieu of Jamaican revival was forged in the period of the post-emancipation, in the Great Revival, and in the aftermath of the Morant Bay Rebellion. The coming of a second missionary wave, with American ascendancy in the region, was taken up in the midst of an established British colonial order. This was an order that sustained a moralized socioracial hierarchy that denigrated the black and poor as superstitious immoralists.

Pentecostalism in Jamaica has responded to this circumstance in two telling ways. Its rank and file have emphasized perfection, the moral and spiritual status of being a saint, as a way of inverting the socioracial order. In this, the enthusiasm of American revival has been conjoined with ideas of African "spirituality" in order to claim for lower-class saints a superior religious standing. In turn, this response has created another: an intense and gendered moral politics concerning fornication and the history of "the fall" as a Jamaican experience.

6

A Modern Pentecostalism:
Ritual Resolutions and
Gender Divides

> In proportion as castes disappear and the classes of soci-
> ety draw together . . . the image of an ideal but always fu-
> gitive perfection presents itself to the human mind.
> —Tocqueville, 1945 [1840]

> [Jamaican] men and women must have freedom to move
> as separate individuals. Symbiotic fusion does not figure in
> the Jamaican idea.
> —Elisa Sobo, 1993

The Jamaican Pentecostalism that I encountered in the 1970s and 1980s was different from that of the early days with its street-corner meetings in the middle of Kingston and enthusiastic progress in northern Clarendon. The movement had spread and secured itself within the world of an independent nation. If Pentecostalism's expansion as a popular religion was aided by the labor migrations, it was helped even more, after the Second World War, by prosperity both in Jamaica and in America that enabled extensive church-building programs. The migrations to England in the 1950s carried trinitarian and unitarian churches to the center of the British colonial world.[1] They created trans-national networks for the saints that remained important after the colonial era had passed. There also have been growing links between immigrant groups in America and their local churches in Jamaica. When they migrate to the United States, saints generally prefer their own style of worship. These transnational groups are given life today by the constant traffic of expatriate Jamaicans coming home and Jamaicans resident in Jamaica traveling to stay with relatives overseas (cf. Basch, Schiller, and Blanc 1994). Greetings and testimonies that are carried from metropolitan centers give the saints within Jamaica a sense of expanding possibilities. The regular acknowledgment of visitors from "foreign" in the course of Pentecostal rite secures the sense of development and change that is part of the Pentecostal milieu.[2]

In the larger churches, Jamaican Pentecostals who are prominent in their organizations can avail themselves of training and experience in metropolitan centers. Talented young pastors from the Jamaican New Testament Church now go regularly to the Church of God in Cleveland, Tennessee, to take degrees in theology.[3] If the male elders of many churches still have the parochial style of rural Pentecostals of the past, their younger colleagues exude the confidence of urbane metropolitan preachers. And women rather seldom wear the cover-all dresses and long, unstraightened hair captured in nets that were once hallmarks of Pentecostal women. Some pastors of the New Testament Church of God repudiate the type of "indefinite period of desperate seeking in prayer and fasting" that once preceded Holy Ghost possession. They deplore the attitude in the past that always assumed some "unconfessed sin" whenever a repentant was slow to be "filled" (Campbell 1984, 54). One pastor from the New Testament church described the "highly emotional" style of worship in which early Clarendon Pentecostalists were involved. "They worshiped with a lot of noise and often kept service all the night, coming up morning. They set themselves against the government. They had all-night singing and prayed too hard." These were Pentecostals who had three-day fasts to "purify the heart" and promoted the idea that religion was simply "a matter of feeling." This religion, the pastor observed, was still too close to the old revivalism where "people, for days, not go to work and meditate on religion." Zion Revival was "a wild religion with beating drums, clapping, jumping, [and] falling on the ground." A unitarian pastor noted a similar change but rued instead the lesser conviction of modern youth. The old commitment to "righteousness," she said, was no longer present in the church.

Pentecostal churches have hosted politicians and officers of state in the rites that mark National Heroes' Day.[4] Their larger organizations have been consulted on contentious social legislation. They appear on television as a voice of the people and support a radio station devoted to their cause. This distance between forms of religion parallels the experience of the Baptists. Like the Orthodox Baptists before them, some Pentecostals now distance themselves from the "wild" religion "against good order" that they, and other Jamaicans, associate with the lower classes.

In June 1986, Pentecostal groups, both trinitarian and unitarian, held a symposium in a Kingston resort. Representatives from most major churches were there and expounded their doctrines in measured terms that emphasized also the churches' contributions to social welfare. Later in the evening, rank-and-file saints were given a chance. One likened the birth of the Pentecostal churches to human birth:

> Ladies and gentlemen, if the church was born normal, then the church was born speaking. Do you know my wife tol' me, you can question her, don' question me, that when babies are born, if they do not cry, they slap and slap, until they get the sound to prove that the baby is normal. Yu know, I believe what we really need is some good doctors to deliver these

babies so that the whole church that don' speak in tongues can have a proper birth.

This observation was met with loud applause and cries of "Amen," "Hallelujah," and "Praise the Lord." Its imagery of doctoring people yet to be "born," albeit with authoritative vigor, struck a familiar chord of bodily care articulating with a care of the soul, an address to bio-moral malaise. A little later, another pastor told of a woman in St. Thomas parish who had been driven from her house by a malignant duppy, described by the pastor as "devil servant him." The ghost flew about and possessed the woman, who became "mad" as a consequence. The ghost, named Coppi, he said, was a well-known force in St. Thomas:

> When we reach the house, the lady say to us, "Gentlemen, don' come in, for it only one set o' people can manage Coppi. It's dem people yu hear speakin' tongues." Because she didn' e'en know she was talking with the speakin' tongue people!

There was exuberant applause and praise from the audience. Then:

> We stood that night, an' went in the room where they said no-one should have gone. The Spirit of the Lord came on us, and we spoke in different tongues, and we pray. All the window and doors start to rattle. And then we find that Coppi gone; he chased out the house by the Spirit of the Lord.

The audience responded with deafening applause and then broke into choruses. The choice of St. Thomas was by no means random. It is known as a parish in which Zion Revival is still very strong, and the observation that only "tongue-speaking" people could exorcise Coppi was a declaration of power for the Pentecostalists (see also Schuler 1980).[5] This power involves the ability to heal and to transform the human person.

Jamaican Perfectionism

Pentecostalism is concerned with the transition that changes a person into a saint. This ritual address to the person is consistent with a cosmology that proposes in rite and trickster myth that change comes through normative breach and not through systematic practice. The trick as a circumvention of hierarchy is integral to Jamaican life and familiar to the many Jamaicans who both scold and laud "Anansi" behavior. In the realm of Jamaican Christian practice, the power of possessing rite stands as homologous to the trick. Both are acts that create a breach in a recalcitrant order. In Pentecostal rite, a sinner is turned into a saint, and this sinner is often a person cast as Africa's descendant. From the viewpoint of the orthodox Christian, this person stood at the base of the system, steeped in superstitious magic and unable to assume the "moral greatness" that a civilized "religion demands." This African immoralist born in concubinage becomes through rites of healing and possession a Jamaican Pentecostal saint. This creole cosmological frame informs Pentecostal rite as it is experienced by the saints. Its meaning is specified for daily life by Jamaica's socioracial order.

It is the poor, black, and supposedly immoral who are the saints of most Jamaican churches. And saints, like other Christians before them, embrace a form of morality in which the sanctifying of sexuality has become a major concern.[6] This central sign of saintly practice is, for many saints, however, situated in a social context that presents other forms of union. Among Jamaica's lower classes, patterns that exclude early marriage and pursue it only later in life inform the lives of the poor. Marriage itself has been a sign of superior social status that lower-class Jamaicans often engage in only in maturity (Smith 1987, 1988). Among Jamaica's poor and black, common-law or visiting unions are more usual among young adults. This is a pattern especially marked in Kingston and other urban areas (cf. Smith 1966, xxi).[7] Perfection conferred by a Pentecostal rite has as a central sign the cessation of "irregular" unions described by the saints as "fornication," "freeness," or the "sweetheart" life. This re-arranging of a social-moral order embedded in a socioracial world has been the substance of a politics pursued through Pentecostal rite. The maid negotiating with her mistress and the revivalist confronting the state both have been able to see the inversion involved in Pentecostal rite. Those cast aside by the orthodox church can be sanctified as perfect saints. Yet forfeiting the "sweetheart" life to realize that "moral greatness" of which the Reverend King wrote (see chapter 3, above) requires of Pentecostal saints that they change the norms of lower-class life. Either they must marry early, or else they must adopt a celibate life. This normative tension in the lives of saints is experienced as a battle against the flesh. In the terms of their own experience, saints must vigilantly search for sin and constantly bring the power of rite to diffuse its corrupting influence.

Perfection and Morality

The Pentecostal rite that allows perfection is realized through Holy Ghost possession and signified by speaking in tongues. Only glossolalia confirms that a person has been filled by the Holy Ghost. But glossolalia also only hails an initial working of the Spirit that may be repeated again or not, depending on the Spirit's design. Healing and the assumption of morality signal, on a more regular basis, that both the body and the soul have changed to become a perfect saint. They are indicative of a change completed, not of a mere apprenticeship to grace. In this context, morality becomes metonymic for perfection. It is not the totality of faith but rather the sign of a completed faith. When practiced initially, morality is a discipline on the self. Following in-filling, however, it becomes a sign of saintliness. It need not be a discipline but rather articulates a transformed state.

For Calvin, moral practice was a form of vocation in the world in response to the calling of God. The vocation was practice in the world that accompanied the call to grace but was not, in and of itself, a realization of that grace. Weber proposed that this position encouraged a pessimistic puritanism. The individual pressed on without assurance of grace to realize God's will on earth (Weber 1958, 102–9). This was the mode of moral being brought by the British Baptists to Jamaica. It contrasts with the newly confident perfectionism that developed in the United States. Through the teachings of Wesley and Charles Finney, this latter doctrine would propose that morality could be a true sign of present grace and perfection.[8] The early genre of Pentecostalism brought to Jamaica as a missionary religion included this perfectionism. Yet the notion that morality can be a sign of saintliness was not without its critics. As Sceats has observed, "A major problem for the perfectionist . . . concerns the moral verifiability of the perfection he claims. Very few have actually suggested that all moral defectibility is expunged in the state of perfection. More commonly the claim to perfection is made on the basis of a careful and specific limitation of what is meant by sin" (Sceats 1988, 506). Among rank-and-file Jamaican saints, perfection is interpreted in practice. Their own responses to the doctrine have not involved explicit ideology but rather implicit understandings of what is involved in being a saint and in avoiding sin.[9]

The morality that is relevant to Jamaican saintly perfection bears on an understanding of the body as a vessel for the Holy Ghost about to conjoin with the body of Christ. The soul's transformation in the body involves its assimilation to the logic of Spirit, but such a soul can inhere only in a body that is undefiled. The salient signs of Pentecostal transformation, a moral healing of the self, are signs of cleanliness concerning the body. One set of signs involves health itself. Pain often signifies spiritual anxiety, and healing through the laying on of hands re-asserts the dominance of Spirit. Jamaicans employ an idiom of health and pain to signify their general state of being (see also Sobo 1993). To make the observation that a person is "hearty" is almost always to say as well that the person is spiritually content. To experience "pains" in "meh inside part" is also an expression of incorporeal unease. If a person is a member of a church, this unease will precipitate a prayer request to try to set the matter right. In this idiom, Jamaicans affirm the experiential complex of affliction that sees moral and physical malaise conjoined. Sobo captures the situation well:

> People who "live good" cannot, ideally, be caught by socially precipitated sicknesses: sickness instigated in a response to perceived affronts by an

animate being (a neighbor, a demon, God or a duppy sent by a "science man" hired by a "grudgeful" villager). In an ideal world, a moral sociable person could never anger anyone enough to attack. And should anyone really want to "sick" a physically and spiritually "clean" person . . . God and his angels provide protection. (Sobo 1993, 294)

To be hearty, then, is to be spiritually at peace, and although not all forms of malaise are seen as indicative of moral failing, it is generally assumed that a morally clean body also will be a healthy one.

Another set of signs of spiritual transformation includes the moral signs of the saved. These signs revolve around sexuality and around the idea that any sexual practice not sanctified in marriage will sully a vessel and make it unclean. Manifesting the moral state thus becomes the active rejection of fornication and the rejection of other practices that independently make the body unclean or else may lead to fornication: the rejection of dancing, smoking, drinking, jewelry, cosmetics, swearing, and engagement with the unsaved. For Jamaicans, these restrictions also have involved a ban against straightening curly hair and, for women, once involved leaving the hair uncut. A purified life that sustains clean bodies is central to the Pentecostal progress. It provides the saved with two related statuses that are integral to being a saint. One is to be, as part of the church, a bride awaiting the Bridegroom's approach. The other, as part of the "body of Christ," is to be the vessel for his Holy Spirit. As embodied vessel for the Holy Ghost, both beyond and around his holy essence, it is imperative that the saint be clean.

The signs of healing and morality are Jamaica's own interpretation of the Pentecostal notion of "signs that follow." The transformation of sinners into saints that is central to Pentecostal belief demands that their practice and bodily being give signs of this altered spiritual state. For all Pentecostals, these signs are described in the Bible as those that "follow them that believe":

In my name they cast out devils; they speak with new tongues; they shall take up serpents; and if they drink any deadly thing, it shall not hurt them; they shall lay hands on the sick and they shall recover. (Mark 16:17–18)

In Jamaica, these signs are interpreted in the standard way as exorcism, glossolalia, and healing. To these three is added, however, the practice of morality. And within the realm of morality, it is the signs of cleanliness that count. A saint may express a jealous sentiment, be angry, lie, say "bad words," or even perpetrate a violence that demands a penance and prayer to God. A saint may remain unemployed for years and never demonstrate that duty in a calling indicative of the ascetic Protestant. But even one act of fornication would signify a fall from grace. Likewise, if a saint went to dance halls or started smoking or drinking liquor, this would be a sign of a fall from the perfect state. It would signify beyond any doubt the reversion of the vessel to an unclean state, separation from the body of Christ, and departure of the power of the Holy Ghost. While other failures or transgressions can be construed as failings of the flesh that merely frustrate the capacity for perfection, these moral signs are signs of defilement that mean that capacity for perfection is lost.

Second- or third-generation Pentecostal women often relate that their mothers counseled them that they were "too young" to receive the Spirit when they attended church in their teenage years. According to Pentecostal doctrine, this never could be the case provided that the person knew the gospel message and was able to perform the acts of contrition involved in signifying repentance. For young Jamaican women, however, this concern with youth pertained to the likelihood that they would bear children out of wedlock prior to settling with a partner. It was less momentous for a woman to be pregnant who was saved and not sanctified or not saved at all than it was for a saint actually to fall and, for a time, be suspended from the church. An older saint addressed on this issue observed, "The young gal' do not like t' fast han' tarry. Dey are too young to open de'r heart t' Jesus." Consistent with this pattern of expectations, it is more often older women, over forty, who have placed their childbearing time behind them, who are richly endowed with spiritual gifts, and who are leaders in evangelism.

The moral signs indicative of being a clean vessel also bear on why practitioners are more often women than men. While childbearing more than sexuality itself is central to definitions of femininity, it is the persona of sexual practitioner that is far more central to Jamaican men (Chevannes 1985; Sobo 1993, 173–243; cf. MacCormack and Draper 1987). And this persona is more readily recognized in the maintenance of "inside" and "outside" relations, in constant and more peripheral relations that mark men in control of their "business" (cf. Austin 1984a, 119–30). It is not simply issue that is important to men but that more than one "'omen 'ave pickney fe we." In addition, smoking and drinking are activities that bind men together in the groups that meet after work at a street corner, a domino game, or a small rum bar (Austin 1984a; Wilson 1973; Manning 1973). Gambling is also a Pentecostal taboo, and gambling on Chinese number games, domino games, or the horses is integral to men in groups. Men who become Pentecostals, then, often pursue a leadership role at least as deacon or elder in the church that through its assertion of a patriarchal status mitigates the inevitable denial of these signs of masculinity. Poor women in Jamaica very often do not smoke or drink, and neither are jewelry and cosmetics especially important signs for them. Hats and stylish clothing are, and in the years since Pentecostalism began, this particular sign of femininity has been accommodated in the churches. Even the Pentecostal white worn for communion services can be fashioned in a stylish way. Women join churches with alacrity when they decide childbearing is past. The aporias of these transitions, however, fuel gender tensions in the church.

This discussion of morality as a set of signs shows that being saved as a sinner and turned into a saint is not the relentless systematicity that Weber described as the Puritan calling (Weber 1958, 133). It is, rather, like perfection itself, the assumption of conventional signs as indicative of a transformed state. Central to these conventional signs is the view that for women, and for men, unclean substances infusing the body, whether through sex or other social habits that are deemed connected with fornication, must be removed in order to make the body a vessel. The ethical rationalism brought to Jamaica thus has been made subordinate to rite; morality serves to make the body suitable for transformation and subsequently serves as a set of signs that transformation has taken place. The signs allow morality to be an embodied experience for the saints that makes perfection real to them as a consequence of miraculous rite.

Perfection and Eudemonic Rite

It is because of this revision of ethical rationalism that aspirations to moral being can cohere in fact with eudemonic rite. Notwithstanding the exhortations against fornication, and even in the midst of them, Jamaican Pentecostals do not exhibit that "fundamental antagonism" to "sensuous culture" that Weber attributed to the Puritan. Nor is the individualism of the Pentecostals "disillusioned and pessimistically inclined" (Weber 1958, 105). Jamaican Pentecostals do not embrace "the strict avoidance of all spontaneous enjoyment of life . . . devoid of any eudemonistic, not to say hedonistic" element (Weber 1958, 53). And, contrary to Phillippo, lively bodies in Jamaica need not purvey the message of sin (see chapter 2, above). Pentecostal services are joyful celebrations of the sanctification conferred on saints by the Holy Ghost. Jamaican women come to church prepared to sing and dance for hours. The services are vast outpourings that resemble the West African Bwiti "pleasure domes," a world of rite within the world, with "strong euphoric sentiments" (Fernandez 1982, 533).[10] There is a distinct aesthetics of bodily movement and harmony involved in choruses that makes of Pentecostal services a musical performance of unusual force. In his account of Jamaican Pentecostal music, Hopkin observes that music in the church is a principal form of religious "realization" (1978, 34). Hopkin comments:

> The importance and significance of worshipping lies in the worshipper's being filled by the religious spirit. And . . . most of the energy of the service is directed toward achieving this immediate experience. It is in the manner in which the worshippers bring on the experience and the surrounding circumstances that are conducive to it, that a difference between

American and Jamaican Pentecostal styles of worship becomes manifest. In the Jamaican church the music, rhythm, and movement of the service take on a religiously potent quality in themselves. Where white Pentecostals bring on the experience of the Holy Spirit by concentration and prayer, the Jamaican church members bring it on by cultivating religious fervour and excitement through these sense-oriented forms of self-expression, and through losing themselves in their active participation in the communal events of the church. . . . Where for the Americans singing a hymn is an act of praise, for the Jamaicans the song and all the dancing and rhythm that accompany it are a religious experience in themselves. This experience does not come about independent of the God that the songs praise; rather, the songs act as vehicles of the God's power, and a means of experiencing Him. (25)

Music is the embodiment of power, the means of realizing the "trick." Hopkin also refers to the sanctification of the eudemonic, the alignment of joy and morality, in the following observation: "The ideal of banishing earthly pleasures and rejoicing in the Lord alone clashes with a religious motivation that always tends toward enjoyment in song and dance. . . . But these two characteristics manage to co-exist, for they are the most essential elements of the religion" (26). They co-exist within Jamaica because the use of rite to realize perfection has subsumed the practice of morality.

Lodged within these services, however, are forceful exhortations to desist from sin. For the saved, the filled, the fully sanctified, these exhortations on the power of sin are testimonies to their own achievement, a further celebration of the saintly state. They allow the display of biblical erudition and knowing engagement with the pastor. But saints are not the only ones who hear these exhortations. Their drama and emotional pitch are designed to influence those in the church who are still unsaved. These sermons bring a fearful image into the midst of eudemonic rite: the image of a judging God who is happy for a sense of joy only among the saints. Jamaica's eudemonic here becomes a gift from God for which the neophyte should pay by taking God's spirit within his or her person. And this is a process that can be achieved only by an act of contrition, the admission of sin. The story-telling, the song, the dance, and even the murmuring flirtations that informed a Jamaican rural life all are retained by the Pentecostals as integral to their experience. The eudemonic is sustained, however, only as the sanctified practice of saints in the service of God (cf. Bloch 1992, 5).[11] This is the resolution that Pentecostalism provides for that antithesis that Claude McKay portrayed between Jamaica's mission order and the peasant eudemonic (see chapter 4, above).[12]

Pentecostalism has been taken up not only as an egalitarian form but also as a ritual form that reconciles orthodox religion with the enthusiasm of revival practice. The re-introduction of healing rite in the face of an ethically

rational religion still sustained by the orthodox churches contests the moralized social order that informed the mission and colonial life. This challenge
to the social-moral order involves a hegemony, however: the acceptance of
the logic of Judeo-Christian sin and its implications for that social order.
Jamaican Pentecostals can be saints but only through the repudiation of
common-law and other unions defined as "fornication."

Pastors, Gender, and the Rites of Saints

In the following chapters, the politics of embodied rite will be explored in a
detailed way. The saints' claim to be morally perfect inverts a socioracial order that would normally confine the poor and black to a subordinate position.
Part of this perfection, however, involves the cessation of "irregular" unions,
a requirement that clashes with conjugal patterns common in the lower
classes. Men and women experience this clash as the propensity to sin that
they attribute to each other in varying degrees and ways. Women are pre-
ponderant in the churches, though men hold most authority positions. The
position of men is weakened, however, by Pentecostalism's moral signs which
seem to challenge the identity of men more immediately than they do that
of women. Men in the church respond to this by asserting male authority in
the figure of the pastor. Yet the pastor's status is precarious for reasons embedded in Pentecostal practice. Consequently, in the eyes of women and
those beyond the church, the pastor can appear as a trickster figure rather
than as a moral leader. Aspects of Pentecostal rite and belief contribute to
the pastor's position.

The "callings" in the Pentecostal church beyond the station of a saint are
deacon, elder, evangelist, and bishop, who heads a number of congregations
(Ephesians 4:11; 1 Timothy 3). Pastoring is not a formal calling but rather a
role prescribed by convention, a leader who emerges from the elders, who
are generally men. In Paul's Epistles and the Book of Acts, which are principal sources on the early church, elders are mentioned as religious leaders
who engaged in discussions with the apostles. It is clear that these were
meetings of men. Along with the Pauline injunctions to feminine modesty in
worship, this legacy imparts a patriarchal ethos to the church.[13] The larger,
more highly organized churches promote a male pastorate, and in the rural
areas they service, male pastors are strongly preferred even by women Pentecostalists. The larger churches justify males on pragmatic grounds. Men,
they claim, find it easier to move about as they circulate through different
congregations. In addition, some of the bishops observed, Jamaican women
prefer to be led by a man rather than a woman. Two women pastors of independent churches, both of whom were acquaintances of mine, also gave
this explanation for the fact that their elders were uniformly male. Yet this is

seen as conventional practice and not indicative of spiritual worth. Pentecostals do not exclude the possibility of women pastors, who are sometimes recruited from among the deacons or evangelists. These women pastors are found more often in independent churches and in urban environments. In more conservative rural areas, women pastors are very rare. One male pastor observed, "Woman is more firm to the gospel. She is a more humble spirit. Men want to get material thing. The Spirit cyan work wid dem so well." This comment sought to explain both the preponderance of women in Pentecostalism and the leadership role of men.

In the process of justification and sanctification, the acts of contrition and ritual in-filling, it is the pastor's role to awaken the inquirer to the need for sanctification. He does this through the practice known as exhortation. He preaches forcefully to the unsaved concerning their position in the world. It is also the pastor's role to teach an inquirer how to pray so that he or she can engage with Jesus. As a principal exponent of prayer, the pastor' leads the saints in their worship of God. Through the power of his engagement with Jesus, he helps saints to "set the church alight." Such a meeting may save a soul, give further spiritual strength to saints, or confer on a saint a spiritual gift. The pastor's spiritual power may be enlisted in an exorcism, and he will baptize the truly contrite. It is also the pastor who "lays on hands" to secure a range of mundane healings. He celebrates in the midst of the saints the Lord's Supper and the foot-washing rite.

Virtually all of these activities, however, can be assumed by saints who are not pastors of a church. The evangelist, a position often taken by women, is usually adept in these regards, and so are the deacons, also often women, who are principal salvationists. Elders of prominent standing can baptize and preside at the Eucharist. This pull to egalitarianism works against patriarchal rite, and other aspects of Pentecostal practice also limit the pastor's role.

Pentecostal rite is a revelation that defines a community of saints involved in praise and supplication of God. Yet its divine service and Lord's Supper rite are derived from earlier practice, and the inherited logic of these forms is at variance with Pentecostal rite. In earlier Christianities, perfection was a rarity and was often linked with the advent of death. Saints were unusual as living beings and resided mostly in the world beyond. The ritual process of the living involved baptism into the community of the church, confirmation following a period of tutelage, and then practice of the Eucharist which ministered to the Christian who remained for life a perennial sinner. The logic of Pentecostalism is different because in every act of in-filling, it assumes a completed act of grace and thereby an immanent transcendence that should provide perfection for the saint. Beginning, then, from the practice of baptism, Pentecostals turn and modify rite to embody the meanings of their revelation.

Because baptism signifies a real contrition or justification in faith, Pentecostals only practice believer's baptism, which is also baptism by complete immersion. There is no baptism of very small infants, the "christening" of some established churches. Though Pentecostalists often "bless" a baby and call out its names in the church, baptism as such can involve only one who is cognizant of the teachings of Christ. This need not necessarily be an adult, and it can be a child of ten or twelve, but never a baby or very young child. Because baptism is a justification in faith, Pentecostals stress complete immersion, the comprehensive washing away of sin. Pentecostals often define themselves as "dippers" and not mere "sprinklers" of water (Austin 1981; 1984a, 103–15). Owing to this particular conception, there can be no practice of confirmation within the Pentecostal church. The Bible tutelage involved in confirmation comes every week at Sunday school and proceeds throughout the life of a saint. Sunday school is not a children's occasion but rather an activity for the whole church. And, consistent with the idea of a saint, endowed with capacity for sinless life through a completed act of grace, the celebration of the Eucharist is also transformed in significance. The rite becomes a memorial service rather than the re-enactment of a sacrifice made for the remission of sin.[14] The name for the rite is "Lord's Supper," which signals its status as remembrance. It is practiced at most once a month, and in some churches only once a year. In addition, it is usually accompanied by a foot-washing rite. This rite is understood as a re-enactment of the cleansing involved in baptismal rite. It also is seen as an act of humility following in the footsteps of Christ. The rite is said to follow Jesus' injunction "If I then, your Lord and Master, have washed your feet; ye also ought to wash one another's feet" (John 13:14). Importantly, in the gospel of John, this rite substitutes for the Last Supper.[15]

In both Catholic and Reformation churches, the interpretation and mimetic presentation of Jesus as lamb and sacrifice underline the sinful nature of man and the need for recurring sacrifice. This is the meaning of the Eucharist. For saints who have received the capacity to be perfect, this recurring need is much diminished. The Lord's Supper is therefore seen as a memorial of the time when Christ's blood was shed for sin. It is also a memorial of commensality between Christ and his disciples. Remembering the last meal Jesus shared with his disciples, saints look forward to that time when the totality of the Kingdom will come again. Then, as one pastor observed of the supper, "de Bridegroom welcome we de bride to de table." Jesus will welcome the Church of God to commensality in his Kingdom. The practices of Zion Revival and of the Bedwardites attest to the fact that commensality, represented in forms of "table," is especially important for Jamaican religious. The gathering to enact a "table" is indicative of heaven come to earth. It also recalls a colonial past in which separation from European tables was a forceful image of cultural defilement, with the black Jamaican, descendant of Africa, outside the world of civilization (see Austin 1979, 1984a). Just as marriage is a sign of hierarchy and of moral legitimacy, so the furnishing of a table at which an assembled group partakes asserts the civility of the group. Pentecostalism conjoins these imageries in a Lord's Supper that includes the bride understood as the Afro-Christian church.

This spiritual intimacy between saints and their Christ is augmented by the aspiration of every saint to see new Christians "born again." Divine service each Sunday morning follows a standard form of lessons, sermon, and collection of tithes, interspersed with chorus singing and united vocal prayer. "Vocal prayer" involves the church praying as a whole and as individuals. Each saint raises his or her own voiced supplication to God. Learning the practice of vocal prayer, conversing with God in a lyrical manner, is integral to being a saint. It is a substantial representation of the church as the living body of Christ. It is also a witnessing, however, for individual saints. The evangelical service on Sunday evenings extends this individualism. It is a rite in which testimony and choruses predominate along with dancing in the Spirit. Tambourines and electric guitars are prominent in these services, and in the poorer churches saints will bring pots or pans to hit. As the name suggests, these services are specifically designed to draw unbelievers in through both the enjoyment of song and dance and the individual stories of saints. Both divine and evangelical services end with altar calls that provide the opportunity for saints to pray for the saved and the unsaved alike. These altar calls, which involve the laying-on of hands and sometimes the anointing of the forehead with oil, are also the occasions for routinized healing of minor ailments among the saints (Austin 1981). Though the pastor is prominent here, so also are other saints.

Around these principal rites revolve other practices: fasting to cleanse the body further, prayer, and especially tarrying in intensive prayer for those who have been baptized but not yet filled. In larger churches, there will be specific prayer and Bible meetings for men and women, meetings for elders and deacons of the church, and also an evangelical night for youth. Larger churches, especially in Kingston, engage in outside evangelism, frequently targeting an area where it is known that there are relatively few Pentecostal churches. Smaller churches evangelize simply by making their Sunday evening services extraordinary entertainments for local observers. In all these forms, the focus is evangelism, so that even the Sunday morning service, meant as a service for the church, consistently becomes an evangelical effort. Consistent with this tension between the practice of liturgy and evangelical effort, Jamaican Pentecostals vacillate between the practice of a church and that of a sect (see Yinger 1946; Wilson 1961). Because the order of the world and the church ultimately depends on individual souls, Pentecostals must strive to save them all. As a consequence, there is no rite in the church that is not a rite that beckons to conversion. And in these acts of evangelism, every saint can be equal to every other. All are entrusted with the holy duty to bring the unbelieving to God.

In this Pentecostal milieu, the pastor's role as leader in the church can be compromised (cf. Weber 1964, 28–31). His ritual practices as a pastor often can be assumed by others. His role as head, although conventional, is not sustained by biblical text. The Pentecostal ritual process that decentralizes the Eucharist puts in its place an image of the church as the bride seeking commensality with the Savior, Jesus Christ. The evangelical dynamic of saints cultivates a view of the church as a rank-and-file domain, and because so many saints are women, this domain is often feminine.

The ambiguous position of men, and of the pastors in particular, encourages a vigorous response. In his leadership role, the pastor becomes a ritual performer who often has the principal task of offering exemplary exhortations and exorcising fallen women. He seeks powerfully to augment the church by inducing his women to morality so that they may become the bride, and in this task he deploys the biblical myth of the Fall and a historical image of women as morally weak (see chapter 8, below). Yet, especially in urban churches with large congregations, women spiritually can supersede the pastor. Realizing their own power through rite and evangelism, they can view the pastor as a trickster figure who relies on them for his effect.

Notwithstanding their perfectionism, saints still fall in Jamaica, and socioracial hierarchy persists. This is the Pentecostal perception of a world that interprets marriage as a sign of status and other unions as "concubinage." The church proposes through a process of rite to turn a sinner into a saint and sustains a sense of moral perfection by exulting the power of rite. Rite creates a eudemonic experience as it confirms the world of saints. The experience of being perfect is maintained beyond the moment of rite by a series of moral signs that define the Pentecostal saint. These are not simply the signs of a transnational world. They are also interpreted from within a Jamaican milieu. Women, who suffer more than men the moralization of their position, flock to the Pentecostal churches. They engage the community of saints and become part of the bride of Christ. Men, outnumbered in the church and more ambivalent at its signs, nevertheless use their power to assert their pastoral influence. Youths aspire to be pastors and elders who present themselves as gateways to God. The ensuing politics of fornication, and of men's and women's holiness, reflects a church in which perfection remains a precarious state.

PART THREE
THE PRACTICE

7 Pentecostal Experience and Embodied Rite

"Yu dance, m' dear, in the Spirit of the Lord."
"I would feel the Spirit in my body; some great Power just taking over."
"The Spirit come up through the belly and reach like blood to the heart."

—Pentecostal women talking of the Spirit's in-filling, 1986–87

The answer to the question "Who creates life?" lies at the core of religious belief. . . . God's word, God's breath creates. The metaphor of the divine breath as life-giving is elaborated in Genesis.

—Gerda Lerner, 1986

In the poorer areas of Kingston, a person might be drawn to a Pentecostal church simply as an observer on a Sunday evening. Living in crowded and noisy yards, people often take to the lanes at night. They stroll about, greet friends, and possibly stand across the street from a Pentecostal church. From within the church, voices and tambourines send ripples of music across the neighborhood.[1] Curiosity raised, and possibly feeling vulnerable in the city, a young man but more likely a woman might begin to attend divine service. She might find a friend to go with her, and she might gradually draw closer to the congregation. In the Pentecostal view, however, mere attendance at a church will not accomplish a Christian transformation, no more than "joining" the church of one's parents. A Kingston Pentecostal pastor said:

> It is a wicked thing to "join" the church. Because you are [actually] born of the Spirit of God, and it is the Holy Spirit puts you in the body of Christ. People go an' join church for the most part. They stand at that door and they obey dogma and theology and they keep out souls that want to get to Christ and they not getting into Christ neither. So the church-joining business is very bad, because people join church and they think that they are Christian and they are not Christian. And they remain at that stage for thirty, forty years, and they die non-Christians and they don't know God. Some cyan even pray.
>
> A man or a woman with the proper understanding will come to our church, and they hear the messages and they are convicted and convinced.

133

But as they are convinced some of dem don' return. "For fear I get saved,"
they don' return, but they go an' join some t'ing somewhere where they
carry on all the worldliness. And they have to give up certain thing, give
up drinking because drunkenness a sin. They have to give up cursing and
swearing and fornication 'cause a sister or brother will stumble on that.
And that's what the gospel preaches.

Pentecostal pastors are inclined to emphasize the rigors involved in being a
saint. Though they hold the view that those who are filled will be moral in
being a saint, pastors still underline the discipline involved in becoming an
appropriate vessel for Spirit, in preparing the way for sanctification. Even in
the face of this discipline, however, the diffusely Christian world of Jamaica
presents real and present problems that often impel the curious forward.

Such "inquirers" are seen by saints as people who are often in the power
of the devil. They are people who need to be saved. A Pentecostal sister gave
the following account of how she managed to save a man. The incident was
especially important to her, for through it, she believed, numerous other
women in her neighborhood were saved. The sister, telling me of a danger-
ous situation, had asked that I turn my tape recorder off. It was also an expression of embarrassment that the world that she was about to recount was
one disparaged by "uptown" or "educated" people in Kingston, people she
regarded as being unsaved. This is my record of her account:

There was a man who used to live in Allman Town, and he practiced
obeah. He enticed young girls from all the areas around and tricked them
into all sort of evil thing; wrong doing and working trick and other thing.
He used the de Lawrence books of magic—two of them—and they were
his most treasured possession.[2] He carried them with him when he walked
about. One day I saw him walking down the lane past my brother's yard.
There were dark clouds above and darkness all about. I could feel the evil
whirling about him as he began to pass by the yard. I immediately fell to
my knees and praised the Lord and implored him to protect my family.

I saw the man with the de Lawrence books crossing the gully and walking toward me. Suddenly, he ran up and said he was tired of the evil bad
ways, and he wanted to get rid of his books. He began to build a fire in
front of my yard, and he threw the de Lawrence books in the fire. He
danced around it and told the books to burn. But Satan was angry because
he was burning the books, and I saw little devils coming out of the fire.
They pounced on the man and wrestled him to the ground, and he writhed
and screamed and shouted as the devils went into his body. They lifted him
up, and he ran away still screaming and shouting.

A week later he came to the church and said, "Mother, will you pray for
me?" I looked at him, and as he came closer I could still feel the forces of
evil around him. I said I wouldn't pray for him because he was really trying
to enlist my power for his evil purpose. I sent him to [another sister] and
left the church. The sister prayed for him, but he was not released. Later

that day he crossed the gully to my yard again. As he came, I called my husband and told him to get the oil.[3] The man came and begged me to pray for him. I told him to kneel down in the house, and I rubbed the oil over his face and arms. Then I began to pray and hit him really hard on the back. I also pushed my hands down on his head. He fell over and made an awful noise and flung his arms and legs around. My husband had prayed with me, and the man was released from the devil.[4] After that, the church received a great blessing. There were many, many young girls who came to be saved. That devil man had walked all around the place and his sinfulness had captured many, and especially the young ones who don't know how to stand for the Lord.

Contrition, Discipline, and Transformation

Testimonies from saints concerning the circumstances in which they were saved very often emphasize the burdens of life, the sorrows for sin, and finally the desire to "give it all over to Jesus." Behind this heavy and burdensome life is a devil who leads people on in sin, which in turn elicits retribution from God in the form of a constant stream of misfortunes. The misfortunes then become a sign that Jesus is calling the person to repent.[5] Naturally, when this course is followed, misfortune and suffering are relieved. The following testimony from a lower-middle-class woman shows the salience of "Satan" in her everyday life:

> I wasn't thinking about getting saved, but I went to church on this particular Sunday and sat with my friends. We had a visiting minister, somebody from the States, I think. They had an altar call, and people started going up. I didn't want to go because I had a friend I liked a lot and I didn't want to pass him up. But my life had been hard, hard, you know. I couldn't get a good, proper job, and my mother was very sick. The rent for our apartment was high, you know, and my little brother was too young to look a job. I sort of felt that maybe God was punishing me. I feel that maybe I should send my friend away. He used bad words and drank a little rum, and sometime I thought, "Maybe he's bringing evil," you see. Anyway, [that day] the pastor kept on saying that somebody was putting off the Lord and he was talking to someone today, but that person was proud because of Satan. And when I heard, I felt different, you know. I knew the Lord was talking to me. I felt uneasy. I was restless. I knew there was a battle going on within me. Something was telling me I should get saved, that I should really give my heart to the Lord, and something else was saying, "You're too young for this. Your friends will think you are mad. You'll have to put your earring away." And I felt really bad inside. I felt as though my stomach hurt.

This account emphasizes the reasons for the teller's being beset by Satan, the evidence of Satan's presence, and the battle between the devil and her inclination for the Holy Ghost which ensued as she listened to the pastor's message. The pain she felt was a sign of the devil telling her not to hear, to turn herself away from the Lord. Pain in relation to spiritual conflict is often felt by women in the "belly." As this is the initial locale of the Holy Ghost in the body, it also becomes the place where disorder is readily felt (see chapter 9, below). Pain signifies that the body, especially the belly, is not open as a vessel to the Spirit. Notwithstanding this battle, the young woman was "called" to Christ:

> But somehow, I seem to decide in my heart, and then what happen, I don't know how I reach to that altar. I can't tell you that I got up off that bench there, but I know I found myself [at the altar,] and this is the first time I am going to pray. I started crying, crying, crying, because I just felt sorry for myself. I didn't know what repentance was then, but I knew myself sorry. And I asked the Lord to forgive me for anything, for the sins I did, and I would become a good girl. I said I wouldn't friend or walk about, and I asked him to help me keep Satan out. They prayed for me at the altar, and I went home. And I was different. Although I wasn't yet baptized in Jesus or filled with the Holy Ghost, some change had come over me.

The woman related that she was baptized a short time later. In one such baptism, following the sermon in the divine service, the seats for elders and the choir arranged on the dais of the church were drawn back so that the lid from the baptismal pool could be lifted and leaned against a wall. Previously, the pool had been filled to the waist level of a man of average height. As the pastor stood before the pool and prayed aloud before the congregation, a deacon or evangelist beckoned the candidates forward and into the pastor's room at the side of the dais. When they reappeared, the candidates, both women and men, were garbed in long white surplices. The women had taken off their shoes in the pastor's room, while men took off theirs at the front of the church. A male deacon entered the pool with the pastor while the candidates lined up in front of the dais along a side of the church, two men first and then seven women. The deacon called out the name of each candidate as he or she stepped into the baptismal pool. Each candidate, as he or she entered the pool, either clasped or stretched out the fingers in a praying position. Holding the candidate behind the back and under the elbows, the pastor said, "Do you believe in the Lord Jesus Christ? Do you promise to seek for the Holy Ghost? By your confession of repentance you are now justified before the Savior. I baptize you now in the name of the Father, and of the Son, and of the Holy Ghost." Some candidates replied "I do" to the questions, others "Yes, sah" instead. All entered the water barefoot, were completely immersed by the pastor, and were thrust up again into the arms of the deacon. Most of the candidates came out quietly, but two, one a woman and one a man, came out praising Jesus and were immediately filled.

The man fell to the ground, jerking his torso up and down and waving one hand in the air while the other hit on the planks of the dais. He called, "Praise be to Jesus! Hallelujah! Calabarra, shallarrana carranana lalla nan! Glory! Glory! Praise the Lord!"[6] Saints in the church responded in kind and, as the last candidate rose out of the water, broke into a chorus. At this, the pastor leaped out of the pool and appealed to the unsaved to come to the altar. No one responded this particular day, and with a final hymn and united vocal prayer, the service closed. Women changed their clothes in the pastor's room and came out with the men to receive congratulations. The two men, including the one who was filled, were wet and quickly left for home. For those who remained unfilled would ensue a period of tarrying to receive the Holy Ghost, intensive prayer among other saints and the saved accompanied by twenty-four-hour fastings. Through this practice, the young woman called by the American pastor also would seek to sanctify herself, to render herself as a vessel for the Spirit:

> And I remember I went on for a period [after my baptism], nothing differ-ent, really, and then one night I had the opportunity to tarry. I went first night and I didn't get the Holy Spirit; the second night, didn't get the Holy Spirit; and then Sunday night again, a week apart. And the third night I went, and I said, "Jesus, you know, I'm not saved yet, because the steps that I have started are not complete, and Lord, if you should come tonight I shall be lost." I stopped a minute in my prayer, and I thought of the people around me, because people, you know, always are around the al-tar singing to encourage the people who are kneeling. And I stopped and I said, "Lord, if you come tonight it means that all these people who are around who are filled with the Holy Ghost will be called to your table and I will be lost." And I really started praying, and I don't know what happen. I can't tell you, but something happen.
> I heard myself speaking in tongues, glorifying God. You know, some-thing was evident, marked. I got up off my knees, you know, after the Holy Spirit had sort of subsided, and I couldn't get up because I was weak. I felt that all strength had gone from my body, but I felt a love that I didn't feel before, something big and swelling and bubbling, and I feel that I could just love everybody around. That was really the mark, you know. I felt great swelling love for the Lord and for people. Then I didn't feel like I was me. I felt like I was all, like I was not here. Something had happened, I was "walking on air," as it were. I had to tell myself, "What has hap-pened? What has happened?" I felt different. I was no longer the woman who had been saved from July, baptized from July. I felt different, and that went on for the whole week, you know. The presence of the Lord was so near that whenever I took up a book to read, a Bible, or a hymn book to sing, you know, the presence of the Lord would just fill the room, and I would feel the Spirit in my body, some great power just taking over.
> It has been like that through the years, you know. God has been near.

He has been here. It's not just, you know, something imaginary. He's close, and he's real, and he's dwelling in me. Whatever it is, whatever you need, whatever you desire, you can talk it over with him. He's a personal friend and more than a friend, because when your friend can't help you, he can.

As the woman's account draws to a close, it also becomes a testimony, an evangelical act, as she seeks to draw the listener into her world. Her praise for Jesus as a friend only follows the account in which she underlines the signs, the "marks" that she experienced and manifest that were indicative of her transformation into a saint. As a Pentecostal evangelist, she knows very well that the appealing description of Jesus as friend is one that often arrests unbelievers. The emphasis in her account, however, is also on the holy signs that follow transformation, on the magical experience by which she is changed into a saint. Another account from a country woman emphasized the experience of tongues as the sign of in-filling:

You see, yu living the holy life, goin' on now, feelin' yu free from things. . . . And we used to have house-to-house prayer meetings, you know. We had a very warm time, a real spiritual time. And then, one day I felt a different feeling, just like somethin' come over me and overshadow my life. And so I got to my feet, and I jump and kick all over the place. And another brother was there, Brother Richards, I remember. And he got the Holy Spirit as well. And I tell you, something strange happen. I found me'self talkin' in different language. I just feel that I was a new person, that I was renewed, and that something really strange had happened. . . . That's why I really love the church, because how could a man get a different feelin' and get a different tongue to speak? We didn' know of such a language. We only know our own way to talk, but in the time of receiving the Holy Ghost, another language come to you. . . . It is like the apostles. They got the Holy Ghost and tongues. You see, my sister come from Frankfield and speak in tongues, too. You dream, and it is strange, but how could it be anyone but God? And the scripture says, "thou, and thy children and thy children's children [shalt be near unto me]." (Genesis 45 : 10)

Once again, the woman underlines the real and mysterious transformation in her person, evidenced by speaking in tongues, that is integral to becoming a saint. It is, in turn, this real transformation that allows the woman to "draw near" to God, to have the capacity to ensure that her children commune with divinity. Women underscore this experience of envelopment that starts with a presence in the belly, moves to "touch" the heart, and pushes itself out through the mouth as the transformation and incorporation are accomplished.

Signs for men, on the other hand, deal not so much with embodiment but rather with the renunciation of social habits that defile the body:

I didn't love church first of all. When people invite me to church, I just couldn't accept that, because church to me, well, was something imaginary you know, about the God business? Then one day, there was a sister that I met there and she told me about the goodness of God. And I could remember when she was speaking to me, there was something from her, stirring up within me. And I was a gambler, I loved on Sundays to go about and play dice and friend and things, you know.

It happened at the Monday [prayer]. She told me about God, and I stood and listened to her, to what she was saying, you know. And immediately after leaving, I find myself singing, "Pass me not, oh gentle Savior, hear my humble cry!" And after singing that song, I could hear myself shouting, "Hallelujah!" I was so surprised, because I didn't know what it was all about.

And I went and left to work with some cigarettes in my pocket. At that time, I didn't feel like smoking any cigarettes. Get back from work late in the evening, to reach home. And at home I intend to buy sardine to go and have somethin' to eat then. And I bought six cigarettes and I smoke two, leave the remaining portion in my pocket. And after finishing eat that sardine, a voice spoke to me, "Throw away the cigarette, because after eatin' you are goin' te want te smoke." And immediately I took the cigarette out of my pocket and I throw it away, and I took up the Bible, and the first thing that came to my eyes was, I think it said Matthew 5:6: "Blessed are those that hunger and thirst after righteousness, for they shall be filled." And I close the Bible and put it underneath my pillow, and I went to sleep.

Next morning I get up, I feel like a different person. The voice came back to me and spoke to me and said, "Go on up te Sister Daley." That was the sister that was speaking to me about God. I went, and I didn't say anything to her. I went inside and I sit down, and she came to me and say, "Do you want me to pray for you?" Well, I didn't answer, because, you know, I felt away. She went around the back with me. She said, "The Lord is dealing with yu." I didn't answer. Anyhow, she said, "Let's go inside," and she took me inside, and she begun te pray, and after she begun te pray, I felt my body begin te shake. She said, "Say 'Praise the Lord!'" and I didn't want to say it because, you know, I was ashamed. Anyhow, we begun to pray, and she went to the next sister now. And I was sitting down in a chair with the rest who wanted to have a prayer, you know. And she said, "All right, why don't you pray, now!" and she went for her hymn book. When she went for the hymn book, I begun to pray, and I was sitting down and she start to sing a song. And then I find myself shouting and praising God, speaking in another language that I never taught before. I didn't know that language before, and therefore I glorify God for this. And from thence I give God thanks and praise his name.

Both this account and the one involving the obeah man portray powerful women taking men to task. The young woman's account of being saved depicts an American male pastor exhorting her to an act of contrition, which she recounts as a spiritual struggle ending in humility. These accounts-cum-testimonies mirror the drama of Pentecostal practice which regularly, at the altar call, brings neophytes into the arms of pastors and their assisting saints intent on the practice of conversion. The experience of conversion or being "in-filled" is described as a moment of transformation, an instantaneous and total reclamation of the human body by the Holy Ghost.

The male account also carries important forms of ambivalence. As one of his disciplines, the man recounts the fact of being called by a woman. It is common for men to suggest in this a humbling prior to sanctification. They then attest to their gratitude for the sanctification brought by a sister. The implied idea that Holy Ghost possession can even re-arrange gender relations is taken as further evidence of the fact that this is a change from God. The ambivalence also reflects that Pentecostal Holy Ghost in-filling is a process closely associated with women. Their bodies are more readily seen as vessels defiled by fornication that the Holy Ghost must cleanse. Among men, the importance of cigarette smoking as a defiling habit terminated at sanctification lies in the parallel drawn between smoke and semen. Both are defiling substances in a body that should be a vessel for the Holy Ghost. Women, as we will see below, are both empowered and disempowered by this association of in-filling with their lives and bodies.

The accounts presented so far are also accounts of signs, the ritual signs of a transformation that cannot be a "man-made" change but only a change from God. Each of the testimonies cites speaking in tongues as the central sign of initial in-filling by the Holy Ghost. This signifies that Spirit has entered the body and tangibly forced itself out through the mouth. In passing through and transforming the body, by making it subject to a transformed soul, the Spirit also has equipped the saint to engage in the task of evangelism. In this, these Jamaican saints evoke the original Pentecost from which all Pentecostals take their name. These signs are also manifest, however, in the disciplines that precede in-filling. The woman would separate from her friend and from a company of drinking and swearing. Later she would marry another saint and socialize only in a network of churches. She was also undergoing a process of tarrying that involved repeated acts of contrition manifest in constant weeping until the time when she was filled. Yet neither her removal from "the world" nor her ability to acknowledge her sins would have been possible without at least an initial engagement with God that propelled her forward in her quest. Morality as an initial discipline is made possible through engagement with God (cf. Asad 1993, 125–67). The man recounts two forms of discipline integral to his seeking God. One involves being called by a woman, and the other involves the rejection of cigarettes. Poor people in Jamaica commonly buy cigarettes in ones or twos. To purchase a packet intact requires too large an expenditure. It is therefore common for Pentecostal men to recount that on hearing the call of God, they threw away a cigarette pack or a number of cigarettes. In a male urban environment, accounts of this type of material sacrifice are similar to those that describe small farmers giving portions of land or fruit-bearing trees to the church. They attest to the spiritual power of the call. Discarding cigarettes, and being responsive to a woman, show that the man is truly changed.[7]

Notwithstanding these moral signs, the three accounts of ritual in-filling all emphasize the status of the event as one that occurs beyond normative life. The young woman observed, "I went on for a period, nothing different, really." The country woman says, "yu living the holy life, goin' on now, feelin' yu free from things and goin' on." The expression "goin' on" means to continue, almost relentlessly, in the regular way. And in the case of the man's account, he emphasizes a regular routine: "I loved on Sundays to go about and play," and he returned from work with some cigarettes in his pocket and went to his "shop" to buy a tin of sardines. These evocations of an everyday life are remarkably similar in mood to the evocations of normative activity involved in trickster tales, when Anansi performs an ostensibly mundane act over and over prior to the trick. This process often is hailed in the tales by the repetition of the line of a song (cf. Tanna 1984, 29–43).[8] The teller of the tale, having established the norm, then relates, as the Pentecostals would say, "something different." In the words of the three Pentecostalists: "And I really started praying, and I don't know what happen. I can't tell you, but something happen"; and again, "then, one day I feel a different feeling, . . . something come over and overshadow my life"; and finally, "Next morning I got up and I feel like a different person." As in a trickster tale, suddenly something mysterious happens that sets events on a different course. In the case of Anansi, this moment of magic concerns his ability to act on the moral ambiguity of relationships and draw out of them unnoticed possibilities. In the case of Pentecostals, the Holy Ghost addresses the moral ambiguity of the person and acts to realize a latent potential for saintliness.

Pentecostal accounts of the in-filling experience are also performances. They conform to Jamaican conventions of story-telling, and in these conventions, Anansi tales provide a paradigmatic model. A tale describes a scene with its anomalies, sets up a sense of normative order, introduces the trick as a magical occurrence operating on those anomalies, and confirms the subsequent state of affairs as enduring. When saints give their testimonies in the company of others, they work to a pitch of excitement relating the progress toward conversion. The audience, as it listens, expresses wonder at the moment of transformation. Frequently, both story-teller and listeners break into song at that moment. As in Anansi tales, the moment of magic is often realized in music. Initial in-fillings and further visitations from the Holy Spirit often occur, as Hopkin observes, in the midst of chorus singing (Hopkin 1978, 25).[9]

That Pentecostalism should grow so quickly to become the major popular faith of Jamaica is indicative of this cultural congruence (cf. Comaroff 1985,

30; Sahlins 1985). The aspiration to individual perfection that became a part of American revivalism required in Jamaica that believers perform a rite in order for the project to be sustained. Homologous with the trick in an African cosmology which realizes change through mysterious means, this rite activates a latent potential to saintliness through a transformation of body and soul. Rite, as an intervention in the normative, issues in morality.[10]

Being a Perfect Saint

When Pentecostals offer these testifying accounts, they terminate with a phrase that proclaims a continuing state of being: "It has been like that through the years," "And from thence I give God thanks and praise," "I am continuing up until now," "I can hear his word and grow in grace." These statements all propose that saints can continue praising God because they remain an appropriate vessel continually empowered by the Holy Spirit. It is only through this continual empowering that the saint can lead a holy life, a righteous life in the service of Christ. When the saints sustain their moral signs, they take this as indicative of the fact that they do indeed lead saintly lives, described by early Pentecostals as "perfect" and by the saints of contemporary Jamaica as "righteous" or "holy" lives "growing in grace even to perfection." I sought instruction from a pastor on this point, and he made the following observation to me in a loud voice of rumbustious conviction:

> I went somewhere today, and a sister get up an' give a testimony. And she finish, just when it all over, "We all sinners now to the end." Well, I went up there and say to she, "You are God righteousness! Yes!" "You are God righteousness!" cried Jesus. You mus' read the scripture. How could you be God righteousness and a sinner at the same time? The son of God or daughter of God is God, our God righteousness! And we must live as such by the grace of God. And if we do err, we have an advocate with the Father. But if we don't want to err, we don't.

The pastor here quotes from Paul's epistle to the Romans, which says in part:

> Know ye not, that to whom ye yield yourselves servants to obey, his servants ye are to whom ye obey; whether of sin unto death, or of obedience unto righteousness?
> But God be thanked, that ye were the servants of sin, but ye have obeyed from the heart that form of doctrine which was delivered to you.
> Being then made free from sin, ye became the servants of righteousness. . . .
> For when ye were the servants of sin, ye were free from righteousness. . . .
> But now being made free from sin, and become servants to God, ye have your fruit unto holiness. (Romans 6:16–18, 20, 22)

This passage, which talks of freedom from a servitude culminating in righteousness, is quoted frequently by Jamaican Pentecostals. Its popularity rests on the fact that the description of a passage from servitude to freedom confirms the same conjunction of temporal and spiritual passage that the original missionaries sought to evoke when they encouraged free villages of Christians as the morally superior counterpart to slave plantations. "Full free," the term that is often applied to the status of Jamaicans after the apprenticeship, is also applied to Christians who have been born again. They are "full free" because they are "free from sin." This is a conventional definition of perfection that plays on particular signs of sin and on signs of morality. These signs seek to mediate the ambiguity in perfection as a human and a super-human condition.

Pentecostals refer to themselves as saints because they are completely transformed. This is the completed act of grace that they must expect, in faith, from the Spirit because of its omnipotence. Nonetheless, saints do backslide as they live their hierarchized being, and the spiritual gifts beyond redemption only come as the Spirit wills. This ambiguity of perfection, and backsliding through fornication in particular, questions the completeness of the Spirit's work unless backsliding is explained in other ways. The nature of the in-filling process and its completeness both for women and for men become the focus of these explanations. They rehearse, this time in a gendered arena, the politics of moral order integral to creole religion. Who intervenes in the project of perfection, whether intentionally or not, becomes the concern of the saints.

Transformation and Embodiment

Apart from the outpourings of glossolalia, which are often quite short and frequently mixed with words of praise, in-filling is accompanied by characteristic movements. As a neophyte is kneeling at the "altar rail" with the hands of a deacon or a pastor on her shoulders, choruses swelling all about her along with fervent vocal prayer, it is usual for the neophyte to twitch involuntarily in the shoulder, arm, or possibly the thigh. This twitch is known as "a touch of the Spirit" and signifies that the Holy Ghost is present and ready to enter a contrite heart. Once a person is saved and sanctified, she may manifest a full in-filling rather seldom but simply realize these touches of the Spirit as she attends her congregation. The pressing physically on the neophyte by the pastor, deacon, or evangelist is intended to focus her concentration in prayer and is normally accompanied by the attendants themselves speaking closely in the woman's ear. Although it is only a repentant heart within a clean vessel that can be transformed into a saint, it is clear to the non-believing observer that the pressing on the neophyte, particularly at pressure points behind the neck, often serves to bring on the convulsions that embody the in-filling of the Holy Ghost. As these more pronounced convulsions occur, the repentant may jerk out and up from a kneeling position and either begin to leap about or else fall to the ground with flaying arms and legs. Convulsions that embody the passage of devils out of the body generally also throw a person to the ground and often are accompanied by voiced obscenities or noises taken as indicative of anger. Convulsions that embody the in-filling experience and are accompanied by tongues may involve a "toss" to the ground, but just as commonly a person leaps on the spot or convulses her body as she moves at a walking pace up and down the church.

In these latter forms of convulsion, the suppleness of women is evident. Far more commonly than men, they undulate their bodies as they move, swinging their hips this way and that and moving both their shoulders and their breasts in rhythmic response to chorus singing. Male possessions generally involve more vigorous use of the arms and legs in reaching up to praise the Lord and leaping about as a form of dancing in the Spirit. The relative inertness of male torsos in their forms of possession suggests to Pentecostals themselves that women "move more easily in the Spirit." When, at evangelical services, women almost trot together, undulating their torsos in concert and with their arms around one another's waist, the impression of "dancing" in the Spirit is a striking, and feminine, one. Saints take particular pleasure in this dancing, understood as joyous engagement with the Spirit. Given the central place that dancing has as a mode of *jouissance* in Jamaican culture and given that Pentecostals cannot engage in any form of temporal dancing, these expressions of Holy Ghost possession, along with testimony and chorus singing, are the ones most instrumental in creating a eudemonic in the church.

The tongues that come at an initial in-filling are interpreted in the biblical form as the pre-eminent sign that the person is empowered to be an evangelist for God. Tongues also are seen as the tangible evidence of the passage of the Spirit as it moves through the body, transforming both its soul and its substance. Saints are very aware that the tongues they speak are not in fact a practical aid in evangelism. This leads many to cite the biblical rendering of tongues as the "unknown tongue" of "mysteries" that a saint articulates when speaking to God (1 Corinthians 14:2). The common Jamaican rendering of the situation is that glossolalia rather than xenoglossy is the sign that a saint can evangelize for Jesus.

It is important to return, however, to that aspect of the in-filling experience that actually involves the Holy Spirit filling and transforming soul and body. Saints rather seldom describe this process, which is understood to be a "personal experience" of mystical engagement with the Savior. For this reason, it is simply common sense to the saints that the process is a phe-

nomenon beyond description. Indeed, requesting a description of the unsay-
able is a sure sign of being unsaved oneself and further confirms the experiential distance between saints and one who remains a knowing sinner. There
were three different renderings of the in-filling experience given to me as a
recognized sinner that are instructive nonetheless. One describes the assimilation of body to Spirit; another describes the transformation of the soul as
conceptualized as a circumcision of the heart; and the third interprets in-
filling as being the acquisition of a friend. From these accounts emerge the
themes that reflect gender tensions in the church.

The following account of spiritual in-filling came from a woman evangelist:

> Being sanctified, which is generally called being in-filled, has buffeted
> quite a lot of person, but the scripture is there. So, in-filling is simply this.
> That a person realizes her shortcomings and sinfulness before God and
> really cannot live as she wants to live because of this sin question. Today
> up, tomorrow down, and all like that. She goes to God. She reaches a point
> where she goes to God and there is a crisis. . . .
>
> I'm dealing with being born now. When a person went to God, that per-
> son's spirit was dead in trespass and in sin. So that person was only a living-
> dead-walking. Her spirit is dead because of the Adamic Fall and her
> Adamic nature, and Satan had been the real father and possessor of that
> precious soul, as all of us have been before committing it to our precious
> Jesus.[11]
>
> God, upon the request of that penitent heart, God himself breathe his
> divine nature into that defunct nature-spirit. God's nature is eternal life,
> and that God's nature being breathed by him into that dead spirit recreates
> that dead spirit, and that soul is revived and can now understand spiritual
> matter. And that soul now make the body a temple so that nature-spirit
> can be one. In other words, then, God in his almighty power breathe out
> eternal life into that seeking soul and body, and John 17:3 say, "And this is
> eternal life, that one know God the Father and His son Jesus Christ."
>
> So it is the experience of God's Holy Ghost that comes. You know God
> as your personal savior, and of course he drives out Satan's nature and gives
> you his nature, and you know it. It is an experience. Spirit, your spirit, wit-
> nesses through the Holy Spirit that something has happened.

This account indicates very precisely how a person is transformed from a
sinner into a living saint. God breathes his Spirit into a body. The Holy Spirit
engages with the "dead spirit" or Satanic soul and revives it as a living force
which stills and thereby assimilates body to it in the role of temple to the
being of soul. This is the unification of "nature-spirit" that allows a human
person to be a saint. In so doing, Spirit drives "Satan's nature," as embodied
in a sullied soul, out of the body. This process resolves the contradiction
inhering in a person as a "living-dead-walking," that is, a soul that is dead
through sin residing in a "living" natural body. The ultimate demonstration

of this transformation is that while a "living-dead-walking" will in fact die, the revived "nature-spirit" has "eternal life" (cf. Bloch 1992).

This rendering of the in-filling process as interpreted here is gender-neutral. In Jamaican interpretations of the process, however, the rendering has a distinctly feminine bias. The Hebraic imagery of God's "breath" entering the body is clearly evocative of the body as vessel, and this is a vessel that acolytes must strive to cleanse, insofar as they are able, prior to the Spirit's approach. The focus on fornication (to be examined in chapter 8, below) makes clear that the paradigmatic sullying of a vessel is the sullying of a female vessel through unsanctified insemination. Jamaican women commonly have an image of their own torsos as largely occupied by a womb that fills the space of the stomach and abdomen, with the heart placed above it adjacent to the breasts (cf. MacCormack and Draper 1987; Sobo 1993, 30–35). Most often, these different organs below the heart are classified under the one term "belly," so that a "big belly 'oman" or "belly woman" is also a pregnant woman. When a woman has had a child, the central sign of feminine maturity, she often will express this transition with the observation, especially to her mother, "I am my own big woman now." And in *drop pan,* the Chinese numbers game played daily in many lower-class communities, the number eight is the number for a woman, for a pregnant woman, and also for a hole, a ring, or a bag (Chevannes 1989, 47). All these imageries reaffirm the notion of a woman as a form of vessel.[12] The heart, which also gives life to the belly, is seen to be conjoined and attendant on it. Pentecostals with whom I have talked have a clear sense that the heart pumps blood, and in the case of women, there is an image of the heart pumping blood to the baby in the belly. This Jamaican image is the image of a body in mature pregnancy. And the emphasis on just two organs, the heart and the belly, is indicative of women's own sense of precedent. The heart is the seat of soul and spiritual health, while the belly is the seat of fecundity and physical health. They are conjoined by blood, which is pumped from the heart throughout the body. Physical health is thereby connected with spiritual health, but the womb-endowed bodies of women also bear on spiritual health.

Women have a strong sense that in-filling involves entry of the Spirit through the vagina—a process not described as such but sometimes signaled by tapping the abdomen. The Spirit fills the cavity of the belly, now cleansed of unsanctified semen, and moves up to the heart in order to revivify the soul. The heart as the seat of soul and blood is made meaningful by the metaphor of "Jesus' blood," used to refer to "the saving grace" that transforms a sinner into a saint. In this experienced bodily transformation, sheer sense of mass is very important. Senior women saints are often stout, curvaceous women, and their sense of in-filling involves not only the power of the Holy Spirit but also the power of their bodies as vessels to receive a plenitude of Spirit that renews and re-invigorates the heart. In everyday speech, the comment "belly full" refers to satisfaction after a meal. Although the term is not employed in other contexts, it connotes very well the emphasis on women as maturely pregnant beings and also on women filled with the Spirit. Once a woman is filled in this way, revivified soul embodied in blood moves from the heart to infuse the entire body.

Lower-class women with whom I have spoken commonly believe that irregular sexual activity, and certainly abstention from sex, can make a female body unhealthy. There is a notion of health that involves keeping "channels" open, and coitus is seen as an instrument of openness. A woman who has a disappointing sexual partner may use this view to explain her turn to an "outside" relationship. It is a necessity for maintaining her health (cf. Sobo 1993, 179). The anatomical rendering of the in-filling experience is concerned both with body image and with sustaining a cultural homology between notions of a "living" and thereby healthy body rendered physically in the world of sin and notions of an eternal body rendered spiritually in the context of a heavenly life. In both these aspects, the rendering of body as vessel to be filled is feminized in the Jamaican milieu.

Mary Douglas has observed that sexual interdictions related to bodily pollution represent concerns about intrusions into bounded social space (1966, 122–24). And Jean Comaroff has demonstrated in her account of Tshidi initiation the manner in which men's bodies are represented as bounded and women's bodies are represented as open and thereby subordinate (1985, 114–18; cf. Boddy 1989, 141–42). If the idea of body as vessel is highly feminized in Jamaica, this is also partly because of a Judeo-Christian view discussed by Gerda Lerner. She observes that the Hebraic God with his creation of the world through word and breath usurped the generative process from earlier figures of the "Mother-Goddess" (Lerner 1986, 180–82). So, although in their Pentecostal rite Jamaican women own in-filling, they do this only as instruments of an androcentric creative process.

Male pastors in Jamaica temporalize and socialize this process. They seek the closure of "their" women's bodies conceived as open through concubinage to the exploitation of a secular order. They must be re-made as moral beings through the breath of the Father. Yet this subordinating openness of women also makes them accessible to Spirit, to conjoining with the Spirit of the Bridegroom Savior in a manner that peripheralizes the pastor. The very closure of male bodies leads them to emphasize smoking and drinking. These proscriptions allow Pentecostal men to assimilate, to a degree, the imagery of the saint as vessel for Spirit that seems so much more amenable to women. They, too, can go through a process of cleansing the body that allows them to render body as vessel. Yet this rendering cannot match the feminine association of body-womb-vessel, and this is reflected in the fact that bodily possession behavior among women is generally more vigorous and more confident. Men perennially find it more difficult than women to sustain the lived experience of being filled. To extend Bloch's theme of vitality, Jamaican women with their wombs seem more able than men to capture the Spirit's vitality (Bloch 1992).

The anomalies for men in the imagery of the body as vessel turn them to another representation. This second representation concerns the heart and proposes, after Paul's epistle to the Romans 3:29, that sanctification is a "circumcision of the heart." In this passage, Paul proposes that circumcised Jews who do not keep the law become the "uncircumcision," for circumcision is not "in nature," or "outward in the flesh," but rather "in the spirit . . . [for] those whose praise is not of men, but of God." This notion appeals to Jamaican Pentecostals, who understand themselves to be subordinated in the "man-made" world but elevated in the spiritual world. They may not keep the laws of "respectable" society, and yet they are among the chosen.

The use of this image, "the circumcision of the heart," was made popular by Wesley in his series of sermons on sanctification (Campbell 1984, 85). And this image of the circumcision of the heart is very often associated by Jamaican Pentecostals with the idea that in the possession of the Holy Spirit, they are infused with the breath of God that becomes the cleansing blood of Christ. This sacrificial blood circumcises the heart by "cutting" it and washing it clean. This use of the notion   of cutting is related to an old Revival idea of "cutting and clearing" evil out of a person and out of a natural environment. It evokes machete cuts, metaphorically, to mean dealing vigorously with a phenomenon. The meaning also is employed in the notion of "cutting" language when it is spoken vigorously and with great facility. Glossolalia is occasionally described as the "cutting" of tongues (cf. Cassidy 1971, 147–48). The shell of the heart being cut from its essence, the heart acts to pump redeeming blood through the body. This imagery proposes a similar mechanism to the previous account for assimilating the body to the soul. It lacks, however, the feminine emphasis on the filling of the womb as a dynamic process that in itself overpowers a sullied heart. A male Pentecostal deacon said:

> Jesus came not to be minister of, but to minister and give his life. He died for us. For the truth of Christ, as a kernel of wheat, is also true for all the Christian. Except he [the Christian] die in the whole of his life, he abideth alone. Jesus said further, "If any man serve me, let him follow me." In other words, I am going to die, and those who follow me must die, too, must die to self. And again, Jesus declared, "If any man wishes to follow me let him renounce self and take up the cross." And so we might follow Mark 8:24 which gives it that he [the Christian] must give up all to follow [Jesus]. The new divine life begotten out of the cell of life is the life that glorifies God bearing much fruit. And this is the circumcision of the heart. Before I was dead to the carnal life, anything troubled me, but since the Holy Spirit came and sanctified me, I am dead. I am glad that I am

dead to this earth-life since the blood of Christ reached and cut my heart.
I love Christ, and it is my mind to serve him until I die.

The statement proposes that a saint can only be an evangelist for Christ. He or she should not aspire to position in the church. The central point of the statement, however, is its observation that to follow Christ is to be dead to one's temporal self so that the "cell of life," the circumcised heart, can bear "much fruit." Elsewhere in our discussion, the deacon described the "self" as "the fleshly husk-life of natural man," and this is the life that he also describes in his statement as "the carnal life." Thus, the circumcision that washes the heart with Jesus' blood also involves the cutting away of the carnal self that is natural man like a kernel of wheat shedding its husk. In this statement, the deacon can be taken to say that the only cell of life that glorifies God is the purified heart that leaves the "husk-life" dead. This statement, although it owns in-filling with a masculine trope, is also very striking in a Jamaican milieu, where "bearing much fruit" through the fecundity of the phallus is a central representation of masculine power. Here the deacon proposes that it is not the phallus that plants vital seeds but rather Jesus' blood that transforms the heart into a seed, cell of life, capable of generating further spiritual fruit.

This powerful rejection of male sexuality, which seems more dramatic in its implications than the gestatory imagery of the feminine vessel, acts to disarm Pentecostal men even as it seeks to give them a presence in the discourse of sanctification. In the feminine imagery, a homology is drawn between the womb as a vehicle for physical gestation and the womb as a vehicle for spiritual gestation. For men, the "circumcision of the heart" is a cutting away that is unseen, within. It draws a parallel, as Paul intended, between male circumcision as a rite of inclusion and spiritual redemption as a comparable rite wrought on the heart within. Yet the cutting of the heart, the shedding, casting off of the external "husk" of man in this process of redemption, seems also, in a powerful way, to place man's masculinity at risk. The womb as procreative organ facilitates transformation of the heart. The phallus as procreative organ is part of the husk of heart to be shed.

Lerner's (1986) account of the Bible legacy suggests a view that in Christian rite, patriarchy is pre-eminent. In the Jamaican context, however, local understandings of the body deflect this inheritance to create a more subtle interplay. In conjunction with the larger ritual logic of the church, discussed in chapter 6, above, these meanings of embodied rite create gender relations that are finely balanced.

Mundane Meaning and Pentecostal Rite

The two statements discussed above fall within the realm of dialogue with religious specialists. And in my interpretation of these statements, I have brought my own knowledge of Jamaican Pentecostal embodiment to eluci-date what I believe to be the cultural implications of this specialist dis-course.[13] To assume that these representations are equally salient for all Pentecostals would be radically to exoticize Pentecostal meanings. The lan-guage of Spirit, breath, blood, and vessel is shared by both men and women. "Circumcision of the heart" is a less usual trope mainly employed by men. Yet it is a very common understanding among Pentecostals that the in-filling transforms soul embodied in the heart. The soul, like a blood transfusion from the heart, then infuses its influence throughout the body. This imagery is aided by the fact that Jesus' blood is a metaphor for Spirit, which, like baptismal water, cleans and heals the repentant. And it is through the me-dium of this blood that Pentecostals gain the sense not only of healing but also of empowerment. New, strong, sanctifying blood is what the Holy Spirit brings.

But rank-and-file Pentecostals seldom dwell on the ontology of their bod-ies as realized through the in-filling process. They think of it, rather, in re-lational terms. It is through the empowering for sinlessness that a saint becomes a companion to Jesus and someone whom Jesus can constantly attend. For most Pentecostal practitioners, the principal importance of spiri-tual in-filling is that the newly transformed saint can look to Jesus as a friend:

> He has proven to me as being a very good friend.
> There were times when the devil would try to push himself in the little loopholes. He would try to force in himself, but then, since the Lord is the conquering Savior, he is always victorious. And the Lord has been very good to me.
> He is my daily companion. He is my guide.
> I can't live without Jesus, and if I should stop loving him, I really feel that something serious would happen.

These radical personifications of God's spiritual power in terms of the Son are extremely common among Jamaican Pentecostals. And in evangelism, the idea of changing oneself in order to obtain this powerful companion is the most common positive inducement to repentance. Four different choruses provide the relevant senses here of transformation leading to friendship. On transformation, it is common for the saints to sing:

> Shackled by the heavy burden, 'Neath the load of guilt and shame,
> But the hand of Jesus touched me, And now I am no longer the same. He touched me,
> And O the Joy that filled my soul . . . , He touched me and made me whole.

And also:

> Here like empty earthen vessels, Lying at the Master's feet,
> Small but clean through Jesus' merit, Wait till through thy work complete,

> Welcome, welcome, welcome, Holy Ghost we welcome Thee:
> Come in power and fill Thy temple, Holy Ghost we welcome Thee.

Subsequent to this in-filling, the saint may have Jesus as a Friend:

> What a Friend we have in Jesus, All our sins and griefs to bear,
> What a privilege to carry, Ev'rything to God in prayer!
> Oh, what peace we often forfeit, Oh, what needless pain we bear—
> All because we do not carry Ev'rything to God in prayer!

And again:

> Tell it to Jesus, tell it to Jesus, He is a friend that's well known,
> You have no other such friend or brother, Tell it to Jesus alone.[14]

This mundane discourse of contrition, in-filling, and "friending" with Jesus is also very amenable to women. The notions of being touched and made complete through a male and of being wrought as a physically small vessel by a male are clearly gendered imageries that appeal to inclinations toward feminine dependency. Moreover, these choruses underline the real acts of contrition in which sinners must be involved prior to their transformation into saints (cf. Jules-Rosette 1975). It is the subordinating power of Jamaica's larger gender hierarchy that makes women more inclined than men to be this "humble spirit" before God. But following the act of contrition, women take Jesus up more vigorously than men as a companion who can and should "fix" their world. Women pursue the forms of active intimacy with Jesus enunciated in the statements above. They cultivate the intimacy, often in the absence of a male temporal partner, that will make them a completed bride to Christ. They also revel in a familiarity with Jesus that is typical of heterosexual partners. I once heard a saint in vocal prayer say, "Glory Jesus, me waiting on yu nuh! Listen nuh?" This type of discourse often occurs in evangelical services that may be conducted entirely by women. They come to these gatherings on a Sunday night and leave their children sleeping in the pews in order to dance with sisters in the Spirit and prepare for a week of work ahead. These are also women in contemporary life who often give allegiance to male politicians as powerful foci in their world. I watched an experienced politician lead his women followers in the singing of a chorus, "Leaning on the everlasting arm of Jesus." The homology was very clear.

Men, on the other hand, have a more formal relation with Jesus. They praise, glorify, give thanks to the Lord, they "walk" with their Lord and "know Him" as their personal savior but less often refer to him as "friend" and never style themselves, like their sisters, as individual "brides" of Christ. The metaphors and analogies for men flow principally from the relationship between the apostles and Jesus Christ. Men are "followers," "pupils," "servants," and "aids." Although the figure of Paul as a leader who was once a sinner is a popular touchstone for Jamaican men, Paul's subordination to the Savior is never in any doubt. To "friend" in Jamaican parlance is also to be sexually involved in a "visiting" relation.[15] In its everyday connotations, this usage reduces the distance between "friend" and "bride" as forms of relation and underlines the theme of heterosexual love. The conjoining of a bride with Christ is never conceived in sexual terms. But the fact that Jesus is a male means that the notions of intimacy involved in this discourse are ones that apply more readily to heterosexual love relations than they do to friendly relations between men.[16] Indeed, male references to Jesus imply the relation between a subordinate and a superior, while female references, though never claiming equality, suggest an intimacy that mediates hierarchy.

Gender and Perfectionism

These highly gendered images are the medium through which Pentecostals try to resolve the ambiguities of perfectionism: soul assimilates body but never completely. The saints are perfect, and yet they are not. The saved are saints, and yet they may fall. Notwithstanding the feminized imagery of Pentecostal churches, it is through the rendering of this central ambiguity that male Pentecostals assert their authority. And this rendering is concerned with body as vessel and with the nature of men's and women's "minds." Because the body is a vessel that harbors revivified soul, and from time to time the Holy Spirit itself, it remains something identifiably different from soul, even though in a practicing saint it is assimilated to the nature of soul. In the in-filling, the mind is turned to contemplate "spiritual matter," and the carnal sensory faculties are made "dead" or latent. Yet, without the constant reinforcement of an intense concert with Jesus, these senses can reactivate and defile the vessel, whereupon the power of transforming Spirit departs. This is the process known as "backsliding" or a "fall."

Although the human mind cannot itself propel in-filling, it can through wavering resolve allow the re-activation of sensuous faculties. That is the role of mind or "brain part," now empowered by the Holy Spirit, to preside over sensuous body and restrain it from corrupting the soul. This can happen only when the saint has acted through the Holy Spirit to still the mind in the sense of voiding its orientation to the temporal world. The mind then becomes a servant of soul, displacing its more prevalent role as servant to desire.

There is a strong suggestion in the Pentecostal churches that men who are saints are more likely than women to employ the mind effectively in stilling the senses and realizing the power of Spirit. Women saints themselves say that pastors are more often men because they have the greater power to "call down the Spirit and invite him in." The pastor is sometimes called a "lightning conductor," and the congregation is a "power house" charged through his ability to call the Spirit down. He concentrates the power of God in the church so that the saints can be filled. Women, it is claimed, are more emotional than men. They generally suffer more than men and worry more about their everyday condition. Their minds are readily turned to spiritual matters, but just because they are temporally more vulnerable, they are also more readily turned away. Women must be responsible for children and are more inclined to "look a man" even when they are saved and sanctified. A male Pentecostal spoke of his duty in the church:

> Our duty is, make right with God and keep right, and when we are carried by the blood of Jesus Christ, the only thing we need to do is invite the Holy Spirit in. He come in and dwell and give us power. God say in his word that he don' give us the Spirit of fear, but of love and of power and of sound mind. So, the person who is goin' out there [to preach] with fear, then he has not the love of God within him, because there should not be fear in the man of God. Woman, now, is often fearful. She is often of a weaker mind. She is able to make right with God, but she don' talk lively in de Church. What I tellin' yu now is what the apostle Paul say in 1 Corinthians 14:34. That is why man have the duty to invite the Spirit in the church. His mind really work with the blood of Jesus.

These views are sustained in part by the fact that passing through the ritual process of contrition and in-filling, men are very much more likely than women to embrace the church as a full-time career. If men are a minority overall but a majority in senior positions, it is almost inevitable that instances of falling will occur more often among the women. Moreover, women have a propensity to honor their pastors as saints who have exceeded "vile man."[17] Many women, though by no means all, therefore assume that the predominance of men in authority positions proves their superior spirituality.

Not all women have this view, however. Some, and especially older women, express a sardonic view of pastors and especially of younger men:

> He don' have the real sense of sin.
> 'Im don' know how te move de baady.
> Pastor, he still learnin' holiness.

These remarks are made in a social context of women deacons and evangelists, who often, especially in an urban milieu, conduct the major business of the church. The evangelist often will act as treasurer to the congregation. She will convene the evangelical service and organize other evangelism. The pastor for her will be a leader-who-is-male to preach and heal at divine service. He is there to be a male leader of women. But he will be a leader in ritual performance rather than in organization or, very often, in spiritual attainment. This milieu is also informed by the pastor's own ambivalence, which reaches back to the tension between signs of transformation in a saint and signs of masculinity. Sainthood is seen as possibly incompatible with a male sexuality. And if this creates ambivalence in men, it also creates ambivalence in women.

The verbal enunciations by male Pentecostals that they are "dead" to the carnal life are only part of the meaning that is actually practiced concerning Pentecostal masculinity. Very often, male pastors remain "living deads," or men who retain a powerful sensuality constrained by a powerful spirituality. Women may often refer to a pastor as "sweet pastor 'im" or "our sweet shepherd," and when this pastor addresses his saints and talks of temptation and fornication, his small asides and expressive face make it clear that even though he is a saint, he indeed knows fornication's temptations. The designation "sweet" is lavished on fruit and on sexuality as well. A popular and attractive Kingston politician was known in his neighborhood as "Sweet William," and the two meanings are brought together in the calypso lines, "Gal, your apple's sour, Let me make it sweeter." A newspaper account of a prominent Pentecostal pastor offered this description in 1981:

> He is a calmer, cooler version of the loud, frenzied voice of radio. He dresses like a member of the Mod Squad and comes across like a charmer wearing an unholy look. He is the typical sharp guy which is probably how he got the "sweet boy" label.[18]

Notwithstanding the dated language, the message of ambivalence is clear. This "sweet boy" is a man of God and especially enticing because of it. If, then, the pastor is "dead" to sin and his "carnal" "husk-life" is shed, it is only his unusual spiritual power that enables him to displace his masculinity, but without destroying it.

An expected familiarity with sexuality is also reflected in the fact that Jamaica's most popular newspaper column was for many years entitled "Dear Pastor." Most letters to the "pastor" concerned romance or sexually related matters. For example, one woman wrote:

> I would like you to help me because I see where you are trying to help a lot of people. The problem is this. My baby father treats me badly. If I ask him for anything he would tell me plenty of bad words. I bore him two children. We were friends from I was 14. Now I am 21. Pastor he has the world of women. He even took away a married man wife.[19]

And another woman from the country wrote:

> Greetings in the mighty name of Jesus our soon-coming King. I am a worried girl. I am 23 years of age. I have a boyfriend. He said he is going to marry me. He asked me for sex and don't give him. . . . I also have another problem. From I was about 19 I have had an unusual discharge. I don't know what it is.[20]

Letters from men appear less frequently but generally address sexual mal-functions or the infidelity of a "baby mother." One young man in 1986 re-ported that he was growing breasts.[21] The phenomenon of the column clearly indicates the view that sexuality should be subsumed within an umbrella of sanctification. It also may imply, however, that holiness and "rudeness" are complicit companions. Ideas of sanctification are embodied in notions of a patriarch who sustains his sanctity in the world. Parrying the patriarch, however, is a mirthful moral ambivalence that has led a devoted readership to follow whether "pastor lick letter" or "letter lick pastor." Women saints play on these meanings to propose that there will never be a fully realized saint in the person of a male. Their sense of power through procreativity that allows them to harbor God's life-giving breath overrides the patriarchal message of the Bible to make them the church and the bride of Christ. Yet if sexuality as such is not the center of a feminine being, the Jamaican women in Pentecostalism are disinclined to deny it to men. And this logic of everyday conception in the church gives a further turn to ambivalence.

Like spirituality itself, sexuality does remain immanent in the pastor. This cultural nuance is affirmed again in the play procedures of everyday life. In *drop pan,* the number twenty-nine stands for both pastor and masculinity. Number thirty-one stands for the pulpit but is also the central sign for the phallus. Number thirty-five stands for the Bible but is also a number mean-ing "vagina," because, in a society where women abound in church, a Bible is indeed the way to women (Chevannes 1989, 47–48).

It is against this backdrop of expectations that embody both the Jamaican eudemonic and the discourse of the African immoralist that the Pentecostal pastor sustains his control of self and thereby his claim to control his saints. This ability to manifest control is also integral to dance hall forms, where one particular style calls upon the woman to press her torso to the man while neither legs nor arms engage. It is essential for the man to remain not nec-essarily unaroused but unmoved, like a pastor in his pulpit. It is such an expression of power with all its many ambivalences that makes the pastor the lightning conductor, who sets alight or fills his saints by inviting the Spirit into the bride (see also Bloch 1992, 95). In this role, he can subordinate himself to Jesus, for in this subordination he has a power that radically su-persedes other men, and does in fact, within his chosen medium, allow con-trol over many women. From this perspective, the Achilles' heel of the pastor is not his own moral failure but rather the failure of his women, who may not only fall themselves but also tempt him into sin. For this reason, he must constantly exhort his saints and at the same time propose, by implication, that the intractable dynamism of the human sensuous person finds its ave-nue in the weakness of women. And this is not merely a weakness of women but also involves the tendency of women to fix their gaze on men who are prosperous but generally unsaved. For this reason, Pentecostal pastors often characterize their status superiors in terms that are very aggressive and focus on fornication. One pastor linked the nature of "middle-class" men with the moral standing of their "established" churches:

> they can go to some place else where they can go to the little dance, they can drink their little rum, they can curse their bad words, they can smoke the cigarette, same way. They can live their fornication and their adultery life same way, and when they done they gone communion, they take their communion and they say, why mus' I come an' tie myself down?

The pastor's responsibility in sustaining the community of saints is to effect a closure from this larger environment on behalf of his mainly women saints. Through closure, they become truly brides of Christ, and he the empowered servant of Christ. Avoidance of fornication, along with its attendant denials to maintain the cleanliness of the vessel, thereby becomes the principal focus of Jamaican Pentecostalism.

Even from this final perspective, however, the pastor's role is precarious. Not all pastors by their talent or inclination can become lightning conductors and realize in that circumcision of the heart the greater role of intermediary for the Savior. The pastor as leader-performer in the church who is sexuality and spirituality in tandem is a role that only some can play. Neither do many women feel the need to rely on a pastor for their spiritual closure. Numerous women Pentecostal saints are adept at realizing their own in-fillings and setting alight the church of the saints through their direct engagement with Jesus. Their preference for the image of holy power as blood, made real when their vessels are filled, is also an imagery that turns attention back to the original sacrifice of Christ and away from the energies of the pastor. When this feminine assertion prevails, the pastor accepts a modified role that can make him peripheral to his women evangelists and subordinate to his elder women saints.

Through an instant and mysterious change, Pentecostal rite confers the power to be a saint. In realizing this experience, the popular belief and practice of Jamaican Pentecostalism partakes of a cosmology in which normative order is challenged and changed through a "trick," through immediate normative breach rather than "man-made" discipline. Moral practice prepares the ground for this change and becomes the sign of its accomplishment. Moral discipline, nevertheless, remains subordinate to rite.

The ritually conferred state of perfection that turns a sinner into a saint is, still, an ambiguous one. Saints backslide, or fall, or tarry without being filled. And these events bring explanations that promote a politics in the church. The politics of Pentecostal rite is a politics of gender ambivalence. It leads men and women to engage in a discourse that often casts one or the other as the real immoralist. The nature of embodied rite seems to offer the edge to women in this ritual dialogue. Yet this position is also modified by the patriarchy of the Bible. Again, the signs of sanctified morality seem to challenge men's masculinity, as does their attempt to own in-filling through an alternative trope. Nevertheless, masculinity as such is important to women as well as men and produces a representation of the pastor that can be turned one way or the other, either to focus on women as Eves who tend to acquiesce in fornication or to focus on "vile man" as the intractable immoralist who is also a delight. This ambiguity is itself a politics that shows why in Jamaican parlance the pastor is more like Anansi the trickster than James Phillippo's Christian black, a man involved in the mystery of rite rather than ethical rationalism. There is still a further dimension of this moral politics, however. It draws on biblical myth and seems to give a prominent role to men as moralists in the church.

8   Exhorting the Saints

And the Lord God said unto the woman, What is this that
thou hast done? And the woman said, The serpent be-
guiled me and I did eat.

—Genesis 3:13

[I]n the story of the Fall, woman and, more specifically,
female sexuality became the symbol of human weakness
and the source of evil.

—Gerda Lerner, 1986

The feminine body, with its Jamaican inscriptions, represents better than its male counterpart the idea of
the human body as vessel for the Holy Spirit (cf. Lewis 1995). Yet in the
practice of Pentecostal rite, men still assert an authoritative status. They do
this not by owning transformation but rather by presenting themselves as the
sensuous constrained for the purpose of sanctifying life. This holy life sustained by women under the direction of powerful men provides for women
a moral closure from soul-corrupting concubinage. It is from this finely balanced position that the pastors call on further potentials in Pentecostal rite.
One of these is their power as exhorters, as discursive performers in the
church. The other is the message they deploy: Christianity's myth of the Fall
which intersects with a Jamaican origin myth to define a moral burden for
women.

The Poetics of Biblical Exhortation

In the New Testament Church of God, Jamaica's largest Pentecostal church,
before a person is licensed and ordained as a pastor, she, but usually he, can
become an exhorter. An exhorter is one who calls people to the faith through
preaching and prayer and is able to do this without the benefit of training.
In fact, a great deal of Jamaican Pentecostalism, both trinitarian and unitarian, falls comfortably under the description of exhortation to the faith.
Eloquence in the service of the Lord is especially admired in Jamaican
churches, and in Pentecostal exhortations saints appeal to the congregation
but also present the grandeur of God (cf. Abrahams 1983, 35).

The Pentecostal call proceeds through earnest admonitions that create for
the exhorter, and for those who begin to hear the word, the presence of God's

holy order engaging with worldly temptation. Integral to this representation are warnings, reproofs, and urgent advice that help to make real the need for conversion. Pentecostalism proceeds in Jamaica through the sense that God is there. In his account of Appalachian Baptists, Titon seeks to capture this sense of the reality of God through the fact that it makes religious speech performative in its social impact. Titon cites not only Austin and Searle but also Keith Graham's redefinition of performatives to capture the empowering force of speaking that embodies a dynamic Spirit (cf. Csordas 1994, 86). In Titon's rendering, an exhortation is a mode of statement that brings about "the truth of the content it expresses as a consequence of people so regarding it" (Titon 1988, 206–7, citing Graham). In another formulation pertaining to religious "performance," Bauman proposes that the intense "communicative interaction" of preaching draws prestige toward the performer, providing control and ability to transform "social structure" (Bauman 1975, 305–6). Seeking to specify these issues further, Csordas (1987) has proposed that connected "genres of ritual language," in this case "sharing, teaching, prayer and prophecy," create an experience of "self-affirmation" that supports the metaphors and dispositions of a charismatic religion. Genres objectify the meaning of rite and make its message a reality.

These are helpful proposals for addressing the dynamics of exhortation and its impact on believers' lives. Exhorters summon considerable power to their person through the performance of their message. Ritual genres in Jamaican churches do not sustain quite the degree of integration that Csordas describes for an American group (1987). For all but deacons, evangelists, and pastors, this integration is a looser one and involves a different repertoire of exhorting, singing, and dancing as well as teaching and prayer. Nonetheless, the practice of ritual genres, as it articulates with daily life, gives meaning to the morality that signifies a perfect saint (but see also Asad 1983 and chapter 9, below). Yet central to Pentecostal practice is the view that the exhorter's message is true. And these accounts do not address the discursive order or cultural logic in which the message is known to be true not only as an immediate practice but also as a logic for the world that extends beyond the province of rite (see also Bloch 1974, 1977; cf. Austin 1979). Jamaican exhortation rests on a textual truth positioned in a creole discourse (see also Asad 1983). A distinguishing feature of this discourse is that the textual truth of the Bible both is part of Jamaican experience and also underpins experience as the ground of history as such. In a fashion not dissimilar to Derrida's "totalizing discourse," the truth of the Bible is seen to be ensured by a Jamaican metaphysic that proposes God as an absolute present prior to the practice of rite. Ritual acknowledgment of this presence is always a sign of its being, which thereby is never contested as a result of the presence of the text (cf. Derrida 1976, 3–13, 323; 1982). Ritual genres affirm the reality of the text and its world. At the same time, the aptness of rite is grounded in a view of the world mediated through the text.

In the Pentecostal view, the passage from Jamaican slavery to freedom is also the passage from sin to redemption. Like many other devout Jamaicans, Pentecostals believe that becoming free was contemporaneous with conversion and was also realized in conversion. Coming to a known history therefore is identified with coming to God, and as a consequence of this, Jamaican landscape and its events are seen as continuous with the Bible's. People travel to sanctity/freedom through engaging the Bible's events (see chapter 5, above). Within this larger discourse which many non-Pentecostals embrace, saints also construe themselves as beings imbued with God's presence. As vessels for the Holy Ghost, their lives and their very bodies realize the immanence of God. The experience of ritual in-filling and its complement, speaking in tongues, signal for Jamaican saints the real and pervasive presence of God. The fact that history for these Jamaicans is understood to begin with the Word, and that in embodied, ritual being they carry the immanence of God, contributes to an experienced world understood as continuous with the Bible.

Acts of exhortation, mediated by the Bible, therefore signify God's truth working actively in the world. Both ritual genres and discursive uses of the text act to make the Pentecostal world "uniquely real" in exhortation. Part of this role for the text lies in the way Jamaican exhorters use the Bible actually to "say" their particular world. Geertz (1973c) provides a first step in understanding this practice with his observation that ritual symbol is always a vehicle for conception. A more specific account requires a sense of biblical poetics itself.

Exhortations involve extensive citations from the Bible, so that the exhorter deploys biblical passages to "say" the message of the exhortation. To the believer, the exhorter actually "says" the Bible in the sense that Titon describes. In doing so, the exhorter employs two techniques of biblical poetics described by Sternberg in his account of Old Testament narrative (1987). Sternberg makes the observation that "from the viewpoint of what is directly given in the language, the literary work consists of bits and fragments to be linked and pieced together in the process of reading; it establishes a system of gaps that must be filled" (1987, 186). Sternberg demonstrates this point by referring to the account of King David's adultery with Bathsheba. The parsimony of the narration means that the moral and ironized dimensions of the saga only become apparent, but with resounding force, in the final, ostensibly modest observation that David's act "was evil in the eyes of the Lord." The force of the statement is magnified by the reader's realization that relevant meanings have been conferred by the reader on the preceding words. The reader thereby constructs the experience of unified meaning in the world and the work. Sternberg demonstrates how the play of the reader's/hearer's expectations enriches the text as the plot of adultery and murder unfolds (190–222). In all of this, Sternberg seeks to demonstrate studied "ambiguity as a constructive force" in the text. His account is strikingly similar in some respects to Briggs' and Bauman's (1992) account of language genres and their "gaps" (see also Bauman 1974, 1975). In each case, the emphasis is on issues of intertextuality and, especially in Sternberg's case, the power of the Bible to traverse milieus.

Gapping of the type that Sternberg describes is integral to Jamaican Pentecostal exhortation. Many exhortations never specify the ills and identities of the persons and groups with whom the saved will be compared. And only sometimes will exhortations specify current events as objects of comment. Yet the meaning these exhortations carry for saints is as a running commentary on their lives in which every Bible passage cited presents an aspect of Jamaican life. A local and conventional filling of gaps helps constitute a saintly community in which the reality of the Book is co-terminous with the lives of saints. If the Bible is a vehicle for conception, it is here a vehicle for the conception of Jamaican daily life (Geertz 1973c). The logic of gapping and filling is aided in congregations by the ready deployment of the call-and-response style of Afro-Caribbean performance (see Abrahams 1983, 131–32). The congregation is expecting to respond by affirming a pastor's proposals. When those proposals come in the form of lengthy citations from the Bible, affirmation invariably carries a sense supplied by individuals that makes the call affirmable. Thus, the Bible cannot be heard as a mere aesthetic moment. It becomes socially contextualized through being a vehicle for the process of proposition and affirmation.[1] This takes Pentecostal exhortation beyond Sternberg's gapping and filling, though the two forms retain in common the text as the vehicle for construction of a continuous world.

In Sternberg's study, even more attention is given to the phenomenon of repetition and its role in establishing the divine or absolute certainty of events (cf. Bloch 1974). One aspect of this complex and multifarious phenomenon of repetition "woven" into "plot dynamics" is the serial effect that has an event presented as "forecast" in the form of command or prophecy, as "enactment" in the form of performance or realization, and, finally, as a "report" of the initial forecast and enactment (Sternberg 1987, 376). Numerous examples of biblical repetition involve complex permutations of this technique to overdetermine the reality of events. Sternberg demonstrates this strategy to greatest effect in his analysis of the story of Joseph's interpretation of Pharaoh's dream. Joseph affirms the unity of the dream, the forecast and the reality, of seven good years and seven of famine, in the face of the confusion of Pharaoh's magicians (394–400).

In exhortation, repetition proceeds by a rather different, but comparable, logic. The exhorter will announce a general theme and then cite numerous Bible passages, possibly as many as fifteen, which he suggests voice this very theme. The passages can be drawn from very different contexts and yet are singularly brought to bear on the theme that has been announced. The message of this apparent superfluity of meaning is that the totality of the Book and thus God's Word endorses the theme that has been announced. Moreover, the ability of the pastor and of the saints to register knowledge of all these passages makes their own world consonant with God's and God's authority embodied in the pastor. A form of layered spatial completeness, rather than Sternberg's temporal completeness, underlines the reality and truth of the message. The Word is felt to be true for all time because it is true everywhere. This repetition also evokes repetition in Anansi story-telling. Stylistic repetition announces a normative reality to be breached only through extraordinary means, in this case the will of God (see chapter 7, above).

Elsewhere in his discussion, Sternberg remarks that repetition and gapping work as complements, their respective principles of redundancy and parsimony shaping particular forms of coherence (438). This is one of the numerous poetic techniques by which, he suggests, the biblical narrator seeks "to win the audience over to the site of God," a task that must be accomplished, nonetheless, without "dwarfing, betraying or compromising" the God for whom the narrator speaks. Sternberg writes of this narrator walking a "tightrope" between the demands of "heaven and earth." He must proceed without a sense of dissimulation and yet achieve a rhetorical effect (315). Pentecostal exhorters' use of the Bible involves an analogous "tightrope walking" that makes the Bible an absolute ground for their rendering of Jamaican life. The "trickiness" of this type of performance "has few equivalents," Sternberg observes (482).[2]

Sternberg's poetics, as deployed in biblical texts, perhaps reveal the scaffolding of Derrida's metaphysics; they constitute a literary, said, and practiced whole as a natural phenomenon that is simply the believer's world. Derrida, too, speaks of repetition in relation to the sign in a way that may seem but is not necessarily inconsistent with Sternberg's view. Derrida remarks on a "logic which links repetition to alterity" (1982, 315). Each time a sign is re-presented, it appears within a different context that may allow a change of meaning. This does not mean, however, that the meaning must change, but rather that a sign's meaning is always open to change (see also Hart 1989, 13). The poetic of biblical repetition and the repetition of Pentecostal exhortation lies in the fact that the "redundancy" of repetition can present a superfluity of meaning that nevertheless resists any challenge to the encompassing presence and truth of God. Exhortation both extends the meanings of signs so that they have meaning in Jamaica and yet reaffirms the integration of the world under the one God and his Book (cf. Gates 1988).[3]

These comments re-contextualize various scholarly projects to address the symbolic mediations of the Bible in Jamaican Pentecostal exhortation (cf. Comaroff 1985). This mediation involves specific ritual genres and deploys the Bible as a vehicle for social meanings related to the present and to the past. The Bible's role as vehicle for conception of both history and ritual practice ensures that a biblical world is the truth in the world for saints. This grounding of life through the Bible is central to exhortation and evident in a specific way that links gender ambivalence to a politics of moral order. The myth of the Fall in Genesis is made to engage another myth concerned with Jamaica's origins (Alexander 1977). The one myth mediating the other presents a statement of generic events both biblical and historical to describe a Jamaican condition (cf. Turner 1988). The myths construe Jamaican life in terms of the suffering consequent on sin that precipitates the need for redemption. They also address a more particular "fall" that tends to feminize sin and makes it appropriate for Jamaican pastors to exhort their saints against fornication.

The Myth of the Fall and a Jamaican Origin Myth

The iconography of the Watt Town church, known as "the Schoolhouse," suggests the way in which literacy in and around the Bible was taken up by Jamaicans as a tool of civilization but also as a truth to re-order the world (see chapter 3, above). The Bible as a European-rendered text was also the legacy of the free village system and the Great Revival. It became the source of models of life such as that proposed by Phillippo and Knibb. And the early history of education to literacy in Jamaica was mainly a history of church activity (Gordon 1963, 19–78; cf. Halliday 1991, 30–31; Miller 1990, 53–55). The outcome of this practice of Bible-as-textbook is evident today in Jamaican culture. Everyday discourse deploys extensive phraseology from the Bible. Injunctions to "love," to "feed the multitudes," to act as "good Samaritans," to be "fishers of men" and "bear the burden" trip from the tongues of conversationalists, as do numerous and various requests for blessings and for "deliverance" or "redemption." The heavily nuanced speech of Rastafarianism is simply one genre of this larger phenomenon (Semaj 1980; Pollard 1980). Rastafarian speech, which also carries a critique of this biblically articulated order, exemplifies Derrida's rendering of the alterity of the sign (see conclusion, below).

The importance of Christianity to Jamaican culture has not been simply idiomatic or even poetic, however. It also has resided in the Bible's role as a principal medium for grounding a world made fragmentary and painful by the legacies of slavery and especially the racialism of slavery's colonial aftermath. In medieval times, the Bible was viewed as the book in which "all mysteries of the universe [were] written," not merely a compendium but a master work that placed everything in the shadow of its order. For Jamaicans proselytized by dedicated missionaries who were nonconformists with a biblical bent, Dante's claim for God through his Book might have seemed especially apt: that he "ingathered, bound by love in one volume, the scattered leaves of all the universe" (Dante 1965). Certainly, the Bible's affirmation that all "differences are . . . unified in God" would have been a tantalizing truth for a scattered people whose difference was disparaged in the larger colonial order (cf. Hart 1989, 31). But the Bible not only presented an attractive unifying truth to Jamaicans that all were fallen and all might be redeemed. Explaining the suffering of Jamaican people, it presented an explanation for the genesis of difference among Jamaicans of African descent.

As the testimonies of Pentecostals reveal, continued misfortune and suffering are related directly to the perpetration of sin, and it has been a feature of creole religion that the church rather than secular governance has been seen as the route to a better Jamaica. In typifying Jamaican sinfulness, however, not all sins have been considered equal. Special attention has been given both by observers and by Jamaicans themselves to the phenomenon of concubinage and to its rendering as "fornication." This emphasis began, as we have seen, with British observers of Jamaican life. Phillippo, Knibb, Underhill, Eyre, and Nuttall all commented on Jamaican sexual "immorality" and its role in undermining "civilization." This concern is also embodied in Pentecostal notions of the central ways in which a vessel is rendered unclean. Unsanctified sexuality is the paradigm of sinfulness. And these Jamaican understandings have continued to be shaped in dialogue with European observers. More recent foreign consultants on Jamaican church life have continued the focus of the nineteenth-century critics.

In 1942, for example, J. Merle Davis wrote an account of churches in Jamaica for the newly formed Jamaican Christian Council. In tones not dissimilar to those of his predecessors, Davis described the domestic circumstances of Jamaicans:

> The houses of a majority of rural Jamaicans are one-room or, at most
> two-room huts in which families of six to ten people live in closest
> intimacy. . . . When darkness comes, . . . [a]dults and younger children go
> to bed, while the older boys and girls roam about the neighbourhood in
> the dark. . . .
> A major reason for the slow progress of the Church in overcoming the
> many outstanding social evils in the island is that the home, which is the
> cornerstone of a Christian civilization, is lacking. . . . Under such circum-
> stances it is not surprising to learn that the ratio of illegitimacy in Jamaica
> is 71.6 percent—one of the highest of all lands where accurate records are
> kept. (Davis 1942, 31)

Though written with the hindsight of the Moyne Commission Report and in the period when Jamaica began to move to independence, this was still not the last such rendering of Jamaica. In 1962, Donald MacGavran published a further study on "church growth in Jamaica." He eschewed Davis's use of the terms "concubinage" and "illegitimacy," describing them as "loaded words." He continued Davis's imagery of "darkness," however, by referring to the world of extra-marital sexual relations as the "Dark River" into which Jamaicans "fall," thereby denying followers to the churches. In MacGavran's words:

> This never-ending procession of children of God marching down into the Dark River in the prime of life, many of them never to emerge, is a large part of the problem of church growth in Jamaica. (MacGavran 1962, 50)

Notwithstanding this demoralizing scene:

> The churches through their ministers and members are continually searching for couples in the Dark River who can be converted, persuaded to marry, be baptized and join the church. (55)

MacGavran observed that in this task, the churches, including the Pentecostal churches, are aided by "elderly . . . [s]ingle women, many with children and grandchildren, [who] form a large percentage of the membership of many working class churches" (47).

The Bible, as a textbook for Jamaican Christians, accounts for humankind's imperfect state in terms of a "fall" from paradise by virtue of an illegitimate acquisition of knowledge and, more especially, sexual knowledge (Lerner 1986, 196). With the discursive prominence of the Bible in Jamaican life, it is therefore not surprising that readings of the legacies of slavery propose a homologous role for "illegitimate" sexual practice. Jamaicans suffer, it is proposed, for their lack of domesticity, which is caused by unsanctified sexuality. This is a sexuality, in turn, that historically was foisted onto Jamaica in the course of the slavery regime. Whatever the "ignorance" of African slaves, the regime exacerbated the practice (see chapter 2, above).

These forms of representation act to locate the fallen nature of a black lower class either in the legacy of African culture or in the experience of slavery or in a view that one state promoted the other. In all such renderings, concubinage and fornication are seen as lower-class concerns and applicable to both women and men. Yet when this view of a fall is placed in the context of hierarchy, the role of women can be emphasized.

In the historical genesis of society, it was African women rather than men who mated with those beyond their ken, light-skinned men of superior power, bringing forth a brown-skinned stratum that breached the ranks of the black enslaved (cf. Alexander 1977). Orlando Patterson's initial account of the "sociology of slavery" in Jamaica is indicative of a widespread popular view. It does not underestimate the element of force in these interclass relations and yet observes that over time, women were inexorably drawn into an economy of sexual relations. Patterson writes:

> The slave women, of course, did not remain virtuous. Under such tempta-tions [of a high male-to-female sex ratio], with their bodies in such great demand and the economic rewards no doubt bountiful, it is impossible to conceive how they could have done so. Furthermore, there were no social sanctions, no notion of chastity or any ideal of marital status to restrain them. The masters themselves, who were the ultimate source of all power and authority in the society, were completely corrupt and competed with the male slaves for [women's] bodies. The inevitable consequence of the unusually high demand for their sexual services, then, was extreme pro-miscuity. (Patterson 1967, 108)[4]

Patterson proposes here that the slavery regime swept away all institutions regulating sexuality and especially the sexuality of black slave women. This scholarly rendering of a mythic theme is mirrored, we shall see below, in popular accounts of Jamaica's origins, understood as the origins of color-class difference. It also is mirrored in a less direct way in ideas of young Jamaican men about the fickleness of women, who are figured as more ambitious than men (cf. Chevannes 1985, 194; Miller 1986). The Pentecostal view that al-though women embody a "more humble spirit," they nonetheless can be more inclined to "look a man," sometimes higher up the system, articulates this mythic theme in the Pentecostal milieu.[5]

Pastors, who may be mainly concerned with saving lower-class men and women in a lower-class milieu, nonetheless present a message strongly ori-ented toward women that sometimes acts as a vehicle as well for inter-class and status concerns. In this, historical experience articulates with biblical lore to define a Jamaican "fall" associated with slavery.

There follow two examples of exhortation and their milieus. The first of these presents the practice of a Pentecostal eudemonic constituted through exhortation. The exhortation was delivered by a female pastor and embodies that aspect of the Pentecostal life that numerous women, and men, avidly seek as an ideal of the saintly state. The very reality of a bibilical world con-stituted through exhortation convinces saints of their transcendence over the trials of daily life.

This ritual path to eudemonic fervor involves, however, a radical act of contrition in response to exhorters preaching sin. And "preaching sin" refers to a particular style of male exhortation that feminizes sin by casting men as shepherds to the brides of Christ. The second exhortation relies on the intersection of notions of fallen women with perceptions of Jamaican hierar-chy. The feminization of sin and fornication that requires the men to be shep-herds of saints is the central theme of this exhortation. Both deploy a bib-lical poetics of gapping and repetition that makes the Word and everyday life a continuous world of biblical truth. That Jamaican "fornication," and the Bible's, have merged in a creole discourse is suggested by some further versions of the origin myth presented in the light of these exhortations.

An Exhortation to Victory in Kingston

The Kingston church in which this exhortation took place was established in 1963, when its founding pastor and his evangelist wife broke away from the United Pentecostal Church. A few years later, the pastor died, and his work was carried on by his wife, who became the pastor of the church. A well-educated woman, she has built a large and successful organization in the lower-class area where she resides. After various mishaps and difficulties, including the collapse of one church building, a fine large structure was raised on a major road leading out of Kingston. Like many of its kind elsewhere in Kingston, the church was built on vacant land next to a gully. Back along the sides of the gully live the poorer residents of the area, which otherwise is populated by lower-class people living in houses, apartments, and tenements. The church itself is built of concrete block with an upstairs balcony and a large front dais. The dais is furnished with a carved wooden pulpit and large polished mahogany chairs for the pastor and the elders. The interior walls are painted yellow and blue, and these colors are used in gowns for both the deacons and the choir. The church has an electric organ, though frequently services also are accompanied by electric guitars and a full drum kit. The building has meeting rooms attached, a pastor's office, and a basement used for tarrying. All these were financed by contributions from the congregation, either in money or in kind.

The church conducts a successful pre-school for the children of saved and unsaved mothers alike. A youth gathering and service is held each week and an evangelical meeting every Sunday night. There is an annual convention and regular meetings of various committees concerned with the Sunday school, publications, and youths', men's, and women's affairs. Younger church members, especially, participate in campaigns held by American evangelists. The church has a network of American contacts sustained both through the pastor's activities and through those of the rank and file. Nonetheless, the church is staunchly independent both financially and in cultural orientation.

The pastor is devoted to her congregation and identifies the problems of women as important. It is largely through this constituency of women that her formidable community of saints is sustained. She observed of young women in the area:

> We have a lot of young people, you know, standing around, who will not come in. Well, one of the most striking things is, for example, we believe that part of living holy is not to live, you know, in an unmarried situation.

I mean a girl and a boy living together without being married, you know. And so many of these girls come, and we talk with them and say, "You should marry your boyfriend," and that sort of thing. And some of them are so pitiful. It has struck me to my heart, you know. I remember one day, a girl, she was crying so much at the altar, and I asked her then, "Would you like to be baptized?" She was pregnant. She was living with the father. He wasn't prepared to marry her. You know, that's a real problem, and to me, too. I feel that some of the girls, some of them, not all of them, could have asserted a more independent spirit. Maybe I'm not being fair to them. Maybe they didn't have any other way out. And yet, according to my Christian conviction, there is always another way out, if you trust in God. They leave school, and then they just don't have what else to do. And then, you know, they start living with a boy or something. . . .

Now, you may say, "Oh well, these are living in concubinage; these are a visiting relationship," or what have you, and, as it were, "We can't say this is the right or wrong." I mean, this kind of thinking is prevalent. You know what home life is in Jamaica. Many times you don't have a stable home. You don't have a father, you know, in the home, and discipline and guidance are affected. This means we bring up our young people in a sort of non-directive way. I mean, even if you are going to direct them badly, it is better than no direction at all. And I feel that our youth have been brought up feeling, then, who's to say what's right, you know. And they just grow up like that. Jamaicans are traveling more now, and more outside influences come in, and things that are workable in other countries, they are not workable here. One small example is that dating system. You cannot take the pattern of dating in America and apply it in Jamaica, because it is a totally different culture, right? And I think that Jamaicans have tried to copy other patterns not right for here.

The pastor here proposes a specifically Jamaican Christian community, engaged with but different from America. A major role of the church will be to create a closure for Pentecostal women from the sexual openness imprinted on them by their cultural heritage and the conditions of an impoverished urban life that lead some, she suggests, into an economy of sexuality. The pastor ascribes the vulnerability of women to the absence of effective male protectors, though she also places the moral onus on women who can become brides with Jesus' help. Notwithstanding these various opinions, she presents a personal alternative to patriarchy. The pastor avoids "preaching sin" and rather underlines, in a eudemonic style, the possibilities of alternative community in the lives of women saints.

Sunday morning congregations are very large, and often the service begins only around noon. It is generally preceded by a long period of choruses, vocal prayer, and testimony, activities generally led by a deacon. Between three hundred and four hundred people attend these services, and the mood is

generally exuberant. The vast majority of the congregation are women rang-
ing in age from youths to the very old. Some are dressed conservatively in
the old Pentecostal style, wearing "tall" dresses with long sleeves and high,
modest necks. Many younger working-class women attend in smartly cut and
brightly colored dresses set off by high-heeled shoes. These women always
wear hats, and some of these are quite elaborate. In keeping with Pentecostal
practice, women do not wear jewelry or cosmetics. Their young children are
brought to church and frequently sleep in the pews. Some women bring their
own tambourines, which they beat and shake with vigor during the choruses.
Men are a minority in the congregation and would certainly not number
more than twelve percent of the whole. Most are either young men, under
thirty, or else elderly men from the first generation of Pentecostals. A significant proportion of these men are deacons or elders in the church, and they
surround the pastor with a male entourage leavened by some women evangelists. Services can continue for almost three hours and usually assume the
form of celebrations of a Spirit-imbued eudemonic.

At first, the warmup period proceeds without the choir assembled on the
dais. As the saints settle down to vigorous chorus singing, however, the choir,
once again with a majority of women, walks rhythmically to its place on the
dais directly behind the elders' chairs. The entry of the choir with its forceful singing and members witnessing to the Lord raises the pitch of the congregation. Once the congregation has moved into the Spirit, the pastor and
elders enter the church and assume their seats, singing and praying as they
settle themselves. On this day, once the pastor had entered, a hymn was
sung by the congregation as they stood and kept time to the powerful and
somber strains of the organ. With the congregation poised expectantly, a
Bible reading was given by a young woman saint:

> That which we have seen and heard declare we unto you, that ye also may
> have fellowship with us: and truly our fellowship is with the Father, and
> with his Son Jesus Christ.
>   And these things write we unto you, that your joy may be full.
>   This then is the message which we have heard of him, and declare unto
> you, that God is light, and in him is no darkness at all.
>   If we say that we have fellowship with him, and walk in darkness, we lie,
> and do not the truth.
>   But if we walk in the light, as he is in the light, we have fellowship one
> with another, and the blood of Jesus Christ his Son cleanseth us from all
> sin. (1 John 1:3–7)

The reading presented the promise and the program of the Pentecostal
church: saints are promised a eudemonic joy with the companionship of
Jesus Christ. These things are embodied in a fellowship, in a community of

the saints. The only way to this fellowship, however, is through Jesus' cleansing blood, which will lead a saint out of the world of darkness into the world of enduring light.

After the reading, a male elder presented a welcome to the congregation, also enjoining those unsaved to "hearken to the word of God." Then the pastor rose to bring greetings to the saints with an initial observation: "Hallelujah! Doesn't it feel good to praise the Lord?" To this, the congregation responded with its own calls to "Praise the Lord!" Notices were presented concerning a local campaign, the welcome performance of some of the church's children in their school examinations, and a coming important business meeting. Visiting saints from other congregations and from America were greeted, along with a female pastor from Miami. Notice of the various group meetings for the coming week was given, and then prayers were said for two church members suffering illness. The pastor finished this segment of the service by saying, "We're trusting God for a great time today," and handed proceedings back to the elder before she resumed her seat. A collection was taken as more choruses were sung. Members of the congregation filed up to a table in front of the dais to offer their contributions. The rhythmic music meant that the files of saints rocked along, as individual believers passed by the table, placing their coins in a collection bowl. After a series of vigorous choruses, six testimonies were taken, including one from the American pastor. Following these testimonies came another time of prayer led by the pastor, during which she observed that very often saints "look at what they don't have and don't look at what they have." She asked all those who were unemployed to raise their hands and say, "I am blessed with a job." Then she said to the congregation, "The 'blessed' was louder than 'with a job.' Say it again, louder. I want to hear your testimony when by faith you come back with a job!" By these means, she led into her sermon, which concerned "the Lord's victories."

The pastor stood at her pulpit, an attractive, thick-set black woman of slightly less than average height. Her curly hair, streaked with white, was pulled back from her forehead in a bun. She wore a fashionable broad-brimmed hat perched slightly to the side of her head. A very large Bible rested before her on the pulpit. She clasped the sides of the pulpit with her hands and, from time to time, lifted one or both of her arms in the air. Her face was alight with enthusiasm, her voice sure and strong, as she exhorted her community of saints. She addressed them in a biblical idiom replete with gapping and repetition:

> We feel that circumstance is going to put us under. We feel that the demands of life are pressing on us today. I'm going to tell you about some of God's victories so that you can know in truth and in faith that today you're on "the victory side."

The pastor's style was both urgent and intimate, drawing the saints with a beckoning smile into her own engaging theme. Her generalized statement allowed the saints to furnish "circumstance" and "demand" with the terms of their daily lives. Then she read from her massive Bible:

> Finally, my brethren, be strong in the Lord and in the power of his might.
>
> Put on the whole armor of God, that ye may be able to stand against the wiles of the devil.
>
> For we wrestle not against flesh and blood, but against principalities, against powers, against the rulers of the darkness of this world, against spiritual wickedness in high places.
>
> Wherefore take unto you the whole armor of God, that ye may be able to withstand in the evil day, and having done all, to stand.
>
> Stand therefore, having your loins girt about with truth, and having on the breastplate of righteousness.
>
> And your feet shod with the preparation of the gospel of peace.
>
> Above all, taking the shield of faith, wherewith ye shall be able to quench all the fiery darts of the wicked.
>
> And take the helmet of salvation, and the sword of the Spirit, which is the word of God.
>
> Praying always with all prayer and supplication in the Spirit, and watching thereunto with all perseverance and supplication for all saints.
>
> And for me that utterance may be given unto me, that I may open my mouth boldly, to make known the mystery of the gospel.
>
> For which I am an ambassador in bonds: that therein I may speak boldly, as I ought to speak. (Ephesians 6:10–20)

The pastor took up the idea that all the saints are ultimately "ambassadors in bonds," destined to fight "not against flesh and blood" but against "spiritual wickedness" and the "rulers of darkness" in the world. The image of strength she projected in the church was embodied and returned by the saints as they called their rejoinders of "Praise the Lord" and "Hallelujah," feeling, as they praised, the presence of God.

By specifying the "ambassadors" and their "fight" in terms of everyday concerns, the pastor then filled the gapping herself. She enjoined the saints not to become embroiled in disputes in their yards. She suggested that when a fellow tenant taunted a saint, the saint should simply draw away. She should not put herself at risk by employing "bad words" and physical assault. She should remember above all that her fight is a fight of Spirit. Similarly, the pastor continued, the saint should not fight with the landlord. Even when he demanded rent that could not be paid, the saint should avoid argument. Simply be contrite, she proposed, and give the worry "over to Jesus." He would find a way to pay. At work, the pastor pointed out, it was foolish to fight a boss. That person employed you and gave you money. Every injustice in the world was an injustice that God could see. He had always fought for his people, and he fought for his saints as well, if only they would believe. The aim of the saint should be simply to fight the devil: "We wrestle not against flesh and blood, but against the evil day." The pastor furnished the notion of power with a power to transcend a tangible milieu by transferring the "pressure" to God. She then juxtaposed this milieu with the triumphs and trials of Joshua as he fought and believed in the Lord:

> And the Lord said unto Joshua, See, I have given into thine hand Jericho, and the king thereof, and the mighty men of valor.
> And ye shall compass the city all ye men of war, and go round about the city once. Thus shalt thou do six days.
> And seven priests shall bear before the ark seven trumpets of rams' horns: and the seventh day ye shall compass the city seven times, and the priests shall blow with the trumpets.
> And it shall come to pass that when they make a long blast with the ram's horn, and when ye hear the sound of the trumpet, all the people shall shout with a great shout; and the wall of the city shall fall down flat, and the people shall ascend up every man straight before him. (Joshua 6:2–5)

The pastor exclaimed that Joshua's famous victory was just one of many victories that the Lord had achieved for the people of Israel. This was made clear in the Book of Deuteronomy, where it was written:

> Happy art thou, O Israel: who is like unto thee, O people saved by the Lord, the shield of thy help, and who is the sword of thy excellency! and thine enemies shall be found liars unto thee; and thou shalt tread upon their high places. (Deuteronomy 33:29)

Here the pastor began her repetition, which would build in intensity as the exhortation proceeded. And as she began her repetition, she also moved in another way to establish the ground of her message. Many people, the pastor observed, disputed the story of Joshua. Children with a modern education said that the walls would not fall down simply because people blew on trumpets. In reply, the pastor declared, "My God is a great God. My God is great enough to use every law of physics to achieve his aims for the people of God." In this statement, she neatly moved to encompass science in the Word of God. Quoting again from Joshua, the pastor indicated that God could direct the sun and the moon:

> Then spake Joshua to the Lord in the day when the Lord delivered up the Amorites before the children of Israel, and he said in the sight of Israel, Sun, stand thou still upon Gibeon; and thou, Moon, in the valley of Ajalon.
> And the sun stood still, and the moon stayed, until the people had avenged themselves upon their enemies. Is not this written in the book

of Jasher? So the sun stood still in the midst of heaven, and hastened not
to go down about a whole day.

And there was no day like that before it or after it, that the Lord hear-
kened unto the voice of a man: for the Lord fought for Israel. (Joshua
10:12–14)

The pastor described God's total encompassment of the world, and certainly
of Jamaican life. She could propose, then, with assurance, that he would
deliver the victory.[6]

The gapping involved in a notion of war was then filled in a different way.
The pastor proposed that the war of the saints also could be "a war of sickness." It took continual faith, she proposed, to place the trust in God alone
and seek through Jesus deliverance from all the physical suffering. But the
Lord saw all things and could heal all things if only one believed, she observed. The pastor then deployed repetition again to present another set of
absolutes; God ruled not only the sun and moon but also the totality of life
and death. Voicing God's word, the pastor said:

See now that I, even I, am he, and there is no god with me: I kill and I
make alive; I wound, and I heal; neither is there any that can deliver out of
my hand. (Deuteronomy 32:39)

Having established the absolute ground of her message, the pastor expanded with more repetition. There were many other victories of the Lord
in the Bible, the victory of Gideon over the Midianites, for instance:

And Gideon sent messengers throughout all Mount Ephraim, saying,
Come down against the Midianites, and take before them the waters unto
Beth-barah and Jordan. Then all the men of Ephraim gathered themselves
together, and took the waters unto Beth-barah and Jordan.

And they took two princes of the Midianites, Oreb and Zeeb; and they
slew Oreb upon the rock Oreb, and Zeeb they slew at the winepress of
Zeeb, and pursued Midian, and brought the heads of Oreb and Zeeb to
Gideon on the other side of Jordan. (Judges 7:24–25)

All these victories, the pastor stressed, were victories achieved for God's chosen people. Such victories, however, were possible only for those who believed. Saints should remember, she cautioned, that not all the disciples had
a complete faith in Jesus. Even Joshua in his war against the people of Ai took
only five thousand from all "the people of war." The Lord, and the God
named Jesus, would only fight the war for those who believed, and believed
in an orderly fashion through careful study of the Bible. As the pastor paused
and smiled at the saints, she said with quiet emphasis, "I love the word of
God because it is so ordered. Sometimes we are undisciplined, and we need
to learn the way." Here she extolled reliance on the Bible, the key to an

expansive knowledge of victory. The pastor then cited the agreement made by God with his people against the infamous Philistines:

> And Samuel spake unto all the house of Israel, saying, If ye do return unto the Lord with all your hearts, then put away the strange gods and Ashtaroth from among you, and prepare your hearts unto the Lord, and serve him only: and he will deliver you out of the hand of the Philistines. (1 Samuel 7:3)

And this promise, the pastor observed, actually came to pass most triumphantly in the victory of David over Goliath:

> Therefore David ran, and stood upon the Philistine, and took his sword, and drew it out of the sheath thereof, and slew him, and cut off his head therewith. And when the Philistines saw their champion dead, they fled. (1 Samuel 17:51)

In the midst of the cries of enthusiastic saints, the pastor emphasized, finally, that in the war of flesh against flesh, the meek were unlikely to triumph. The only victories to be had in life were through the Spirit of "our Lord" and the glorious encouragement of "our great God." Her closing injunction to the saints was: "Just give God the glory and forget the creature." She followed this observation with a crescendo of repetitions that focused on emancipation and redemption:

> And the Syrians fled before Israel; and David slew the men of seven hundred chariots of the Syrians, and forty thousand horsemen, and smote Shobach the captain of their host, who died there. (2 Samuel 10:18)
> He arose, and smote the Philistines until his hand was weary and his hand clave unto the sword: and the Lord wrought a great victory that day. (2 Samuel 23:10)

And finally:

> And David spake unto the Lord the words of this song in the day that the Lord had delivered him out of the hand of all his enemies, and out of the hand of Saul:
> And he said, The Lord is my rock, and my fortress and my deliverer.
> The God of my rock; in him shall I trust: he is my shield and the horn of my salvation, my high tower, and my refuge, my savior; thou savest me from violence.
> I will call on my Lord who is worth to be praised: so shall I be saved from mine enemies.
> When the waves of death compassed me, the floods of ungodly men made me afraid. . . .
> In my distress I called upon the Lord, and cried to my God: and he did hear my voice out of his temple, and my cry did enter into his ears.

Then the earth shook and trembled; the foundations of heaven moved
and shook, because he was wroth. . . .

He sent from above, he took me; he drew me out of many waters.

He delivered me from my strong enemy, and from them that hated
me: for they were too strong for me. . . .[7]

The Lord rewarded me according to my righteousness; according to the
cleanness of my hands he hath recompensed me.

For I have kept the ways of the Lord and have not wickedly departed
from my God. (2 Samuel 22: 1–8, 17–18, 21–22)

In this exhortation, the pastor proposed an absolute ground for Pentecostal life in God's control of the universe. She deployed the violence of biblical
narrative in perhaps the most important piece of gapping to acknowledge
the violence of a slave history and of a present in "the ghetto." She matched
the magnitude of Israel's history to the history of Jamaicans and proclaimed
that just as God had rewarded the Israelites with victory, so he rewarded his
Jamaican saints.

Pentecostalism's status as a redemptive religion is here clearly demonstrated. The juxtaposition of imperfect world with the belief in transcendent
God requires a definite form of accounting for both the living and the dead
(cf. Weber 1964, 138–39). And yet the declaration of this final accounting is
made with assurance, because the pastor, like her sanctified saints, knows
that she is on "the victory side." In a series of discussions I had with the
pastor, she emphasized that this was the importance of tongues, as the central and embodied sign that a person had become a vessel for Spirit. Tongues
brought the joy of victory:

> I had been taught that you don't have to speak in tongues, and that getting
> the Holy Spirit is a quiet thing. And then I remember, well, I looked up all
> the references in the Bible, and one in particular, maybe that one, didn't
> even mention speaking in tongues. But the whole gist of the story made
> me realize that there was some kind of outward visible sign to receiving
> the Holy Ghost. And this was the story of Peter and John going down to
> Samaria. And the sorcerer, Simon, offered Peter money, you know, so that
> he could get the same gift: whoever he laid hands on would also receive
> the Holy Ghost. You know that story? It's in Acts of the Apostles, chapter
> eight: "And when Simon saw that through laying on of the apostles' hands
> the Holy Ghost was given, he offered them money, saying, Give me also
> this power, that on whomsoever I lay hands, he may receive the Holy
> Ghost."[8]
>
> Now, you know, when I saw that and I reasoned it, I felt that there must
> be some outward sign, because if it was just a matter that they laid hands
> on you and said, well, "You have the Holy Ghost," Simon wouldn't have
> offered money, because he could have deceived them anyway. . . . But
> something follows when the apostles lay hands on them that Simon

couldn't do, you know, so he said, "I'll give you money to give me this same power, that when I lay my hands on people they receive the Holy Ghost, too."

In these Pentecostal services, even women who remained unsaved could partake in the eudemonic enthusiasm of saints assured of their own salvation. Owing to the size of the congregation, a certain anonymity was assured the participant who did not seek to enter the world of the saints. In consequence, the gatherings acted as massive social-religious occasions in which the particulars of Jamaican life were situated in the absolutely real of the Bible. The meetings, on a scale with political rallies, were of mainly lower-class women seeking an embodied sense of hope in the midst of often difficult lives. Not surprisingly, women could come to these meetings unsaved and, hearing the exhortations of the pastor, experience an unforeseen in-filling. Some others, becoming familiar with the church and seeking greater engagement, would be drawn into a process of prayer and tarrying as they sought to be saved and sanctified. In this process, they would attend prayer meetings in the room below the church set aside for tarrying, and often they would be addressed by male elders or deacons. In a milieu that even the pastor described as one of "concubinage" and not "living holy," male authorities often turned to the issue of fornication. Exhorting these unsanctified women to examine the ways in which they might yet be unclean, male officers sometimes focused on the personal moral status of women. Her being an "unclean vessel" was the chief explanation offered for the Holy Ghost's reluctance to enter a woman.

In one such reflection, an elder observed that the Lord cared only for "chaste virgins" and not for the "knock-about virgins" of Jamaica. He reminded the women, "Yu don' want to be slaves today. Yu 'ave the freedom to come to Jesus if yu wish to come to Jesus." The elder observed that if women desired to be filled, they must cease to live a "knock-about" life and put their trust entirely in Jesus. The elder also observed that this would not be done through a "little cry" or feeling "a little bit sorry" for themselves but only through a major change. He then invoked a range of biblical sources in support of the truth of his proposition:

> For thy Maker is thine husband: the Lord of hosts is his name; and thy Redeemer the Holy One of Israel: the God of the whole earth shall he be called. (Isaiah 54:5)

In this passage, he identified the life of a Pentecostal woman with a life of wifely restraint. He then considered the responsibilities of the saint-as-bride in relation to the Lord and the Lord's representative, here identified as Paul. The elder employed repetition with marked effect on the listening women, who were presented with a threat and then with the means to avoid its implications:

> For I am jealous over you with godly jealousy: for I have espoused you to one husband, that I may present you as a chaste virgin to Christ. (2 Corinthians 11:2)
>
> For I am the Lord thy God, the Holy One of Israel, thy Savior: I gave Egypt for thy ransom, Ethiopia and Seba for thee. (Isaiah 43:4)
>
> Rejoice greatly, O daughter of Zion; shout, O daughter of Jerusalem: behold thy King cometh unto thee. (Zechariah 9:9)

The elder observed that this could be the joy of a chastened vessel awaiting her King. Like all women descended from Eve, Jamaican women, the elder proposed, should wait on a husband. For the rest, "yu on the road t' Babylon." The whore of Babylon was presented to the women as a real feminine persona. The elder quoted extensively from the seventeenth and eighteenth chapters of Revelation, which include this lurid description:

> And the woman was arrayed in purple and scarlet color, and decked with gold and precious stones and pearls, having a golden cup in her hand full of abominations and filthiness of her fornication:
>
> And upon her forehead was a name written, MYSTERY, BABYLON THE GREAT, THE MOTHER OF HARLOTS AND ABOMINATIONS OF THE EARTH.
>
> And I saw the woman drunken with the blood of saints, and with the blood of martyrs of Jesus. (Revelation 17:4–6)

Several of the younger women burst into tears as the elder enjoined them to study their lives. And in this ritual drama, the very rhetorical effect of the male elder was mediated and magnified by mythic themes from Jamaica's past. The contrast between slaves and saints, and between whores and wives, positioned their being as women within a mythic repertoire from which they were invited to choose one or the other course.

These small-scale ministrations to women, which I observed in numerous churches, were always emotionally charged situations in which men combined kindness and threat in a strategy to bring women into the fold. Bible passages were used to contrast an idealized state of male guardianship embodied in submission to the Savior, with a state of degradation and perpetual danger.[9] Women often became extremely emotional in the course of these sessions and were sometimes filled with the Spirit forthwith. The pressure created in this environment was in marked contrast to the eudemonic community embodied in the regular Sunday services. The acceptance of an act of contrition for being an embodiment of the Fall became the rite of passage for women to enter the community of saints. In the smaller and especially independent congregations of numerous urban and rural churches, these different moments of a Pentecostal progress often were collapsed into one. This occurred most commonly in male-led churches with exhorters adept at "preaching sin."

Exhorting the Poor to Be Rich in Spirit

The small Pentecostal Spirit-Filled Church is located just outside the rural center of Mandeville in Manchester parish. At the exhortation described below, the preacher addressed a congregation that was largely comprised of women, though the church also had a number of young male members. The church was located in an impoverished area, and it is in such areas that Pentecostalism tends to attract young male deacons aspiring to the pastorate, a pastorate they can reach through revelation and Bible knowledge, especially if they are good exhorters. The service was an anniversary service for the bishop of the church, who had occupied his bishopric for twenty-three years.

That night, the bishop sat in the church slightly to one side of the dais. He was a gaunt little man, very black, with glasses and dressed in a light brown suit. Next to him, on his right, sat a visiting bishop from Westmoreland parish, who would deliver the exhortation. On the home bishop's left sat other male officers of his church, including a couple of junior pastors and some deacons and evangelists. Behind this row of men sat the women: missionaries, deacons, evangelists, and also wives of the male officers. Further left from the bishop sat the choir, mostly young women, clothed in blue and wearing small blue hats. The few male choir members were dressed in rather shabby clothes and not to any particular style. To the left of the choir stood the band: three young men playing a drum, a guitar, and a small electric keyboard. Centered above the heads of those seated on the dais was a large painted sign:

> Repent, and be baptized every one of you in the name of Jesus Christ for
> the remission of sins, and ye shall receive the gift of the Holy Ghost.
> (Acts 3:38)

On either side of this sign, enclosed in heavy wooden frames, were two black-and-white photographs of the bishop and his wife.[10] The church itself was perched high on a hill just a few miles from Mandeville. The housing around it was more in the style of a shanty town than a rural village, though one could stand outside the church and look beyond the settlement to the countryside. The members of this church were people from rural backgrounds who had come to live in this satellite of Mandeville. They were seeking service and laboring employment in the town, which had lost its rural demeanor over the previous twenty years. A large open-cut bauxite mine had slashed through the countryside close to Mandeville, and although these people were not engaged with the mine, their migrations had been part of a secondary development as Mandeville expanded as a service center. They embodied the twentieth-century social milieu in which American Pentecostalism first had begun to grow in Jamaica, a milieu of rural-to-urban migration encouraged by American investment in the region.[11]

The interior of the church was lined with masonite board. Weighed down by the damp of tropical rains, the ceiling was beginning to buckle. The walls, like the ceiling, were water-stained. The floor was tiled, and on it stood rows of spartan wooden pews. The only kneeling cushions lay along the front of the dais. Older saints went there to pray. In front of the dais, in the body of the hall, stood a table covered with a white lace cloth and on it two wooden collection plates shaped like frying pans with handles extending from the bowl. A large vase of flowers cut from ginger plants also stood on the modest table. Further down the central aisle of the church was a blackboard on a trestle. At the head of the board was written in capital letters, "SICK PRAY-ERS," and below it were scrawled a number of names of the sick for whom the saints should pray.

Because the service was an anniversary, a large part of the proceedings was taken up with representatives of the Sunday school, men's and women's groups, the choir, and the church band, each offering a song, a prayer, or a recitation in honor of the bishop. After each performance, a representative from the group would give the bishop an envelope, saying, in effect, "This is not payment, for you cannot be paid for the work of God. Rather, this is a tribute of esteem for all you have done." Each speaker kissed and was kissed in turn by the bishop, who was greatly moved. Young members of the church in particular expressed a very obvious affection for the bishop in their recollections. Several said that they knew he had blessed them as babies and "talked them out of sin" when they were old enough to understand. The bishop's own son, taller than his father and strikingly handsome, with his father's shining eyes, talked of how strict the father had been with him. The man had never relented in his stand against sin. He was unforgiving, and yet he was able to guide the son "in the way of Spirit and of truth." One member spoke of how the community had been in spiritual and literal darkness before the bishop had arrived on the scene. He had improved people's' lives by bringing them the gospel and by petitioning "the politician" to provide them with lighting and better roads.

One young woman testified that it was not only "Bishop" but also his wife who came to her when she was having her baby and was out of work. The bishop's wife had said, "I know things hard." She had helped with food and also brought Jesus' message. Another spoke of a sick woman living near the bishop's house, who would say all day, "Potato, potato." The bishop had a plot of potatoes in his yard and realized the woman was pining for food. The bishop's wife cooked some potatoes and took them across to the woman. Because of the potatoes, she was saved. This very practical aspect of the church also was reflected in the "sick list" noticeboard, which ensured that anyone praying in the church would know immediately who was sick. Most of those who offered tributes were young people whose parents had brought them into the church. One, however, was an elderly woman evangelist, very thin with a gray complexion that suggested ill- health. She sang a song for the bishop and then presented him with a boutonniere as she recollected the twenty years they had spent evangelizing together. Her testimony elicited a rapturous reply from the saints, as many sprang to their feet, praising Jesus and saluting the Lord.

This was a multi-generational church. It was clearly embedded in the lives of the people, even as it stood in the midst of a transitional milieu of a rural people moving inexorably toward town. The very simplicity of the church and the immediate engagement between officers and saints revealed it as a site of creole religion. Yet the milieu also reflected a religion in which I, a stranger, could enter and credential myself through a range of accepted signs. A personal association through Kingston Pentecostals, a knowledge of hymns and choruses used, a working knowledge of the Bible, a catalogue of phrases repeated, and the ability to be "touched" by the Spirit were all that was required for acceptance and fellowship. These aspects of the Pentecostal movement allow saints to be mobile beyond the boundaries of a childhood church. Notwithstanding a common nostalgia for the milieu of their Pentecostal beginnings, saints can move from one location to another with confidence that "God will find you a place" and "slot you in!" This aspect of Jamaican Pentecostalism underlines its modernity, the retention of a local knowledge, and also a trans-nationalism.

After these tributes to the bishop came the call for a church collection and then the visiting bishop's exhortation. The visiting bishop was Afro-Indian and came from a very impoverished background. He had built a major church in Savannah-la-Mar and was, as well, successful in business. He was well known in Pentecostal circles in Kingston and some years later would receive an "Achievement Award" from the government for his impact and influence on his region. He was a handsome man of above-average height and with a powerful frame. His face was firm, almost chiseled, and his eyes were bright and keen. His sermon, an exhortation to remain with the Lord, ruptured the homely intimacy of the church. And yet the delivery was judged by those present as a fine example of "preaching sin," an appropriate exhortation on this anniversary occasion. The sermon was at once an attack on Jamaica's and America's wealthy. It was also a gendered injunction concerning the status of saintly brides. It exemplified the lower-class pastor criticizing his status superiors and simultaneously reaching for the sexual closure of his women.

The preacher began speaking quietly and slowly in a casual, even off-hand manner. He stood with his body only half turned to the microphone and with his gaze directed back to the officers on the dais. With his Bible in his hand, he proceeded without notes of any kind, flicking through the book to the relevant passages, most of which obviously had been committed to memory. His first Bible reference came from the Book of Psalms and, like other such opening statements, embodied the corpus of Pentecostal belief:

> Have mercy upon me, O God, according to thy loving kindness: according unto the multitude of thy tender mercies blot out my transgressions.
>> Wash me throughly from mine iniquity, and cleanse me from my sin.
>> For I acknowledge my transgressions; and my sin is ever before me.
>> Against thee, thee only, have I sinned and done this evil in thy sight; and thou mightest be justified when thou speakest, and be clear when thou judgest.
>> Behold, I was shapen in iniquity; and in sin did my mother conceive me.
>> Behold, thou desirest truth in the inward parts: and in the hidden part thou shalt make me to know wisdom.
>> Purge me with hyssop, and I shall be clean: wash me, and I shall be whiter than snow.
>> Make me hear joy and gladness; that the bones which thou hast broken may rejoice.
>> Hide thy face from my sins, and blot out all mine iniquities.
>> Create in me a clean heart, O God; and renew a right spirit within me.
>> Cast me not away from thy presence; and take not thy holy spirit from me.
>> Restore unto me the joy of thy salvation; and uphold me with thy free spirit.
>> Then will I teach transgressors thy ways; and sinners shall be converted unto thee.
>> Deliver me from blood guiltiness, O God, thou God of my salvation: and my tongue shall sing aloud of thy righteousness. (Psalm 51:1–14)

The passage underlines the conviction of sin and uncleanliness, the moment of truth and subsequent repentance, the ensuing joy of being relieved of sin, and the commitment to bring others to the Word. The "blood guiltiness" of the sinner, however, is also a guilt realized at the very point of conception through the mother's own sexual-procreative moment. And the truth that will relieve this sin and make for wisdom also will make the sinner "whiter than snow." Jamaican readings of the Bible are steeped in ambivalence, and this was revealed in the bishop's exhortation.

The preacher began his sermon on a theme of civilization. He observed that owing to the history of Jamaica, many people who lived there had plenty of ideas about who was "civilized" and who was not. Some people said that clothes made one civilized. Others said that it was only with education that a person could become civilized. Still others maintained that living in a fine house and having plenty to eat made one a civilized person. Some said that to be civilized, a person had to learn how to obey the law. Yet the Bible saw things differently. The law, in fact, was not made for the righteous but only for the unrighteous, the uncivilized before God. The bishop then spoke through his Bible:

> Knowing this, that the law is not made for a righteous man, but for the lawless and disobedient, for the ungodly and for sinners, for unholy and profane, for murderers of fathers and murderers of mothers, for manslayers,
>   For whoremongers, for them that defile themselves with mankind, for men stealers, for liars, for perjured persons, and if there be any other thing that is contrary to sound doctrine. (1 Timothy 1:9–10)

Reiterating the point, the bishop observed that it could not be the law that made a man civilized, for the law was there for those who were unrighteous. Education could not be the route to righteousness, for some who were educated were also criminals. The route could be only through God. And even though the righteous suffered for the Word, it was God's civilization that would triumph:

> Yea, and all that will live godly in Christ Jesus shall suffer persecution.
>   But evil men and seducers shall wax worse and worse, deceiving, and being deceived.
>   But continue thou in the things which thou hast learned and hast been assured of, knowing of whom thou hast learned them;
>   And that from a child thou hast known the holy scriptures, which are able to make thee wise unto salvation through faith which is in Christ Jesus.
>   All scripture is given by inspiration of God, and is profitable for doctrine, for reproof, for correction, for instruction in righteousness:
>   That the man of God may be perfect, thoroughly furnished unto all good works. (2 Timothy 3:12–17)

The bishop's deployment of the scriptures here, in conjunction with his observations on civilization, made the "lawless and disobedient," "evil men and seducers" gaps that the saints filled in by reference to their own Jamaican hierarchy. The people who were these things were also the people who believed that civilization was realized in material prosperity and education. It was in the face of these "middle-class" views that the saints received the bishop's "instruction" that they might be "perfect, thoroughly furnished unto all good works." He repeated that above all others, it was saints who knew that being Spirit-filled made a person civilized. This was the only form of civilization that could possibly work in Jamaica. It was the only "manners" that could really change a people. This time, the bishop spoke against the common middle-class charge that lower-class people have no manners. He proclaimed that manners come from God, as do life and victory:

> Be not deceived: evil communications corrupt good manners.[12]
> Awake to righteousness, and sin not; for some have not the knowledge of God: I speak this to your shame. (1 Corinthians 15:33–34)
> For this corruptible must put on incorruption, and this mortal must put on immortality.
> So when this corruptible shall have put on incorruption, and this mortal shall have put on immortality, then shall be brought to pass the saying that is written, Death is swallowed up in victory.
> O death, where is thy sting? O grave, where is thy victory?
> The sting of death is sin; and the strength of sin is the law.
> But thanks be to God, which giveth us the victory through our Lord Jesus Christ. (1 Corinthians 15:54–57)

This message of victory over the oppressive claims of the Jamaican un-Godly, also people of superior status, was met with enthusiasm by the saints. The bishop was interrupted by a loud outburst of Spirit possession, as some saints were thrown, rejoicing, to the floor. Others paraded, dancing, up and down the central aisle, some speaking in tongues and all waving their arms in the air. The bishop seemed to relax and turned now to face the congregation squarely and give them the full fury of his message. He warmed to their enthusiasm and engaged them in the language of their everyday lives.

Only those who have been baptized, the bishop continued, could follow the path of righteousness. Anyone else was a "fallen angel," one of the "living-dead," an "obeahman," or else a poor "fool" possessed by devils. Very few people could be trusted to preach the proper path. Therefore, saints needed to take care to whom they listened. This was so especially with foreigners who came to Jamaica or preached on the television. If one looked carefully at television, one would see that women in American churches did not wear hats. They put on lipstick and curled their hair. They wore maxi-skirts sweeping the dirt. These people were "devils" still, and the men who preached to them were devils. When these men came to Jamaica, they were the "living-dead" preaching to the living. And why would the living wish to listen to the dead? No woman saint, he observed, would wish to join a community of devils. "African woman nu need te lipstick." The preacher then exclaimed, "Anyone tell yu different, mus' be obeahman yu listen te." The bishop thereby claimed for his saints a superior status not only in relation to Jamaicans but also in relation to the more affluent and white Pentecostals whom Jamaicans see on their television screens. He both racialized and gendered relations between communities of saints. Having positioned the congregation, the bishop addressed its own concerns.

To follow in the path of God, the bishop proposed, means that there can be no "sweetheart life." And here, from addressing the saints as "righteous men," the preacher turned to address the women. He exclaimed: "Thou shalt not commit adultery" (Exodus 20:14). Moreover, he observed that all God's women should cover themselves:

> But I would have you know, that the head of every man is Christ; and the head of the woman is the man; and the head of Christ is God.
>
> Every man praying or prophesying having his head covered, dishonoreth his head.
>
> But every woman that prayeth or prophesyeth with her head uncovered dishonoreth her head: . . .
>
> For if the woman be not covered, let her also be shorn. (1 Corinthians 11:3–6)

Women, he continued, must wear "the hat" to church and live every day the life of the "bride." It was only thus that the church would be sustained:

> Who shall change our vile body, that it may be fashioned like unto his glorious body, according to the working whereby he is able to subdue all things unto himself. (Philippians 3:21)
>
> For this is the will of God, even your sanctification, that ye should abstain from fornication:
>
> That every one of you should know how to possess his vessel in sanctification and honor;
>
> Not in the lust of concupiscence, even as the Gentiles which know not God. (1 Thessalonians 4:3–5)

In proposing that the women should assimilate their bodies to God's, the bishop also interposed himself as an embodied man of God. His power to subdue desire was offered as a model for the women. He thereby confidently instructed women in a task he saw as especially theirs.

The preacher's uncompromising challenge to the saints brought a hush to the church. His voice had risen to an extraordinary pitch as he now stood facing the saints with his body leaning over the microphone. He modified his delivery again and observed that if the demand seemed hard, the saints must think of what that demand would save: "The living saint mus' ne' fear gonorrhoea; no saint mus' worry she catchin' AIDS." Having made women the site of the ravages of the devil, he deployed repetition and gapping to impress the necessary course on women: "Marriage is honorable in all, and the bed is undefiled" (Hebrews 13:4). But:

> [If] the tokens of virginity be not found for the damsel:
>
> Then they shall bring out the damsel to the door of her father's house, and the men of the city shall stone her with stones that she die: because she hath wrought folly in Israel, to play the whore in her father's house. (Deuteronomy 22:20–21)

The bishop then observed that the woman's body is the sanctuary of Christ and must be kept clean. Saints followed Christ so that "ye may put difference between holy and unholy, and between clean and unclean" (Leviticus 10:10) The bishop then addressed all the saints again with a statement that the body must be kept clean and could be kept clean only while saints were prepared to put aside the life of the whoremonger:

> But fornication, and all uncleanness, or covetousness, let it not be once named among you, as becometh saints;
>   Neither filthiness, nor foolish talking, nor jesting, which are not convenient; but rather giving of thanks.
>   For this ye know, that no whoremonger, nor unclean person, nor covetous man, who is an idolater, hath any inheritance in the Kingdom of Christ and of God. (Ephesians 5:3-5)

The bishop moved quickly to underline that it was still the women who concerned him most: "Woman, yu listen to de word of de Lord":

> For true and righteous are his judgments: for he hath judged the great whore, which did corrupt the earth with her fornication, and hath avenged the blood of his servants at her hand.
>   And again they said, Alleluia. And her smoke rose up for ever and ever. (Revelation 19:2-3)

The saints themselves endorsed the words, as many expressed the need to listen to the Word of God: "Thus saith de Lord," "Follow him in truth and righteousness," "His word comes in being and in truth." The bishop pressed his advantage as he sensed a strong consensus from the saints: "Mos' people don' like it an' wa'an trouble te do it. Dem t'inking money, position, and make ev'ert'ing soft, soft, so big congregat'un come collect plenty money, build big concrete block church. Fly te America." But all these churches, the bishop argued, are "devil churches": "Ev'ry person in dem, open 'imself to the devil." Even a prominent Pentecostal bishop in Kingston, proposed the exhorter, naming the pastor, was clearly not a real Christian. "No way," he said, would an "obeahman" like that pastor preach in this holy, Spirit-filled church. The bishop turned aside to other officers on the dais and expressed his view again that the prominent Kingston pastor was probably an obeahman. The preacher then observed, "In him church some women have no hat on; dem raise de arm an' do a little wave; wave an' tink dat save them." Here the bishop referred to the restrained modes of Spirit possession that are common in some more respectable churches that are also churches that do not "preach sin."

He concluded with the final observation that no -one could believe that he or she was saved except through baptism in Jesus' name. Everything else was sin and damnation everywhere in the world. The saints should understand that they, too, would be damned unless they made themselves right with

Jesus and right with the bishop of their church. Civilization was theirs if they
followed the Word of God. Otherwise, the saints would be like Jamaica's
fallen and indeed all the Godless fallen of the city of Rome:

> Being filled with all unrighteousness, fornication, wickedness, covetous-
> ness, maliciousness; full of envy, murder, debate, deceit, malignancy;
> whisperers,
> > Backbiters, haters of God, despiteful, proud, boasters, inventors of evil
> things, disobedient to parents,
> > Without understanding, covenant breakers, without natural affection,
> implacable, unmerciful:
> > Who knowing the judgment of God, that they which commit such things
> are worthy of death, not only do the same, but have pleasure in them that
> do them. (Romans 1:29–32)

The exhortation was received with enthusiastic approval and followed with
a round of choruses and united vocal prayer that closed the celebration.
There being no altar call that night, many saints, particularly the women,
rushed forward to greet and praise the visiting bishop. It was the moment of
jubilant affirmation of faith that saints had desired to confirm and expand
their own tributes to the elderly bishop. The exhortation was a fine example
of "preaching sin" in which the women, though given the central duty of
chastity on behalf of their male counterparts, were nevertheless lifted up in
moral and spiritual celebration beyond the domain of more wealthy Jamaicans, and even beyond the domain of their American counterparts.

That the bishop, in his exhortation, assessed the moral standing of others
through the persona of their women was unremarkable for these saints. His
injunction to avoid higher-status pastors and their churches, which were also
"devil" churches, reflected a pastoral care in this milieu. His combination of
"sweet" or "good" talk, the only genre for women pastors, and also "broad
talk" or "nation language," was a special delight to these women. Its implicit
mixing and reversing of statuses—the broad talk spoken as an aside but used
to comment on respectable views, and the good talk used for Bible citation—
evoked the very inversions of status in which Pentecostal rite is involved.[13]
The embodied spiritual power of the bishop deployed on behalf of his en-
feebled brother was therefore remembered later in the church with gratitude and great affection.

I had come to the church on the advice of friends in Kingston and through
a fortuitous meeting with a "bus boy" at a local hotel who had asked me if I
had come to Mandeville as a missionary. Over time, I befriended the young
man's mother, a woman of thirty-one years, who had only casual domestic
employment in Mandeville. From a poor rural family on the border of Manchester and Clarendon parishes, she had come to Mandeville as a live-in
domestic at the age of fourteen. She had left that position a year later, on the
occasion of her first pregnancy. She since had had a series of domestic posi-

tions of varying durations. Her life was hard, but she was supported in some degree by an aunt, her mother's sister. The aunt came to market in Mandeville and regularly brought a modest supply of provisions from the young woman's family in the country. The food was generally brought home by the son, who also worked assiduously for tips to supplement the household income. The woman's son was her first child by a man who had soon left her. She had two daughters by another man who had worked for a while in Mandeville but had now returned to his family settled comfortably in Kingston. He occasionally sent money, but the first "baby father" sent none at all. The woman lived in a tiny wattle and daub house roofed with corrugated iron. It was perched precariously on the side of a hill. The house had neither water nor electricity. One room was used for eating and living, the other for sleeping. Newspapers covered the holes where the walls had caved in.

The woman had been saved two years previously, and her two older children had followed her soon after. The son said that he studied his Bible, even at work, so that one day he might become a deacon. The younger daughter did not go to church. She had sickle-cell anemia and was too weak to move from her tattered couch. The mother showed me photographs of herself before she was saved. She indicated that she wore earrings then, which she called an adornment "of the devil." Her divestment of jewelry, cosmetics, and other adornments has been a sign of the "hidden" change within that made her into a saint. She had exchanged the "sweetheart life," which had proved untenable in the midst of migration and fragmenting kinship networks, for a framework of communal living presided over by her bishop.

This acceptance of a patriarchal spiritual comfort does not leave women merely abject. Their embodied practice of rite is often the dominant experience of a church, and women saints often prevail in the constitution of communities based in neighborhood locales (see chapter 9, below). Yet the process of preaching sin, of feminizing moral disorder, has become a cultural implicit among many Pentecostal believers. In small churches, such as the Pentecostal Spirit-Filled Church, women experience a genuine patriarchy that requires of them a humility before men, as it offers them an alternative community. And even in the larger churches, the notion of women as promiscuous like men but also as responsible for moral renewal gives constant plausibility to male exhortations. This plausibility is based not only in the patriarchy of the Bible but also in Jamaican mythic themes that, juxtaposing brides to the Babylon of slavery, make reference to concubinage and socioracial hierarchy.

From Bride to Babylon and Back

In his account of the culture of race in middle-class Kingston, Alexander (1977) wrote of the "origin myth" that informed middle-class notions of race:

> Informants believe that the middle class originated in the nonlegal union
> of a white male master and a black female slave that produced an illegiti-
> mate brown offspring midway in status between slave and master. This
> belief is clearly expressed in the genealogies of those informants who see
> themselves as of middle-class origins; they trace their genealogies back to
> a white male master, black female slave, and mulatto or brown offspring.
> (Alexander 1977, 431)

Elsewhere, I have written of this myth as it is seen through the eyes of lower-
class women (Austin 1979). From their social position, the myth records a
history that has placed both men and women, paradigmatically women and
their children, "outside" respectable society. They are the dark-skinned illegitimate offspring of a larger socioracial order. In the account that I recorded, the woman identified both her family and herself as distanced from
power and status and also from cultural legitimacy. The perception of these
and other lower-class people was not that concubinage meant social mobility
but rather that it was a concomitant of illegitimacy and lower-class life. Concubinage is, in fact, most common among status equals in the lower class
rather than between status unequals (cf. Smith 1987, 188). Nonetheless,
from a lower-class point of view, and especially from a male view, it has been
hierarchical relations that conferred this condition on the lower class, and
this conferral came through women (cf. Patterson 1967, 108). The play of
meaning in the word "*concubinage*" is instructive in itself, a relation involving
men and women but a status that is feminine. Conjoined with a reference to
the slavery past, discussions of concubinage focus on the role of women in
introducing this particular status into Jamaican life.

Just as the biblical myth of the Fall, with its feminization of sin, seems to
inform Jamaican myth, so this Jamaican origin myth seems to inform Pentecostal exhortation. Notions of "the whore," "the whore of Babylon," "concubinage," and "the knock-about virgins" descended from "slaves" refer to a
present identity but one that is referenced to a mythic past. In conjunction
with the patriarchy of the Bible, these descriptions give a special status to
women as mediators of hierarchy, even when now, and in the past, they have
been involved mainly in intraclass unions.

Three examples of this myth form follow, statements made to me by men
who, although not Pentecostals, resided in their neighborhood milieus.

> *Version I:* You see, in the old colonial days, the serfs then, as the slaves
> were, enjoyed no benefits, no social recognition. They were just there for
> work, what they could produce. Well, as time went on, this gradually
> change. The slave master went to look a woman among the slaves. A child
> was born to that woman, the father being a slave master. Now, that child
> wasn't treated exactly like a slave. There was a little bit of human feeling
> there, so that you find that as time went on the institution [of slavery]
> change slightly. As a matter of fact, education really start in Jamaica, not

for Jamaicans [but] for the children of the white slave masters. The idea
was that these children would at least be ahead, way above the children of
the slaves. . . . So you find these children never really went to school [for a
long time], but they weren't really bullocks as the slaves were. So all that
really go along with the concept of how exactly the different classes come
about; the elite, you could call it. That woman, the slave woman I'm talking about now, she was trying to do better, but she really create a difficult
situation there.

A second version carries the impact of the initial encounter into the period
of Crown Colony rule.

> Version II: Well, I can only say from what I have actually read and heard
> from the pages of history, and from older people, that it [shade prejudice]
> had its origin in the time of slavery, when black people had to be continu-
> ously subservient to the white people [and] with the sex involvement of the
> white masters with the black slaves, the women. That brought about a gen-
> eration of people that was not of the original black and they weren't exactly
> white. They have something of a mulatto complexion, because they could
> be usually distinguished from their darker brothers or sisters. They were
> influenced, definitely, that if the whites are the fathers of these children
> and he is the master of the slaves, then the offspring should not be far
> away from him and much better than those who are the slaves themselves.
> And that seems to have taken root into the minds and soul of a lot of the
> offsprings.
>   And this, really, you know, with the English colonialists, it served their
> purpose. It served their purpose, because if I can remember a slogan that
> was used, the psychology of the British was "divide and rule," and the divi-
> sion is through the medium of the person who is the mulatto. They could
> be the whipping boy, or they could be the one in charge, the one left in
> charge of the people, the masses, the slaves who are actually doing the
> hard labor and the hard work and the dirty work, and has to wash himself
> in filth and what have you, while the mulatto, he is given priority treat-
> ment, not in equity with the white, but he is given treatment that excludes
> him entirely from the slime and slut of slavery itself.

In both these accounts, the black woman is crucial as the origin of a division
of rank among the slaves. She is the route through which the masters could
pursue a policy of "divide and rule." Moreover, that initial breaking of ranks,
in imagination and the making of myth, is associated directly with the hierarchy of twentieth-century society. As another man made clear in a further
brief comment, this issue became focused between black and brown as whites
themselves became increasingly peripheral to the society.

> Version III: But then it is not so much the white who the tyrannies were
> against. It's the mulatto who the black feel, we all feel, well, we are all
> black people and feel it is a deep prejudice why the white people would

take the mulatto and don' take the black because of color. And that is because of that black woman. She really create the brown-man class.

This origin myth, with its gender ambivalence, also comes in a more diffuse
form as a myth of social reproduction.

In 1986, a leading Jamaican educationist, Errol Miller, presented the In-
augural Aubrey Phillips Lecture. The lecture is an annual event in memory
of one of Jamaica's most distinguished educational psychologists. Miller's
topic was "Marginalization of the Black Male: Insights from the Development of the Teaching Profession." The substance of the lecture concerned
changing Crown Colony policy toward teacher training in the elementary
system. In the years following the Education Law of 1892, which made the
colonial government responsible for recurrent school funding, various measures were taken that had the end result of feminizing the elementary teaching profession. By the turn of the century, three of the four colleges that still
trained teachers recruited only women. This development had come in the
wake of male migration to Central America and the formation, in 1894, of a
quietly militant Jamaica Union of Teachers (JUT). The membership of the
JUT was, at the time, significantly male. Miller, quoting H. D. Golbourne,
argued as follows:

> the move to make elementary school teaching a feminine occupation "is
> suggestive of a deliberate attempt to keep salaries down, [and] release men
> for agricultural work since agricultural labour was perceived by the less en-
> lightened planters . . . as one of the crucial problems of the period. An-
> other reason for such action may also have been to undermine the mili-
> tancy of a political occupation." (Miller 1986, 60)

These moves came, Miller argued, in the wake of an economic downturn
at the end of the century and a political climate characterized by a loss of
impetus on the part of the older mission churches as they withdrew from
primary education (67–68). The political vacuum left by the churches, which
the JUT aspired to fill, was one the government would seek to sustain by
populating the teaching profession with ostensibly apolitical women. Miller
also remarked that a contemporary outcome of this process has been a society wherein male youth among the poor are encouraged to see themselves
as marginal. Women, he observed, are prominent in religion, constitute the
majority of household heads, and now control the socialization of the young
through the elementary schools. One outcome of this situation is that boys
perform less well than girls in the important scholarship examinations that
admit children to Jamaica's high schools.

Miller's argument concerning the institutional re-organization of teacher
training is a plausible and interesting proposal. It seems very likely that a
conjunction of events biased the recruitment of trainee teachers in the early

years of the century and that this new feminine bias was seen to act in the planters' interest. Yet Miller's argument is also more ambitious. He has not proposed simply an interpretation of teacher training at a particular point in history but rather a much more general rendering of institutional history in which, once again, it is the liaison between black women and white men that becomes the focus of attention. Miller's argument is best stated in his own words:

> The restrictions placed on the number of black men that are permitted up-ward mobility benefits the black woman since by definition the amount of opportunity open to blacks exceeds the number of black men coopted, thus she has more opportunity and greater access to mobility. . . . This has the effect of giving the impression of the liberation of the black woman. In addition, her greater mobility is a means by which the ruling minority can defend themselves of the charge of racism. It is also a useful means of neu-tralising potential rebellion on the part of the black man. It suggests that the black man's failure to rise socioeconomically is his own fault. More importantly also, it establishes an alliance between the black woman and the ruling [white] minority. . . . This alliance creates division in the ranks of the blacks and frustrates unity and mobilization to resist and oppose exploitation. (5–6)

Miller acknowledges that women very seldom achieve real power in more prominent areas of society. Nonetheless, his account suggests that black women have allowed themselves to be used by the colonial authorities and possibly have conspired with those authorities in the marginalization of males. Notwithstanding the pertinence of his substantive argument, Miller's more general thesis reveals itself as a variation on the Jamaican mythologi-cal theme of the black woman as the instigator of difference among black Jamaicans.

In the midst of this Jamaican discourse, biblical assertions on the status of women have taken on an additional resonance. The engendering of morality that occurs in the Western tradition as it is mediated by the Hebrews and Greeks has overlain the Jamaican milieu. In the story of the Fall, two types of knowledge were forbidden to Adam and Eve. One was a self-discriminating moral knowledge, the knowledge that proposed humans rather than God as the arbiter of good and evil. The other was the knowledge of sexuality that would make Adam and Eve aware that "they were naked," aware of shame. In her discussion of biblical patriarchy, Gerda Lerner argues that the reprisal for the acquisition of this second form of knowledge fell unevenly on the woman, who was made to forfeit control of her own sexuality. In Lerner's words, "Creativity is reserved to God; procreativity of human beings be-comes the lot of women. The curse on Eve makes of it a painful and sub-ordinate lot" (1986, 197). Yet in the act of procreation, men and women retain a slender grip on creation. In the succeeding generations, they can see their own humanity perpetually reproduced as woman and man labor in their own particular ways. Lerner writes:

> Here is the redemptive aspect of the Biblical doctrine of the division of labor between the sexes: not only shall man work in the sweat of his brow and woman give birth in pain, but mortal men and women depend on the redemptive, life-giving function of the mother for the only immortality they shall ever experience. (197)

But what of the Jamaican mother involved in miscegenation, who became the bridge for a succeeding generation to repudiate the laboring creativity of the fathers? What of African men confronting their lack of control over the destiny of their sisters, women no longer their source of status and alliance but rather used to forge alliances against them? The Jamaican origin myth, in locating the source of color class division, also locates a source of black male efficacy challenged. The significance of "Babylon" and the "whore of Babylon" in the creole religious discourse rests on the construction of this historical experience. Sin seen as a dynamic of history and the feminization of sin mark the Bible's mediation of a Jamaican experience.

This concern with the re-ordering of black lower-class sexual relations, which was also, ironically, the concern of missionaries such as Phillippo, has been a central characteristic not only of Pentecostalism but also of Marcus Garvey's black separatism and of the Rastafarian movement. All have sought a subordination and privatization of women as an integral part of redemption, where the issue of the relations involved can be an intra- as much as an inter-class concern (cf. Austin-Broos 1987b). That Phillippo should share an orientation with the later religious movements is simply indicative of the integration of the myth of the Fall into Jamaican perceptions of being. The movements all have clear affiliations with a Christianity focused on the redemptive Savior and the pursuit of a new Jerusalem in which the agonies of Babylon will be overcome. The identification of women with hierarchy and with a historical fall articulates this influence in a specifically Jamaican milieu.

Garvey's black separatism conjoined a strong affiliation with Christian religion, in which the life of the Savior was seen as a model for African struggle, and an equally strong sense of the need to reconstruct Africans as a nation, both procreative and cultural. On this latter issue, Garvey observed in 1923:

> The abuse of our race was, up to eighty-five years ago in the West Indies and fifty-seven years ago in America, beyond our control, because we were then but chattel slaves of our masters; but since emancipation we have had full control of our own moral-social life and cannot, therefore, complain

against anyone other than ourselves, for any social and moral wrongs inflicted upon us.

The Universal Negro Improvement Association realizes that it is now our duty to socially and morally steady ourselves, hence our desire to bring about a united race with one moral code and principle. The types in our race should not be blameable to our generation, but to the abuse and advantage taken of us in the past; but that should not be a reason for us to further open ourselves to a continuation of this abuse and thereby wreck our racial pride and self-respect. (Garvey 1969, 55–56)

With this injunction to African people not to stratify their ranks through a misguided allegiance to the "color caste" system, Garvey would conjoin a strong sense of redemptive mission modeled on the life of the Savior (Garvey 1969, 62). Neither was Garvey a stranger to the Christian perfectionism current in America, which would constitute such a central element in Jamaican Pentecostalism (cf. Burkett 1978). The constitution of a "Negro" nation redeemed and moral before God also would involve following "the life of Christ, the spotless life, the holy life, the life without sin," and a life of African exclusiveness from the ranks of whites (Garvey 1969, 28).

These ideas, which appear to have been regional ideas of the 1920s and '30s, were the ones out of which were forged important dimensions of Jamaica's Pentecostal and Rastafarian movements. Both movements shared in common a strong male imperative not simply to control sexuality but to control the sexuality of women associated with the movement (cf. Chevannes 1994, 28–30, 256–60). This tenet was seen as a central Christian requirement and also the requirement of a people once enslaved and then made subordinate in a sociated order.[14]

Where Pentecostalism, because of its mainly mission origins, has emphasized acceptance of the social-racial order, Rastafarianism, in the spirit of Garvey, has emphasized black separatism. And integral to this separatism has been the promotion of patriarchal unions for women with men that bind them as firmly as marriage but without a specifically Christian rite (Barrett 1968; Cumper 1979; Austin-Broos 1987b). This distancing from Christianity nonetheless acknowledges its moral politics by creating "African queens" who cannot be "whores of Babylon" and who, in rural regions, "view the male as almost if not equal to Jah" (Chevannes 1994, 260). Especially for Rastafarian men, the movement promotes the experience of an existential transcendence as part of everyday life. The parallel with Pentecostal perfectionism is striking. Both movements have promoted the desire for separation from Babylon, understood to involve a moral degradation with its source in slavery. Both movements have also designated women as the major if unintentional agents of a historical "fall," who now should be re-positioned as a pre-condition of redemption.

Contrition induced through preaching sin is the passport to a eudemonic life steeped in perfectionism. Though women through their bodily inscriptions and their majority presence in the church move to own Pentecostal rite, the political dynamics of exhortation reveal a really experienced world in which the poetics and performance of male exhortation act to confer on women a particular moral burden. The feminization of sin often found in Pentecostal exhortation is sustained not merely in text and rite but also by the articulation of the Bible with Jamaica's socioracial hierarchy. The rhetoric of missionaries and others has condemned both lower-class men and women for their concubinage, and in the biblical language of "fornication," Pentecostalists continue this critique. The prominence that is given to women in these Pentecostal exhortations, however, suggests a further dimension of meaning: an intersection of the Bible's myth of the Fall with a Jamaican origin myth. In this intersection, the biblical myth becomes a vehicle for figuring a historical "fall" in which women are given a significance beyond their everyday circumstance. In effect, the burden of immoralist is moved from a culture or "race," and from a social class, to the persona of lower-class women in rites that sustain and also transpose a politics of moral order.

Despite the tenor of male exhortation, Pentecostal pastors are not simply moralists, and women in different moments of their lives as saints can endorse and subvert a patriarchal stance. Pentecostal practice also involves healing, change, and the birth of saints. Notwithstanding the moral politics of rite and its gender ambivalence, these are creative moments for the saints in which men and women both participate. Both seek to heal the sins that keep their fellows from a new life, from the "born again" experience.

9 Hierarchy, Healing, and the Birth of Brides

> For all their appeal to advocates of free love, and other so-
> cial reforms, the kinship systems of . . . the West Indian
> slave societies were rooted in the soil of hierarchy—not
> egalitarianism.
>
> —Raymond T. Smith, 1988

> If religious symbols are to be thought of as the patterns by
> which experience is organised, can we say much about
> that experience without considering how it comes to be
> formed?
>
> —Talal Asad, 1983

Terence Turner has defined myth as "an attempt to for-
mulate the essential properties of social experience in
terms of a series of 'generic events.'" These generic events can subsume and
render in a meaningful order the "particular relations" and "events" of history (Turner 1988, 252). In this formulation, Turner, like Alexander, takes
from Lévi-Strauss the idea that myth proposes categories that are universal
for a culture (cf. Alexander 1977, 432; and Lévi-Strauss 1963). Yet notions of
the Fall and fornication, as they are presented in "preaching sin," are also,
after Roland Barthes, "alibis" for a point of view. This view concerns a male,
mainly lower-class rendering of the "generic events" involved in the socioracial order. In this view, hierarchy is caused as much by the failures of
women as it is by the inequalities of men (Barthes 1973, 123; also see Ricouer
1986b). Preachers cast fornication, initially in the form of plantation concubinage, in the role of generic event that explains not only gender relations
but also a lower-class condition. And the ritual object of the Pentecostal pastor is thereby rendered not simply in terms of saving and sanctifying Jamaicans but also in terms of producing "brides": vessels rendered clean for the
Holy Ghost who, as spiritual representations for men, can circumvent a moralized order. Women, in turn, engage with this imagery, which can act as a
subordinating force but also offers them ritual power through embodied
transformation.[1]

Hierarchy, Dual Marriage, and Pentecostal Brides

This representation of a transcendental bride, produced through an act of mysterious rite and signified by morality, both mirrors and extends a major aspect of Jamaican practice. Raymond Smith (1987, 1988) has argued that a marriage system that included both concubinage and legal marriage was integral to slave plantation society. In this system, white men married white women of similar status while they sustained non-legal relations with women who were brown or black and judged to be of inferior station. The practice of marriage became appropriated as a sign of relatedness between status equals who were also superior in status to others. And this pattern was indicative not only of white and non-white relations but also of powerful male slaves and their spouses. As Smith observes, "they might marry—either legally or according to some customary form . . .—but they would also have 'outside' unions, and those usually with women of lower status in the racial hierarchy" (Smith 1987, 177; cf. Higman 1976, 146–47). Non-white women of superior status, freed or enslaved, were the brown "outside" daughters of white men. The freed among these women often commanded significant property and personal liberties that gave them a special place in the hierarchy (Smith 1965b). Notwithstanding, they seldom would marry. They sustained concubinage relations with higher-status men, and possibly some secret liaisons with men of their own station or men who were black.[2] These women were reputed to prefer their non-legal relations with white men to offers of marriage from their brown male counterparts (Smith 1987, 180).

Black slave women within this system could look to non-legal relations with men of similar or somewhat higher status. They could seek through mating to mitigate their own position and move their children slightly up in the hierarchy. The position of the black woman become brown concubine, and placed more favorably than black and brown men who were denied access to lighter-skinned women, is the aspect of this larger system on which the male lower-class origin myth has focused. It is important to note that in this system, male power, nonetheless, had its own expressions: first, in securing a wife from other men; and, second, in demonstrating fecundity, and possibly sexual charisma, through having multiple women bear children for them (see also Austin 1979).

This system changed when, with emancipation and Crown Colony rule, "the creole white and coloured population began to converge" (Smith 1987, 183). Powerful positions in the society now were filled by expatriates from Britain who remained a relatively closed social group. Creole white and colored classes gradually conjoined in the "middle class" and continued to practice the dual marriage system. There also was emerging in the aftermath of the Morant Bay Rebellion a stratum of modestly prosperous Christian blacks, the inheritors of the free village system (Hall 1953; Paget n.d.; Mintz 1974a, 1974b; Austin-Broos 1992). These cultivators stood in marked contrast to the very poor and tenant farmers, and also to that portion of Jamaica's population that remained as mainly plantation workers. It was men from among these latter groups who would become migrant laborers overseas.

During this late-nineteenth-century period, "illegitimacy" emerged as a prominent issue. In this, Jamaicans from the middle class identified an aspect of the larger system as exclusively a problem for lower-class blacks (Smith 1987, 187–89). The phenomenon on which these critics focused was the fact that marriage and concubinage had become alternatives for the lower classes. This was taken to indicate a lower-class disorganization, immorality, and lack of education (cf. Austin 1979, 1983, 1984a). In this, middle-class women in particular overlooked the extra-marital relations of their spouses, often with women of a lower class, in order to focus on their status inferiors. Their view presented a counterpart to the view of Phillippo and Eyre, among others, concerning the particular immorality of Africans. The position of Jamaica's Christian blacks was and remained rather different. Like Bishop Nuttall, they saw illegitimacy as a problem spread throughout the system (Smith 1987, 186–87). And while they condemned fornication in their own class, they also condemned it in their status superiors.

Smith proposes that the lower-class alternatives decried by the middle class in fact continued to manifest the hierarchical relations of the dual marriage system: "the structure was compressed within the confines of the lower-class in such a way that a lower-class man could use any status factor, even masculinity itself, as the basis for insisting upon casual rather than a legally sanctioned union" (Smith 1987, 189). The major impact of this system is now felt by "the lower-class woman of limited means attempting to raise several children, forced to work if and when she can, and often passing through a series of unions" (188). These women, Smith proposes, are placed in this position both as a matter of practical necessity as they search for "an adequate provider" and through a certain construction of their being which pronounces that they, as the lowest rung in a socioracial and gender hierarchy, are women, generally black, who "cannot do better" (190–91, 169). This particular sense of being a black woman is underpinned by inequalities in men's and women's wages and the extremely high rates of unemployment that persist among lower-class women (Gordon 1987, 15–17; 1989, 75–77).

A distinguishing feature of Smith's account is his view that while legal and non-legal relations are alternatives for the lower classes, they nevertheless carry with them the social meanings of hierarchy, of superior and inferior, with which they have been invested by a distinctive history and culture. The marriage system as articulated through the classes is not the same as it was during slavery, but the general notion remains that marriage is appropriate to superior status equals, and concubinage to status unequals or inferiors.

The concerns of Pentecostal women and men are consistent with Smith's proposal that marriage and hierarchy are closely related. This hierarchical significance of marriage, however, derives not only from the eighteenth-century socioracial order but also from that hierarchy and its structural trans-formations in engagement with the transformations of the mission. Where marriage is concerned, its hierarchical significance is not only of a legal-social nature but also of a ritual-moral nature.

With the development of the missions and the free village system came a value hierarchy and forms of hegemony that in various limited but salient ways replaced the controls of the slavery period (Mintz 1974b; Austin-Broos 1992). For missionaries concerned to save followers from sin, marriage was a priority in constructing Christian blacks. Marriage saved the emancipated slaves from the condition of promiscuity. Missionaries also recognized the moral obligation of men to guard the "honor" of women, howsoever poor a man might be and certainly irrespective of his color. It therefore involved no contradiction for the missionaries to recommend marriage among Jamaicans who were poor and black. This ritual-moral view of marriage, which involved its own incipient hierarchy, confronted the established dual marriage system based on a system of legal hierarchy. The position of the missionaries' appeared to democratize marriage and therefore might be presumed to have been popular. Yet this position also intervened in certain expressions of power and freedom to which Jamaicans had become accustomed.

For men, power was realized both in securing a woman as a wife and in further demonstrations of fecundity. While only the fortunate among the black emancipated or men who had worked for most of their lives might feel able to take a wife, most men were able through alternative mating forms to express the power of their fecundity. The missionaries' marriage excluded this course, and from this exclusion has grown a Jamaican discourse on the desexualizing power of Christianity. This is reflected in various literary sources, including Claude McKay's portrayal of the theological student, Herald Newton, and the portrayal of the latent sexuality of Roger Mais's Christ-like Brother Man (McKay 1933; Mais 1966). Sometimes this is assumed to be a peculiarly European phenomenon. While I lived in the East Kingston area, I often heard a local expatriate Anglican clergyman referred to as a "picky-picky" man. His finicky nature was assumed to be associated with an imputed chastity. These Kingstonians' view of the clergyman matched McKay's portrayal of the Craig mission regime as redolent with sexual repression.

In the context of these cultural assumptions, men who identified with the church were men for whom the church's empowerment was real but different from fecundity. These men readily gave up "fornication" in order to assume position in the church based on a spiritual superiority, and marriage as a symbol of moral elevation was deployed to augment their modest position. For these men, the fidelity of their "wives" became an issue of central concern. In order that they should not be seen as "picky-picky" subjects of cuckoldry, it has always been important to control their women and sustain a male presence in the church.

Women involved in the dual marriage system would come to have a skeptical view of men, only some of whom could aid their positions. It was only a "good man," as Jamaican women say, who was really desirable as a marriage partner (Austin 1984a, 49). It was important for these women, nonetheless, to demonstrate their procreative ability, both in attracting men and as a sign of maturity (cf. MacCormack and Draper 1987; Sobo 1993, 179). The gender hierarchy of Jamaican occupations, which generally preserved the better jobs for men, still made a marriage partner a very desirable acquisition (Lobdell 1988). And this could be just one partner, for unlike many Jamaican men, women's sense of self has not required engagement with multiple partners. These factors have made the church's democratization of marriage more desirable to women than to men, a fact reflected in their generally greater attendance at church. And this feminization of church congregations has given scope to a proprietorial patriarchy among male pastors who are also married men.

Notwithstanding these different and gendered interpretations, mission teachings concerning marriage have transgressed aspirations of both men and women. The aesthetic of social relations promoted by the mission, a style of austere ethical rationalism, clashed, as McKay portrays, with a Jamaican eudemonic style that had become an integral part of life. This insertion of play in a laboring life was and undoubtedly is enjoyed by men and women irrespective of the power relations involved. So-called "alternative" mating patterns are not simply the product of hegemonic meanings but also result from skepticism concerning "the moral," a skepticism manifest in sexual play and in the "rudeness" of a trickster tradition.[3] This has meant that the status of marriage both in the initial socioracial hierarchy and in the teachings of the mission has always been viewed with ambivalence. Play itself has contested hierarchy, providing a different supersession from a spiritual transcendence with its moral signs. Hence the duality in Kingston today between aspirations to divinity and dance hall, and the appeal of Pentecostalism as it brings eudemonic into the church.

As the plantation system declined in the period after emancipation, the missions' democratization of marriage had its greatest impact in the brown middle class and among those more prosperous farmers, many of whom lived in the free church villages. Henriques has described a more contemporary family type that inherited the early mission tradition:

> The father usually has a regular job and a small cultivation which may be adjacent to the house, or up the "bush." He may be the sole wage earner unless the boys are old enough to be working. . . .
>
> The picture [of the cultivator] which emerges is reminiscent of the respectable Victorian working class family where the husband was a sober and steady person in regular employment. The atmosphere is markedly religious and the patriarchal attitude of the father is constantly reinforced by frequent reading of the Bible.
>
> The maintenance of this type of domestic group is in part governed by the regularity of the man's employment so that there is an economic stability in the family. His sexual needs are satisfied within marriage. If he does feel the temptation to be unfaithful, religion and the concept of respectability are liable to prevent him. To do so would be to betray his group and to place him with the undesirable element of his class. The strength of this feeling is considerable.
>
> Although a larger income is one of the factors which tend to produce monogamy it is only contributory, as there are many instances of better-off couples in the lower class who are not married. (Henriques 1968, 112)

Modest rural families of this type initially deployed the ritual-moral status of Christian marriage to make a claim for superior standing. They thereby set their face against a system whose implicit categories seemed to deny them marriage. This was the first democratization of marriage promoted by the original missionaries. Over time, however, the "literate devout churchgoers" they created, who were also often farmers of minor export crops, came to constitute a particular sector within the rural lower class (Smith 1987, 183). Many sons and daughters of this stratum acquired education and were socially mobile into the middle class (Eisner 1960, 315). And, like the family that Henriques describes, these people guarded their superior status against the "undesirable elements" of their class. They were clearly church members and not mere attenders in the distinction that *Banana Bottom's* Bita Plant describes (McKay 1933, 72).

In this process, the ritual-moral hierarchy of the mission and the socio-racial hierarchy began to converge. Both moral and legal-social views decreed that a man, in return for a faithful wife, should be able to supply an appropriate security. Following the Morant Bay Rebellion and the turn to conservatism in mission circles, the radicalism of mission marriage was lost. Mission churches would act to secure rather than undermine the colonial order. Yet the potential that lay in the Christian view of marriage, to disrupt Jamaica's moralized hierarchy, remained. It was always open to the poor and black to claim marriage as a definitive sign of superior ritual and moral worth in defiance of the meanings of color class. This became Pentecostalism's appeal in the third and fourth decades of the twentieth century. And as the movement has continued to expand, this appeal itself has been transformed. Pentecostalism has addressed at least three different groups that both resemble and diverge from the initial Christian blacks.

Pentecostalism's Contemporary Appeal

In the first instance, Pentecostalism appealed to religiously committed men and women unqualified and yet inclined to the pastorate who also wished to be marriage celebrants (see chapter 5, above). These individuals emerged from a milieu that was characterized not only by a division between the orthodox denominational churches and a creolized Zion Revival. It was also a milieu in which greater mobility in and out of the island, because of labor migration and the banana trade, had brought contact with various forms of revivalism and evangelism active both in North America and Britain. This context, which fostered expatriate evangelists such as Raglan Phillips, gave impetus to the aspirations of Alexander Bedward. He criticized Jamaica's status order but also aspired to recognition as a significant Christian evangelist. Where Bedward was thwarted and all but destroyed by the Crown Colony regime, the early Pentecostal evangelists sheltered under the support of American enthusiasm. Often unable to obtain the forms of qualification expected by the denominational churches, they turned for their accreditation elsewhere.

A second group consisted of poor farmers, possibly on the fringes of denominational practice, who would take up Pentecostalism as a statement of superior Christian status. These people lived in the more remote and smaller villages scattered around larger market towns. The latter are commonly populated by independent farmers growing for both home and export markets. Their towns have a health clinic, a school, and a post office and are serviced with paved roads, electricity, and a water supply. Such communities sustain a number of churches, and farmers belong to the national rural associations. Expansion of mining, tourism, and other industries has brought "an influx of white collar workers to these areas" (Foner 1973, 6). The poorer villages, often placed in proximity to these towns, are

> geographically isolated, often reached only by unpaved roads, and lack
> electricity, water-supply systems, health clinics, and post offices. Few out-
> siders move into such communities, since they are not considered desir-
> able places to live, and social relations within them are organized primarily
> around kinship and territorial ties. There are few associations and
> churches. Many who once lived in settlements of this type . . . [have]
> moved to more prosperous settlements. (Foner 1973, 5–6)

Claude McKay's "Banana Bottom" in its relation to the larger "Jubilee" is modeled on such smaller villages surrounding the market town of Chapelton in Clarendon parish. It was north of Chapelton in the hill villages that Pentecostalism had its first rural expansion. In towns like Borobridge, Johns Hall, James Hill, and Alston, some of which are accessible only by unpaved roads today, Pentecostalism put down its early roots among people some of whom still aspire to a prosperous rural life, one engaged with local associations and a church and based in a patriarchal family form. They are people for whom marriage is a mark of superior status, which they associate not only with ritual-moral imperatives but also with at least the hope of a modestly prosperous and respectable life (cf. Clarke 1966; Foner 1973, 74–75).

Yet these early Pentecostal sites were not simply isolated villages but villages experiencing population movement as the banana and, later, citrus industries in Clarendon provided limited economic expansion and better communications with Kingston. Similarly, members of the Pentecostal Spirit-Filled Church lying on the outskirts of Mandeville are people who have moved to Mandeville from smaller, generally northerly villages and towns over a period of two or three generations (cf. Wedenoja 1980). In the first four decades of this century, rural-to-urban migration in Jamaica had, as described above (chapters 1 and 5), a major feminine component as women moved out of agricultural employment and into forms of service work (Roberts 1957, 152–54; Lobdell 1988; Higman 1983). From the 1920s, this movement reflected over-population in the countryside as the diminution of external migration brought men back into the rural workforce and also bolstered a previously low birth rate (Roberts 1957, 158–64). Women moved both to Kingston-St. Andrew and to the larger market towns, and often this involved a movement away from the kinship networks of rural life, so that living, and mating, in urban areas became a more precarious affair. M. G. Smith proposes that in "comparison with settled peasant communities," these conditions promoted an increase in single-person and women-centered households and a decrease in the incidence of marriage (cf. Smith 1962, 242; 1966, xxiii–iv).

In the period following the Second World War, the circumstances of women would change again. While more than a third of women in the workforce were domestics in 1943, by 1984 this proportion of women had dropped to a mere 16 percent (Gordon 1989, 72). Women were mobile into the middle strata of various clerical positions and also into the "mass professions" of teaching and nursing in particular (Gordon 1987, 15–16; 1991). These occupational movements are indicative of a relative educational success for lower-class women in relation to lower-class men (cf. Miller 1986, 1990). Yet the situation of women is modified by the meager incomes of these occupations, the greater pressure on women to work, and the high unemployment rates they experience (Gordon 1989, 72, 75–77). At all points in the educational spectrum, men in the workforce receive greater returns for their education than women (Gordon 1989, 76). Moreover, the mobility of women, mainly structural mobility, means that they are almost twice as likely as men to find a position that is different from that of the women of their natal home (Gordon 1987, 17; 1989, 77–78).

Contemporary Pentecostalism's appeal to these women is the appeal of a religious movement that places them "on the victory side" in a situation where structural mobility also has brought displacement and individuation in their lives. Large Pentecostal congregations in Kingston recruit feminine personalities drawn from both the first and second moments of this mobility, and it is not uncommon to find mother-daughter combinations, both Pentecostals, that reflect these moments. Younger women, sometimes at the behest of a mother, seek to use the structuring power of the church in order to avoid an early pregnancy, while other women of an older generation come to "give it all over to Jesus" as they pass beyond their childbearing period and struggle to raise a number of children alone on the wage of a domestic, clerk, or shop assistant. These women do not accept that they "cannot do better," and they embrace Pentecostalism as a positive creed. Where the expectation has been that "the man . . . must ask," Pentecostalism situates women so that they can expect a father of their children to marry them (cf. Blake 1961, 134; and Smith 1987, 169). Husbands are often not at hand, however, or else they prove unreliable, and in these circumstances, women embrace the ritual celebration of a transcendental state: they are the purified brides of Christ who have Jesus as their Savior and friend. And by the example of their joyful lives, they also can hope to influence the men.

In a pamphlet distributed in a large Kingston church, heaven was described as a place in which "even men are holy" as well as women, as a place where men can be relied upon. Especially in Kingston, women sometimes introduce a critical element into their Pentecostal worship that contests a patriarchical construal of their being. More often, this alternative rendering of the world in terms of the phrase "vile man" is manifest not in criticism of men but rather in celebrations of feminine community which Pentecostal services often become. And in these forms of celebration, the constant appeals to Jesus as friend often sideline the person of the pastor. In churches that have a woman pastor, the effect is even more arresting.

Healing and Gendered Ritual Practice

Pentecostalism demonstrates the Jamaican cultural acceptance of sin as an explanation for misfortune and malaise. The gender tensions within Pentecostalism are tensions concerning the actual locus of the Christian's propensity to sin interpreted within a Jamaican milieu. The representation of sin as fornication embodies this search for the locus of sin. Observed from another vantage point, however, the Jamaican cultural acceptance of sin also reveals the historical transformation of West African notions of affliction and suffering. It is not only sickness but historical suffering that can be traced to the fact of sin and alleviated by sin's repudiation. Responsibility for human malaise thereby lies with individuals who serially bear the burden of sin. No accidental outcome of life's events, the evil that brings malaise is the product of a person's very being, as is every history of suffering. Benign and malign spiritual forces no longer reside beyond the person as inherent aspects of ambivalent life. Rather, they are stretched between the poles of God's transcendence and the immanence of man. In this Christian scheme, it is man's fallen state that confirms the inherent humanness of suffering. This "morality of being," as John Mbiti calls it, was first introduced to Jamaica by the missionaries of the slavery period (Mbiti 1969). It has been brought to fruition through a politics of moral order that has shaped a creole religious discourse. This discourse now includes Jamaica's Pentecostalism.

With this securing of sin in the cosmos has come a new interpretation of healing. The spiritual in-filling that creates a saint also creates a healed person who becomes a person of sound, healthy body and also a joyous being. Comaroff (1985, 210–11) has proposed that in Botswana, the suffering body is also a sign of the experience of a suffering society. Healing the body among the Tshidi is thereby healing their tortured social world. It is one of Pentecostalism's most interesting features that in the midst of modernity, it still renders cosmology as ontogeny and thereby inscribes moral order on the body. Jamaican Pentecostalism proposes that the cleansed and healed body is indicative of a union with Christ that inevitably re-orders the world of the saint. Yet when they cleanse and heal, Jamaican Pentecostals do not reconstitute their whole society but rather enter a heaven on earth sustained only in saintly practice (cf. Comaroff 1985, 227–28, 231; Asad 1983, 243–44). Their practice does not obviate suffering in a larger Jamaica but only the suffering of the saved. It is therefore imperative that saints evangelize the many unsaved and seek to heal them, too, through Christ.[4] Yet, once again, these healing transformations can bring divergent meanings stemming from masculine and feminine practice.

The male perspective is articulated mainly from the authority position of a pastor or elder and concerns the duty of all church members to make themselves "clean vessels" for the Lord. In this, Jamaica's Pentecostal men show a concern to sustain the virtue of their women that is not peculiar to them alone but integral to creole religion. Among the Pentecostals, however, the moral malaise of fallen women also is represented in a physical mode as forms of malady requiring exorcism. Both men and women exorcise. In fact, as one of the "signs that follow," this ability is potentially there for every saint.

It is principally among male pastors, however, that a mythology of exorcising women is deployed as an indication of special powers that sets them apart from other saints. Exorcism is a radical extension of the "laying on of hands," a mundane healing practice that occurs every Sunday in any Pentecostal church. The "laying on of hands," sometimes with oil, involves praying for a person who is ill or in pain, and transmitting through bodily touch one's own spiritual infusion to the person. The Spirit thereby cleanses the person, purifying body and soul, and dissolves the illness or relieves the pain. Exorcism is a magnified form of this practice that drives a manifest devil from a body that is generally perceived to be greatly disturbed (cf. Kapferer 1979a, 1979b; Csordas 1994, 25–56). Exorcism is the most dramatic act in which a pastor can be seen to heal a woman and thereby allow her to become a saint.

The maladies assumed to indicate an exorcism are generally psychological or gynecological. The former include cases of depression and mild schizophrenia and presumably other forms of evident psychosis. Temper tantrums and other even fairly minor variations in demeanor also can be placed in this class, however. The gynecological cases often involve menstrual flux over many months, acute and regular abdominal pains, and swollen bellies or "bad belly," often assumed to be peculiar pregnancies (cf. Sobo 1993, 286). Descriptions of the relevant cases of flux emphasize the viscous, clotted nature of the blood, its dark color, its evil smell, and the difficulties of dispensing with the substance. Flux can be a sign that a woman has become a breeding ground for devils, which slip out through the contaminated blood to become troublesome agents in the world. The cases of pain and swollen bellies are cured when women eject the cause: a worm, a serpent, or perhaps a snake, in each case understood as an embodiment of evil. This is the pastor's most dramatic expression of a patriarchal power over women that situates him in a central role beyond mere helpmeet to the saints. It presents a dramatic and more serious side of the persona identified in "Dear Pastor."[5]

A feminized engagement with healing is more likely to emerge in an urban setting, where a number of women, not necessarily related but living in adjoining yards, become mutually supporting sisters in a church. This group will include at least two and possibly three generations of women who assist each other in child minding and illness, keep a "partner" together, and occasionally help with marketing.[6] They will attend their church on a Sunday morning and possibly nightly twice a week for evangelism, tarrying, or women's prayer. Most will read their Bibles every day. Saints sustain not merely relations of "mutual dependency" but a relational life of holiness within a larger Kingston milieu (Austin 1984a, 41, 46–47). The moral order that saints create and their heavy reliance on the guidance of Jesus, as it is revealed through prayer and the Bible, give these lives a sense of completeness that is different from other neighborhood lives. The absolute grounding of a

Pentecostal faith is socially embodied in everyday being, made real through circumscribed social interaction within the bounds of a neighborhood.

In the words of Talal Asad, saints act to *create* their religion through "interpreting meanings," through "forbidding certain utterances and practices," and through "authorising others" as an integral part of their daily lives (1983, 242). The idea of "giving it all over to Jesus" is manifest in the neighborhood as becoming a part of a close network that assists with everyday domestic chores. The obverse of this situation is that the constant disciplines of behavior that mark off the Pentecostal world from other milieus of neighborhood life prove at times too restricting and alienate saints from a group. The frequent fissions in local Pentecostal churches are a product of this process. While members of the initial group define the splinter group as "fallen," the individual initiating the split often will represent it in terms of a doctrinal discrimination. The relevance of hand-washing to daily prayer, as an optional or required first step, was one such basis of a division I observed in a local church. The long process that is often involved in women becoming in-filled also may be sustained by an implicit perception that the community of saints can be a very closed one. Other saints, women and men, remain more oriented to their families and resist inclusion in a tightly-knit community. Still, a significant set of women are involved in these groups, and it is often from among them that deacons and evangelists are drawn.

This constitution of community is also a healing for Jamaican women. As they live their created moral order, they revel in a healed and healthy body (cf. Csordas 1994, 26). The power of the force that transformed this body is revealed by the saints in two different ways. One is in the constant and successful experience of "laying on of hands" for minor ills. Women frequently come to church with back pains and pains in joints and muscles. Very often, these pains indicate muscular or spinal strain from heavy work or the early onset of arthritic pain that often comes with repeated and prolonged cold-water laundering. Saints have headaches as well, some of which clearly come from stress. To this repertoire of pain that is integral to environment is added the cultural construction of pain as an obligatory manifestation of saints' need for the Lord. Feeling pain and requiring its cure are a manifestation of holiness that has not become arrogant and over-confident. The curing that comes to terminate pain is a major sign of saintly status, albeit in a human form. It signifies a physical body governed by the power of Spirit.

A healthy woman in Jamaica is also a woman who brings forth children. And one of the disciplines of being a saint is that only married women can procreate. Part of the health of saintly women and of the community of which they are a part involves the substitution of spiritual mentoring for the saints' physical procreation. Saints believe that through their vigorous evangelism, more and more Jamaicans will be reborn to populate their heaven on earth. In Kingston Pentecostal churches that sustain the larger women's congregations, these ideas produce a striking imagery of the church itself "birthing" new saints. Here the imagery of woman as vessel is transferred from the locus of individual saints to their community and congregation. Both in everyday life and in the practice of rite, the role of saints is to nurture and bring forth new souls for God. The healed Pentecostal saint is a woman without pain in her alternative community, who, through her Pentecostal congregation, produces saints who are born again.[7]

The practice that is dramatically individualized by the pastor in the act of exorcism is here made a collective practice in which the imagery is markedly feminine. These divergent meanings, once again, express the structural tension in the fact that although the pastor is a congregation leader, he is also simply another saint who faces a majority congregation of women. Spectacular exhortation and exorcism become the pastor's typical expression to assert his authority over other saints. Women saints, on the other hand, draw attention to their efficacy and numbers through ritual statements of community.[8] More inclined to witness than to exhort, they bring others to God through their fervent collective practice.

These divergent but not mutually exclusive worlds inform the practice of Pentecostal rite. In one aspect, women, as represented by their pastors, bear a heavy burden for sin. In another aspect of ritual practice, which is consonant with their everyday being, women act to make the holy state their own through the sheer intensity of their interactions both within and beyond the church. As they engage with their Savior and friend, often in the absence of effective male partners, women constitute an order in which men can become peripheralized. In both these masculine and feminine aspects, Pentecostalism is a healing cult in which Jamaicans are healed of sin and its suffering through the power of the Holy Ghost. Two different scenes from fieldwork show the conditions of truth that sustain these ritual meanings: healing and cleansing through exorcism, and the communal birth of saints.

Exorcism and Pastoral Practice

I resided for some time with Pastor Downes, who lived in the upper Clarendon town of Frankfield. He lived with his wife, a fellow evangelist, who was also trained as a primary schoolteacher. Pastor and Sister Downes had two children and two other relatives living with them. One was a young boy who was the son of a cousin of Sister Downes, the other the pastor's younger half-brother who had been involved in gang activity in Kingston. He had been in jail for a number of months before his mother sent him to stay with her elder son. The new arrival had been saved recently, but his commitment was questionable, and the pastor watched him with a cautious eye. Both these lads, like Sister Downes and her children, called the pastor "Sir" in the household.

"Alvin Downes" pastored two churches in his district, preaching at them on alternate Sundays. He also preached in the early afternoon for a missionary outreach group that met in the yard of one of his members. During the week, the pastor visited the other churches in his charge, often walking long distances. He kept fairly close associations with the three young pastors, each of whom led one of these churches, acting to assist them and guide them in their work. With two of these men, he was especially friendly. They sometimes visited during the evening and helped the pastor work on a small car that had been out of order for quite a long time. Once a month, Downes traveled to Kingston to return his district tithes and other takings. At this time, he would report to the island overseer or bishop on the spiritual and financial welfare of his district. When he returned from these visits, always in time for the Sunday services, he generally brought small presents for his children. Pastor Downes was in his late thirties, dark-skinned, cheerful, and a forceful preacher, who frequently accompanied hymns with his guitar. He was popular in his district and particularly solicitous of women saints, one of whom had donated land for a church. He was known to be able at healing and exorcism and often offered exhortations in the "preaching sin" style. His aspiration was to become a full-time evangelist for the church. Pastor Downes believed that if he were allowed to work freely in Kingston, he could "plant" at least four churches in a year. He found the "book-keeping" side of his work onerous and believed that his real contribution was spiritual.

Downes was a pastor for Jamaica's New Testament Church of God, which at the time (in 1986 and 1987) had 337 churches and 65,000 saved and sanctified members.[9] Many more Jamaicans attended its churches regularly on a Sunday morning. Within the church were a number of influential families, most of whom were second-generation Pentecostalists. Some of these families had close links with the United States. A past island overseer, for instance, left his permanent residence in Florida to return to be the Jamaican bishop. Others among this particular group had tertiary qualifications from the United States. Within this still fairly fluid organization, there was, nonetheless, a stratification evident at island-wide conventions and ministers' meetings. Depending on the families from which ministers were recruited and their backgrounds in rural or urban milieus, their courses and prospects in the church could vary. Alvin Downes stood not at the base of this Pentecostal hierarchy but rather in its middle reaches. The nature of his career and practice in this context demonstrates the manner in which men like Downes are both embedded in the themes of healing, fornication, and brides, and also stretching out to an institutionalized center linked to the power of America. The pastor recounted his own career, which I noted in the following form:

Pastor Downes began with the observation that his mother was not married to his father. She had had children by other men, and he had had children by other women. So the youth in his household was a half-brother only. His mother was a small-scale country higgler, and his father had been a "mechanic." He had grown up in a village in the parish of St. Mary and there attended all-age school. After his schooling was finished, he stayed on as a "monitor" to help the teacher. There was very little work in that part of the parish.

He was saved when he was seventeen years old, and after that event he acquired a job. He worked as an assistant in a dry goods shop, cleaning, lifting, carrying, and serving customers. He was paid seven dollars (Jamaican) a week in his first year, rising to fourteen dollars in his second year. He complained to his employer about his wage, but nothing was changed. He was offered employment in another shop, and when he started they paid him forty dollars a week. The money was better, but he had already received a calling to the ministry. He was a deacon in his local church, and he used the extra money to buy his guitar. He then asked the pastor if the church would assist him in his desire to attend Bethel Bible College [in Mandeville in Manchester parish,] where he could train as a Pentecostal minister. The pastor, however, said that there were no funds. The church was a very poor community.

God led Pastor Downes to "put pen to paper." He wrote to a great-uncle in Portland, whom he had never seen, and told him of his calling to the ministry. The uncle himself was a born-again Christian and agreed to fund Downes through Bible College.

At the college, Downes was "miserable." The food was particularly poor, and he missed the meals provided by his mother. He found the first-year classes difficult and then developed a stomach ulcer. He was spitting blood. He was very sick just before his first-year comprehensive exams. The exams were dreadful, and he did very poorly. He went home to St. Mary, assuming that that would be the end of his ministerial career. He consulted a doctor about his stomach ulcer, but the doctor's medicine did not help.

Finally, he prayed to the Father for direction, and the pain from the stomach ulcer went away. He did not experience any more bleeding. Soon after, he received a letter from the college saying that in spite of his poor results, they were prepared to allow him to return. From that time on, he had little trouble handling the course.

His first ministry was in Clarendon in a church that was very badly run down, with fewer than thirty members and very few tithes. Sometimes his income was only fourteen dollars a month, though the saints did give him gifts in kind. The church had only half a roof. There were no windows, and the floor was dirt. A large tree growing beside the church was cracking the walls with its roots. Gradually, he built up that church, though it was a very difficult experience. It was the Lord who really showed him the way.

He met his wife, "Shirley," on a visit to a pastor friend in St. Thomas parish, and they were married by the younger brother of the bishop of the time. Downes's church could not maintain a married couple, so headquarters moved him to Trelawney parish to pastor two churches there. Giving him this responsibility was also a way of testing him. His first child was born there, and after two years he was moved to Hanover parish.

In Hanover, he had three churches to pastor. It was during this period that he bought an old Land Rover. The roads were very bad over there, and he had to move about a lot. He also cultivated a vegetable garden with pumpkins, red peas, and even tomatoes. He was living in a very good yam area, and church members offered him plenty of yams. After he had been in Hanover for a time, friends said that he was being considered for a district pastor's job. He did not believe this was possible, but he said, "Let the will of God be done."

He was called to headquarters and offered his present position in Clarendon. He really found it very surprising and blessed the Lord for blessing him. He sold his Land Rover and bought a small sedan, but the car was a constant problem. He would prefer to live elsewhere in Jamaica, especially if he could become an evangelist in Kingston. Then, perhaps, he could travel overseas to America, and even to Australia. Everybody he met agreed that Jamaicans were the best evangelists.

Pastor Downes and his wife both came to the church from impoverished backgrounds. Their career together had included hardships. Yet the pastor had high status in his district, marked even within his household. On his trips to Kingston, he was careful to cultivate members of one of the families that is influential in the church. Concurrently, he was also careful to offer to his local congregations the healing and preaching that saints required.

I visited a village with Pastor Downes to attend a conference of the local church. High up in the northeast corner of Clarendon, we trudged along a winding road that took numerous sharp turns around hazardous corners. The village was spread out along the ridge of a hill with a number of small houses, some timber, some of wattle and daub, and also a few of concrete block, lined up along either side of the road. There were also a couple of barracks-like structures more common in cane-cutting districts. The road dwindled to a track past the village and crossed the mountains into St. Ann's parish. The little village was a mixed farming community with the emphasis on yam, banana, the root crop coco, and everywhere a few stands of sugar, sometimes with a cocoa tree or some ginger plants. Donkeys were in fairly common use, and for public transport, including transport to school and the nearest health clinic, villagers had to walk almost a mile to an intersection leading to a larger village. There they could catch a local bus. This particular Church of God was the only church in the immediate vicinity. The other church closest to the village was a Congregational church more than three miles away. The village had its own all-purpose shop stocked with tinned foods, flour and syrup, matches and cigarettes, various cleaning and household utensils, water crackers, biscuits, sweet buns, and a little cheese. The shop also doubled as a bar and sold aerated waters, beer, and small flasks of rum. The district pastor acted as an overseer for this and churches in the area. He not only supported the local pastors but also co-ordinated the collection of that portion of the tithes paid to the central organization. Whereas a part of the district pastor's income was paid by the central administration, local pastors were dependent on the support of their congregations.

The church, which had an old timber structure standing beside it with a bell suspended at its pinnacle, had not been completed and had a section at the back walled up with corrugated iron. A number of pews were arranged in two rows with a central aisle. They were turned to face a dais at the front on which stood items of furniture common not only in Pentecostal churches but also in Revival churches. There was a small table covered with a white lace cloth and on it a vase of artificial flowers. To one side was a modest pulpit covered by an old red velvet cloth fringed in gold. The only decorations in the church were a tapestry portrait of the Last Supper and a calendar with a colorful picture of Jesus of the Sacred Heart. As in the Watt Town Revival Church, large wooden hat pegs were nailed to the walls beside the doors to take the hats of male members.

The conference was akin to an annual general meeting and involved a discussion of church funds and past and future projects. The name of each member of the church was called by one of the male elders, who also called the total of tithes that each person had contributed to the church for the year. There were, at the time, sixty-one members listed for the church, and thirty-two were present for the conference. In addition to these sanctified saints, there were about thirty more people who attended as saved or unsaved sinners who had not yet received Holy Ghost in-filling. In this farming community, the conference was held on a Tuesday morning. Those with waged employment were unable to attend.

There was considerable concern on the district pastor's part that the congregation had been unable to complete its church. The meager tithe tallies told the story, particularly when it became apparent that those tithes were to pay the local pastor after almost 40 percent had been taken by the central organization to finance district and central administration, the district mission fund, a central radio program subscription, and a "feeding" program for student pastors. These payments had been quite bitterly discussed by an all-island pastors' gathering held in May Pen some time before. The major focus of the conference, however, was on a more immediate matter. The district pastor was there to chastise the saints for not supporting their pastor through tithes. The points of contention between the pastor and his saints were two. Although the young pastor was very firm on "right living," he did not "preach sin," and the saints did not feel that they were really "being preached." Two daughters of older saints had fallen in fornication, in this case resulting in pregnancies, and older saints felt disappointed with the pastor. The young ones required more "firmness," it was said, for "Pastor, him don' mek dem stay good."

One old man, concerned to explain the situation, introduced himself to me with his wife. I recognized him as the person who regularly arrived at the district pastor's house in Frankfield on a donkey bringing produce for the pastor's family. Along with other modest donations, these contributions could amount in a week to four full stems of green bananas, four or five large pieces of yam, and, in season, perhaps a couple of breadfruit, some avocado pears, and a small variety of citrus. The man's wife volunteered that when they were first saved and sanctified, they were living "the sweetheart life" and had subsequently married when her husband was "filled." She said that the church had been "full fire" then and that people all around had a very "warm" time. She had heard some of the early great Pentecostal preachers, and that had drawn her away from "the Methodist." She said that it had been hard to make her husband come to church, but he too had learned to "jump and dance," and the church had kept them "well and good." The old man said that he was happy in the church, because he knew that the devil blew "breezes" in the air that required the Holy Spirit for protection. To catch a "breeze," by which he meant a ghost or a duppy, could make a person sick or do "bad thing." This was why people needed to be "preached," to keep them safe from "devil power."

The second disagreement concerned the fact that some older members were expecting that when they died, their framed photographs would be hung in the church. Similar practices were evident not only in the Mandeville Spirit-Filled Church but also in the Revival Church at Watt Town. The young pastor had demurred and suggested that the practice was no longer appropriate in a "modern" church. Once again, older saints were disappointed. They believed that the influence of "old and righteous saints" was more than ever required in the church. Coming from their creole tradition, they did not share the young pastor's fear of a nascent ancestral iconography that echoed an African past.

During the airing of these grievances, the young pastor sat silent, looking at the ground. When the saints paused to hear a response, it was the district pastor who replied. He told the saints that their pastor was very young and that all they did was "keep malice" with him. They had failed to encourage him. He observed that their tithes were a duty to the Father and were not simply paid to their young pastor. To refuse the tithe payment was to break the Father's commandment. It was the Father's commandment, not the pastor's. Some of the saints looked rather disappointed. The district pastor was very popular, and perhaps they had expected another reaction. Later, the young pastor asked me for news from Kingston. He ruefully observed that he seldom had contact with the "outside" world. Yet he was hurt and saddened by his situation and resolved over lunch with the district pastor to try harder with his preaching to the congregation. He defended himself a little, however, when he observed that some of the women were not "trying" with their "daughter" when men were away on their cultivations or going "to meeting" in other towns. There was too much "friending about" at night, he said. All he could do was pray and preach both for the saints and for himself. The district pastor was sympathetic and proposed that he put more "fire" in his preaching. He privately observed, however, that if the young pastor could not "keep the saints holy," as overseer he would have to speak with the bishop in Kingston.

This was not the only congregation in which there was a tension between a local pastor and his saints. Yet the contrast in attitudes toward the local and the district pastor was marked. The district pastor was regarded warmly both by his own saints and by others in his district. Despite his youth, he was a fiery preacher who lit up the church with his guitar. He was ready to exorcise the sick and disturbed. He was known to keep evil at bay, to bring more people into the church, and to exorcise those who were troubled by the devil. It was therefore not surprising in the course of my stay that I should witness an exorcism.

The process involved a young country girl, probably about thirteen years old, who seemed to be emotionally disturbed. Although not saved, the girl attended church with her mother, who was a well-known saint in this region of the Clarendon hills. She was a plain girl who had been quiet and "mannerly" prior to an unfortunate experience. She had had a sexual encounter with an unknown assailant whom she still refused to name. Whether this was assault or seduction no-one had been able to discern. Now she ran about the country town, often with her blouse undone, and sometimes swore in a vehement way at people who happened to be passing by. The fury of her responses to her mother's inquiries had convinced the congregation that the unknown man must have filled the girl with devils. She was brought to the church on a Sunday morning to be exorcised. As the girl stood by her silent in the church, the mother told me they had been fasting for days. She prayed, she said, to her "dear Jesus Savior" that he might make her daughter well. The mother made the girl lie on the floor of the church, where she remained for the duration of the service. Occasionally, the girl muttered to herself and tried to meet her mother's eye. She was dressed in a soiled white blouse, short-sleeved and buttoned down the front, a short purple skirt, and worn black shoes minus the backs and the laces. Her curly black hair was plaited in tiny "pigtails" and matched the skinny arms and legs thrust out on the polished wooden floor. It had been a very lively morning, with a number of women speaking in tongues and both men and women dancing in the Spirit. At the altar call after the exhortation, the senior woman evangelist sent a young man with money to the local shop. He returned with a small parcel wrapped in newspaper, which he gave to the evangelist. As other deacons prayed with members of the congregation who had answered the altar call, the pastor and the evangelist devoted their attention to the girl.

The pastor knelt down beside the girl and placed his palms on either side of her head above her ears, with his fingers overlapping at the top. He pressed very hard on her head with both his palms and fingers and at the same time prayed aloud, saying, "Devil, we have come to cut and clear the sin away!" Both he and the evangelist, who was standing beside the two on the floor, then shouted in the direction of the girl, "Come out! Be gone, devil spirit!" The pastor said, "I can feel there is darkness and evil around you. Clear it away, Holy Jesus. Let her know you as the Savior!" The evangelist unwrapped the newspaper from a bottle of patent eucalyptus oil and knelt down beside the girl as the pastor stepped back. She poured oil liberally onto one hand and then rubbed it with the other. With both hands oiled, she then ran her hands firmly down the full length of the girl, telling her to be healed and let the darkness go. She turned the girl over on her back and rubbed the oil right over her face and into her hair, then moved to her arms and legs. The evangelist later directed me to Mark 6:13, where the disciples were said to have "cast out many devils, and anointed with oil many that were sick, and healed them."

The girl remained impassive in her physical movements, though her face showed resentment and possibly fear. Her hands were shaking slightly, but not in a fashion that saints would interpret as indicative of Spirit. She seemed frightened of the ministry, and some of the saints commented later that this was the working of the devil within her. Once more, the evangelist called to the evil inside the girl to come out. The pastor then took up the task again, kneeling beside the girl and running his hands from her neck down her arms. He said firmly but also quite gently in her ear, "If I cast out devils by the Spirit of God, then the Kingdom of God is come unto you." As he said these words, he lifted the girl to a sitting position and slapped her forcefully on the back. The girl's shaking suddenly stopped. She loosened herself from the pastor's grip, curled her body up, and began to weep in large, violent sobs. The praying of the saints had ebbed almost to a hush as they observed this miracle of healing. The girl shuddered all over her body and let out a screeching, anguished cry as her face screwed up and her mouth drew taught. Suddenly, the mother burst forward from the congregation, crying, "Praise God! Praise be to God!" As the pastor and the evangelist stepped back, the mother helped the girl to her feet and took her to sit beside her in the church. The pastor immediately struck up a chorus:

> It was Jesus, my Savior, who wrought this change in me,
> It was Jesus, my Savior, blest Lamb of Calvary,
> I came to him just as I was, from sin he set me free;
> It was Jesus, my Savior, who wrought this change in me!

The sermon preached by the pastor that morning had concerned the Pentecostal power to heal through Jesus Christ. The text had been from the Gospel of Mark–:

> And one of the multitude . . . said, Master, I have brought unto thee my son, which has a dumb spirit;
> And wheresoever he taketh him, he teareth him: and he foameth, and gnasheth with his teeth, and pineth away: and I spake to thy disciples that they would cast him out; and they could not.
> He answereth him, and saith, O faithless generation, how long shall I be with you? how long shall I suffer you? bring him unto me. . . .
> And he asked his father, How long is it ago since this came unto him? And he said, Of a child. . . .
> Jesus said unto him, If thou canst believe, all things are possible to him that believeth.
> And straightway the father of the child cried out, and said with tears, Lord, I believe; help thou mine unbelief.
> When Jesus saw that the people came running together, he rebuked the foul spirit, saying unto him, Thou dumb and deaf spirit, I charge thee, come out of him, and enter no more into him.
> And the spirit cried, and rent him sore, and came out of him. . . .
> And when he was come into the house, his disciples asked him privately, Why could not we cast him out?
> And he said unto them, This kind can come forth by nothing, but by prayer and fasting. (Mark 9:17–29)

The pastor had told the saints that everyone who is sick is sick in the heart and needs the healing power of Jesus, because every sickness, and not just the one shown by the "mad man," was in fact the work of the devil. He reminded saints that healing was a sign "that followed," though some had a "special gift" of healing which was a spiritual gift from the Holy Ghost. The pastor demonstrated that he had such a gift as he set matters right with the girl. The Bible passage on which he had based his exhortation both diagnosed and prescribed for her malaise in a way that made the process eminently biblical, as the ritual made the Bible real. The gapping of the biblical text was filled here not in imagination but in the very practice of the saints. The pastor himself was thereby elevated as a real practitioner blessed by God, a man engaged both in "preaching sin" and in healing through exorcism. He was a man who kept the congregation safe, and, sustaining the blessing of transformation, its members could lead a "proper" life. The expectations of the saints were given forceful voice in the evangelist. She was a powerful woman in the congregation, who had provided the land on which the church was built. It was she who instigated the exorcism and placed herself at the center of the rite. Dressed in white as a bride of Christ, she juxtaposed herself to the penitent. Yet, as evangelist, she deferred to the pastor to bring the rite to its fruition. His ability to realize the rite and sustain the community's moral being marked him as a successful pastor.

The reality of such an exorcism that heals a devil-induced disorder is captured not simply in its practice, however, but also in the mythology that surrounds it. In this myth, supposed sexual transgression is represented as the transformation of a woman's body into a vessel for a loathsome creature, frequently a snake or a lizard. This Jamaican imagery of exorcism calls on Jamaican trickster tales that represent the deceiving suitor as the Garden of Eden's serpent in disguise. The handsome prince turning into a snake on the wedding night is a familiar motif in tales akin to the Anansi type. The exorcism I witnessed in Clarendon was five years later described in this way. On a return visit to the Clarendon hills, I was reminded by some church members of the exorcism I had seen. It was said that after the girl was rubbed with oil and "prayed on" by the pastor, a snake had emerged from between her legs and slithered across the floor. Other like accounts are common in the Pentecostal world.

In another part of rural Jamaica, the bookstall at a major pastors' conference was replete with a number of exorcising manuals, and these were eagerly bought through the day. It was at this conference, as I toyed myself with an exorcising manual, that I was told of the following incident by a pastor who had recently moved from the country to Kingston. As he spoke, a small crowd gathered around. Both other pastors and their wives listened intently to his story:

> The pastor told me that he was, at the time, a newly appointed minister in St. Mary. His bishop had counseled him to stay fairly quiet because "tongue-speaking people" were still rare in the area. He was holding "missionary church" in the yard where he lived and being careful only to give a "little cry" even at the evangelical service. One day after Sunday service, a man came and spoke to him. He said that his wife had been pregnant for almost three years. No matter how she tried, or what the doctors did, she could not be delivered of the child. "She grow fat-fat, and she growl a lot," so that now she never went outside the house. She just lay about and was "miserable" to the man whenever he tried to help her. The man observed that the pastor was a "powerful praying man" and requested that he visit his wife.

At first, the pastor was reluctant and said that he was very busy in his immediate vicinity. But the man kept returning, and finally the pastor said to himself, "Lord, this mus' be your will." One day, the man came, and the pastor followed, and they walked for many hours to arrive at a house beside a cultivation. Even as the pastor approached the house, he could hear the groaning and mumbling inside. He felt a powerful force around the house and hissing whispers in some nearby trees. He knew that the power of Satan was about. The pastor told the man he should come inside with him. And when he entered the house, he saw the most horrible sight. The woman was lying on an old bedstead with only papers as a mattress. Her hair had grown long and knotty, and she was dressed in just a ragged "duster." Her belly was huge, and there was sweat on her face. She was crying, but at the same time there was a dreadful moan coming out of her. The pastor knew straight away that there were devils inside her. He walked to the woman's side and stood there for a moment. She seemed to "quiet" and began to say to him, "Please, sah, help." Just as she spoke, however, she began to moan, and terrible noises came from her body so that the pastor could not hear anymore.

He decided to act immediately and asked the husband to stand at the head of the bed and hold her down firmly by the shoulders. The pastor crouched down beside the woman and placed one hand on top of her belly and the other underneath her back. Then, as he pushed up under her back and began to push his other hand along her belly toward her legs, he shouted out with all his might, "I can do all things through Christ which strengtheneth me!" "Hold thy peace and come out!" (Phillipians 4:13; Mark 1:26). The pastor said he was immediately filled with the Holy Ghost and burst into the most glorious tongues. And as he spoke the tongues and felt the power through his own body, screams came from the woman's body, and she immediately began to give birth. Eventually, seven octopus-like creatures came out of the woman's belly. They were slimy and slippery and smelled "bad and evil." Their little "legs" waved about on the ground. When they were out, the woman's belly went flat, and she began to weep and weep. Both she and her husband praised the Lord, and the pastor knew that he had saved two souls that day. He sent the husband to gather newspaper and banana leaves. They wrapped up the "foul devil creature" and carried them a long way from the house. They were buried next to a path, not on the farmer's land.

News of the exorcism spread. Both a Methodist minister and a Roman Catholic priest came to tell the pastor that they had heard what he had done. The Methodist witnessed to the Lord and became a Pentecostalist. After that, the pastor said, he "free up" his services, and many people in the area were saved.[10]

The pastor did not care to speculate on how the woman had become devil-possessed. I suspected, however, that the seven octopi were very likely a reference to the seven devils that came out of Mary Magdalene (Luke 8:2).

When I asked, he affirmed that this was a case like Mary Magdalene's. The account was a potent representation of an empowered male who could render a vessel healed and clean. The pastor's story was also a statement of the view that powers must be demonstrated and not hidden "under a bushel." In this respect, the account was a mild rebuke of the bishop, who had told him to proceed with discretion. In the larger context of Pentecostal discourse, the story also communicated that, unlike doctors, obeahmen, or Revivalists, Pentecostals do not charge for healing. Yet the powers of healing that they possess are equal to the worst forces in Jamaica. In this account of the Holy Spirit's superior power to heal and cleanse, there is no doubt left that the affliction healed is the affliction of Christian sin. It is the evil that distorts the body's functions and can be combated only by an act of God that demands repentance on the part of the sinner.

The woman wept. The pastor's description was also the Pentecostal representation of contrition and the story in toto presented a fallen woman relieved from the effects of her sin by powerful men who were acting as the agents of the Father. In less dramatic forms, this is the complex of meanings acted out as male Pentecostal pastors address their congregations and lay their hands on suffering women in order to have them be born again.

A third example of exorcism comes in the form of a newspaper report concerning a notable Kingston Pentecostalist, Brother Herro Blair. Himself the son of a Pentecostal pastor, Blair, like a number of his male siblings, became a pastor in a Pentecostal church. Blair built his own organization in Kingston known as the Deliverance Center and developed a television ministry popular throughout the island. The report began:

> His bottles of medicine are labelled "faith" and must be taken in large doses. He charges no fee and asks no other commitment than the demonstration of that intangible but powerful something called faith. And his "patients" go their way rejoicing and singing his praises.
> They claim that through him incurables have been made whole. Cancer victims whom doctors gave up are reported to have been cured in a matter of days and growths have reportedly disappeared overnight.

The report then observed that a controversial healing by the pastor had brought him to "national attention" when it was discussed in a radio broadcast.

> A woman claimed she gave birth to a creature that looked somewhat like a snake after she sought the help of the preacher. Confessing to have developed a sick stomach and to have experienced agonising pain for years because of this, she said she found no relief even after she had had seven operations.
> Her name is Etta Reid. In a tape-recorded testimony a week before her deliverance, the 31-year-old woman told how her stomach showed signs of

mysterious bite-marks and how an insect sound which often times emanated from her, played havoc on her nerves. . . .

Last September, she said, she had another operation at the University Hospital. She said she was unconscious for three days but claimed that the people there "heard the roaring around of a beastly creature coming from her but they could not find out what was wrong."

The report related that Etta Reid had heard Brother Blair preaching on the radio.

That same night between one and two o'clock, she said, she hobbled to a phone booth and called Brother Blair. He prayed for her. She went back home and was able to use the toilet, something she had not done for three weeks.

She followed up her telephone conversation with a visit to the Deliverance Center.

The report recounts that Etta Reid began to feel better, and then one night there was a dramatic occurrence

Says Ms. Reid, "I started having pains like when you are going to have a child." It was then she went to the toilet and passed out what she said looked like a snake.

"It was yellow, white and black with scales like a fish. It was alive and it went into the toilet with a hissing, bubbling sound," she tells us. She raced to tell her husband the news. "He said he knew I was possessed by a demon. It was Satan or some demonic spirit." She ran to the phone booth afterwards to tell her pastor of the unusual birth.

Now Etta Reid says she is healed and strong. . . . Her experience has made her more desirous of serving God. . . .

With the "snake's" ignominious fall from grace, it did a disappearing act down the drain. And with it went the only bit of concrete proof. Many have taken her story with a grain of salt. . . . [Yet,] of some 200 calls Brother Blair received just after the testimony was aired, he said only one caller doubted the incident really took place.

Brother Blair sides with the believers. It is his view that hers was a "clear case of demon possession," the likes of which is found in Mark chapter 5 (the case of the Gadarene demoniac). Besides, the Reverend says, she looks years younger; the big jacket she usually wore to cover the bulge has since been discarded for a "nice little dress."

The report cited Blair as saying, "There are no strings attached to what I do. God is working. I am just His instrument. Everything I do is done before the people so that they can see." The article finished with this comment on Blair's other activities:

According to him the interest being shown [in the Deliverance Center] is "a direct result of what is being done for the community. We use the church as an employment center, finding jobs for the jobless and clothes for the needy, financing school fees for the children of poor parents and doing just about anything we can to fill the social gap."[11]

The pastors who assiduously "preach sin" also are recognized by Jamaican observers as trickster figures who play with the imaginative worlds of their saints in exorcisms. The report itself evokes the image of the obeahman dealing with malignant infestations and then distances Blair from this identity through reference to his social welfare work and his affirmation that his healing is unpaid. The account both gives credence to the pastor and hints at the naughtiness of the enterprise as the snake disappears "down the drain" and the woman ends up in a "nice little dress."

If Jamaica's history of Christianity is a history of affliction's transformation into sin, it is also an enduring saga of forms of suffering seeking release. That release has come in healing practices as various as divinations, balm-yard baths, dipping in a river, consecrated handkerchiefs, and the Pentecostal laying on of hands. And in this long and various history, practitioners of Christian rite have engaged the repertoire of folk healing rite, including the rite of the obeahman. The theater and the magic of the images of exorcism draw from this Jamaican trickster environment. Yet pastors ministering mainly to women confront not a generalized need for healing but the socially embodied experience of a people defined through a confrontation of cultures and in the midst of hierarchical relations. This particular historical experience has made women, marriage, and fornication matters of particular concern to men and to the women within the church who define themselves as the brides of Christ.

The images of Pentecostal exorcism focus on forms of feminine disorder related to the organs involved in procreation. Paradigmatically, the images propose that women have misused their bodies or else, through other forms of sin, have made these particular parts of their bodies vulnerable to spiritual and physical corruption. It is this malaise the pastor heals by claiming the sufferer for God and cleansing her body of polluting substance. In each of the three images of exorcism, the woman was held responsible, even in the case of the country girl whose experience was never entirely known. This Jamaican rendering of woman as Eve, as the person who, if not a deliberate transgressor, nonetheless is inevitably deceived, brings the practice of Pentecostalism into engagement with the origin myth and thereby with the hierarchy of Jamaica's dual marriage system. Exorcism leads to redemption/deliverance and to the creation of saints who are brides, realized in rites controlled by males who nimbly represent their God. In so doing, the Pentecostal pastor shores up his community of saints. He helps create a patriarchal order in which elders and evangelists of the church can know that their women are secured from sin. This status of a morally superior life, within the confines of the lower class, becomes a sanctified eudemonic in which the status of Pentecostal men is secured by the healing and cleansing of women.

Some of the pastors from this base then can strike out through their organization to link with American institutions. These links may come through the headquarters group of organizations such as the New Testament Church or through a more modest association with a church established in the United States, perhaps by migrants from a pastor's district. In either case, the pastor may come to distance himself from "wild" religion, but even more of Jamaica's pastors will remain in this healing milieu and make it the center of a saintly life.

Living Holy and Giving Birth to Brides

In the course of my Kingston fieldwork, I befriended some saints, one of whom was a short, stocky woman who lived very close to my own adopted yard. "Jenny Clarke" resided in a two-room apartment with her four children by two different men. The apartment was located in an East Kingston yard. She was a devout trinitarian Pentecostalist and attended an independent church in the area. She was forty-three years old at the time and had grown up in East Kingston, where her mother had worked as a seamstress until her eyes deteriorated. The mother lived nearby in a room and frequently had one of Jenny's children stay with her. The mother was sixty-eight years old and had come to Kingston from rural Westmoreland after a sojourn as a seamstress in Panama. She, too, was a devout Pentecostalist, though she went to church less often than Jenny. She had been married to a man who worked on the wharves, although he had died sometime previously. This man had come from Portland parish to Kingston, and his relatives mostly remained in that parish. Old Mrs. Clarke's' relatives were scattered in Westmoreland, St. James, and Kingston, and only one younger sister had regular contact with the East Kingston Clarkes.

Jenny Clarke had two brothers and a sister, as well as two half-sisters in Panama who grew up there with a paternal aunt. Jenny had never met her Panama sisters. One of her brothers also worked on the wharves and came occasionally to see his mother. Jenny explained that he did not like the Pentecostal church and very seldom visited her. The second brother worked as a watchman in a north coast tourist resort and had struck up contact with his father's kin. He came to Kingston at least once every couple of months and stayed with his elder brother. He enjoyed his visits to his sister and mother and, like his elder brother, helped his mother financially. Jenny's younger sister worked as a private secretary in a successful mercantile company. She had married and moved to St. Andrew, whence she seldom came to visit her mother and sister. She attended a church but was not born again. In Jenny's eyes, she was not a Christian.

Jenny worked at Kingston's central postal exchange as a sales clerk in customer service. She had worked there for a number of years and hoped to obtain a position as a supervisor soon. She said that her wage was very "mean," but nonetheless she felt fairly secure in the job. Her eldest child was a girl of seventeen years who had left school and was working part-time in the administrative section of an "uptown" bookstore. Three nights a week, the girl attended secretarial college. She was saved at the age of fifteen but had not yet been sanctified. The girl had won a scholarship to secondary high school. On a number of occasions, she had been socially embarrassed by her residential address and the class identity of her mother and father. Her engagement with the Pentecostal church gave her a secure social environment in which she could meet, so she observed, some "better" people who would value her "goodness." Jenny's three other children were boys ages thirteen, twelve, and eight. Two were attending an all-age school, and the eldest boy attended a secondary school. He had already been saved, had exceptional Bible knowledge, and wanted to become a deacon later on. The mother propelled all the children to church twice on Sundays and generally took them to prayer meetings as well. The daughter's father was socially distant and came occasionally with a gift for the girl. He lived in Passmore Town, where he had another family. The father of the three boys visited more regularly and was living not far away with another woman and the two children she had had for him. He worked in a mechanics yard in the West Kingston area. He was a personable man and drank regularly and played dominoes with friends in a small local bar. Jenny said that they had co-habited for five years. They separated when, as a sanctified saint, she could not persuade him to marry her. He had said that her praying made his "head hurt." He also had been quite a heavy drinker, Jenny said, and had entered his present relationship even before he and Jenny had parted. This combination of factors had led her to drive him from the apartment. As she recounted it, she did this berating him and also praying he would change his ways. He had been resentful and still quarreled with her but nonetheless gave money for his sons. Jenny said that she prayed for him constantly and hoped that one day Jesus would "show him the way."

Jenny's household lived a pristine life. She sometimes called on another saint to "help" her with laundering, but otherwise she and her daughter did the chores and tended her mother as well. Two boys slept in the room where the family ate. Jenny, her daughter, and the younger son slept in the other, smaller room. The family shared cooking, toilet, and bathing facilities with others living in the yard, though Jenny had her own small stove standing in the communal kitchen. To relieve the congestion in the apartment, one of the elder sons often went to stay with his grandmother. Jenny regularly cooked for her mother as well as for her children at home.

Jenny was a deaconess in her church. Her religious duties kept her very busy, especially in conjunction with her job. She was supported in the care of her children by her mother and also by two other saints who lived in her yard, one a married woman with her own children, and the other a young woman whom Jenny had saved, who boarded with an older couple also resident in the yard. Jenny was at church every Sunday morning and evening, attended a deacons' prayer group on Tuesday night, and sometimes went to tarry with the unsanctified on a Friday evening. Once a fortnight, her mother held a "cottage meeting" on a Thursday night which Jenny generally attended with her children. The two saints from her yard and one other saint who was struggling to convert her common-law husband also regularly attended this meeting. The sheer demands on her time, in addition to the church's financial demands, meant that Jenny's whole life was integrated into her saintly community. The pastor of her church was a small, wiry man especially adept at "preaching sin." Jenny respected him, but her affection was reserved for the tall, rather stately woman evangelist who was prominent in the Sunday night evangelical service. Jenny's proudest moment had been when the young woman from her yard was saved and sanctified under her guidance. She told me that she prayed constantly that the Holy Spirit would give her gifts of evangelism similar to this admired evangelist.

The small group of women saints who lived in and around Jenny's yard passed back and forth to church together at night. Although the neighborhood was relatively safe for most of its permanent residents, saints still worried that gunmen from the Wareika Hills nearby might suddenly emerge and threaten them.[12] Walking together in a group brought Jesus' protection into their midst. On these walks, as I became familiar with the saints and their church, I would discuss aspects of practice and belief. One night, I asked Jenny what it meant to be a saint. She explained that in her Church of God, they were all saints through spiritual grace, "holy ones and brides of Christ." She told me, as we walked through lanes that daily teemed with unemployed youth, and past a putrefying dog that had made the small lane smell for days, "You see, we are saints livin' here; livin' here in heaven on earth." And this displacement into a holy and mainly feminine domain was sustained not simply by exuberant rite but also by this network of saints which supported a daily round of practice.

This was a healing from an experience of urban "pressure" and meager means in the context of an individuation wrought by waves of urban migration. It made the lives of women like Jenny seem full and open to optimism. If, like Jenny, they experienced disappointment with men, this life filled in "the social gap" and gave women of modest means a superior status dressed in white. The intimacy of this healing community is revealed in the prayer meeting to which Jenny went at her mother's apartment every fortnight.

When I arrived at just after seven-thirty p.m., the meeting had already begun. A hymn was being sung. The meeting was held in the little house in which Mrs. Clarke had her apartment. It was one of the better rooms at the front. The room itself was furnished with a single bed, a cabinet in which there was crockery and glassware, a coffee table, and a number of chairs, including two rocking chairs. A dresser stood in one corner, and by the door leading to the back of the house there was a tall wooden stand, almost six feet high, with shelves on which a number of photographs perched. In addition to this furniture, two wooden school benches had been brought for the meeting, and six children, Jenny's and two others, were sitting there. The baby of one prayer group member lay sleeping on Mrs. Clarke's bed. Mrs. Clarke sat in a large wooden chair in a focal position. It was she who was leading the meeting. Another woman from Mrs. Clarke's yard sat quiet and gaunt in a corner. The young saint from Jenny's yard was there with Jenny, and another woman and a man. This woman was around thirty years old, and her companion was possibly ten years older. The baby was theirs. There were a number of religious pictures on the walls. One was a version of the Last Supper, and another pictured Christ in the garden of Gethsemane. On top of the dresser were Bibles and hymn books. All the girls and women wore hats.

Opening prayers had already been said. Following the hymn, each person presented a Bible quote of his or her choice. Next, the group addressed various "questions." These included "Who was Barnabas?" "Who was the first man in the world to shed blood?" "What did Jesus say to the Samaritan woman at the well?" "What will be the signs of Jesus' second coming?" "Name some of Joshua's battles," and "Recite a verse from Jeremiah." In both the reciting and the questions, a tremendous emphasis was placed on verbatim Bible knowledge. The children were scolded when their knowledge fell short and were anxious to please the grandparental figure. After the quiz, another hymn was sung. There followed united vocal prayer in which all, including the children, participated, with the one exception of the man. These prayers thanked Jesus for his kindness, related evangelical efforts, and were punctuated by the sighs and sucking of breath that are characteristic of Pentecostal prayer.[13] The reading was taken from Mark 11:12–24. Jesus, encountering a fig tree, caused it to wither when it had no fruit. Questioned by Peter, Jesus proposed that those who believed would have his blessing while those who did not believe would wither.

The lesson that Mrs. Clarke drew from the passage was that Christians must give their will entirely to the Lord, and he would protect from any harm. She then told a story of her days as a young seamstress in Panama. She was called to the house of one of the officers' wives. The woman came with a dress and a length of material and told her she wanted a new dress cut in the style of a dress that was already made. Mrs Clarke said that the made-up dress had a broadly flared skirt; it was material "cut on the cross" and a style that she had never made. She was sick with worry and so nervous that she could not even eat. The material from which she was to cut the dress was beautiful black satin, and she feared that she would ruin the cloth. Mrs. Clarke prayed to the Lord, asking how she might possibly make the dress. Suddenly, she knew what to do, and she knew that the Lord was leading her. She gathered up a lot of newspaper, laid the dress on the ground, and laid the paper over the dress so that she could cut the appropriate shapes. Then she laid the pattern over the satin and finally began to cut. She knew that everything would be all right, and her hands were not shaking in the least. The officer's wife came back for the dress. She tried it on, and it was perfect. She was thrilled, and kept swirling around in front of the mirror looking at herself and admiring the dress. She asked Mrs. Clarke, "How do you Jamaican girls become such good dressmakers?" Mrs. Clarke replied that she did her work by the grace of the Lord, and that he guided her hands in her work. The story ended, and Mrs. Clarke called for a testimony.

Jenny stood up. She did not relate specific events in her life but gave a description of how her life with her children and even her relationships with their fathers had improved since she "turned it all over to Jesus." She noted that her sisters in Christ were better friends than those of her past, that her boys' father did not drink so much, and that her children were more obedient. She knew that her own conduct was better, and that she had influenced her friends and her children. At work, her efforts had been noted more often, and now she hoped a promotion was near. Her back, which had given her a lot of pain following the birth of her children, now hardly troubled her at all because she had given it over to Jesus. She had been able to follow in her mother's path and hoped that she could serve the Lord as well as her mother had.

The meeting broke up as everyone said a prayer of his or her own and then repeated a benediction. I shook hands with everyone present and left after various pleasantries. The one man at the meeting was the common-law husband of the young woman saint. We encountered each other fifteen minutes later in a restaurant on the area's main street as he darted in for a quick drink of beer on his way home to his common-law wife.

Jenny's constitution of a feminine community was experienced as a blessing from the Lord. Saints like Jenny, feeling a transformation in their bodies at the moment of sanctification, can experience a more diffuse change in life sustained by these neighborhood relations. More than merely symbolic mediation, these creations of a social and moral field interlink with the organization of the church to define a distinctive practice. When Jenny went to church on Sundays, she went to witness and praise her Lord for this diffuse experience. Especially in the evening evangelical service, this witnessing also encouraged others to seek the born-again experience.

Jenny's church had been born in the early 1970s, when a wave of enthusiasm swept through her East Kingston neighborhood.[14] The group of about fifty saints that attended the church in the late 1980s had fluctuated in the previous decade from a height of more than one hundred down to thirty in the late 1970s, creeping up again in the 1980s. It was an independent trinitarian church housed first in a large corrugated iron shed and then rebuilt in the early 1980s in a permanent concrete block structure. The church never had been completed, however, or even properly painted. Suggestive but unfinished murals of the Nativity and the Last Supper were painted gaudily on the interior walls. The first pastor had left to pastor a related group in Florida. Although his successor was a forceful exhorter, the group's cohesion came from the senior evangelist, an impressive and committed woman, nonetheless exhausted by the vagaries of the church. Throughout its checkered history in the area, the church was, in fact, a group of women saints, including Jenny, ministered by a male pastor but sustained by the community of women.

Saints walked from their yards to attend the church's Sunday evangelical service. The new concrete block church was built on a lot one block behind the main street of the area, a street populated by an ice-cream parlor, a shoemaker, a bicycle repair shop, two barbers and a tailor, numerous small shops selling general provisions, a hardware store, and six bars. On Sunday evenings, the streets were crowded, and many stood in the street outside to observe the Pentecostal service. Inside, a number of chairs were arranged on a dais to accommodate the pastor, the evangelist, and the choir. In the center of the dais stood a lectern on which a large Bible always rested. Below the dais, two rows of wooden pews stood on either side of a central aisle leading to the main door at the back of the church. Along walls hung a number of plaques, placed in the new church below the murals: "Thou shalt be saved," "If any man be in Christ he is a new creature," "Old things are passed away; behold all things are become new," and "Unto them that look for Him shall He appear a second time without sin unto salvation."

As the church began to fill, the mostly women saints kneeled on the floor to pray. In their vocal prayers before the service, God or Jesus was addressed directly as the worries of the week, personal ills, and the troubles of family and friends were recounted. Soon, someone began a chorus taken up by others and accompanied by hand clapping and shaking of tambourines. Generally, choruses were sung from memory at a lively pace, which quickened with each successive round. For those less familiar with the words, most of the choruses sung could be found in a small red book, entitled *Redemption Songs*. As the choruses proceeded, women and children rose to their feet

Figure 10. "Redemption Songs," the Pentecostal hymnal

and began to sway from side to side, clapping out a repertoire of rhythms (Hopkin 1978, 28–29; Jules-Rosette 1975). Choruses conveyed the friendship of Jesus and the encompassing nature of his blood which gives victory over life to the saved:

> Tell it to Jesus, Tell it to Jesus; He's a friend that's well known,
>   You have no other such friend or brother; Tell it to Jesus alone.

> I'll be present when the roll is called; Pure and spotless thro' the crimson flood.
>   I will answer when they call my name; Sav' thro' Jesus' blood.

Sing glory, hallelujah; I'm living on the victory side;
　　Since Christ my soul hath sanctified; I'm living on the victory side.

As the third or fourth chorus died, another was struck up by the choir, which walked swaying, singing, and clapping to the dais. Even at this point, one or two saints left their pews and danced and jumped in the center aisle with arms outflung and eyes raised to the ceiling. The volume of singing, clapping, tambourines, and vocal prayer rose as the officers took their places on the dais. A deacon stepped forward and crossed his arms above his head, the signal for activity to stop. The singing ended quite abruptly, and the saints seated themselves. When the church was quiet, the deacon greeted the saints and turned to the crowd outside. He entreated them to come inside as the saints joined him to cry, "Praise the Lord, praise God," "Hallelujah," "Praise Jesus!" The deacon offered a short prayer for blessing on the service, and as he resumed his seat, he called for a sister to lead "the gospel part of the service."

Jenny stepped forward from the congregation. She struck up another chorus as she walked to stand facing the saints directly in front of the dais. As she positioned herself, those who wished to testify rose to their feet. Testimonies alternated with choruses, Jenny pointing to each testifier in turn. As most saints testified each week, their testimonies comprised a continuing oral history of their lives in the Spirit of Jesus. A saint would begin a testimony with a cry of "Praise the Lord" in which others would join, and then embark on a catalogue of the week's events with a comment such as "I am happy to be cleansed in the holy blood of Jesus' name," "Jesus has been so good to me this week," or "I would like to tell you tonight of the goodness of that man Jesus." Very often, saints described minor sicknesses or pains and thanked God that they could "turn out" that night. Often, feuds with landlords and other creditors were mentioned. Saints were asked to pray for the souls of these antagonists. Fellow saints would be told of children's achievements either at school or in the workplace. God would be praised for his benevolence. Such announcements often were followed by a request for God's assistance in a personal problem. Individual missionary activities were recounted along with any conversions made. All ended their testimonies with comments such as "It is my determination to carry on in the way of the Lord," "I shall remain steadfast in the way of the Lord," "It is my intention to carry on until the end," and, frequently, "Pray for me, saints!" Choruses were sung after every few testimonies, and a pattern of rising and sitting was established as chorus singing and testifying flowed out of the saints in turn. While testimonies were being given, other saints interjected with comments and encouragement. Saints became convulsed and danced in the Spirit, while others spoke in tongues. This would prompt the testifier herself to break into glossolalia. The congregation moved as a body as saints sat, rose, sang, swayed, clapped, sat, cried out, and rose again. The saints became one body in a fervor that only began to subside after some thirty saints had testified. When no saints remained standing, Jenny closed this testifying effort. To complete this gospel part of the service, she offered her own testimony, quite long and incorporating the deeds that her fellow saints had recounted. She called once again on those outside to come into the Church of God and be saved. Jenny then announced that the service would pass back to the young male deacon.

The deacon called the saints to their feet for a prayer and then announced a hymn. This was sung to a strict beat without clapping or tambourines. Next, a Bible reading was presented from the body of the church. Finally, an offering was collected while saints listened to a hymn from the choir. This quiet preceded the "laying on of hands." As the deacon beckoned forward those requiring prayer, the saints rose to sing softly and slowly a chorus that began, "Spirit of God, spirit of God," or another, "Touch me, heal me," or yet another "Blessed hour of prayer." These choruses were sung for the duration of prayer requests and the laying on of hands.

The pastor now actively entered the service. He said a prayer for each person kneeling at the dais while the deacons, elders, and evangelist stood in a semi-circle around those kneeling, praying in quiet but audible voices. Those who had requested the laying on of hands then rose. The pastor took a small bottle of oil from under the lectern and made the sign of the cross on each person's forehead. He went to each person individually, placing one hand on the side of the neck and the other on the back. He called on the Holy Spirit to come down on each person and drive evil away. One of those standing was a friend of Jenny's, and she moved close to the woman, whispering in her ear. As the pastor proceeded along the line, sometimes Satan was addressed directly as the pastor called, "Out, out, out, evil spirit!" He then pushed down and back on each person's shoulder to drive evil out of the body. Some were convulsed by this process and fell onto the ground weeping, shouting, or flailing arms. Others testified to relief from pain and returned more quietly to their seats. The saints were roused by these acts of healing and broke into loud cries of "Praise the Lord" and "Praise God."

The pastor returned to the dais and, when the congregation was seated, began his exhortation. The exhortation was delivered on a loosely defined theme pertaining to the dangers of the outside world. The pastor's own words and biblical verse were run together in a stream of staccato comment eliciting the engagement of the saints. Saints were enjoined to study their Bibles and not to "lipstick" and "mini-skirt." The time was coming when Bibles and churches would be destroyed by sinners who placed their faith in the world. Education, the pastor claimed, was taking over society. Even in the newspaper, education was lauded, but never the force of the Holy Ghost. As he proceeded, the pastor thumped his Bible and jumped from the dais onto the floor of the church. He moved up and down the aisle, stamping his feet and slapping his thighs. He ran between the rows of pews and peered through the windows outside to ask if their faith was in education or in the blood of Jesus Christ. Gradually, the saints came to their feet in support of their pastor as he exhorted all who listened to resist Satan and turn from sin. As the sisters began to dance, Jenny cried out to another saint, "This is the Spirit speaking, moving in you now! Praise him! Praise him!" and so it went as the pastor preached and the saints began to dance with one another. As the pastor finally sat, some turned to those outside, entreating them to come into the church. Others danced in the Spirit.

The evangelist, tall and thin, with a stately bearing, now came to the front of the dais. Her gray hair was pulled back loosely in a bun, and she wore small steel-rimmed glasses. Her hair and glasses framed a creased African face. Her dress was long and mauve, with a neckline reaching up under her chin. The evangelist opened her arms wide and called "any who desire to seek the Lord, to be strengthened in the Lord, to come to the altar of God." As she made the altar call, saints began to pray aloud, a number speaking in tongues. Through their dancing, many had moved out of their pews and were standing in the center aisle or grouped at the front around the dais. The pastor and elders descended from the dais and joined Jenny and the other deacons around the unsaved, who were praying. The entire congregation dropped to its knees. Saints now entered a period of intensive united vocal prayer as they strained forward in a womanly wall and kneeled close to those seeking to be saved and sanctified. The whole congregation appeared to push forward in one concerted effort of prayer. The voices rose and rose again in an extraordinary patterned crescendo, while the unsaved trembled and wept and sighed. They sensed the force of the saints' prayers and called for God's spirit to descend upon them. A woman saved by receiving the insight that she must serve her God suddenly received the Holy Ghost, which burst from her mouth as glossolalia. Her body threw itself forward across the dais, and then she turned to face the church. Some saints rose and danced in the Spirit, while others struggled to embrace the saint, newly born. Others kneeled and praised the Lord. As the women rejoiced in God, the young deacon raised his voice and concluded with the saints, "For his name's sake, amen."

A few years ago, one of Jamaica's leading women pastors marked her "fiftieth spiritual birthday." In her testimony on this occasion, she thanked her mother, her grandmother, and her late husband, who all had helped her in her course. She also thanked her "former pastor, Mother Russell, whose sacrifice, dedication, and commitment were God's channel for bringing me into this relationship with Him." This pastor is also referred to as "mother" and has herself been the "channel" through which many other saints have been born again. For her and other Pentecostal women, the metaphor of birthing saints, whom one will "slap and slap" to give voice, is a common representation of their being as women who are saints of God. The healing power of Jesus Christ for these women comes in both these aspects: through the constitution of community and as midwife to Jesus' saints. One meaning of this feminine eudemonic was defined by another Jamaican woman writing of her experience with God:

> [I]t would seem to me that female sexuality and reproductivity, in themselves, may be appreciated for being shades of the larger yearnings of God for union with His creation and with mankind, the cause for which He sent His Son to die. They are reflections of His own reproductive and creative ability as seen in His creation of the natural world; His setting of human beings on the earth; and the process of reproduction of Godly and positive qualities within people. In short, it seems that if you look long enough, and think long enough, you might appreciate the women for how suggestive they are, of eternity.[15]

This Jamaican woman's linking of God's creative spiritual power with women's creative procreative power acknowledges that same relation in myth that Gerda Lerner (1986) has identified as the generic site of Judeo-Christian gender relations. The woman's statement feminizes creativity as it also eschews the feminization of sin. Her comment resonates with the Pentecostal sense of women as vessels for the Holy Spirit. As vessels, they become the brides of Christ and provide a channel for the birth of saints. In Pentecostal evangelical rite, with its feminized congregations, women become both singular vessels and also a collective vessel for a God who is immanent in all his saints. Contextualized in the midst of a service, the pastors' exorcism and "preaching sin" purvey a sense of the trickster's performance engulfed in a larger congregation. Still, it is often this trickster's performance that actually creates a saint so that even cast in the role of Eve, women revere their pastors for their spiritual immanence. Yet as they enter the domain of saints, women also enter a feminized world in which they become the church united, which is the bride of Christ.

CONCLUSION

I accept this archipelago of the Americas. I say to the ancestor who sold me, and to the ancestor who bought me I
have no father, I want no such father. . . . I have no wish
and no power to pardon . . . . I give the strange and bitter
thanks . . . that exiled from your own Edens you have
placed me in the wonder of another, and that was my inheritance and your gift.
                                                    —Derek Walcott, 1974

Although this account has dealt sequentially with a politics of moral orders that is cultural, enclassed, and also
gendered in Pentecostalism, it is not my intention to suggest that these negotiations occurred as a sequence of discrete events. The engagement of
Africa with Europe, and of North America with the creole, has been a confrontation of cultures transposed into color-class relations. Dealt with historically in my account, this transposing has been complemented by a politics
of gender relations acted out in Pentecostal rite. This latter transposing of a
cultural theme, mediated by the myth of the Fall and Jamaica's origin myth,
has been recorded through ethnography rather than traced historically. In
view of the teachings of Phillippo, however, and his other missionary colleagues, against the backdrop of women's experience in the course of the
slavery regime, it is impossible not to think of a politics of gender extending
farther in this Christian world. The records consulted for this account have
not contained sufficient material to allow a retrospective view. But perhaps
my analysis of the present can be an invitation to others to plumb the historical record.

Transposing the Politics of Moral Orders

This transposing of a cultural theme has forged a creole religious discourse
among Pentecostals with whom I engaged. The source of this discourse lies
in those mighty cultural engagements not only between Africa and Europe
but also between Jamaica's creole and a North American practice. The discursive "shape" I have given to this process has been through reference to
different ontologies and moral orders. At the outset, Europe brought a sense
of sin located in the person and addressed through moral discipline that
allowed transcendence only in death. West Africa brought a more nuanced

experience of good and evil as companions in the world, controlled by rite and a sense of the trick. Able to transform good into evil and evil into good, African ontology allowed a present though inconstant joy in life.

When this creole negotiation intersected with North American revival, the ritual practice of Jamaican Revival was redefined in terms of sin. This would prove to be, however, a sin experienced as bodily malaise to be healed by embodied transformation rather than moral discipline. A once African joy in the world intersected not only with a sense of "freedom," following the emancipation, but also with North American ideas of perfectionism. In Jamaican Pentecostalism, this has produced an acute sense of transcendental immanence and eudemonic rite realized in being a saint.

The gendered politics of Pentecostal rite has turned on the nature of this perfection (can it be sustained in human form?), on the intersection of Jamaican and biblical myth, and on the typical relationship between a male pastor and his mostly women saints. All these relations are mediated, however, by the figure of the pastor, who embodies the trick and the mystery of rite. Although there is a gendered politics of rite, Pentecostal women's views of men and men's views of women are articulated through a cultural logic that mitigates the exercise of power. Pentecostal women are not "against" men, and men, like the women who are pastors, strive to save all who are seeking God.

This politics of moral orders within a creole religious discourse was once a politics pursued by the mission between Europe and Africa. The transformation of this initial politics, which proposed African culture as sinful in relation to the European, produced in color-class and gender relations a politics of moral practice within one larger regime, Jamaica's socioracial order (cf. Smith 1987). The moralization of the socioracial hierarchy, especially through the dual marriage system, at numerous points in its history has led Jamaica's ritual practice to engage with the larger social order. It was into this nexus that Pentecostals introduced perfectionism and through this intersection that Pentecostal rite would become creole. Perfectionism was used to address a history that had become Jamaican and thereby able to redefine the new meanings that were introduced. Perfectionism became not simply a holy state but a state that inverted the socioracial world. Pentecostalism's transnational order, with its variety of powers, also has embodied another change. Close linkage with American churches has been one way in which Jamaicans have responded to a new regime and to the decreasing influence of Britain. Change has been shaped by American forms and mediated by creole religion (cf. Basch, Schiller, and Blanc 1994).

Gender and the Politics of Rite

In the preceding chapters, I have represented the negotiations of Pentecostal rite as being fairly evenly balanced. Men deploy the myth of the Fall in conjunction with an origin myth and seem to subordinate women. When they engage in the myth and practice of exorcism, they also seem to position themselves in a way that commands the birth of saints. Again, in the small rural churches especially, Pentecostalism seems a patriarchal order. Yet in the larger urban churches, these practices of men can become set pieces overtaken by the practice of women. And even in the small rural churches where patriarchy seems to prevail, women as the active members of a church can withhold their tithes, the pastor's wage. The moralism of the pastors is tempered by the trickster tradition and by a skepticism concerning ethical rationalism.

Nonetheless, two further factors should bear on any final assessment. In Gerda Lerner's (1986) account, Christianity does emerge as an eminently patriarchal scheme. God in word and breath creates life through his being, and God is most definitely male. In Jamaica, women strive to be brides as a realization of their being. This process brings together the gendered power of the dual marriage system as described by Raymond Smith, and Christianity's ideology with its patriarchal bias. Women realize as a form of transcendence that which they cannot attain easily in the practice of social relations. Freud would look on this scene with satisfaction and pronounce their religion a "fantasy" (1971). It is certainly a re-valuation and certainly, in part, a hegemony. That women pastors are still quite rare and that women often are led by men seem to confirm this hegemonic side.

From this factor emerges another, also pertinent in a final summation. Not all of the Pentecostal world is linked with large American institutions. Of the four Pentecostal sites described in chapters 8 and 9, only one of these, in northern Clarendon, falls under the umbrella of a church that is affiliated with a United States group. This circumstance is not representative, however, for a majority of Jamaica's Pentecostal population is encompassed by organizations that have strong links with American churches. The impact of these larger churches is tangible in the lives of pastors. In the New Testament Church, for instance, pastors at the level of overseer and above have part of their income paid from the central office in Kingston by proceeds from tithing all over the island. Men further up the scale, for the organization has few women pastors, are supported entirely by the organization. Although the church is now self-supporting, the ability to command an extensive income has been aided in the past by church-building programs that were assisted from the United States. Occasionally, in this and other churches, men who have risen in Jamaica find a position in an American church bureaucracy and pass from Jamaica altogether. More commonly, senior men and even bishops must return eventually to pastor a church and lose many of their advantages. Nonetheless, the conditions of practice close to the center are very different from those in the small local churches. Where independent and indigenous churches are concerned, pastors may allow their churches to be sponsored by an American group. They may use this link to facilitate a personal relocation in the United States. Again, individual pastors and bishops may seek a career on America's Pentecostal lecture circuit speaking on foreign evangelism to American groups all over the nation. All of these are possibilities, and although women have access to the individual routes, this trans-national world of Pentecostalism is occupied mainly by men. It gives them authority in the church and a positioned power that exceeds that of women.

There are many worlds in Pentecostalism, and men are advantaged in this trans-national one. Yet if women are subject to an imaginary Bridegroom and to male hierarchies in the larger churches, these powerful and urbane men are themselves subject to another order. In Kingston, at a pastors' meeting, I heard the wife of a church bishop propose that the wives of future delegates to the United States should be instructed in table manners so that they would not offend or detract from their own religious standing. A bishop, established on the American lecture circuit, nevertheless complained of Americans' arrogance, their lack of understanding of Jamaican people, and their indifference to cultural preferences in food (see also Austin-Broos 1996). Another bishop, from one of Jamaica's larger churches, mused about a separate Caribbean conference. He observed that his United States counterpart was unlikely to agree. If the Caribbean churches split off, it might be seen as a sign for a similar move from the black churches in America. Black Americans, he observed, were the majority membership of the church even though whites predominated in most of the more powerful positions. For these men with ostensible power, their sometime ritual peripheralization is paralleled by a confined position in a regional trans-national order extensively informed by racialism. If power is considered in terms of hierarchy, the formal capacity to control those below, Pentecostal men prevail over women. Yet this hierarchy engages a racialism that definitely tempers the joy of power.

Power and the Constitution of Religious Worlds

To learn more from the Jamaican situation, I here propose to dwell for a moment on this issue of power. It is a popular bent in discussions today to speak of "empowerment" as well as "power," and behind this usage lies a divergence in ideas about power as represented by Thomas Hobbes and the philosophy of Friedrich Nietzsche (Patton 1989, 1993). In his account of the state of nature and the need for sovereignty, Hobbes rendered power as a zero-sum game (cf. Geertz 1980, 121–23). Objects of desire being scarce and some human beings wishing to prevail, power, Hobbes proposed, would ever be the process of some prevailing over others, the genesis of hierarchy. Nietzsche offered a different view of power in his notion of persons as sovereign agents, beings able to secure for themselves a positive, satisfying sense of self through a process of self-overcoming, a continuing revaluation of lives (cf. Austin-Broos 1991–92). As Paul Patton has observed, Nietzsche's view depends on the acknowledgment of qualitative and different powers as well as mere quantities of power (1993, 158). It involves a process of constituting and valuing being in ways that facilitate agency, shucking off the "mental slavery," as Bob Marley once proposed. The process is a social one and not a solipsistic re-presentation. It involves, in Peter Berger's words, the creation of new "plausibility structures," new forms of moral order and new subjects as well (Berger 1969, 45–51; cf. Bourdieu 1977 and Taylor 1989). In colonial and neocolonial society, people do resist redefinition in particular ways that they are capable of. Even when systems are forced upon them, they turn to use the rules of these systems in ways different from those intended (de Certeau 1984, xiii). In the process, they move to deflect reconstitutions of their being and construct themselves in different ways, albeit as lived experience and often unconsciously (Comaroff 1985, 4–6). This is the genesis of creole subjects different from both the "fathers" that Derek Walcott invokes.

These politics of moral orders are often a politics of the subject confined to micro-social relations encountered in the day-to-day. They depend not only on the ability of people to re-present themselves but also on circumscribed social arenas that objectify these representations. These domains, defined by practice, become the "spaces of disclosure" in which a moral order is sustained (Taylor 1985). For this reason, the women of Pentecostalism can be empowered through their action because they can command the domain in which they sustain their local practice. They socially create a world for themselves between their yards and activities in the church (cf. Csordas 1987). This becomes a sufficiently powerful social base to inform their neighborhood and working lives. The politics of moral orders finds its nemesis, however, in the experience of Jamaican Pentecostalists confronting a regional racialist order. Here, although saints involved can sustain a critical view, they cannot redefine in and of themselves the social order of which they are a part (cf. Comaroff 1985). They can be critical, however, and thereby denaturalize the regional order in which, perforce, they must interact. To this extent, hegemony is limited by a local Jamaican practice that can offer these women, and men, an autonomous sense of being wrought through their own religion. As de Certeau observes, they become "other" within the confines of the "colonization that outwardly assimilated them." They are able to "escape" the larger order without necessarily "leaving" it (1984, xiii).

These remarks about power also invite an observation on religion and its anthropology. The preceding account shows in a number of ways how a Christian world is real for Pentecostalists. In chapter 5 on the early preachers, Jamaicans related how they were converted and couched their accounts in a language that also evoked the landscape of Palestine. Donkey carts carrying bananas and sugar cane also were carrying a Christ-like figure and an ark. Miraculous healing occurred as an integral part of Jamaican life. In the reports on Raglan Phillips and the practice of exorcism, this healing was seen by some as the same as that recounted in the Bible.

The representation of Jamaica through a biblical landscape and narrative becomes even more powerful with the intersection of biblical and Jamaican myth. The parallel that many Caribbean peoples have seen between the Hebraic and African enslavements has been given an additional salience in Jamaica by the role sectarian missionaries played in the course of the emancipation (cf. Walcott 1974). Whatever the later vagaries—social, political, or religious—of the missionaries, their role has encouraged many Jamaican Christians, including Pentecostalists, to associate closely, as does the Bible, the passage from slavery to freedom with the passage from sin to salvation. The proposals in Romans 6 that "servants of sin" are "made free" to be "servants of righteousness"; in 1 Corinthians that "victory" over "sin" is victory over "death"; and that, as stated in Ephesians, Christians should become "ambassadors in bonds" for the "gospel" (see chapters 7 and 8) all employ bondage or slavery and freedom as metaphors for religious passage. It is from within this redemptive model that the myth of the Fall and Jamaica's origin myth seem to speak to each other in Pentecostal exhortation. The very violent preaching to women of sin and, especially, fornication is indicative of the concerns of pastors seeking a closure for Pentecostal women from others among the lower class. The representation of women, however, as those who might be more inclined to breach the ranks of the black lower class invokes an understanding of Jamaica, once again, as read through the Bible.

This symbolic mediation of Jamaica through the Bible that becomes a vehicle for Jamaican conceptions both informs ritual genres and also is supported by them. Saints experience a transformation when they are filled by the Holy Ghost, a real change in the constitution of body, soul, and mind that has inevitable implications for health and for moral capacity (cf. Csordas 1987; 1994, 107). And yet this symbolic mediation rests on sustaining practices that can construct a world within a world, a creativity shaped by constraint. When saints fall through a prominent transgression such as smoking or becoming pregnant, they are suspended from the church until they either redeem themselves or entirely cease to be saints. A mother who has had an "outside" child and been associated with a church is required to discipline herself if she wishes the baby to be blessed by the pastor of her church. In larger churches, part of an overseer's duties to his central organization is to report on those newly sanctified and also those who have been suspended. The conditions of truth that allow saints a transformation in body and soul are also conditions that confine their human social experience in ways that are highly contested within Jamaican culture itself (cf. Asad 1983, 243).

In Asad's (1983, 1993) critique of Geertz's (1973c) view of the self-sustaining power of symbols, important elements can be found of this dual Pentecostal circumstance. The presentation of a Jamaican history through a Hebraic history, including its history of sin, has been a focal symbolic moment for Jamaica's creole discourse and central to that society's poetics. This moment is one of extraordinary power registered by groups as disparate as the Orthodox Baptists, Zion Revivalists, Pentecostalists, and Rastafarians. Yet underlying this symbolic moment, which Geertz has explored in many texts (e.g., Geertz 1968, 1980), has been the sustained role of the churches both in the past and in the present as alternative modes to the secular order that challenge that order in varying degrees and depend, also in varying degrees, on a Euro-centered metropolitan power and its influence. Religion's ability in Jamaica to empower its local practitioners also has been its ability, in part, to engage with the regional order without offering it a major threat. Jamaican Christianity, and Pentecostalism specifically, show both these aspects of religious practice. They invite the type of analysis that gives " 'real analytic weight' to the process of colonial domination and also [treats Pentecostal] churches adequately as modes of signification" (Ranger 1986, 12).

Pentecostalism and Rastafarianism

These observations inevitably invite a comparison with Rastafarianism, which is easily cast as the critical religion in the face of Pentecostal hegemony, as Jamaica's religion of explicit symbolic defiance. Rastafarianism also constructed a world—albeit an avowedly African one—out of a biblical poetics that is integral to Jamaica's creole religious discourse. Rastafarianism is a product of this milieu and definitely not independent of it. Nonetheless, Rastafarianism, as an explicit discourse, has made important innovations within this larger religious milieu.

The Rastafarian figure, and his engagement with Hailie Selassie, emperor of Ethiopia and the re-incarnate Christ, subverts the master-servant relationship embedded in relations between the pastor and Christ, especially when those relations are infused with notions of a Euro-Christ and an African disciple. No Pentecostal with whom I have spoken has proposed that God and Christ are other than "colorless." Yet centuries of European iconography are a formidable legacy to contest. This Rastafarianism does in one powerful stroke, conferring on the biblical text an explicit politics of race. Likewise, Rastafarianism puts aside the emphasis on sin as the earthly state and contrition as its accompaniment. The Rasta doctrine seems to propose transcendence on earth as a humanly created state and not as only conferred from heaven, through God's power brought to earth (cf. Bloch 1992). Rasta-farian transcendence suggests more of Sartrean existentialism than Chris-tianity as such (cf. Lloyd 1985). It is for this reason that Rastafarianism has become as much a cultural mode as a ritual practice. Its very rendering of religion as politics has about it a rationalist cast in which redemption is an earthly act. This process parallels Jamaican art, in which painters including Mallica "Kapo" Reynolds and Osmond Watson, among many others, have produced Jamaican male figures as striking images of Christ. Where Rasta-farians live the image, Pentecostal saints assume the image, and only through the grace of God.

Barry Chevannes describes the process whereby many "young men and women from middle-class backgrounds become Rastafari" as one involving "first, a kind of shock treatment, perhaps to leave a feeling of guilt, but defi-nitely to mark a separating distance between the oppressed and the oppres-sor and the sacred and profane; and second, an appeal to step across the threshold and join the oppressed" (1994, 228). This process is similar to Pen-tecostal conversion but carries within it the departures I have mentioned. Nonetheless, a marked parallel can be drawn between the Rastafarian com-mitment to ganja (marijuana) smoking and Selassie—smoking ganja is a commitment to blackness that also signifies commitment to Selassie—and Pentecostal ideas of speaking in tongues and commitment to the Holy Ghost and God. Both complexes represent the point at which practitioners "cross the threshold separating the righteous and the saved from the unrighteous and the damned" (Chevannes 1994, 219).

In short, the shared cultural logic of these two religions is marked at many points and bears further comparison for a better understanding of Jamaican religion. A further point connects the movements and is perhaps the most crucial and complex one. Each movement positions itself in terms of Jamai-ca's origin myth, and although these positions are different ones, they seem to address the same historical problem that bears on aspects of gender rela-tions (see also Austin-Broos 1987b).

Both forms of religious practice operate in Jamaica with the assumption that earth-bound social relations are mediated by issues of race. As Alexander observes, while Jamaicans generally regard socioracial hierarchy as being a contingent and historical matter, it is far more common for people to assume that "races" have associated with them "distinctive life styles and power po-sitions" (Alexander 1977, 428). Alexander observes that "in the cultural defi-nition, the solidarity that arises out of racial sameness is an intrinsic property of racial sameness," not least because historical experience is thought to be rooted "in the experience of people's' bodies" (Alexander 1977, 432–33).

Pentecostal attitudes toward women revolve around these types of assumption magnified by biblical writ. Women have been the agents for a "historical process of mixture" that has also been an immoral act. Pentecostals do not propose black exclusivity because they look to a utopian heaven in which both black and white move beyond the cultural specificities of race. In Pentecostal practice, where saints reside in a heaven on earth, they strive to integrate that world, although not always with success. As the preceding account relates, racial tensions are manifest at many points in the Jamaican church. Rastafarianism, clearly enough, tends toward black exclusiveness. Skeptical, like the Pentecostals, that these race-culture divisions can be overcome even in miscegenation, Rastafarians opt to redefine their world within a delineable utopian present. They do, however, present a dilemma for some among their humanist supporters unable to embrace racial exclusion, even when sustained by the oppressed.

On first observation, the Rastafarian transcendence would appear to be a transcendence simply from a white-dominated order. Yet Rastafarians in Jamaica are no more able than their Pentecostal counterparts entirely to circumvent the dominant powers of the region. They become renouncers, in a sense, rather than inverting the regional order. In what, then, does their powerful sense of transcendence reside? Rastafarianism draws significantly from a biblical poetics in which the transcendence of the man is thought to come through feminine subordination. Jesus, like other great prophets, frees himself and his disciples from family and the domestic domain. He addresses the circumstance of "all men" and creates new values in the world. The transcending hero in the Judeo-Christian tradition frees himself from "species life," from unreflective lived experience, and defines new values for the self (Lloyd 1984). Rastafarian men seem to do this, but at the expense of their women, who have only belatedly sought to claim a comparable path (Rowe 1980). Rastafarianism's well-known gender order, which confines women mainly to domestic life and out of the public and ritual sphere, is now being challenged. Yet the recent research of Imani Tafari Ama (cited in Chevannes 1994, 258–60) suggests that women in Rastafari are still quite widely denied the very active participation in the ritual realm that is claimed by Pentecostal women (cf. Cumper 1979; Dreher and Rogers 1976; Austin-Broos 1987b). Pentecostal women, as I have shown, deploy the experience of their own bodies to reposition themselves significantly within the biblical patriarchal order. By remaining part of the larger society, they also command certain powers as their period of childbearing passes and they emerge as self-sufficient household heads. They thereby offer a challenge to the cultural logic that positions them at the intersection of the origin myth and the myth of the Fall. As I have indicated, this creates a politics of moral order between Pentecostal men and women.

These are options for women that are less developed in Rastafarianism, possibly not by accident. Without organizational structures that objectify standing in the world, as occurs in the larger Pentecostal churches, Rastafarian male transcendence can tend to subordinate women as the major controllable mark of its status in a circumscribed milieu. It is interesting to note Chevannes's observation that rural Rastafarian men and women are more conservative on these matters than their urban counterparts (1994, 259–60). This, too, has been my observation within the Pentecostal domain and suggests that if large-scale Pentecostal organization is an avenue mainly for men, it at least allows space for women to be prominent in Jamaican public spheres. These are comments offered in the hope that other researchers will consider these movements together and not bifurcate Jamaican religion in ways that may illuminate but also obscure.[1]

Jamaican Pentecostals and America

It is apt to finish where I began by situating Pentecostalism in relation to the Jamaican state and America's modernity. Weber can be invoked to characterize the Pentecostals as people disposed to a salvation religion (Weber 1968, 486–500). Yet not all Christian cultures that are modern states sustain this form of salvation religion or do so with Jamaica's enthusiasm. Here, three additional factors are important: the uneven capacity of the state to act as a structuring power in social life, the expanding structures of foreign churches partially funded from abroad, and the corresponding forms of collective life in which Jamaicans have been involved. The Baptists secured a role for the church and for religion in Jamaica when they, with other mission groups, encouraged free villages. Although this process was fairly short-lived, the churches sustained their commitment to educational institutions. As the twentieth century proceeded, the state assumed responsibility first in primary education and then increasingly in secondary education (Eisner 1960, 326–37; Miller 1990). Nonetheless, the notion that churches should sustain a pastoral role was firmly established in Jamaica. Pentecostalism has entered this milieu in a different capacity. Numerous churches in Jamaica maintain pre-schools for their adherents' children. More importantly, in a more prosperous century, the churches in themselves provide significant organizational structures in which adherents can become involved. For many Pentecostalists, the church is a total way of life, a comprehensive moral order that sustains coherence in their lives. It also reaches out to America and England to define the full extent of Pentecostalism. This trans-national and metropolitan world, rather than Jamaica's nation-state, becomes the Pentecostal milieu. And this world is informed by a cosmology that places trust in Jesus and God rather than in a political process.

The church can become, in significant part, an alternative world for Jamaicans. And this is achieved at least in part because the modern state has continued to have an uneven presence in Jamaican life (cf. Stone 1991, 93). Pentecostal churches thereby bring an order that is alternative to other groups, including trades unions and parties. Where the latter construct a reality based on the power of humankind and its legal institutions to arrange the goods of a social life, Pentecostal churches address the dilemmas of the person by proposing a moral reconstitution informed by God's spiritual power (cf. Weber 1968, 484–86; Sombart 1906, 77–79). These operations on the subject become manifest in collective practice that sometimes aids mobility both within and beyond Jamaica (cf. Asad 1993). All these factors come together to create a world in which the appeal to God, and especially to Jesus as redeemer and friend, is an eminently real resort in life.

The reality of this alternative world of transcendental being is bolstered by the structural links between Jamaican Pentecostals and the metropolitan world. The transcendental mode brings opportunities because Jamaicans change themselves and become perfect saints. They do this, however, in a milieu that has carried resources from the metropole and made them available in Jamaica, largely independent of the state. This, perhaps, is the significance behind the census returns for 1982 that show large and comparable numbers of Jamaicans as either Church of God or with no religion (see appendix 1, below). Two powerful worlds reside in Jamaica and often interact and merge: ritual practice and secular politics. The world of ritual practice, however, is also bolstered by links beyond the state that are politically relevant.

A number of writers have remarked on the forms of secularization that followed the development of capitalism and its legal institutions. These writers also have remarked on the fact that this secularization very often involved the acceptance of man rather than God as the measure of things in social life (Sombart 1906, 75; Weber 1968, 484–86; Dumont 1977, 11–44; de Certeau 1988; cf. Austin-Broos 1991–92). Sombart and Weber, in particular, focused on markets in the modern state that gave even workers a singular sense that it is man rather than God who controls social life. Weber described the emerging perception that "power relationships [are] guaranteed in law" rather than by transcendental forms (Weber 1968, 485; cf. de Certeau 1988, 149). De Certeau's reading of Weber's Protestant ethic is consistent with this typification. The shift from a focus on rite to one on ethics introduces the notion of a "theory of behaviors" as a principal focus for religion rather than a statement of cosmological order. In time, Christianity largely becomes subservient to political forms; transformed, it becomes "a sacred theatre of the system that will take its place" (de Certeau 1988, 157).

This brief genealogy of denominations is challenged by Pentecostalism, which, beginning as a sect in Yinger's sense, can expand to become a large organization that claims the status of a universal church (Yinger 1946, 19, 550–60; cf. Simpson 1956, 339–41; and Wilson 1961).[2] This status rests on the treatment of religion as an integrative truth, and of Pentecostals as the only church, along with a muted hostility to the state. The various arms of the Protestant Reformation found it impossible, in the age of the secular state, to assert themselves as a universal religion. Twentieth-century American evangelical sects that have populated weaker nation-states in the less developed world now present a different prospect. Believing in the essential corruption of man, they also propose that man-made laws and their attendant institutions are themselves invariably corrupt unless brought under the governance of God (Wilson 1975, 22–25). They present a return to revelatory truth that supports a universal claim even as they themselves abide in a particular political milieu.

Jamaican society and culture, with its discourse of creole religion, has been sustained in the course of this century by the intersection of local conditions with this expanding trans-national religion. The religion in Jamaican culture today is not there simply as a legacy of the slave plantation's immediate aftermath. It is informed by this legacy extensively, but its orientations and practices, including its politics of moral order, have been reproduced and transformed by this American intersection. The impact of this regional event, now sustained through most of the century, infuses Jamaican culture. The religion that results from this process is not a lag in secularization but rather a modern condition, a new condition articulating with older ones that manifest as a creole milieu.

Missions, both old and new, can and should be seen as a globalization that acts as a vehicle for peoples residing in less powerful states. As I have proposed throughout this account, this circumstance has its creative moments as well as its hegemonic ones. It is, however, a modern condition manifesting itself in a circumstance where the autonomy of nation-states remains at best precarious (cf. Appadurai 1990, 1991). These are the conditions in which Jamaicans negotiate through Pentecostalism issues of race and culture and also gender and class. Saints heal in order to redeem a people who will be the bride of Christ. Their sense of a Jamaican history, so extensively shaped by the Book, is itself confirmed by the Book as the revealed Word of God.

APPENDIX I: TABLES

Table 1. Population by religious affiliation, by sex, all Jamaica

Religious affiliation	Total	Male	Female
Church of God	400,379	175,140	225,239
Baptist	217,839	98,700	119,139
Anglican	154,548	71,287	83,261
Seventh Day Adventist	150,722	67,129	83,593
Pentecostal	113,570	47,974	65,596
Roman Catholic	107,580	50,769	56,811
Methodist	68,289	30,770	37,519
United Church	58,938	27,154	31,784
Moravian	31,772	14,924	16,848
African Methodist Episcopal Zion	30,530	12,761	17,769
Jehovah's Witness	25,016	10,991	14,025
Brethren	22,961	10,029	12,932
Rastafarian	14,249	11,661	2,588
Salvation Army	11,131	5,040	6,091
Disciples of Christ	8,483	3,706	4,777
Muslim/Hindu	2,238	1,311	927
Jewish	412	202	210
None	385,517	244,191	141,326
Not stated	243,614	122,834	120,780
Other	125,091	56,889	68,202
Total	2,172,879	1,063,462	1,109,417

Source: 1982 Population Census (final count). Statistical Institute of Jamaica. Count for 1991 census not available to author at time of writing.

Table 2. Adherents for selected faiths

	1921	1943	1960	1970	1982
Baptist	205,483	318,665	306,037	319,730	217,839
Church of God	1,774	43,560	191,231	305,412	400,379
Seventh Day Adventist	5,416	27,402	78,360	117,059	150,722
Pentecostal	—	4,907	14,739	57,055	113,570
Rastafarianism	—	—	—	—	14,249

Source: Jamaica, Department of Statistics, Census of Jamaica: 1921, 1943, 1960, 1970, 1982 (1991 count not available to author at time of writing.).

APPENDIX II: THE PAULINE INJUNCTIONS TO FEMININE SUBMISSION

1 Corinthians 14

34   Let your women keep silence in the churches: for it is not permitted unto them to speak; but *they are commanded* to be under obedience, as also saith the law.

35   And if they will learn anything, let them ask their husbands at home: for it is a shame for women to speak in the church.

2 Corinthians 11

5   But every woman that prayeth or prophesyeth with *her* head uncovered, dishonoreth her head: for that is even all one as if she were shaven.

6   For if the woman be not covered, let her also be shorn: but if it be a shame for a woman to be shorn or shaven, let her be covered.

Ephesians 5

22   Wives, submit yourselves unto your own husbands, as unto the Lord.

23   For the husband is the head of the wife, even as Christ is the head of the church; and he is the savior of the body.

1 Timothy 2

8   I will therefore that men pray everywhere, lifting up holy hands, without wrath and doubting.

9   In like manner also, that women adorn themselves in modest apparel, with shamefacedness and sobriety; not with braided hair, or gold, or pearls, or costly array.

10   But (which becometh women professing godliness) with good works.

11   Let the woman learn in silence with all subjection.

12   But I suffer not a woman to teach, nor to usurp authority over the man, but to be in silence.

13   For Adam was first formed, then Eve.

14   And Adam was not deceived, but the woman being deceived was in transgression.

15   Not withstanding she shall be saved in childbearing, if they continue in faith and charity and holiness with sobriety.

NOTES

Introduction

1. The sources of American Pentecostalism were in English Methodism and the Holiness movement, reinforced, of course, by influences from the English Keswick Convention. Dayton (1975, 1980, 1987) is an excellent source on the theological roots of the movement in America. See also Synan (1971). Not all, but the most influential forms of Pentecostalism in Jamaica came from churches in the United States, located principally on the East Coast. See chapters 1 and 5, below.

2. Chevannes (1994) is the most comprehensive account of Jamaican Rastafarianism. For discussion of Zion Revivalism, see chapters 3 and 4, below.

3. The very first Christianity in Jamaica was Roman Catholicism brought by the early Spanish settlers. Catholicism's influence in Jamaica, however, has been dwarfed by that of the Protestant churches. The Christian culture that this study addresses is therefore a Protestant culture. Stewart (1992) has some comment on the Catholic church in Jamaica.

4. For my initial record of that early fieldwork, see Austin (1984a).

5. "Nation language" comes from Brathwaite (1984) and proposes a view of "patois" that characterizes Jamaican popular speech in positive terms, rather than as mere deviation from a European norm. Roger Abrahams's (1983) accounts of stylistics in speech are another contribution in this area.

6. The preponderance of women in Jamaican and Caribbean Pentecostal churches has been remarked upon frequently (see Austin 1981, 1984a; Austin-Broos 1987b; Calley 1965; Dreher and Rogers 1976; LaRuffa 1971, 1980; Smith 1978). It also has been remarked upon for other regions of the world (see Hollenweger 1972; Pope 1942; Sundkler 1961; Williams 1974). Other recent accounts discuss the matter in more detail (see Rose 1987, Cucchiari 1990, Gill 1990, and Scott 1994).

7. The status of "Pentecostal saint" is explained in chapter 1, below.

8. Compare this account of Pentecostalism with Mintz (1960).

9. The form of ethnographic history writing in which I engage has been influenced by Foucault but also by Marxist notions of what constitutes a structuralist history. In taking some ideas from Foucault, I do not feel compelled to reject ideas of structure altogether. Certainly, however, this mode of history writing is very different both from Mintz (1985; cf. Taussig 1984, 1987b) and from Price (1983, 1990; cf. Hobs-

247

bawm 1990). In conjunction with Trouillot's (1988, 1990, 1992) substantive and critical discussions of Caribbean history and ethnography, these works constitute a rich
framework of historical anthropology for the Caribbean.

10. I take "moral ontology" from Charles Taylor (1989, 5–8), who describes it as
the condition of any people's moral judgments. This circumstance involves "the belief
that we are discriminating real properties, with criteria independent of de facto reactions" (1989, 6). On Taylor's account, sinfulness would be a real property of some
actions and intentions within a Christian moral ontology. Taylor's own example is of
our likely response to racists who might claim that skin color determines to whom we
should give respect. Taylor observes, "Racists have to claim that certain of the crucial
moral properties of human beings are genetically determined: that some races are
less intelligent, less capable of high moral consciousness, and the like. The logic of the
argument forces them to stake their claim on ground where they are empirically at
their weakest. Differences in skin color are undeniable. But all claims about innate
cultural differences are unsustainable in the light of human history. *The logic of this
whole debate takes intrinsic description seriously, that is, descriptions of the objects
of our moral response whose criteria are independent of our de facto reactions*" (1989,
7, my emphasis).

11. I have rendered Orthodox Baptist practice as "ethical rationalism" in accord
with Weber's notion of the "rational ethics" of ascetic Protestantism. The British Baptists who came to Jamaica were neo-Calvinist in outlook but also, like their American
counterparts, sympathetic to nineteenth-century revival (see chapters 2 and 3, below). Weber proposed that this rational ethics had developed in an "elective affinity"
with the "economic rationalism" of capitalism (1958, 27 and passim). In his famous
work, Weber traced the genesis of a style of religion through Luther, Calvin, the Pie-
tists, Moravians and Baptists, and the Methodists, to the enthusiastic "renewals" of
New England and other North American locales that preceded the rise of American
Pentecostalism. While Troeltsch (1912, 1949) has covered some of this ground more
thoroughly and Tawney (1926) has disputed Weber's more particular thesis of the
relation between a form of religion and capitalism, Weber's work still remains un-
matched as a brilliant sketch of a specific religious milieu. Weber's characterization is
built on the dual foundations of Luther's "calling" and Calvin's "predestination" as they
would be interpreted in subsequent protestantisms.

He summarizes the important point for this account of a creole religious discourse
in the following passage: "the conception of the state of religious grace . . . as a
status . . . could not be guaranteed by any magical sacraments, by relief in the confession, nor by individual good works. That was only possible by proof in a specific type
of conduct unmistakably different from the way of life of the natural man. From that
followed for the individual an incentive methodically to supervise his own state of
grace in his own conduct, and thus to penetrate it with asceticism. But, as we have
seen, this ascetic conduct meant a rational planning of the whole of one's life in accordance with God's will. And this asceticism was no longer an *opus supererogationis*,
but something which could be required of everyone who would be certain of salvation. The religious life of the saints, as distinguished from the natural life, . . . no
longer lived outside the world in monastic communities, but within the world and its
institutions" (Weber 1958, 153–54). This shift in Christian practice from a focus on

rite to "a theory of behaviors" was the central characteristic of Moravian, Baptist, Congregational, Methodist, and Presbyterian missionaries who would be active in Jamaica at the time of emancipation (de Certeau 1988, 157; see also Turner 1982). Their intersection with a Jamaican concern for healing the body as a way of ritually (or "magically" in Weber's terms) reconstituting the world was formative for a creole tradition. This intersection created the type of fertile tension that would generate a particular religious style. Weber comments of the Baptists in another passage that they "carried out the most radical devaluation of all sacraments as means to salvation, and thus accomplished the religious rationalization of the world in its most extreme form" (1958, 147). The British or Orthodox Baptists will be a central focus of the account of creole religion in the chapters to follow.

12. "Living-dead" is used by Goody (1962) to refer to the ancestors in his account of a West African religion. The term seems entirely apt to describe some relevant features of these religions that influenced the Jamaican milieu. It should be noted, however, that Jamaican Pentecostals sometimes refer to the unsaved as the "living-dead" or, more specifically, as the "living-dead-walking." I believe these to be independent usages.

13. In his introduction to Paul Radin's work, Stanley Diamond's (1971) relatively unknown discussion of the morality of Job as compared with the trickster has been a source of ideas for my own analysis of a creole religious discourse.

14. I have desisted throughout my discussion from defining the "eudemonic" in sociological terms. The word is used to mean exactly what it describes, a fleeting "happiness" experienced in both rite and performance. I have not wished to load the term with the import of Turner's "communitas," for, rather than being an "anti-structure" or "resistance," it is an aesthetical experience that in my view echoes an ontology, West African-become-Jamaican, that is antipathetic to a Protestant Christian world. I have offered an extensive critique of Turner in an earlier work (cf. Turner 1969; Austin 1981). The eudemonic probably has more in common with Fernandez's "pleasure dome," which "satisfies by providing a whole experience to those to whom life does not provide enough of anything they feel they need" (Fernandez 1982, 4). In Jamaica, however, the eudemonic is also involved in a politics of moral orders that can contest its meaning.

15. Raymond Smith (1987) puts a similar argument in his analysis of Jamaican kinship and marriage. It may not be an exaggeration to say that my study supplies a Jamaican cosmology for Smith's analysis and, perhaps, libidinizes Alexander's (1977) related account of "the culture of race."

16. My study relies not to so much on a notion of *"ideology"* but rather on *"hegemony,"* which I use in conjunction with *"discourse"* and *"culture."* By *culture,* I intend a broad and internally connected symbol system, and by *discourse,* a more specific and transforming genre of meaningful practice within that larger field. Geertz (1973a) has been most influential in shaping my view of culture (but see Austin-Broos 1987a). My notion of *"discourse"* is derived from Foucault (1972, and also 1977, 1980). I have discussed Gramsci's rendering of *"hegemony"* in two previous works (Austin 1984a, xx–xxiv; 1984b, 5–45). A more recent and detailed discussion of hegemony from the point of view of anthropology can be found in Comaroff and Comaroff (1991, 19–27). Another recent treatment is Linger (1993), while Williams (1991) also has used the

concept for the Caribbean. Gramsci (1971) is the standard reference to his work on hegemony. Issues of hegemony and New World religion come together in Genovese (1976) and Mintz (1960). The latter work interprets Pentecostalism entirely as a hegemony, while the former sees Christianity among American slaves in these terms. Compare Levine (1978) and Raboteau (1980).

My study also moves beyond the notion of hegemony, and this involves two separate steps: (1) initially, "hegemony" was steeped in class analysis and in the notion that classes are the principal collectivities of society. An excellent alternative to this view, which has been undermined in modern thought by Weber, Sartre, and Foucault, is the statement by Bourdieu (1991) which makes varieties of collectivity available for analysis. Recently, anthropologists including Williams (1991) and Turner (1994) have taken up a notion of the politics of cultural struggle that once again sets the focus on certain types of collectivity described best, perhaps, as "ethnicities." Williams goes to considerable lengths to avoid reification of these cultural groups, whereas Turner is not quite as successful. Both treatments tend, however, to naturalize a new focus on just one type of collectivity. (2) Owing to my interest in religion, and in acknowledging varieties of collectivity or nascent collectivities within the one society, I have preferred to speak of "politics of moral orders" rather than "cultural struggles." These politics may be understood as forms of the politics of identity in which it is acknowledged, however, that subjects must have a social field or a "space of disclosure" in which to live. Struggles for identity, therefore, can never be entirely individual. Adopting this level of analysis reveals a similar suspicion to that of Foucault (1985, 1986) of tying analyses up in standard collectivities (e.g., the holy family of race, class, and gender). Foucault expressed this suspicion as the shift from politics to the study of ethics and to micro-processes of power. (This is not to say that all collectivities are of equal import or that theories of history that privilege some collectivities over others are useless. It is to say, however, that such theories or "holy families" can hide other important realities.)

In writing of a politics of moral orders, my position also has been influenced by a group of thinkers in philosophy called "communitarians," who acknowledge that ethical systems of individuals must be grounded in socio-cultural orders. These philosophers include Paul Crittenden (1990), Alasdair MacIntyre (1981, 1988), Ross Poole (1991), and Charles Taylor (1986, 1989). The term *"communitarian"* is problematical, implying that "communities" are unproblematical units in society. Notwithstanding the label attributed to his work, Taylor at least is well aware of the difficulties of such a notion. He argues, nonetheless, for the contextualization of individuals' ethical judgments.

17. I discuss these issues of power and empowerment and their relation to the analysis of religion more fully in the conclusion, below.

18. The problematic of the subject began at least as early as Saint Augustine's *Confessions* (1991) and his passage to a knowledge of evil and good. The issue is intimately linked in the Western tradition to the relation between history and theology. Lloyd (1993) demonstrates this when she gives an interesting account of Augustine's views on time: "If you would understand yourself in relation to time, [Augustine] is saying, you will do so not by looking to the external world, but rather by looking inward—to

the inner world of consciousness where you can understand yourself in relation to eternity" (1993, 37). What Lloyd describes as the "shift" between "seeing consciousness as in time" and "seeing time as in consciousness" is also the uneasy relation in the Western tradition between theories of history and theology. The relation and the tensions between Hegel and Marx in this regard are well known. Lloyd herself in an earlier work also sketches out the close relation between Hegel's and Sartre's notions of transcendence, which she argues convincingly have an anti-feminine bias in addition (1984, 1985). Notwithstanding his *Genealogy of Morals* (1967), Nietzsche's idea of self-overcoming also has roots in this tradition of movement between history and theology, time and consciousness. Finally, very modern ideas about politics of identity or authenticity and notions of "re-making" the self have their sources in this ambivalent relation among theology, morality, and history.

19. Gaining a sense of the "cultural meanings" or "lived experience" of Pentecostalism was not without its difficulties. The most common view among Pentecostals was that anyone attending church who was not a seeker after salvation was thereby motivated by the devil. The implication of this view with which I had to contend was that the status of "observer" or "researcher" was not a recognized or morally neutral one. Only among a very few church leaders was the status of researcher accepted. This created an ethical dilemma for me in the practice of my field research. Following the observations of Asad (1983, 1993), my main access to the experience of Pentecostalism came through repeated practice of Pentecostal rite both within and beyond the church. In this practice, however, I always stopped short of manifesting the in-filling of the Holy Ghost. Given that I was not in fact a seeker after salvation and that for Pentecostals these manifestations have an unambiguous meaning, I would have been caught in an act of bad faith which I was not prepared to perpetrate. In none of the senses we might attach to the term was I "converted" in the course of my fieldwork. Rather, I identified as within the Christian arena, as being of good will and open to argument. Even on this basis, there were only relatively few churches in Jamaica with which I could sustain a constant relationship over more than four or five months. Pentecostals would therefore confirm that I did not gain the meanings of *their* religion, and with this I would have to agree. Nevertheless, I believe that between chapters 5 and 9 of this work, I do convey a tenor of experience that is faithful to the Pentecostal world that I saw.

In her review of Peshkin's (1986) account of a fundamentalist school, Harding (1988) criticizes Peshkin's objective stance that constrains him from delving into the culture of the "born again" experience. The totality of the study at hand is a sustained argument for addressing the lived experience of Christianity and, especially, of Pentecostalism within Jamaican culture. However, there are particular dilemmas involved in Western anthropologists studying a Christian tradition with which their discipline has been in direct competition over the construction of "truth." My own way around this matter is a fairly eclectic though considered one in terms of methodology. It strives to engage Pentecostal experience without being a part of it. This I believe is necessary for myself, positioned as I am principally within history rather than theology. I seek, however, a sympathetic understanding of Jamaican friends who define the world through theology.

Chapter 1

1. Bustamante's statement may be found in Hill (1976, 53). George White's statement was reported to me by Bishop O'Hare of St. Ann's Bay in 1986.

2. The formal doctrinal features of Jamaican Pentecostalism are very similar to its American counterpart. On the latter, Marsden (1980) and Sandeen (1970) give background to the Pentecostal movement. Anderson (1979) gives a comprehensive coverage of movements and central doctrinal disputes. Hollenweger (1972) is a comprehensive survey of movements world-wide. Dayton (1975, 1980, 1987) discusses the theology of Pentecostalism. T. G. Gordon (1989) offers a theory of religious movements that is particularly pertinent to understanding Pentecostalism in America and Jamaica.

3. Patterson (1983) has interesting observations on the Redeemer in relation to slavery. Also see Garvey (1969, 27–33).

4. On Pentecostal perfectionism, see Dayton (1975), Jones (1974), and Peters (1956). Passmore (1970) gives a more general account of forms of perfectionism and their logic. Also see chapter 6, below, for a discussion of perfectionism. For accounts of possession in Jamaica, see Wedenoja (1978), and for some psychological accounts of possession in Trinidad, see Ward (1979–80) and Ward and Beaubrun (1980).

5. Williams (1975) discusses some theological aspects of speaking in tongues. Goodman (1969, 1972) is the anthropological authority on the phenomenon. Goodman has debated Samarin (1972, 1973). Hine (1968) offers another view.

6. In Jamaican parlance, "rudeness" can simply mean sex, or else forms of play and innuendo relating to sex.

7. For an account of Jamaican healing techniques, see Long (1973) and Barrett (1976). Simpson (1956, 383) describes the use of these techniques within Revival religion.

8. Tithing is one among other fundamentalist practices of the Pentecostals. The biblical precedent for glossolalia is Acts 2:1–12; and 1 Corinthians 12; for offices in the church, 1 Timothy 3, Acts 6:1–8, and 1 Corinthians 12:28; and for tithing, Genesis 28:22 and Hebrews 7:2.

9. Dayton (1980, 11) comments on the lack of accounts of the American 1857–58 revival that preceded Jamaica's Great Revival of 1860–61. See also Orr (1949), Beardsley (1904), and Sweet (1944).

10. Personal communication, Reverend Aubrey Steward, Assemblies of God in Jamaica, Kingston, June 20, 1986.

11. See chapter 5, below, for an account of the origins of the Pentecostal Union.

12. The historical and ritual relationships between Orthodox Baptist practice and Zion Revivalists or "Native Baptists" are described in chapter 3, below.

13. The "triangular trade" was the three-cornered trade of Britain with the West African coast, the Caribbean, and the east coast of North America. See Williams (1944) for an account.

14. It is remarkable that the major commentators on Jamaican religion, including Moore, Simpson, Hogg, Chevannes, and Wedenoja, have not made greater use of Weber's sociology of religion or of developments from his ideas such as those proposed by T. G. Gordon (1989). The changes in Jamaican society noted here, which involved gradual changes in the ontology of the people, are crucial to the analysis,

though they are not regarded as the "causes" of religious movements (cf. Gordon 1989, 161–65)

15. The period known as the "Harlem Renaissance" extended from around 1917 to 1929 and involved an effusion of New World African music and literature. Jamaicans Claude McKay and Marcus Garvey were prominent in the movement. For a study of its impact on another Caribbean society, Haiti, see Berrian (1978).

16. Post (1978) is the standard work on Jamaica's 1938 rebellion. For my critique of Post's approach to Jamaican society, see Austin-Broos (1991–92).

17. For accounts of Norman Manley's career, see Nettleford (1971) and Reid (1985).

18. Madeleine Kerr (1952, 10) reports the following statement about marriage from one of her female informants: "Some people fond a married, and some people don' married at all. Since me husband dead about four times marriage offered to me. Me wouldn't married again, not if the man rich as gold. Them only want you to work for them. Them may support you at first and then you have to work and mind yourself. You can get no rest. As Parson did preach, I am once bitten and twice shy."

19. The complex of domestic service, Pentecostal religion, and contemporary matrifocality are clearly interrelated in Jamaica. See Austin-Broos (1987b) for an earlier formulation.

20. See Huggins (1967, 109–22) for an account of her activities and of opposition from Wills O. Isaacs. A report in the *Daily Gleaner* described the Mass Wedding Movement thus: "The Jamaica Mass Wedding Committee of which Lady Huggins is chairman and Counsellor Mary Morris Knibb, pioneer of mass weddings in the island, a member of the Executive Council, will be advocating a programme of intense publicity of the movement between June 9 and July 9. A booklet is also being compiled in which will be recorded the aims of the committee and other information relevant to mass weddings. Lady Huggins has kindly agreed to give a message to the booklet. In connection with this method of publicity, pamphlets will also be distributed to the public.

"A drive as the effort to raise the sum of 2,000 pounds follows this campaign. This money will be used to equip the brides for their wedding, and in cases only where it is extremely necessary, to help the men.

"The next mass wedding is scheduled to take place in November. Lady Huggins has kindly seen about the importation of 400 rings from Britain and as there is a scarcity of gold at the present time, the gesture is considered a great help" (*Daily Gleaner*, May 22, 1944, p. 6).

Also see chapters 3 and 9, below.

Chapter 2

1. By "magic," I intend "mystery" or the mysterious character of events. See Thomas (1973) for a detailed account of the manner in which orthodox religion sought to distinguish itself from the mystery of the unorthodox by pronouncing the latter "magic." Early anthropologists, including the notable James Frazier, took this distinction for granted, so entrenched had the terminology become in English. Thomas's account is a good counter-balance to Frazier's position.

2. The Christian cosmology referred to here is primarily a European Protestant

cosmology of the post-Enlightenment period. Weber has typified this cosmology most vividly from a sociological point of view (1958; 1968, 611–23). Also see Troeltsch (1912, 1949) for his account of the Christian view of man as "an individual in relation to God." An important addition to these well-known works is Herbert Marcuse's collection of essays *From Luther to Popper* (1983), which explores the post—Enlightenment idea of perfect freedom within to correct the soul, accompanied by inevitable social constraint without. Brown's (1985) account of changing conceptions of Jesus can be read as a rewarding complement to Marcuse's text. Latourette (1975) situates the Great Awakening and the Reformation in their historical contexts. "Kingdom come" is a common expression, but see also Ireland's (1991) study of Brazilian religion.

3. Fortes (1965) would argue that West African people did not consciously reflect upon these issues. This view is compatible with the observation that implicit understandings might nevertheless conflict with Christian attitudes. See below in the text and also note 20 for my account of West African ontology relevant to the present study.

4. The standard work on the British Baptists is Whiteley (1932). Torbet (1950) surveys the missionary activity of the Baptists. Raymond Brown's (1986) is a more recent treatment of the period of British Baptist history relevant to the initial missionary outreach in Jamaica.

5. All the general Baptist histories carry accounts of the mission initiative. See particularly Brown's (1986, 109–32) account of William Fuller's efforts to redefine Baptist Calvinism away from "its inhibitions about evangelistic preaching" toward an evangelism that would spread "the gospel to the distant parts of the habitable globe." Carey (1923) gives an account of William Carey and the founding of the Baptist Missionary Society in 1792 at Kettering. The society was called initially the Particular Baptist Society for Propagating the Gospel among the Heathen (Brown 1986, 120). Brown also describes the impact of the slave trade on Baptist ideas: "London, Bristol and Liverpool were the main centres of the [slave] trade and in each place Baptists gave expression to a sense of public concern about this inhuman traffic" (1986, 121–23).

6. Turner (1982, 1–37) gives an excellent survey both of the relation between the slave trade and the formation of mission societies in England and of the arrival of various missionary groups in Jamaica. Her account underlines that most missionary efforts began in agreements between particular slave owners and missionaries. Phillippo (1970, 285) gives an overview of mission work on the island directly following emancipation.

My own account here, and in later chapters, is concerned with cultural configurations and therefore focuses on the ideas of British Baptists and their clergy in Jamaica, who built Jamaica's most populous church after the emancipation. The Black Baptist George Liele began preaching in Kingston in 1784. He was a freed slave from America who had established the first black church in Georgia. He was joined by Thomas Swigle, a free Jamaican convert, and Moses Baker, another black American. The Baptist Missionary Society sent its first missionary to Jamaica in 1814, encouraged by the work of Liele (Turner 1982, 11, 17–18). Phillippo (1970) puts these dates at 1782 and 1813, respectively. The Wesleyan-Methodist mission began after Dr. Thomas Coke's tour of the West Indies in 1789 (Turner 1982, 7). The Moravians had entered the field early in 1754 but expanded their activities only slowly (Phillippo 1970, 279; Turner 1982, 7). George Blyth, a missionary for the Scottish Missionary Society, was established in Trelawney in 1825, and the Congregationalists' London Missionary Society arrived in 1834 (Grant 1985, 1; Turner 1982, 23, 36). For more detailed accounts of missionary efforts in Jamaica, see Clarke (1869) on the Baptists, Buchner (1854) and Furley (1965) on the Moravians, Samuel (1850) on the Wesleyan-Methodist mission, and Grant (1985) on the London Missionary Society. For the latter, also see Gardner (1873).

7. Phillippo's use of "apostasy" is somewhat idiosyncratic here. Generally the term refers to an explicit falling away from faith rather than to the intrinsically fallen state of man proposed in Genesis. It is the latter meaning that Phillippo seems to employ.

8. These emphases of the Jamaican missionaries came not only from their ethical rationalism but also from the important fact that the slaves, through the plantation system, were already significantly socialized into a European-informed regime. This allowed the missionaries to identify forms of behavior that were "wrong" and "change-able" within a regime that they understood. Comparison of this situation with various other "contact" situations is instructive for understanding the extent of missionary influence in Jamaica. See Price (1990, 54–75) and Comaroff and Comaroff (1991, 171–97). These particular accounts, in turn, also can be compared with Genovese's excellent account of slave Christianity in the American South (1976, 161–284; see also Sobel 1988).

9. For an account of the early days of the Religious Tract Society, see Martin (1983).

10. God's redeeming grace in exchange for a yeoman life is evocative of Nietzsche's account of the German term for guilt, "*Schuld*," and its derivation from "*Schulden*," to be indebted. Moral guilt of the Christian type, Nietzsche suggests, is an exchange relationship based on "the contractual relationship between creditor and debtor" (1967). See Poole (1991) for a discussion of this attempt by Nietzsche to relate modern Christianity to the institutional dominance of market forms.

11. Jacqui McGibbon (1987) has given an anthropological account of this element of slave culture.

12. See Turner (1982, 10) for an account of the manner in which the Anglican church became Jamaica's "established" church and also a church that "ignored [its] 'home heathen.'" In Jamaica, the Anglican church was disestablished in 1870.

13. Compare the contemporary comments of Raymond Smith (1982) on Long, who remains Jamaica's most infamous historian.

14. It would be misleading to suggest that Africans were thought of in terms more extreme than other indigenous peoples. Consider, for instance, a Baptist comment on the "Hindoo": "As Hindooism is incapable of carrying forward a nation in the career of improvement, so neither is it adapted for a high state of civilization; they cannot coexist together; but while there is no species of improvement to which Hindooism is not hostile, there is none which Christianity does not foster" (quoted in Potts 1967, 2).

15. Compare Laqueur (1976) on Sunday Schools and working-class culture in England during the period 1780–1850.

16. Africanists themselves are not consistent in their views of the nature of particular high gods. Compare, for instance, Herskovits (1938, 238) and Parrinder (1961, 11–12). For a general survey of African views of God, see Edwin Smith (1950).

Both Patterson (1967, 134–44) and Curtin (1969, 127–62) comment on the mix of coastal and hinterland slaves brought from the Gold Coast and the Bights of Benin and Biafra. The cultural influence from the hinterland, where sky gods were less pronounced was probably considerable.

17. The Jamaican ritual practice most closely related to forms of West African ancestral possessions is the dance known as Kumina, sometimes treated as integral to myal practice and sometimes as a separate cult. Buchner's is the clearest early description and seems to align Kumina with myal practice (1854, 139–40). Also see Moore (1953, 2467), Barrett (1976), and Brathwaite (1978, 45–63).

18. I adopt "interdiction" from Evans-Pritchard (1956) in order to indicate a generic notion of prohibited action not necessarily identical with the Christian concept of "sin."

19. Where such possessions were often transitory in Africa, driving out a malignancy, in Jamaica and with a Christian influence these possessions could come to mean a permanent and desirable change of state. A comparison of Bascom (1969) on divination and Dayton (1987) on the genesis of Pentecostal Holy Ghost possession demonstrates the differences in these forms and suggests that in the Jamaican case, that rite has been involved in a complex transformation.

20. Related to these divergent constructions is the issue of soul in West African religions. Lucas (1948, 246–52) and Goody (1962, 364–70) provide clear discussions of the manner in which two West African peoples have conceptualized the "parts of human nature." Although the soul was associated with the vitality of the person, it was not as such a register of moral worth. More often, the soul was associated with the heart and in addition with physical well-being. A soul could be attacked through the workings of witchcraft, and this would be manifest in physical malaise. But in these West African schemes, there was no direct equivalent to the Christian soul as a seat of moral behavior or "indestructible essence" (Fortes 1965, 128; cf. Foucault 1985). Moreover, the God creator of these religions was in no way the nexus of normative life. Correlatively, the moral status of the West African was not assessed by a generalized relation to God as represented in a state of soul. Moral norms were expressed through lineage obligations and other clan and personal concerns that were tested in a nexus of social relations and not in a personal encounter with God. This social-cum-moral order did not exclude specific culpability for a wrong, or even restitution in an afterlife (Goody 1962, 372). Yet this afterlife was, in Goody's view, just one among other forms of restitution. It was not a final judgment in a Christian sense, still less a culminating transcendence (Goody 1962, 376).

21. Pelton (1980) is the fullest treatment of the West African tricksters. Compare, however, Beidelman (1986).

22. Jekyll (1907) is not only a collection of Anansi and other folk stories. It also has extensive and neglected data on Jamaican rural culture at the turn of the century.

23. As well as *Banana Bottom* (1933), two of McKay's short stories dwell especially on the situation of women: *Crazy Mary* and *The Strange Burial of Sue* in McKay (1979).

Chapter 3

1. See note 5 in chapter 2 on the origin of the Native Baptists and below in this chapter for Gardner's characterization of their practice.

2. After the initial emancipation in 1834, an "apprenticeship" was imposed—an interim period of preparation and a concession to planters that preceded the final emancipation. Nonpredial slaves were to serve four years and predial slaves six years of apprenticeship. Full emancipation for all was finally declared on August 1, 1838. See Hall (1953) and Wilmott (1985).

3. The British Baptist missionaries practiced adult or "believer's" baptism by complete immersion. This practice was incorporated in revival religion, both orthodox and unorthodox. In the latter case, it often was identified as a form of healing rite.

4. Victor Turner, in his study of the cure of affliction among the Ndembu in East Africa, also describes this practice of eliciting objects from the body of the sufferer (1968, 161–73).

5. Arminianism is a doctrine named after the Dutch theologian Jacobus Arminius (1560–1609). He proposed that Christian election only followed man's pursuit of grace. As "God decrees to save all who repent, believe and persevere," election depended, Arminius believed, on a willingness to heed the call. John Wesley took up the doctrine and made it a cornerstone of Methodism, which stressed the "human appropriation of grace," along with the possibility that a person also might fall from grace. The doctrine provided a "voluntaristic view of faith" that made individuals accountable for their salvation (see Letham 1988). It also introduced a ground for the expectation that receipt of grace might be signaled in some way or other. Arminianism is intimately related to the later doctrine of perfectionism (see note 7, below) and to the emergence of "tongues" as a visible sign of receipt of grace.

In the context of this study, Arminianism is important for its association with forms of enthusiasm and, ultimately, notions of spiritual "in-filling" that diverted metropolitan Christianity from the austere ethical rationalism of Calvinism. It was the intersection of this dynamic with Jamaican "myalist" notions of possession that were definitive for Zion Revival and, later, Pentecostalism.

6. Dates for the Church of Christ in Jamaica and the Seventh Day Adventist Church were obtained from their respective secretariats in Kingston. These churches do not have published histories. For the Salvation Army in Jamaica, see Hobbs (1986), and for the Holiness Church of God in Jamaica, see Graham (n.d.).

7. Sceats (1988, 505–6) observes that Finney was a principal proponent of perfectionism and makes this comment on the doctrine: "At all times Christians have been faced with the tension between [the] calling to reflect in their lives and conduct the perfect holiness of God, and the fact, all too evident to experience, of the continuing presence within the personality of the sinful tendencies of their former lives. It is hardly surprising that, from time to time, Christian teachers have argued for the attainability of such a perfection in the present life as a way of dealing with this tension."

Sceats notes that Wesley's views were a bridge to perfectionism and comments further, "Perfectionism played an important part in the thought of William Booth, the founder of the Salvation Army, and it is perhaps not entirely surprising that it was in American perfectionist circles that modern Pentecostalism, with its emphasis on a two-stage Christian experience and the baptism of the Spirit, first appeared" (506).

See my comments on Jamaican Pentecostal understanding of the two stages of conversion in chapter 1, above.

8. Smith (1957) is incomparably the best text for the course and the cultural implications of revivalism in nineteenth-century America. There is no equivalent text for revivalism in Great Britain, although a more significant part of this movement was perhaps subsumed within Methodist enthusiasm. In this regard, the influence of E. P. Thompson's study of English Methodism (1963) has not always been salutary. He shares with other Marxists a difficulty in addressing religion as an autonomous experience rather than simply as mystification. In this, he has been a little too influential on anthropologists addressing religious movements in colonial and post-colonial situations.

9. Phillippo estimated that in 1840, there were 21,777 members attached to seventy-three different "congregation stations" and, in addition, another 21,111 inquirers attending these stations. Beyond these strongly committed followers, there were possibly 52,000 others, Phillippo proposed, who attended Baptist chapels—in all, he thought, close to a quarter of the entire population (Phillippo 1970, 294).

In the wake of the "Baptist War," an uprising in 1831 led by Baptist sympathizers (see Turner 1982, 148–72), many sectarian chapels were burnt by supporters of the planters. The Baptists received compensation in England amounting to 24,000 pounds, and it was with the aid of this sum that they began to realize their scheme for free villages (Knight 1938, 7, 30). Phillippo's optimism was, in part, built on this circumstance, and certainly the response from the emancipated was enthusiastic, if short-lived. Rental and other disputes between freemen and planters diminished through the 1840s, making some workers less inclined to leave plantations. Others squatted on remote land out of reach of the missionaries, while still others leaving the estates found, with the economy in decline, that it was difficult to purchase land or make the hoped-for contributions to their chapels (see Underhill 1879, 5; Holt 1991, 139–40). These circumstances preceded the visit of Underhill and Brown, to be reported on extensively by Underhill when he returned to England (Underhill 1862, 1879; see also Wright 1973).

10. Swithin Wilmott (1985, 1986) provides excellent accounts of the British Baptists' engagement in the politics of the Jamaican Assembly. In brief, the Baptists focused on two issues related to taxation: contesting the need for immigrant indentured labor to replace slaves and to be paid for by taxation, and advocating the disestablishment of the Church of England as the state church once again in order to leaven taxation devoted to the Anglican clergy's support. Fewer than one percent of Jamaicans were involved in the state church, and yet their taxes were the substantial contribution to its upkeep (Campbell 1976, 230–31; Wilmott 1985, 4).

To change the tax regime, however, required influence in the Jamaica Assembly, and this, in turn, committed the Baptists to struggles over the enfranchisement of their freeholder followers. In 1840, a Franchise Act was passed that extended the franchise among the newly freed (Campbell 1976, 239–40; Heumann 1981a; Holt 1991, 217). Baptists had some initial success with the enfranchisement of their followers (Wilmott 1986, 49–50), and eventually, between 1849 and 1851, six candidates were elected to the Assembly with freeholder support. However, subsequent economic decline and cholera and smallpox epidemics destabilized the population of the island (Eisner 1960, 134, 136). William Knibb had died in 1845, and without his strong political leadership, Baptists became more inclined to join with others who were fearful of representative government in favoring the imposition of Crown Colony rule (Wilmott 1986, 59; Campbell 1976, 314–16, 329). Governor Eyre's distrust of the British Baptists at the time of the Morant Bay Rebellion was, in some respects, an irony.

11. Stewart (1983; 1992, 66–109) gives an outstanding treatment of color and cultural prejudice not only in the Orthodox Baptist church but also for the Anglicans and other mission groups.

Perhaps the only point that I would labor over and above Stewart's comments is the impact that prejudice against "native" pastors had on the staffing of Baptist churches. In the course of the 1850s, it was usual for a pastor to command two churches, and in the case of European pastors, this was a necessity, for, in Underhill's words, "few churches are strong enough . . . to support alone a European pastor, even at the present low rate of salary" (Underhill 1862, 433). Though European ministers often complained of overwork, they needed multiple congregations in order to support their families (Underhill 1879, 11). And it was unthinkable that the Europeans could be reduced by increasing the number of Jamaican ministers. Underhill observed, "It appears to me essential to the continued advancement of the people, and to the training of an indigenous ministry, that a certain proportion of Europeans should, for years to come, be pastors among the churches. Their higher standard of learning and piety, their disinterestedness, their devotion to their work, the encouragement they afford to every effort for the elevation of the people, their freedom from prejudices of colour and race, and their interest in everything which concerns the well-being of the negro, are of invaluable worth and service in the good cause of raising the African from his degraded condition" (Underhill 1862, 437).

This view was consistent with Phillippo's ideas of European tutelage over the African. It meant, however, that churches and chapels were poorly staffed and that the tendency toward heterodoxy always was marked, even prior to the Great Revival and the Morant Bay Rebellion (Underhill 1862, 434–35).

Stewart's initial 1983 work is more detailed than the subsequent published work, and therefore I have cited it more extensively in my own text. My differences of interpretation in relation to Stewart stem mainly from the governing observation of my work that Pentecostalism is today the dominant popular religious practice in Jamaica, rather than, for instance, Zion Revivalism. As I elaborate in my introduction, above, one's interpretation of a Jamaican present tends to influence one's reading of the past.

12. Gardner (1873) gives details of the manner in which Anglicans after the emancipation began to address evangelism among the people and thus began the growth of a popular following for the Church of England. At no time, however, has the identity of the church been able to match the ethos of the Orthodox Baptists so closely associated with emancipation. Also see comments on Bishop Nuttal in chapter 4, below.

13. Most writing on Jamaican religion has concerned Zion Revivalism. The principal texts are Moore (1953), Simpson (1956), Hogg (1964), Barrett (1976), Wedenoja (1978), Schuler (1980), and Seaga (1969).

Minor details of my brief account, based on the two Revivalist bands I have observed, vary from these other accounts as they vary from one another. I suspect that a focus on the Holy Spirit has grown with the advent of Pentecostal churches alongside Zion Revival ones. In both the Revivalist groups that I observed, there were participants who clearly were familiar with the ritual style of Jamaican Pentecostal churches. Wedenoja compares Zion Revival with Pentecostalism in a manner that is different from my own account, regarding it as an American-derived intrusion that is essentially antagonistic to Revival. Yet even Simpson (1956) in passing notes ideas of "getting the spirit" and "tongues" that are similar for the two movements. Seaga (1969, 2) notes that both groups are counted in Jamaican terms as "spiritual" in contrast to the "temporal" orthodox denominations.

14. Of "trumping" and "laboring," Simpson (1956, 353–54) comments, "The most frequently employed technique for encouraging spirit possession in a meeting is 'labouring in the spirit.' Here the leader, followed by the officers and leading members of the church, circles counter-clockwise the altar, or the 'table' inside or outside the church, or the 'seal' in the yard. 'Labouring in the spirit' or 'spiritual dancing' consists of (a) 'trumping' and (b) 'sounding.' 'Trumping' is the trampling of evil spirits underfoot, and consists of stamping hard with the right foot while the body is bent forward from the waist and breath is expelled, and stamping more lightly with the left foot as the body straightens up and as the maximum amount of air is breathed in. Revivalists groan as they over-breathe on the up-swing, and this is called 'sounding.' 'Labouring in the spirit' is believed to increase the religious understanding of participants."

Also see Seaga (1969, 7). "Sounding" is sometimes called "groaning."

15. Pseudonyms are indicated by quotation marks. Some religious to whom I spoke wished to be identified. Others did not. Others I have chosen not to identify as a matter of ensuring privacy.

16. Long (1973) has the most extensive treatment of balm or curing yards. Also see Barrett (1976).

17. The "seal" is sometimes identified with the Schoolhouse proper, or with the part of it where the Revivalists labor. Seaga (1969, 6) observes, "The most sacred area of the 'ground' is known as the 'seal' . . . in Zion, it is usually in the 'mission house.' The 'seal' is the centre for the most important ritual activity."

18. A "band" or "bands" is simply a group of Revivalists. Seaga comments, "A 'bands' usually consists of both members who 'have the spirit,' that is, have experienced possession by a spirit, and those who have never" (1969, 7).

19. See Eisner (1960, 334, 336) on the growth of literacy in Jamaica, especially during the second half of the nineteenth century.

Chapter 4

1. *Jamaica Baptist Reporter,* January 1929, p. 4.

2. Weber's discussion of the routinization of charismatic authority comes in his analysis of "types of legitimate domination." Charismatic authority, among which may be counted a Christian revelatory authority, has a character, Weber notes, "specifically foreign to everyday routine structures" (1968, 246). Among these are administrative and economic structures which become increasingly systematized as a movement consolidates itself. Weber also comments, "Only the members of the small group of

enthusiastic disciples and followers are prepared to devote their lives purely idealis-tically to their call. The great majority of disciples and followers will in the long run 'make their living' out of their 'calling' in a material sense as well. Indeed, this must be the case if the movement is not to disintegrate" (249).

This was the process that precipitated debate among Jamaican Orthodox Baptists in the 1920s. On the circumstance of the Baptists, also see Knight (1938, especially Dillon and Meredith), Payne (1933), and Timpson (1938). A similar process of rou-tinization accompanied by similar debates has been evident in the larger Pentecostal churches during the last twenty years.

3. *Jamaica Daily Gleaner*, April 17, 1929, p. 2; *Minutes of the Western Sub-Committee of the Baptist Missionary Society*, April–October 1931, no. 18; *Jamaica Baptist Reporter*, February 1929, p. 5; *Jamaica Baptist Reporter*, March 1929, p. 3.

Two major issues in the course of this debate were the status of the Baptists' Cala-bar College and that of the Missionary Society (see Payne 1933, 76–81; Meredith 1938, 33). The Jamaica Baptists Union, formed in 1854 out of the previous Jamaica Baptist Association, was the central administrative group that wished both to rational-ize its activities, in relation to mission society, and to expand its control in relation to Calabar. This precipitated long and heated debate between the principal of Calabar College, Dr. Price, and the Baptist Union (see Price 1930).

4. Letter signed by T. A. Jones, R. G. Chambers, J. A. Black, L. M. Beverley, R. L. Knight, and Glaister Knight in the *Jamaica Baptist Reporter,* January 1929, p. 5.

5. The debate in Caribbean ethnography, often couched in terms of "heteroge-neity" and "homogeneity," sometimes overlooks that homogeneity also can include the *construction* of difference as part of its discourse. The historical, conceptual, and analytical tangle involved in understanding transformations of difference that are con-structions mediated by different forms of power barely has been addressed in the Caribbean corpus, though discussions of the nature of "creole" make a beginning (see Bolland 1992). For a look at some of the issues in a different cultural context, see Clifford (1988, 277–346).

6. Williams (1934) argues strongly that Ashanti forms have been dominant among all Jamaican rite. Hogg (1964, 56–57) queries this, as does, by implication, my own discussion.

7. The importance of North American church newsletters such as the *Church of God Evangel* cannot be underestimated in the spread of new religions. If the Watt Town Schoolhouse made literacy an icon of power incorporated in rite, forms of reli-gion from a literate world that also seemed to incorporate elements of Afro-Jamaican practice and beckoned to the allegiance of the poor and black inevitably would have had a powerful appeal.

8. The moral politics of these gender relations are developed in chapters 6 through 9, below.

9. In 1991, the Church of God of Prophecy in Jamaica lifted the ban on the wear-ing of wedding rings, which previously had been considered as a pagan representation of a spiritual union. Personal communication, Bishop Lesmon Graham, Kingston, January 7, 1992.

10. Using "inside" here is a deliberate play on meanings to point to my earlier discussion of the cultural construction of class cultures in Jamaica (Austin 1979). The

notions of "inside" and "outside" statuses connoting ideas of civilization and its lack
are intimately associated with notions of literacy and recognized institutionalization
as embodied in permanent building structures. This is as true of religious life as it is
of the domestic domain in Jamaica.

11. Although Raglan Phillips and William Booth were to go their separate ways, it
is interesting to note that Booth was influenced in England by the doctrine of perfectionism that would later be a part of Jamaican Pentecostalism, including the doctrine
of the Kingston City Mission (see Sceats 1988, 506). Also see chapter 6, below.

12. Letter from Reverend George Henderson, *Jamaica Daily Gleaner*, August 18,
1924, p. 10.

13. *Daily Gleaner*, August 19, 1924, p. 8.

14. *Daily Gleaner*, August 19, 1924, p. 8.

15. *Daily Gleaner*, September 3, 1924, p. 10.

16. *Daily Gleaner*, August 18, 1924, p. 10.

17. McKay portrays the demise of the initial missionary influence, Baptist, Anglican, and Congregational, in *Banana Bottom* (1933). The novel and also a short story,
The Great Revival, describe a Revivalist who was almost certainly Raglan Phillips
(McKay 1933, 230–33, 242–58; 1979, 40–47). His north Clarendon revival occurred
in 1906–7 and was based at the James Hill Baptist Church. McKay describes such a
revival occurring in 1906, and also a Revivalist who conforms in description to accounts given to me by current members of the Kingston City Mission of Raglan Phillips. In 1907, McKay went to Kingston (Cooper 1987, 20–21). In the description
offered in *Banana Bottom*, McKay contrasts this new revivalism both with the initial
missionary religion and with the practice of Zion Revival and does this in terms of a
newly ferocious moralism that differed from the Baptist/Anglican accommodation
with people's practice over time, and with the ritualistic and possession-governed
practice of Revival. In his fictional representation, McKay, like numerous Pentecostal elders in Clarendon with whom I spoke, chose to represent Revival in terms
of "supple-jacks" used to whip and thereby heighten the possession states of
practitioners.

Chapter 5

1. *Church of God Evangel*, April 14, 1919, p. 4.

2. Personal communication, Reverend Milton Davidson, Church of God in Jamaica, October 1986.

3. Among the early Church of God in Jamaica workers was A. S. McNeil, who
became pastor of the Frankfield church and also opened a church at Chapelton. G. S.
Cohen worked for sixteen years from a base in Port Antonio and proselytized throughout the parish of St. Mary, beginning his work in 1911. These men had both had
former associations with the Baptist Union. McNeil was a schoolteacher and a graduate of Calabar College who had studied theology in the United States. Cohen, who
was employed initially in the Jamaica Public Works Department, had aspired to the
Baptist ministry. Another schoolteacher, J. A. Mason, began a church at Baileston in
Clarendon (Graham n.d., 13–15).

4. *Jamaica Daily Gleaner*, April 8, 1922, p. 21.

5. Also see *Daily Gleaner*, March 14, 1922, p. 5.

6. *Daily Gleaner*, June 11, 1926, p. 11.

7. Personal communication, Bishop O. B. O'Hare, St. Ann's Bay, and Sister Russell, Jr. Also see *Daily Gleaner*, June 11, 1926, p. 11.

8. *Evangel*, August 11, 1917, p. 2.

9. Ackee is a West African fruit imported into Jamaican during the slavery period. Its unripe fruit is poisonous and, if eaten, can cause death.

10. *Daily Gleaner*, March 27, 1918, p. 11.

11. *Evangel*, March 2, 1918, p. 3.

12. *Daily Gleaner*, May 14, 1918, p. 3.

13. *Daily Gleaner*, December 24, 1925, p. 17.

14. Ibid.

15. *Evangel*, March 11, 1922, p. 2.

16. Personal communication, Percival Graham at Pennants and Brother Henry Richardson at Borobridge, 1986.

17. A. J. Tomlinson, cited in *Cyclopaedic Index of Assembly Minutes (1906–49) of the Church of God*, p. 207.

18. Information on Smith's career came in personal communications with Percival Graham and with his son, Bishop Lesmon Graham, of the Church of God of Prophecy in Jamaica and with Reverend Adrian Varlach of Church of God of Prophecy headquarters in Cleveland, Tennessee, the latter two interviewed in November and December 1991. Further materials came from Hawkins (n.d., 3) and *Triumph,* January–March 1986, 4–5.

19. Jamaica n.d., ccvii, cclvi. These incorporations that were always denied the Zion Revivalists allowed the church to hold property on behalf of its members and independent of the persons of individual officers. It has been common in Jamaica for peasant believers in revival religion to make grants of land to a favored pastor. Initially, these grants were made to the person of the pastor, who, if he determined to break away from a church organization, could treat that land as private property and use it as the base for an independent church. State recognition involved not only the formal registering of a pastor as a minister of religion but also the power to incorporate and secure property as an important financial base of a church. A fundamental difference between nineteenth-century and twentieth-century popular religion in Jamaica has been the ability of Pentecostal churches to incorporate. This degree of routinization along with ritual enthusiasm has given Pentecostalism a unique position in Jamaica.

20. Personal communication, Bishop O. B. O'Hare, St. Ann's Bay, and Sister Russell, Jr., Kingston, September 1986.

21. *Daily Gleaner*, November 14, 1924, p. 13.

22. *Daily Gleaner*, April 22, 1927, p. 12.

23. Personal communication, Bishop O'Hare, St. Ann's Bay. Also see *Daily Gleaner*, February 17, 1928, p. 13.

24. *Daily Gleaner*, September 20, 1929, p. 18.

25. *Daily Gleaner*, June 5, 1931, p. 21.

26. *Minute Book of the General Convention of the "Jamaica Territorial Council" of the "Pentecostal Assemblies of the World" Incorporated, 1931–32*, p. 4. The 1931 convention was held June 21–28, 1931.

27. *Daily Gleaner*, April 8, 1932, p. 19.

28. *Daily Gleaner*, September 9, 1932, p. 19.

29. *Daily Gleaner*, April 28, 1933, p. 21.

30. Personal communication, Bishop O'Hare, St. Ann's Bay, September 1986.

31. *Daily Gleaner*, June 12, 1936, p. 21.

32. Personal communication, Bishop O'Hare, St. Ann's Bay, September 1986.

33. An account of these events comes in the *Minute Book of the First Convention of the Jamaican Union of Apostolic Churches* (1941). The report begins, "On Monday 17th March, saints from the various Apostolic churches all around the Island started to gather at Emmanuel Temple, 167 King Street, Kingston, for the purpose of holding the first Convention of 'The Jamaican Union of Apostolic Churches.'"

34. Personal communication, Bishop O'Hare, St. Ann's Bay, October 1986.

35. See note 18, above.

36. Personal communication, Bishop Beason, Kingston, January 13, 1992.

Chapter 6

1. Foner (1979) and Calley (1965) between them give a good account of the circumstance of Jamaicans, generally, in England, and of those who were or became affiliates of Pentecostal churches. Among them, status issues concerning their position in comparable churches in Jamaica were underlined even more by their minority status in England.

2. Trans-nationalism has become a general theme in the writings of many Caribbean anthropologists. See, in addition to Basch, Schiller, and Blanc (1994), Dominguez (1975), Sutton and Chaney (1987), Gmelch (1992), and Olwig (1993).

3. Personal communication, Dr. Joseph Byrd of the Pentecostal Research Center, Church of God headquarters, Cleveland, Tennessee, November 1991.

4. Jamaica's National Heroes' Day is designed to celebrate the memory of heroes including Bustamante and Norman Manley but also the Maroon leader "Nanny" and Paul Bogle of Morant Bay Rebellion fame. The church service is held on the first Sunday in October.

5. Schuler's really excellent account of the arrival in St. Thomas parish of free African immigrants after the emancipation offers significant explanation of why it should have been in St. Thomas that Zion Revival and Kumina were sustained more strongly than in other parishes (1980, 66–80). Schuler's work overall also offers a caution both to historians and to anthropologists who would assume that religious history in St. Thomas is simply a delayed version of a similar history elsewhere on the island. Missionaries stayed away from St. Thomas at the time of emancipation because of its limited plantation development. The additional importation of Africans there, at a later date (from 1848 to the 1860s) than elsewhere on the island, means that St. Thomas and to a lesser extent Westmoreland, where similar importations occurred, have different histories from the rest of the island.

6. For an account of early Christian preoccupations with control of the body, see Brown (1988). The issue became a major concern for Foucault (1978, 1985). The collection edited by Asuncion Lavrin (1989) on the church in Latin America is influenced by the work of Foucault and provides interesting comparisons with Jamaica. See especially Lavrin's own article, pp. 47–95. Also see the discussions of Alexander (1984, 147–82) and Gutierrez (1984, 237–63).

7. The debate over "matrifocality" in the Caribbean, especially as part of the larger plural society debate between M. G. Smith and R. T. Smith, is too well-known to be rehearsed here again (M. G. Smith 1962, 1984; R. T. Smith 1995). Suffice it to say that my own interpretation of Pentecostalism relies on the systematicity of R. T. Smith's account as it has been elaborated in his recent work (see especially R. T. Smith 1987, 1988). M. G. Smith's observation on urbanization, however, and the greater incidence of female-headed households in this circumstance also bears importantly on the differences in ethos between rural and urban Pentecostal churches. I explore this issue more fully in chapter 9, below.

8. American revivalism, and particularly Pentecostalism, extended the tendencies Weber saw in Pietism and Methodism. Pietism encouraged an intensely emotional salvation experience, and Methodism a sanctification that entirely negated the power of sin and certainly presaged perfectionism (Weber 1958, 130–31, 140–41; cf. Dayton 1987, 35–59). These tendencies were drawn together in American Pentecostalism. It is a practice that pursues the individual's experience of completed grace or sanctification, the experience of being born anew with abilities to realize moral perfection if not a completed spiritual perfection. These individual experiences, a form of mysticism, become the bases of communal life (cf. Fogarty 1972). This trajectory was there in ascetic Protestantism as soon as Arminian ideas challenged Calvinism.

The care of the self in Pentecostalism overshadows ascetic utilitarianism and provides in the practice of morality and rite a sense of individual divinity. Pentecostalism's idea of "God in me," the inhering of divine possibility in the person, is the index of Pentecostalism's modernity. Ironically, this theological notion is a modern equivalent to Marx's demand that people reclaim the transcendental God and make his powers immanent in them all. This very response to transcendentalism Dumont describes as Marx's "individualism" (Dumont 1977, 111–44; 1986). Marx, so Dumont argues, identifies a society in which all its possibilities are contained in the person as representative of civil society. Dumont's typification of Marx's "individualism" captures an element of the modern individualism involved in Jamaican Pentecostalism. Just as Marx proposed that workers should reown the alienated God through reowning the state, so Pentecostalism has asserted that saints embrace the immanence of God by dissolving structures of church organization within an egalitarian community of saints. And, ironically, just as the state does not "wither away," so God for Jamaican Pentecostalists is in but always beyond the believer, sustaining new forms of church organization. The inescapable opposition of immanence and transcendence is indicative of this individualism that finds its reification and alienation in churches that deny they are "man-made" concerns.

In his discussion of America, Tocqueville contrasts the view of humankind sustained in societies of aristocratic rank and in egalitarian societies. In aristocratic societies, where there is little mobility, people in their various stations become the measure of human potential (Tocqueville 1945, 34–35). In egalitarian societies, however, mobility is a common occurrence, and as a consequence of this mobility, "imperishable monuments" "melt into air" (Marx 1972b, 338). In these circumstances, Tocqueville argues, misfortune and reverses abound and militate against the view that a particular class is the author of good. Yet improvement also is everywhere at hand, and, because it seems perennially attainable, individual desire for improvement abounds: "forever seeking, forever falling to rise again, often disappointed, but not discouraged. . . . Aristocratic nations are naturally too liable to narrow the scope of human perfectibility; democratic nations, to expand it beyond reason" (Tocqueville 1945, 35).

The impact of America on a colonial Jamaica was tantamount to a juxtaposition of these two principles. The firmly established hierarchy of colonial color class was shaken by the mobility and individual opportunity that seemed to lie in regional migration. The arrival of Pentecostalism, with its opportunities offered to aspirant pastors, communicated the hope of the modern while hiding its racialist hinterland.

9. My account of Pentecostalism here and in other parts of the book is based principally on field observation and on discussions with Jamaican saints. I have sought clarification of some technical points, such as the meaning of Calvinism and the history of perfectionism as a doctrine, from writings in theology and the sociology of religion. My sources are indicated clearly in the text. The account of Pentecostalism given here is, however, principally an account of Pentecostalism as I found it among rank-and-file practitioners, and their pastors, in Jamaica.

10. The reference is to James Fernandez's (1982) outstanding ethnography of a neo-Christian sect among the Fang in Gabon. His focus on the way in which a people construct a world for themselves in the midst of change is salutary. What one awaits in the African ethnography, Ranger's (1986) discussion notwithstanding, is a clearer formulation of the differences in ritual dynamics that occur in the different circumstances of the absence or presence of stable, non-migratory waged labor. Degrees of incorporation within modern urbanism and the state seem to affect radically a people's capacity to sustain purely local symbolic structures and imaginaries. Rather than the concepts of political economy being "imageless," as Fernandez suggests, it is more a matter of these different positionings producing different modes of symbol and representation.

11. It is here that I am most inclined to adopt Bloch's account of ritual as a particular form of violence that alienates the vitality of the self (1992). By way of introduction to his own studies, Bloch observes: "If the rituals dramatise a journey of the person to the beyond and a conquering return, this mirrors a similar two-way experience which is felt as taking place inside the person. The first part of the rituals involves an experiential dichotomisation of the subjects into an over-vital side and a transcendental side. Then, as in the external drama, the transcendental drives out the vital so that the person becomes, for a time, entirely transcendental. This victory of one side of the person over the other is what requires the first element of violence in the rituals.

"This violence is, however, only a preliminary to a subsequent violence which involves the triumphant experiential recovery of vitality into the person by the transcendental element. However (and again as in the external drama), this recovery of vitality does not compromise the superiority of the transcendental identity, because the recovered vitality is mastered by the transcendental" (1992, 5).

My interpretation of Pentecostalism in Jamaica involves the proposal that Pentecostals have sanctified a eudemonic that once was seen by missionaries as antithetical to the practice of their ethical religion. The scope for Bloch's style of analysis is obvious, and the use of it would allow an elaboration of the parallels with Marxist thought: the view could be propounded that Pentecostalism involves the transcendental rendering of the process of dealienation of the human subject foreshadowed by Marx. My disinclination to adopt this course involves a disinclination to define transcendentalism as a human construction opposed to truth, rather than as one of many forms of human cosmology that may become ideology and even hegemony but do not intrinsically have this status. Whether or not Pentecostal women in particular can or would realize their human "vitality" in any other ways remains, for me, an open question.

12. See note 22 for chapter 2, above, for the relevant writings by McKay, some notable examples of which are dominated by Jamaican women's struggles with morality.

13. See note 2 for the introduction, above, for references pertaining to women's position in Pentecostal churches. Appendix II lists the Pauline injunctions to women in the church.

14. Bloch's recent account of "sacrifice" in anthropological literature is evocative for the Pentecostal milieu. In his account of rite as rebounding violence, Bloch observes that spirit possession can be seen as a form of sacrifice: "because spirit possession is a matter of the triumphant penetration of a transcendental being into the conquered body of a medium, we can see that this is also what sacrifice is about. . . . In [rite,] the sacrificial animal is made to stand for the vitality of the body of the sacrificer" consumed and subsumed by the transcendental force (Bloch 1992, 35). In Pentecostalism, it is in-filling rather than the Eucharist itself that reenacts the sacrifice of Jesus, the giving of vitality over to God. As a consequence, the Eucharist becomes a communal meal which celebrates, in Bloch's words, "a legitimate increase in vitality since the vitality that is now being recovered is conquered and ordered by the transcendental order" (37). The Lord's Supper of Pentecostalism is a confirmation of powers received rather than an enactment of sacrifice in itself, already achieved in the in-filling experience. Bloch's account builds on recent critiques of Smith (1959) and Hubert and Mauss (1964). Clearly, this resituating of sacrifice within a Christian ritual practice is consistent with the idea that saints can be perfect beings on earth and therefore beings who do not sin and need not require a communal rite of propitiation.

15. Many saints stressed to me that foot washing within Jamaican Pentecostalism was an important sign of humility in which all social classes and colors could be brought together, remembering that they came from a background of slavery in which human beings of one color had been absolutely privileged over others. Humility, as a central sign for the saints and embodied in the foot-washing rite, often seemed to be more important than the celebration of a Eucharist.

Chapter 7

1. The setting for these observations, which stem from my initial fieldwork in Jamaica in 1971–73 and in 1977, are elaborated more fully in Austin (1981, 1983, 1984a) and Austin-Broos (1995). Similar conditions prevailed, however, throughout the 1980s, when I pursued fieldwork on Pentecostals in both Kingston and Mandeville and in upper Clarendon.

2. "De Lawrence" was the name of a Chicago publishing company that produced books early in the century with titles including *Sixth and Seventh Books of Moses*, *Black and White*, and *Egyptian Secrets*. These books have something of an apocry-

phal status in Jamaica. Reference to them is used to designate people involved with obeah. Sometimes a person called "de Lawrence" is identified as a sage of obeah men and women. I have never actually seen de Lawrence books, although other books on "black magic" are quite common in Kingston bookstores, along with manuals on exorcism. Also see Barrett (1976).

3. The oil referred to here is a patent eucalyptus oil generally sold in small bottles at local shops. Saints claim biblical precedent for the use of oil in healing from sin. Apart from the famous passage from Psalm 23, "Thou anointest my head with oil; my cup runneth over," the other passage saints often cite as a basis for this practice is James 5:14: "Is any sick among you? let him call for the elders of the church; and let them pray over him, anointing him with oil in the name of the Lord." It is firmly denied that this Pentecostal practice has any connection with the use of oils for healing by obeah practitioners. One such, interviewed by Barrett, made this comment on healing oils: "we have 300 or 500 different kinds [of oil] sold in the drug store. They are sold in small 50, 60, and 75-cents phials. Some of the names are: High-John-the-Conqueror, Compliance, Ten Commandments, Lover's Delight, Love oil, Lover's oil, Lily-of-the-Valley, Prosperity Magnet, Lucky Mojo oil, Seven-Eleven-Holy oil, Auntie Sally Good-luck oil, and all those oils. Many people use them in their daily life. Many people believe that these oils will help them get a job here and there but the oil alone is not sufficient. *You have to do something else*. There is Oil-of-Sunday through Saturday; these oils are used according to the day on which you were born. You must bathe in these oils on that day. Then you have oils of miles. These go from 1 mile up to 100 miles. If you are travelling and want to keep away evil spirits you drop a little of these oils at certain distances. . . . There is another oil called Oil-of-Hundred. It is made by Kai-ka-hi-chih of Egypt. There is Oil-of-Fifty and Oil-of-Thunder. These three oils are made by the same Egyptian" (Barrett 1976, 86).

4. The sister actually gives an account of an exorcism, in which her husband also was involved. Among Jamaican Pentecostals, however, exorcism is implicitly assumed to be principally a male concern. This account therefore lacks many of the representations specific to male accounts of exorcism. See chapter 9, below.

5. Cucchiari (1990) describes similar circumstances for Pentecostal women in Sicily. Indeed, there are striking parallels between Cucchiari's account of gendered Pentecostalism in Sicily and my own account for Jamaica.

6. In my observation, "voice" speaking styles varied systematically among different churches. Saints in particular churches, especially smaller ones, tended to adopt similar-sounding chains of articulation. See note 5 for chapter 1, above, for some scholarly accounts of Pentecostal tongues. I have not made this topic central to my account of Pentecostalism, which focuses, rather, on perfectionism and the experience of ontological change in the body, both of which tongues signify. In fact, to focus on tongue-speaking as the distinguishing feature of Pentecostalism misses the point that Pentecostalists themselves regard it as important *only as a sign of spiritual transformation*.

7. Talal Asad (1993, 65) asks the question, "by what systematic practices are particular moral dispositions and capacities created and controlled?" His accounts of monastic discipline have a resonance with Pentecostal practice, where the assumption of morality through disciplines is seen as central to the preparations involved in becom-

ing a vessel for Spirit. Once a person has been in-filled, however, morality is sustained as an integral part of being a saint. Many saints have stressed to me that following in-filling, morality is not experienced as a discipline.

8. See especially Tanna's analysis of the story performance by Adina Henry, *De Missus fe Me and De Gal fe Yu, Suh*. Anansi seeks Dog's aid in charming a woman, all the while promising that her maid will be Dog's reward. With the repeated promise of "the gal fe yu, suh," he leads Dog on, as well as the woman, until he finally performs the trick that leaves Dog outside where he belongs, while Anansi gains his prize. Tanna comments, "Ten times the song is repeated with only one word changing as Anansi advances from gate, to half-gate, to yard, to doorstep, to living room, to room door, to bedroom, to bedside. The performer delays Anansi's victory by drawing out the climax, having him sit on the bed and finally lie on it, a delay which heightens the audience's anticipation of the seduction" (1984, 43). It is just this rhetorical device that saints often use when explaining how they received in-filling (independently of their own willed attempts) after a series of disciplined procedures.

9. A striking difference between Jamaican Anansi stories and their West African counterparts is the introduction of music in the form of the fiddle as a means of realizing the trick. Adina Henry's tale recounted above (note 8) is a good example of this Jamaican genre. Compare Rattray (1969).

10. The reason for my disinclination totally to accept Bloch's (1992) analysis of rite as rebounding violence and alienation that transform a human vitality into a transcendental vitality lies in this proposal that for Jamaican Pentecostals, ritual transformation shares a cultural homology with the notion of the trick in Anansi tales. The two together propose a characteristic feature of popular Jamaican culture: skepticism regarding normative regulation which is sourced in the forms of domination that initiated Jamaican society. The idea that change comes through a trick rather than the accretion of normative practice is prominent in everyday Jamaican life. That rite rather than ethical rationalism should be central to Jamaica's revival discourse is simply an aspect of this larger cultural complex.

11. As chapter 8, below, will show, notions of the Fall and breach of covenant are central to the discourse of creole religion.

12. This reference to woman as receptacle or vessel also is mirrored in Rastafarian conception. Barry Chevannes has reported an "Elder" reassuring a man with a light-skinned mother of his black identity: "A woman has no lineage. A woman is only a vessel!" (1989, 48).

13. In broad terms, both Comaroff (1985) and Ong (1987) interpret women's possession as a form of "resistance." I have avoided that characterization in this analysis. It is not clear to me that Jamaican Pentecostals are responding especially to a capitalist order, and, although the movement does address potent issues of socioracial hierarchy, the ritual response within Pentecostalism is too ambivalent to make the term "resistance" especially helpful analytically.

14. These choruses can be found in the Pentecostal hymnal, *Redemption Songs*.

15. "Visiting" or "friending" can involve a union in which partners reside in different domiciles. For accounts of the Jamaican repertoire of unions, see Smith (1988).

16. Of this strong implicit association of spirituality with sexuality within the Christian corpus, Bloch comments: "Sexual and marital relations are often merged with

ideas about the conquest of vitality by a transcendental subject for its own purposes. Thus, if Christian theology was the imitation of Christ and if Paul was asking Christians to die with Christ and become transcendental themselves, the virgin birth was the invitation to celebrate the re-entry of the divine into the vital through the sexual conquest of a woman. . . . The idea of the virgin birth then became particularly suitable to a church which saw itself, like Mary, as the continuing earthly vessel of the divine, 'bride of Christ'" (1992, 95–96). Even more thought-provoking, in the same passage Bloch proposes that this image of religious community superseded that of "the law of Moses and of circumcision," the alternative image of community that Pentecostal men sometimes sustain.

17. "Vile man" deployed as a description of men is popular among Pentecostals in Kingston. The sense of the phrase seems to come from Job's description of himself as "vile" in the face of God, and God's vindication of Job after Job's repentance in which he says, "Behold I am vile" and "I abhor myself and repent in dust and ashes" (Job 40:4; 42:6). For his pains, "the Lord blessed the latter end of Job more than his beginning" and so "Job died, being old and full of days" (Job 42:12, 17).

18. *Sunday Sun*, February 8, 1981, p. 14.

19. *Jamaica Weekly Gleaner (North America)*, March 11, 1985, p. 13.

20. *Weekly Gleaner*, October 6, 1986, p. 12.

21. Ibid.

Chapter 8

1. Abrahams takes the ring game as a paradigm of what he describes as "overlap" in communication, the forceful communication of "presence" by all those involved (1983, 131–32). He observes that these games are "serially organized" and "open-ended and therefore can be begun and ended at any time." Pentecostal exhortations share this feature to a degree. Especially in conjunction with testimony giving (see chapter 9, below), services can be open-ended and thus proceed for many hours.

2. I am indebted to Sternberg for his account of biblical narrative as a very special type of trick. It is the creativity in the "tricks" of Pentecostalism that once again disincline me to interpret its rite simply as an alienation in the form that Bloch (1974, 1977, 1992) suggests. It is interesting to reflect on whether this repetition and "trickiness" bears a resemblance to Gates's (1988) account of "signifying" in Afro-American literature and art. Gates is clearly influenced by Derrida, but his ideas on repetition and innovation also fit the Jamaican case.

3. My interpretation of Derrida relies heavily on Hart's (1989) seminal work, which achieves the almost unimaginable: relating Derrida to theology without, at once, destroying theology.

4. Patterson assumes here that among plantation slaves, there were no particular marriage rules. Smith (1987, 177) and Higman (1976, 146–47; 1984) would disagree (see chapter 9, below). The assumption demonstrates, however, a common feature of lower-class views of slavery, wherein elements of West African and adaptive culture relevant to domestic life are conceived, rather, as an absence that awaited the influence of the mission. This construal of slave culture is itself a construction of the mission, Phillippo's views being a paradigm.

5. These views involve an opinion among Jamaican men that women can be dan-

gerous. Chevannes reports an informant observing that it is not advisable to beat a woman, who may retaliate in another way: "A woman can hurt a man easily. . . . Normally, dealing with a woman it is not right to beat her. Put it this way: living and having sex with a woman, you don't really know her intentions. If you go 'round beating her and she might not like it, in the night in your sleep she can harm you [through obeah]" (1985, 194).

This concern is married with another: that women often expect money for sex. Sobo explains the form in which these expectations come: "One woman bluntly denied that she would ever consider having sexual relations without financial gain. Another announced, 'no man no go 'pon my belly unless I got something from his pocket.' But the sex both referred to is not of the solicited sort. It conforms to the traditional model in which sexual relations are initiated by men, ongoing, and only indirectly paid for. Money is properly and respectably exchanged, with a time lag. It serves not to compensate but to attract—to 'keep the women them coming back.' It becomes part of the expression of kinship like altruism that traditionally overlays sexual relations" (1993, 195).

Pentecostal men, seeking more control, preach against fornication in this cultural context.

6. Such a victory, saints said to me, had occurred when their second church was built after the collapse of the first construction. They made a reference to this event, underlining the physical process of collapse and reconstruction rather than the organization of the event.

7. A number of saints have proposed to me, on various occasions, that this reference in 2 Samuel to "waves," "floods," and "waters" alongside the reference to "enemies" and "them that hated me" is a reference to the "middle passage" of slavery whereby West African slaves were transported across the Atlantic to the Caribbean.

8. The exact reference for this passage is Acts 8:18–19.

9. Abrahams (1983, 135) and Wilson (1973) underline the domestic domain (or yard) as the feminine domain and the road as the domain of men. In Jamaica, where lower-class women have been such a prominent part of the workforce, this conception is contested every day. Nonetheless, one dimension of the cultural logic in Pentecostal exhortation may well be to respond to a situation for women seen to be unsatisfactory according to these categories. Fernandez's comment on gender relations in Bwiti among the Fang of northern Gabon is evocative for this Jamaican Pentecostal milieu: "Bwiti faces the fact that the materialistic, the libidinous, and the dominance-subordination aspects of the male-female relationship were coming to be stressed at the expense of the complementary satisfactions that used to exist. Women, formerly always the path to prosperity, were coming to be more the path to weakness and conflict" (1982, 169).

If there was no such "golden age" in Jamaica, there may be, nonetheless, a strong cultural expectation on the part of men that women should remain "inside."

10. The practice of hanging framed photographs of founders in a church has been common in Zion Revival as well as some Pentecostalisms. Chapter 9, below, describes a tense moment in a New Testament Church of God, when this practice was construed by a young progressive pastor as part of a "superstitious" iconography embraced by the Revivalists.

11. Anderson (1979) and Gordon (1989) give the best accounts of the social conditions in which Pentecostalism developed in the United States.

12. Like numerous other Bible passages, this one is part of common Jamaican parlance. See my previous ethnographic account in which an informant, "Miss Furneaux," makes the following statement: "[In the tenant areas,] children are left with themselves, or with another person in the same home until the mother returns and so there is a great mix-up and a kind of evil communication that undermines good manners" (Austin 1984a, 167).

13. "Sweet" and "broad" are from Abrahams' (1983, 111–13). They are not a common terminology in Jamaica, though comparable distinctions are made between "proper English" and "patois." The fact that women pastors are locked within "sweet" talk indicates, in Wilson's (1973) terms, perhaps, that "respectability" and not "reputation" is the special province of women.

14. An interesting comparative case concerning Indian (Hindu) women is document by Kelly (1991) for Fiji.

Chapter 9

1. Throughout the analysis, I have sought to underline that gender tensions in Jamaican Pentecostalism are implicit rather than explicit. Women have prominent roles in churches and are very proud of the fact. They see their moral burden as part of being a saint.

2. These forms of relations are still extant in Jamaica today. During the course of my fieldwork, I encountered a light-skinned woman of the lower class who was mistress to a Chinese businessman. His business was in a slum neighborhood where he had met the woman. She lived with her three children by the man in a lower-middle-class neighborhood to which he had removed her. He visited on Friday evenings and also brought her a weekly allowance. During the week, she welcomed young, mainly black-skinned friends from the slum neighborhood who would visit and sometimes stay with her for a number of days.

3. "Rudeness" here has the meanings of roughness and being ill-mannered as much as libidinous.

4. Jean Comaroff's (1985) formulation seems to be that in curing the body, the Tshidi Zionists cure their world. In Jamaica, this is not so, because saints clearly understand that their "heaven" on earth only encompasses the saved, who must deal on a daily basis with many who remain unsaved. Being saints "in heaven on earth," they conceive a space within an earthly society that is conjoined with heaven and can, through witness, expand itself to subsume a greater and greater portion of the temporal world.

5. Janice Boddy (1989), writing of women in the Sudan, gives a compelling account of the moral politics of wombs in a quite different culture. Women's and men's ritual domains being far more separate, the gender dynamics of the politics is interestingly different.

6. "Partners" are the informal and local credit associations that are maintained mainly by women and extend throughout Jamaica. See Austin (1984a, 50, 248–49).

7. This ritual interpretation of women in Jamaican Pentecostalism brings a novel twist to Lerner's account of the fate of women after the Fall. New Pentecostal saints

and brides are not birthed "in pain." Rather, these births are celebrations for the community seen to extend its eudemonic (cf. Lerner 1986, 196). In this sense, women saints can see themselves as doubly blessed by their Bridegroom Savior. In Bloch's (1992) terms, this transcendental vitality has its attractions.

8. As I indicated in the introduction, above, reference to Victor Turner's (1969) notion of "communitas" is deliberately muted in this work. My examination of gendered ritual is designed to demonstrate that forms of "communitas" are not as unambiguous as they may appear at first (cf. Austin 1981). Foucault's (1986) criticism of the denial of politics within collectivities is relevant to Turner's concept when he figures it as a totalizing anti-structure. The notion of a "politics of moral order" is not far distant in this respect from Foucault's notion of "ethics" in its aim not to mask this politics.

9. Personal communication, Bishop Ronald Blair, New Testament Church of God, August 1987.

10. Sobo devotes an entire chapter to the condition known as "false belly," a pregnancy created by other than natural means and quite often by malignant spirits. She describes such a condition thus: "A spirit pregnancy can mimic a regular one so well that a woman might think it 'natural' until the time of delivery when only clots of 'cold,' 'sinews,' and 'bad' gas or air come out. If she was already pregnant before the attack, or if an attacker's leavings 'catch' one of her eggs, a monster baby can develop. People told of froglike creatures, memberless torsos, and children resembling monkeys. Miss Amelia, who lived up the hill, gave birth to a cow head" (Sobo 1993, 275).

Not only this description but also Sobo's account of Revivalist healers addressing "false belly" (281–86) make clear the cultural continuity between these beliefs and practices and those of the Pentecostalists. Interestingly, Sobo also remarks that the Jamaican view of clearing "channels," or, as she describes it, the "washout" view, represents a gynocentric rather than androcentric view of health. Healthy menstruation is valued and regarded, like child-bearing itself, as a form of purging and purifying the body (299–300).

11. *Sunday Sun*, February 8, 1981, pp. 13-14.

12. During the late 1970s and the early 1980s, gang activity expanded in East Kingston. It accompanied political unrest. Gangs sheltered in the Wareika Hills in order to avoid police. Sometimes they preyed on local residents. This activity diminished in the 1990s.

13. The sucking in of breath between the teeth is thought to indicate reflection and seriousness in prayer. Sighing is often taken to signify involvement and proper seriousness in the task.

14. Compare this description with my earlier account positioning Pentecostal ritual in a different theoretical frame (Austin 1981). The description of "Selton Town" in Austin (1984a) is the social setting for this Pentecostal church.

15. *Jamaica Daily Gleaner*, October 28, 1986, p. 8.

Conclusion

1. In a number of articles, I have put forward the view that Rastafarianism and Pentecostalism should be considered in conjunction with each other rather than in isolation. Just as disturbing is the tendency to treat Zion Revival as the major popular

religion and entirely ignore the denominational and Pentecostal heritage. Driven by a limited notion of "resistance," this view quite radically misrepresents the nature and complexity of Jamaica's religious discourse. See Austin-Broos (1987b, 1991–92, 1996).

2. Yinger (1946, 19) describes "the Sect" and the "Established Sect" as involved in ethical themes of protest, emphasizing personal renovation as well as the evil of society, stressing obedience and the possibilities of perfection. Sects sustain lay forms of religion and are often associated with the lower classes. Universal churches have well-formed authority structures and tend to generate national churches that strain toward the orthodoxy of the center. Albeit at different points in the Jamaican Pentecostal spectrum, it is remarkable that both these modes of religious organization can be realized in significant degree.

◆ BIBLIOGRAPHY

Newspaper Sources
Church of God Evangel. 1917–1942.
Jamaica Baptist Reporter. 1929–1931.
Jamaica Daily Gleaner. 1917–1945, 1986.
Jamaica Weekly Gleaner (North America). 1985–1986.
Sunday Sun. 1981.
Triumph: Quarterly Publication of the Church of God of Prophecy in Jamaica and the Cayman Islands. January–March 1986.
White Winged Messenger. 1929–1936.

Minutes
Cyclopaedic Index of Assembly Minutes (1906–49) of the Church of God, Cleveland Tennessee.
Minute Book of the First Convention of the Jamaican Union of Apostolic Churches. 1941.
Minute Book of the General Convention of the "Jamaica Territorial Council" of the "Pentecostal Assemblies of the World" Incorporated 1931–32. 1932.
Minutes of the Western Sub-Committee of the Baptist Missionary Society. Boxes 18 and 19 1931–1938. Baptist Missionary Society, London.

Secondary Sources
Abrahams, Roger D. 1983. *The man-of-words in the West Indies: Performance and the emergence of creole culture.* Baltimore and London: Johns Hopkins Univ. Press.
Alexander, Jack. 1977. The culture of race in middle-class Kingston. *American Ethnologist* 3:413–35.
———. 1984. Love, race, slavery, and sexuality in Jamaican images of the family. In *Kinship ideology and practice in Latin America,* ed. R. T. Smith, 147–80. Chapel Hill and London: Univ. of North Carolina Press.
Althusser, Louis. 1969. *For Marx.* Trans. Ben Brewser. Harmondsworth: Penguin Books.
Althusser, Louis, and E. Balibar. 1970. *Reading capital.* New York: Pantheon.
Anderson, Robert M. 1979. *Vision of the disinherited: The making of American Pentecostalism.* New York and Oxford: Oxford Univ. Press.

Anonymous. 1968. History of the Churches in Clarendon. Typescript. Clarendon Parish Library, Jamaica.

Appadurai, Arjun. 1990. Disjuncture and difference in the global cultural economy. *Theory, Culture and Society* 7:295–310.

———. 1991. Global ethnoscapes: Notes and queries for a transnational anthropology. In *Recapturing anthropology,* ed. R. Fox, 191–210. Santa Fe: School of American Research Press.

Arscott, Lindsay. 1971. *Forward in faith: The story of the New Testament Church of God in Jamaica.* Kingston: Hallmark Publishers.

Asad, Talal. 1983. Anthropological conceptions of religion: Reflections on Geertz. *Man* n.s. 18:237–59.

———. 1993. *Genealogies of religion: Disciplines and reasons of power in Christianity and Islam.* Baltimore and London: Johns Hopkins Univ. Press.

Ashcroft, Bill, Gareth Griffiths, and Helen Tiffin, eds. 1995. *The post-colonial studies reader.* London and New York: Routledge.

Augustine, Saint. 1991. *Confessions.* Trans. and intro. Henry Chadwick. Oxford: Oxford Univ. Press.

Austin, Diane J. 1979. History and symbols in ideology: A Jamaican example. *Man,* n.s. 14:297–314.

———. 1981. Born again . . . and again, and again: Communitas and social change among Jamaican Pentecosalists. *Journal of Anthropological Research* 37:226–46.

———. 1983. Culture and ideology in the English-speaking Caribbean: A view from Jamaica. *American Ethnologist* 10:223–40.

———. 1984a. *Urban life in Kingston, Jamaica: The culture and class ideology of two neighbourhoods.* Caribbean Studies Series 3. New York and London: Gordon and Breach Science Publishers.

———. 1984b. *Australian sociologies.* Sydney, London, Boston: Allen and Unwin.

Austin-Broos, Diane J. 1987a. Clifford Geertz: Culture, sociology and historicism. In *Creating culture: Profiles in the study of culture,* ed. Diane Austin-Broos, 141–59. Sydney, London, Boston: Allen and Unwin.

———. 1987b. Pentecostals and Rastafarians: Cultural, political and gender relations of two religious movements. *Social and Economic Studies* 36, no 4:1–39.

———. 1988. Class and race in Jamaica. Paper presented to conference on "The Meaning of Freedom," August 25–27. Pittsburgh: Univ. of Pittsburgh Press.

———. 1991–92. Religion and the politics of moral order in Jamaica. *Anthropological Forum* 6:287–319.

———. 1992. Redefining the moral order: Interpretations of Christianity in post-emancipation Jamaica. In *The meaning of freedom,* eds. F. McGlynn and S. Drescher, 221–45. Pittsburgh and London: Univ. of Pittsburgh Press.

———. 1994. Race/class: Jamaica's discourse of heritable identity. *Nieuwe West-Indische Gids* 68:213–33.

———. 1995. Gay nights and Kingston Town: Representations of Kingston, Jamaica. In *Postmodern cities,* eds. Sophie Watson and Katherine Gibson, 149–64. Oxford: Blackwell.

———. 1996. Politics and the Redeemer: State and religion as ways of being in Jamaica. *Nieuwe West-Indische Gids* 70:1–32.

Bakan, Abigail B. 1990. *Ideology and class conflict in Jamaica: The politics of rebellion.* Montreal and Kingston: McGill-Queen's Univ. Press.

Banbury, Rev. R. Thomas. 1894. *Jamaica superstitions or the obeah book.* Kingston: DeSouza.

Barrett, Leonard. 1968. *The Rastafarians: A study in messianic cultism in Jamaica.* Caribbean Monograph Series 6. Rio Piedras: Institute of Caribbean Studies.

———. 1976. *The sun and the drum: African roots in Jamaican folk tradition.* Kingston and London: Sangster's Bookstore and Heinemann.

Barthes, Roland. 1973. *Mythologies.* Frogmore, St. Albans: Granada Publishing.

Basch, Linda, Nina Glick Schiller, and Cristina Szanton Blanc. 1994. *Nations unbound: Transnational projects, postcolonial predicaments and deterritorialized nation-states.* New York: Gordon and Breach.

Bascom, William. 1969. *Ifa divination: Communication between gods and men in West Africa.* Bloomington and London: Indiana Univ. Press.

Bastide, Roger. 1978. *The African religions of Brazil.* Baltimore and London: Johns Hopkins Univ. Press.

Bauman, Richard, 1974. Quaker folk linguistics and folklore. In *Communication and performance,* eds. Dan Ben-Amos and Kenneth Goldstein, 255–65. The Hague: Mouton.

———. 1975. Verbal art as performance. *American Anthropologist* 77:290–310.

Beardsley, Frank G. 1904. *A history of American revivals.* Boston: American Tract Society.

Beattie, John, and J. Middleton. 1969. *Spirit mediumship and society in Africa.* London: Routledge and Kegan Paul.

Beckford, William A. 1790. *A descriptive account of the island of Jamaica.* London: Egerton.

Beckwith, Martha Warren. 1924. *Jamaica Anansi stories.* New York: G. E. Stechert.

———. 1929. *Black roadways: A study of Jamaican folk life.* Chapel Hill: Univ. of North Carolina Press.

Beidelman, Thomas O. 1982. *Colonial evangelism: A socio-historical study of an East African mission at the grassroots.* Bloomington: Indiana Univ. Press.

———. 1986. *Moral imagination in Kaguru modes of thought.* Bloomington: Indiana Univ. Press.

Bell, Hesketh J. 1893. *Obeah: Witchcraft in the West Indies.* London: Frank Cass.

Berger, Peter. 1969. *The sacred canopy: Elements of a sociological theory of religion.* New York: Anchor Books.

Berrian, Brenda. 1978. *Africa, Harlem, Haiti: The great black cultural revolution.* Nuclassics and Science Publishing (U.S.).

Black, Clinton V. 1965. *The story of Jamaica.* London: Collins.

Blake, Judith. 1961. *Family structure in Jamaica.* New York: Free Press.

Bloch, Maurice. 1974. Symbols, song, dance and features of articulation: or Is religion an extreme form of traditional authority? *Archives Europeenes de Sociology* 15: 55–81.

———. 1977. The past and the present in the present. *Man,* n.s. 18:178–92.

———. 1992. *Prey into hunter: The politics of religious experience.* Lewis Henry Morgan Lectures, 1984. Cambridge and New York: Cambridge Univ. Press.

Boddy, Janice. 1989. *Wombs and alien spirits: Women, men, and the Zar cult in northern Sudan*. Madison: Univ. of Wisconsin Press.

Bolland, O. Nigel. 1992. Creolization and creole societies: A cultural nationalist view of Caribbean social history. In *Intellectuals in the twentieth-century Caribbean*, Vol. 1, ed. A. Hennessy, 50–79. London and Basingstoke: Macmillan.

Bourdieu, Pierre. 1977. *Outline of a theory of practice*. Cambridge Studies in Social Anthropology. Trans. R. Nice. Cambridge: Cambridge Univ. Press.

———. 1984. *Distinction: A social critique of the judgement of taste.* Trans. R. Nice. Cambridge: Harvard Univ. Press.

———. 1991. *Language and symbolic power*. Cambridge: Harvard Univ. Press.

Brathwaite, Edward. 1971. *The development of creole society in Jamaica, 1770–1820*. Oxford: Clarendon Press.

———. 1978. Kumina: The spirit of African survival. *Jamaica Journal*, no. 42: 44–63.

———. 1984. *History of the voice: The development of nation language in Anglophone Caribbean poetry*. London and Port of Spain: New Beacon Books.

Briggs, Charles, and Richard Bauman. 1992. Genre, textuality, and social power. *Journal of Linguistic Anthropology* 2: 131–72.

Brodber, Erna. 1980. Life in Jamaica in the early twentieth century: A presentation of ninety oral accounts. Mimeograph.

———. 1984. A second generation of freemen in Jamaica, 1907–1944. Ph.D. thesis. Univ. of the West Indies.

Brooks, A. A. 1917. *History of Bedwardism or the Jamaica Native Baptist Free Church*. Kingston: Gleaner.

Brown, Colin. 1985. *Jesus in European Protestant thought 1778–1860*. Grand Rapids, Mich.: Baker Book House.

Brown, Peter. 1988. *The body and society: Men, women, and sexual renunciation in early Christianity*. New York: Columbia Univ. Press.

Brown, Raymond. 1986. *The English Baptists of the eighteenth century*. A History of the English Baptists, Vol. 2. London: Baptist Historical Society.

Bryan, Patrick. 1985. Archbishop Nuttall and the revival of the "white man's" church in Jamaica. In *Religion and society*, ed. Barry Higman, 1–26. Mona: Univ. of the West Indies.

———. 1991. *The Jamaican people, 1880–1902*. Warwich University Caribbean Studies. London and Basingstoke: Macmillan.

Buchner, J. H. 1854. *The Moravians in Jamaica*. London: Longman.

Burkett, Randall K. 1978. *Garveyism as a religious movement*. ATLA Monograph Series 13. Metuchen, N.J., and London: Scarecrow Press and American Theological Library Association.

Calley, Malcolm J. C. 1965. *God's people: West Indian Pentecostal sections in England*. London and New York: Oxford Univ. Press.

Campbell, Isaiah. 1984. The Church of God Jamaican experience: From Pocomanianism to Pentecostalism. M.A. thesis. Church of God School of Theology, Cleveland, Tennessee.

Campbell, Mavis C. 1976. *Dynamics of change in a slave society: A socio-political history of the free coloureds of Jamaica*. Cranbury, N.J.: Fairleigh Dickinson Univ.

Carey, S. Pearce. 1923. *William Carey*. London: Hodder and Stoughton.

Carlile, Warrand. 1884. *Thirty-eight years mission life in Jamaica: A brief sketch*. London: James Nisbet.

Carnegie, James, 1973. *Some aspects of Jamaica's politics: 1918–1938*. Kingston: Institute of Jamaica.

Carrithers, Michael, Steven Collins, and Steven Lukes, eds. 1985. *The category of the person: Anthropology, philosophy, history*. Cambridge: Cambridge Univ. Press.

Cassidy, Frederic G. 1971. *Jamaica talk*, 2nd ed. Basingstoke and London: Macmillan and Institute of Jamaica.

Cassidy, Frederic, and R. B. LePage. 1967. *Dictionary of Jamaican English*. Cambridge: Cambridge Univ. Press.

Chevannes, Barry. 1971a. Jamaican lower class religion: Struggles against oppression. M.Sc. thesis. Univ. of the West Indies, Mona.

———. 1971b. Revival and black struggle. *Savacou* 5:27–37.

———. 1985. Jamaican men. Final report to the National Family Planning Board on the In-Depth Study of Jamaican Male Sexual Beliefs and Behaviour. Typescript. Institute of Social and Economic Research, Univ. of the West Indies, Mona.

———. 1989. The social and ideological origins of the Rastafari movement in Jamaica. Unpublished Ph.D. dissertation. Columbia Univ., New York.

———. 1994. *Rastafari: Roots and ideology*. Syracuse: Syracuse Univ. Press.

Clarke, Cyril. 1986. *Handbook of Baptist witness in Clarendon*. Jamaica: Clarendon Baptist Association.

Clarke, Edith. 1966. *My mother who fathered me*, 2nd ed. London: George Allen and Unwin.

Clarke, John. 1869. *Memorials of Baptist missionaries in Jamaica*. London: Yates and Alexander.

Clifford, James. 1988. *The predicament of culture*. Cambridge: Harvard Univ. Press.

Comaroff, Jean. 1985. *Body of power, spirit of resistance*. Chicago: Univ. of Chicago Press.

Comaroff, Jean, and John Comaroff. 1991. *Of revelation and revolution*, Vol. 1. Chicago: Univ. of Chicago Press.

———. 1992. *Ethnography and the historical imagination*. Chicago: Univ. of Chicago Press.

Conn, Charles W. 1955. *Like a mighty army moves the Church of God, 1885–1955*. Cleveland, Tenn.: Church of God Publishing.

———. 1959. Where the saints have trod: A history of the Church of God missions. Cleveland, Tenn.: Pathway Press.

Cooper, Wayne F. 1987. *Claude McKay: Rebel sojourner in the Harlem Renaissance*. New York: Schocken Books.

Crittenden, Paul J. 1990. *Learning to be moral: Philosophical thoughts about moral development*. Atlantic Highlands, N.J. and London: Humanities Press International.

Csordas, Thomas J. 1987. Genre, motive, and metaphor: Conditions for creativity in ritual language. *Cultural Anthropology* 2:445–69.

———. 1994. *The sacred self: A cultural phenomenology of charismatic healing*. Berkeley, Los Angeles, London: Univ. of California Press.

Cucchiari, Salvatore. 1990. Between shame and sanctification: Patriarchy and its transformation in Sicilian Pentecostalism. *American Ethnologist* 17:687–707.

Cumper, George E. 1958. Population movements in Jamaica, 1830–1950. *Social and Economic Studies* 5: 261–80.

———. 1979. *The potential of Ras Tafarianism as a modern national religion.* New Delhi: Recorder Press.

Curtin, Phillip. 1969. *The Atlantic slave trade: A census.* Cambridge: Harvard Univ. Press.

———. 1970. *Two Jamaicas: The role of ideas in a tropical colony, 1830–1865.* New York: Atheneum.

Dante. 1965 ([1899]. *Paradiso.* The Temple Classics. London: J. M. Dent.

Davis, David B. 1966. *The problem of slavery in Western culture.* Ithaca: Cornell Univ. Press.

Davis, J. Merle. 1942. *The church in the new Jamaica.* New York: Academy Press.

Dayton, Donald W. 1975. From "Christian perfection" to the "baptism of the Holy Ghost": A study in the origins of Pentecostalism. In *Aspects of Pentecostal and Charismatic origins,* ed. H. Vinson Synan, 54–63. Plainfield, N.J.: Logos.

———. 1980. Theological roots of Pentecostalism. *Pneuma* Spring:3–21.

———. 1987. *Theological roots of Pentecostalism.* Grand Rapids, Mich.: Francis Ashbury Press.

De Certeau, Michel. 1984. *The practice of everyday life.* Berkeley: Univ. of California Press.

———. 1988. The formality of practices: From religious systems to the ethics of the Enlightenment. In *The writing of history,* trans. T. Conley, 147–206. New York: Columbia Univ. Press.

De Lisser, Herbert, G. 1913. *Twentieth century Jamaica.* Kingston: Jamaica Times.

Derrida, Jacques. 1976. *Of grammatology.* Trans. G. C. Spivak. Baltimore: Johns Hopkins Univ. Press.

———. 1982. *Margins of philosophy.* Trans. Alan Bass. Chicago: Univ. of Chicago Press.

Diamond, Stanley. 1971. Introductory essay: Job and the trickster. In Paul Radin, *The trickster: A study in American Indian mythology,* xi–xxii. New York: Schocken Books.

Dominguez, Velez. 1975. *From neighbor to stranger: The dilemma of Caribbean peoples in the United States.* New Haven: Yale Univ. Press.

Dorsey, Odeline W. 1974. *History of the City Mission [on the fiftieth anniversary of the Kingston City Mission].* Kingston: n.p.

Douglas, Mary. 1966. *Purity and danger: An analysis of concepts of pollution and taboo.* London and Henley: Routledge and Kegan Paul.

Dreher, Melanie, and C. M. Rogers. 1976. Getting high: Ganja man and his socioeconomic milieu. *Caribbean Studies* 16, no. 2:219–31.

Drewal, Margaret T. 1992. *Yoruba ritual.* Bloomington and Indiana: Indiana Univ. Press.

Dumont, Louis. 1970. *Homo hierarchicus: An essay on the caste system.* Trans. Mark Sainsbury. Chicago: Univ. of Chicago Press.

———. 1977. *From Mandeville to Marx: The genesis and triumph of economic ideology*. Chicago: Univ. of Chicago Press.

———. 1986. *Essays on individualism: Modern ideology in anthropological perspective*. Chicago and London: Univ. of Chicago Press.

Eaton, George. 1975. *Alexander Bustamante and the modern Jamaica*. Kingston: Kingston Publishers.

Eisner, Gisella. 1960. *Jamaica, 1830–1930: A study in economic growth*. Manchester: Manchester Univ. Press.

Elkins, W. F. 1975. "Warrior" Higgins, a Jamaican street preacher. *Jamaica Journal* 8: 28–31.

Ellis, Alfred B. 1890. *The Ewe-speaking people of the Slave Coast of West Africa*. London: Chapman and Hall.

Emerick, Abraham. 1915. *Jamaica superstitions: Obeah and duppyism in Jamaica*. Woodstock, Md.: n.p.

Engels, Friedrich. 1972 [1890–93]. Letters on historical materialism. In *The Marx-Engels reader*, ed. Robert C. Tucker, 640–50. New York: W. W. Norton.

Evans-Pritchard, E. E. 1956. *Nuer religion*. Oxford and New York: Oxford Univ. Press.

Faubion, James D. 1995. Introduction. In *Rethinking the subject: An anthology of contemporary European thought*, ed. James D. Faubion, 1–27. Boulder, San Francisco, Oxford: Westview Press.

Fernandez, James. 1982. *Bwiti: An ethnography of the religious imagination in Africa*. Princeton: Princeton Univ. Press.

Field, M. James. 1937. *Religion and medicine of the Ga people*. Oxford: Oxford Univ. Press.

Finnegan, Ruth. 1970. *Oral literature in Africa*. Oxford: Clarendon Press.

Fletcher, Duncan. 1867. *Personal recollections of the Honourable George W. Gordon*. London: Elliot Stock.

Fogarty, Robert S. 1972. *American utopionism*. Itasea, Ill.: F. E. Peacock Publishers.

Foner, Nancy. 1973. *Status and power in rural Jamaica: A study of education and political change*. New York: Teachers College Press, Columbia Univ.

———. 1979. *Jamaica farewell: Jamaican migrants in London*. London and Henley: Routledge and Kegan Paul.

Forde, Daryl, ed. 1954. *African worlds*. London: Oxford Univ. Press.

Fortes, Myer. 1945. *The dynamics of clanship among the Tallensi*. London: Oxford Univ. Press.

———. 1965. Some reflections in ancestor worship in Africa. In *African systems of thought*, ed. M. Fortes and G. Dieterlen. London, New York, Toronto: Oxford Univ. Press for the International African Institute.

———. 1987. *Religion, morality and the person: Essays on Tallensi religion*. Cambridge and New York: Cambridge Univ. Press.

Foucault, Michel. 1972. *The archaeology of knowledge and the discourse on language*. New York: Pantheon Books.

———. 1977. *Discipline and punish: The birth of the prison*. Harmondsworth: Penguin Books.

———. 1978. *The history of sexuality: An introduction.* Harmondsworth: Penguin Books.

———. 1980. Two lectures. In *Power/knowledge,* ed. C. Gordon. Brighton: Harvester.

———. 1985. *The use of pleasure.* New York: Vintage Books.

———. 1986. Politics and ethics: An interview. In *The Foucault reader,* ed. P. Rabinow, 373–80. Harmondsworth: Penguin Books.

French, Joan. 1986. Colonial policy towards women after the 1938 uprising: The case of Jamaica. Presented to the Conference of the Caribbean Studies Association, Caracas.

French, Joan, and Honor Ford-Smith. n.d. Women and organisation in Jamaica, 1900–1944. In *Women and development studies.* The Hague: Institute of Social and Economic Research.

Freud, Sigmund. 1971 [1916]. Lecture 35: The question of a Weltanschauung. In *The complete introductory lectures on psychoanalysis,* trans. and ed. J. Strachey. London: George Allen and Unwin.

Furley, Oliver W. 1965. Moravian missionaries and slaves in the West Indies. *Caribbean Studies* 5:3–16.

Gardner, W. J. 1873. *A history of Jamaica from its discovery by Christopher Columbus to the year 1872.* London: Frank Cass.

Garvey, Amy Jacques, ed. 1969. *Philosophy and opinions of Marcus Garvey.* New York: Arno.

———. 1970. *Garvey and Garveyism.* London: Collier Macmillan.

Gates, Henry L., Jr. 1988. *The signifying monkey: A theory of Afro-American literary criticism.* New York: Oxford Univ. Press.

Gee, Donald. 1949. *The Pentecostal movement,* 2nd ed. London: Elim Publishing.

Geertz, Clifford. 1968. *Islam observed: Religious development in Morocco and Indonesia.* Chicago: Univ. of Chicago Press.

———. 1973a. Thick description: Towards an interpretive theory of culture. In *The interpretation of cultures,* 3–30. New York: Basic Books.

———. 1973b. Person, time and conduct in Bali. In *The interpretation of cultures,* 360–411. New York: Basic Books.

———. 1973c. Religion as a cultural system. In *The interpretation of cultures,* 87–125. New York: Basic Books. Originally published 1966 in *Anthropological approaches to religion,* ed. M. Banton. London: Tavistock.

———. 1980. *Negara.* Cambridge: Cambridge Univ. Press.

Geisler, N. L., and J. Y. Amanu. 1988. Evil. In *New dictionary of theology,* ed. Sinclair B. Ferguson, David F. Wright, and J. I. Packer, 241–43. Leicester, England, and Downers Grove, Ill.: Inter-Varsity Press.

Genovese, Eugene G. 1976. *Roll, Jordan, roll: The world the slaves made.* New York: Random House.

Giddens, Anthony. 1979. *Central problems in social theory: Action, structure and contradiction in social analysis.* London: Macmillan.

Gill, Lesley. 1990. "Like veil to cover them": Women and the Pentecostal movement in La Paz. *American Ethnologist* 17:708–21.

Glazier, Stephen D., ed. 1980. *Perspectives on Pentecostalism: Case studies from the Caribbean and Latin America*. Washington, D.C.: Univ. Press of America.

Gmelch, George. 1992. *Double passage: The lives of Caribbean migrants abroad and back home*. Ann Arbor: Univ. of Michigan Press.

Golder, Morris E. 1973. *History of the Pentecostal Assemblies of the World*. Indianapolis: n.p.

Goodman, Felicitas D. 1969. Phonetic analysis of glossolalia in four cultural settings. *Journal for the Scientific Study of Religion* 8:227–39.

———. 1972. *Speaking in tongues: A cross-cultural study of glossolalia*. Chicago: Univ. of Chicago Press.

Goody, Jack. 1962. *Death, property and the ancestors*. Stanford: Stanford Univ. Press.

Gordon, Derek. 1987. *Class, status and social mobility in Jamaica*. Mona: Institute of Social and Economic Research, Univ. of the West Indies.

———. 1989. Women, work and social mobility in post-war Jamaica. In *Women and the sexual division of labour in the Caribbean*, ed. K. Hart, 67–80. Kingston: Consortium Graduate School of Social Sciences.

———. 1991. Access to high school education in postwar Jamaica. In *Education and society in the Commonwealth Caribbean*, ed. E. Miller, 181–206. Mona: Institute of Social and Economic Research, Univ. of the West Indies.

Gordon, Shirley. 1963. *A century of West Indian education*. London: Longman Group.

Gordon, Thomas G. 1989. *Revivalism and cultural change: Christianity, nation building and the market in nineteenth century United States*. Chicago and London: Univ. of Chicago Press.

Graham, Tom. n.d. *The story of the Church of God in Jamaica*. Kingston: Task Printers.

Gramsci, Antonio. 1971. *Selections from the prison notebooks*. Trans. Q. Hoare and G. Nowell Smith. London: Lawrence and Wishart.

Grant, Robin. 1985. The London Missionary Society in Jamaica 1834–67. In *Religion and society,* ed. Barry Higman, 1–19. Univ. of the West Indies, Kingston.

Green, William. 1976. *British slave emanicipation: The sugar colonies and the great experiment, 1830–1865*. Oxford: Clarendon Press.

Gutierrez, Ramon A. 1984. From honor to love: Transformations of the meaning of sexuality in colonial New Mexico. In *Kinship ideology and practice in Latin America*, ed. R. T. Smith, 237–63. Chapel Hill and London: Univ. of North Carolina Press.

Hall, Douglas. 1953. The apprenticeship period in Jamaica, 1834–1838. *Caribbean Quarterly* 13:142–66.

———. 1959. *Free Jamaica*. New Haven: Yale Univ. Press.

———. 1964. The early banana trade from Jamaica, 1868–1905: A descriptive account. In *Ideas and illustrations in economic history*. New York: Holt, Rinehart and Winston.

Hall, Stuart. 1995. Negotiating Caribbean identities. *New Left Review* 209:3–14.

Halliday, Joseph. 1991. Education and society in St. Kitts and Nevis. In *Education and society in the Commonwealth Caribbean*, ed. Errol Miller, 27–58. Mona: Institute of Social and Economic Research, Univ. of the West Indies.

Harding, Susan. 1988. Review of God's choice: The total world of a fundamentalist Christian school. *American Ethnologist* 15:582.

Hart, Kevin. 1989. *The trespass of the sign: Deconstruction, theology and philosophy.* Cambridge and New York: Cambridge Univ. Press.

Hawkins, Charles G. n.d. Jamaica. Unpublished report of the World Mission Department, the Church of God of Prophecy, Cleveland, Tennessee.

Hebdige, Dick. 1979. *Subculture: The meaning of style.* London: Methuen.

Henderson, George E. 1867. Letter of the ministers of the Jamaican Baptist Union to His Excellency Edward John Eyre, Esq. In *Dr. Underhill's Letter,* E. B. Underhill, pp.22–48. London: Arthur Miall.

Henderson, George E. 1931. *Goodness and mercy: A tale of a hundred years.* Kingston: Gleaner.

Henriques, Fernando. 1968. *Family and colour in Jamaica,* 2nd ed. London: Mac-Gibbon and Kee.

————. 1974. *The children of Caliban: Miscegenation.* London: Secker and Warburg.

Herskovits, Melville J. 1938. *Dahomey: An ancient west African Kingdom.* New York: J. J. Augustin.

Heumann, Gad J. 1981a. White over brown over black: The free coloureds in Jamaican society during slavery and after emancipation. *Journal of Caribbean History* 14:46–69.

————.Heumann, Gad J. 1981b. *Between black and white.* Westport, Conn.: Greenwood Press.

Higman, Barry. 1976. *Slave population and economy in Jamaica, 1807–1834.* Cambridge: Cambridge Univ. Press.

————. 1983. Domestic service in Jamaica, since 1750. In *Trade, Government and Society in Caribbean History, 1700–1920: Essays presented to Douglas Hall,* ed. B. Higman. 117–38. London and Trinidad: Heinemann.

————. 1984. Terms for kin in the British West Indian slave community: Differing perceptions of masters and slaves. In *Kinship ideology and practice in Latin America,* ed. Raymond T. Smith, 59–81. Chapel Hill and London: Univ. of North Carolina Press.

Hill, Frank. 1976. *Bustamante and his letters.* Kingston: Kingston Publishing.

Hill, Robert. 1983. Leonard P. Howell and millenarian visions in early Rastafari. *Jamaica Journal* 16:24–39.

Hill, Robert, ed. 1983–85. *The Marcus Garvey and Universal Negro Association Papers,* Vol. 1. Berkeley: Univ. of California Press.

Hine, Virginia. H. 1968. Pentecostal glossolalia: Toward a functional interpretation. *Journal for the Scientific Study of Religion* 8:211–26.

Hinton, John H. 1847. *Memoir of William Knibb, missionary in Jamaica.* London: Houlston and Stoneman.

Hobbs, Doreen. 1986. *Jewels of the Caribbean: The history of the Salvation Army in the Caribbean Territory.* London: General of the Salvation Army.

Hobsbawm, Eric.J. 1990. Review of *Alabi's world* by Richard Price. *New York Review of Books* 37, no. 19:46–48.

Hogg, Donald. 1964. *Jamaica religions: A study in variations.* Unpublished Ph.D. dissertation, Yale Univ.

Hollenweger, Walter J. 1972. *The Pentecostals*. Trans. R. A. Wilson. London: SCM Press.

Holt, Thomas. 1991. *The problem of freedom*. Baltimore: Johns Hopkins Univ. Press.

Hopkin, John B. 1978. Music in the Pentecostal church. *Jamaica Journal* 42:22–40.

Horton, Robin. 1964. Ritual man in Africa. *Africa* 34:36–58.

———. 1967. African traditional thought and Western science. *Africa* 37: 50–71.

———. 1971. African conversion. *Africa* 41:85–108.

———. 1975. On the rationality of conversion. *Africa* 45:219–35, 372–99.

Hubert, Henri, and M. Mauss. 1964 [1898]. *Sacrifice: Its nature and function*. Trans. W. D. Hall. Chicago: Univ. of Chicago Press.

Huggins, Molly. 1967. *Too much to tell: An autobiography*. London: Heinemann.

Iglesias Garcia, Fe. 1985. The development of capitalism in Cuban sugar production, 1860–1900. In *Between slavery and free Labour: The Spanish-speaking Caribbean in the nineteenth century*, ed. M. M. Fraginals, F. Moga Pons, and S. L. Engerman. Baltimore: Johns Hopkins Univ. Press.

Ireland, Roland. 1991. *Kingdoms come: Religion and politics in Brazil*. Pitt Latin American Series. Pittsburgh: Univ. of Pittsburg Press.

Jacobs, H. P. 1953. The parish of Clarendon. *The West Indian Review*, September: 14–21.

Jamaica. 1910. *Handbook of Jamaica*. Kingston: Government Printer.

Jamaica. 1943. *Census of population*. Kingston: Government Printer.

Jekyll, Walter. 1907. *Jamaican song and story: Anancy stories, digging songs, ring tunes and dancing tunes*. London: David Nutt.

Jones, Charles E. 1974. *Perfectionist persuasion*. Metuchen, N.J.: Scarecrow Press.

Jordan, Winthrop D. 1969. *White over black: American attitudes towards the Negro, 1550–1812*. Baltimore: Penguin Books.

Jules-Rosette, Bennetta. 1975. *African apostles: Ritual and conversion in the church of John Maranke*. Ithaca and London: Cornell Univ. Press.

Kant, Immanuel. 1960 [1899]. *Education*. Trans. A. Churton. Michigan: Univ. of Michigan Press.

Kapferer, Bruce. 1979a. Emotion and healing in Sinhalese healing rites. *Social Analysis* 1:153–76.

———. 1979b. Mind, self, and other in demonic illness: The negation and reconstruction of self. *American Ethnologist* 6:110–33.

Kelly, John D. 1991. *A politics of virtue: Hinduism, sexuality and countercolonial discourse in Fiji*. Chicago and London: Univ. of Chicago Press.

Kerr, Madeline. 1952. *Personality and conflict in Jamaica*. Liverpool: Liverpool Univ. Press.

King, Rev. David. 1850. *The state and prospects of Jamaica*. London: Johnstone and Hunter.

Knibb, William. 1842. *Speech before the Baptist Missionary Society in Exeter Hall, April 28, 1842*. London: G. and J. Dyer.

Knight, Franklin W. 1985. Jamaican migrants and the Cuban sugar industry, 1900–1934. In *Between slavery and free labour: The Spanish-speaking Caribbean in the nineteenth century*, ed. M. M. Fraginals, F. M. Pons, and S. L. Engerman, 84–114. Baltimore: Johns Hopkins Univ. Press.

Knight, R. A. L., ed. 1938. *Liberty and progress: A short history of the Baptists of Jamaica.* Kingston: Gleaner.

Knox, Bruce. 1976. The queen's letter of 1865 and British policy towards emancipation and indentured labour in the West Indies, 1830–1865. *Historical Journal* 29: 345–67.

Laguerre, Michel. 1987. *Afro-Caribbean folk medicine.* South Hadley, Mass.: Bergin and Garvey.

Langley, Lester G. 1980. *The United States and the Caribbean in the twentieth century.* Athens: Univ. of Georgia Press.

Laqueur, Thomas W. 1976. *Religion and respectability: Sunday schools and working class culture, 1780–1850.* New Haven: Yale Univ. Press.

LaRuffa, Anthony. 1971. *San Cipriano: Life in a Puerto Rican community.* New York: Gordon and Breach.

———. 1980. Pentecostalism in Puerto Rican society. In *Perspectives on Pentecostalism,* ed. S. Glazier, 44–65. Washington, D.C.: Univ. Press of America.

Latourette, Kenneth S. 1975. *A history of Christianity,* Vol. 2. New York and London: Harper and Row.

Lavrin, Asuncion. 1989. Sexuality in colonial Mexico: A church dilemma. In *Sexuality and marriage in colonial Latin America,* ed. M. C. Meyer, J. D. Martz, and M. Leon-Portilla, 47–95. Lincoln and London: Univ. of Nebraska Press.

Lerner, Gerda. 1986. *The creation of patriarchy.* New York and Oxford: Oxford Univ. Press.

Letham, R. W. A. 1988. Arminianism. In *New dictionary of theology,* ed. Sinclair B. Ferguson, David F. Wright, and J. L. Packer, 45–46. Leicester, England, and Downers Grove, Ill.: Inter-Varsity Press.

Levine, Lawrence W. 1978. *Black culture and consciousness.* New York: Oxford Univ. Press.

Lévi-Strauss, Claude. 1963. *Structural anthropology.* Trans. C. Jacobson and B. G. Schoepf. Harmondsworth: Penguin Books.

Lewis, Gordon K. 1983. *Main currents in Caribbean thought.* Kingston and Port of Spain: Heinemann.

Lewis, Ioan M. 1971. *Ecstatic religion.* Harmondsworth: Penguin Books.

Lewis, J. Lowell. 1995. Genre and embodiment: From Brazilian *capoeira* to the ethnology of human movement. *Cultural Anthropology* 10: 221–43.

Lewis, Matthew G. 1969 [1834]. *Journal of a West Indian proprietor.* New York: Negro Universities Press. Originally published by John Murray, London.

Lewis, Rupert. 1987. *Marcus Garvey: Anti-colonial champion.* London: Karia Press.

Lincoln, C. Eric, and L. H. Mamiya. 1990. *The black church in the African American experience.* Durham and London: Duke Univ. Press.

Linger, Daniel. 1993. The hegemony of discontent. *American Ethnologist* 20: 3–24.

Lloyd, Genevieve. 1984. *The man of reason.* London: Methuen.

———. 1985. Masters, slaves and others. In *Radical philosophy reader,* ed. R. Edgley and R. Osborne, 291–309. London: Verso.

———. 1993. *Being in time: Selves and narrators in philosophy and literature.* London and New York: Routledge.

Lobdell, Richard. 1988. Women in the Jamaican labour force 1881–1921. *Social and Economic Studies* 37, nos. 1 and 2:203–40.

Long, Edward. 1774. *History of Jamaica.* London: Lowndes.

Long, Joseph K. 1973. Balm Jamaica folk medicine. Ph.D. dissertation, Department of Anthropology, Univ. of North Carolina.

Lucas, J. Olumide. 1948. *The religion of the Yorubas.* Lagos: CMS Bookshop.

MacCormack, Carol P., and A. Draper. 1987. Social and cognitive aspects of female sexuality in Jamaica. In *The cultural construction of sexuality,* ed. P. Caplan. London and New York: Tavistock Publications.

MacGavran, Donald. 1962. *Church growth in Jamaica.* Lucknow: Lucknow Publishing.

MacIntyre, Alasdair. 1981. *After virtue: A study in moral theory.* London: Duckworth.

————. 1988. *Whose justice? Whose rationality?* London: Duckworth.

Mais, Roger. 1966. *Brother man.* In *The three novels of Roger Mais.* Kingston: Sangster's Book Stores with Jonathan Cape.

Manning, Frank. 1973. *Black clubs in Bermuda: Ethnography of a play world.* Ithaca: Cornell Univ. Press.

————. 1980. Pentecostalism: Christianity and reputation. In *Perspectives on Pentecostalism,* 177–88. Washington, D.C.: Univ. Press of America.

Marcuse, Herbert. 1983. *From Luther to Popper.* Trans. Joris de Bres. London and New York: Verso.

Marley, Bob. 1992. *Songs of freedom.* Milwaukee: Hal Leonard.

Marsden, George M. 1980. *Fundamentalism and American culture: The shaping of twentieth century Evangelicalism.* Oxford: Oxford Univ. Press.

Marshall, Dawn I. 1982. The history of Caribbean migrations. *Caribbean Review* 11, no. 1:6–9, 52–53.

Martin, Richard D. 1983. *Evangelicals united: Ecumenical stirrings in pre-Victorian Britain, 1795–1930.* London: Methuen.

Marwick, Max. 1970. Witchcraft as a social strain gauge. In *Witchcraft and sorcery,* 280–95. Harmondsworth: Penguin Books.

Marx, Karl. 1972a [1932]. The German ideology: Part I. In *The Marx-Engels reader,* ed. Robert C. Tucker, 110–64. New York: W. W. Norton.

Marx, Karl. 1972b [1872]. Manifesto of the Communist Party. In *The Marx-Engels reader,* ed. Robert C. Tucker, 331–62. New York: W. W. Norton.

Mason, Elsie W. 1985. Bishop C. H. Mason, Church of God in Christ. In *Afro-American religious history: A documentary witness,* ed. M. C. Sernett, 285–95. Durham: Duke Univ. Press.

Mauss, Marcel. 1985 [1938]. A category of the human mind: The notion of the person, the notion of self. Trans. W. D. Hall. In *The category of the person: Anthropology, philosophy, history,* ed. M. Carrithers, Steven Collins, and Steven Lukes, 1–25. Cambridge and New York: Cambridge Univ. Press.

Mbiti, John S. 1969. *African religions and philosophy.* London: Heinemann.

McGibbon, Jacqui. 1987. Culture and power: The anthropology of Jamaican slave plantations. B. A. (honors) dissertation, University of Sydney.

McKay, Claude 1933. *Banana Bottom*. New York: Harcourt Brace Jovanovich.

McKay, Claude 1979. *My green hills of Jamaica and five Jamaican short stories*. Kingston: Heinemann.

McLoughlin, William G. 1960. Introduction. In *Charles Finney, Lectures on revivals of religion*. Cambridge: Harvard Univ. Press.

Meredith, A. W. 1938. The Jamaica Baptist Missionary Society. In *Liberty and progress*, ed. R. A. L. Knight, 32–54. Kingston: Gleaner .

Miller, Errol. 1986. *Marginalization of the black male: Insights from the development of the teaching profession*. Mona: Institute of Social and Economic Research, Univ. of the West Indies.

———. 1990. *Jamaican society and high schooling*. Mona: Institute of Social and Economic Research, Univ. of the West Indies.

Milne-Home, Mary P. 1890. *Mamma's black nurse stories*. Edinburgh and London: William Blackwood.

Mintz, Sidney. 1960. *Worker in the cane*. New Haven: Yale Univ. Press.

———. 1974a. The origins of the reconstituted peasantries. In *Caribbean transformations*, 146–56. Chicago: Aldine.

———. 1974b. The historical sociology of Jamaican villages. In *Caribbean transformations*, 157–79. Chicago: Aldine.

———. 1985. *Sweetness and power: The place of sugar in modern history*. New York: Viking.

Mintz, Sidney, and R. Price. 1976. *An anthropological approach to the Afro-American past: A Caribbean perspective*. Philadelphia: Institute for the Study of Human Issues. Republished 1992 as *The birth of African American culture: An anthropological perspective*. Boston: Beacon Press.

Moore, Joseph G. 1953. *The religion of Jamaican Negroes: A study of Afro-American acculturation*. Ph.D. dissertation, Northwestern Univ.

Moyne, Lord. 1945 [1938]. *Report (with appendices) of the commission appointed to enquire into the disturbances which occurred in Jamaica between the 23rd May and the 8th June 1938*. Kingston: Government Printing Office.

Myers, Fred R. 1986. *Pintupi country, Pintupi self: Sentiment, place, and politics among Western Desert Aborigines*. Washington, D.C.: Smithsonian Institution Press.

Nadel, Sigfried F. 1946. A study of shamanism in the Nuba Mountains. *Journal of the Royal Anthropological Institute of Great Britain and Ireland* 76:25–37.

———. 1970. Witchcraft in four African societies. In *Witchcraft and Sorcery*, ed. M. Marwick, 264–79. Harmondsworth: Penguin Books.

Nettleford, Rex. 1970. *Mirror, mirror: Identity, race and protest in Jamaica*. Kingston: William Collins and Sangster.

———. 1971. *Manley and the new Jamaica: Selected speeches and writings, 1938–1968*. Trinidad and Kingston and Port of Spain: Longman.

Newton, Velma. 1984. *The silver men: West Indian labour migration to Panama, 1850–1914*. Mona: Institute of Social and Economic Research, Univ. of the West Indies.

Nietzsche, Friedrich. 1967 [1888]. *On the genealogy of morals*. Trans. W. Kaufmann and R. J. Hollingdale. New York: Random House.

Norris, Katrin. 1962. *Jamaica: The search for identity*. Oxford: Oxford Univ. Press.

Nuttall, Enos. 1896. *Letter to professing persons and congregations in Jamaica, 1896*. Kingston: J. McGraw Reeves.

Olivier, Sidney. 1910. *White capital and coloured labour*. London: Independent Labour Party.

———. 1936. *Jamaica, the blessed island*. London: Faber and Faber.

Olwig, Karen Fog. 1993. *Global culture, island identity*. Camberwell, Paris, etc.: Harwood Academic Publishers.

Ong, Aihwa. 1987. *Spirits of resistance and capitalist discipline*. New York: State Univ. of New York Press.

Orr, J. Edwin. 1949. *The second evangelical awakening*. London and Edinburgh: Marshall, Morgan and Scott.

Paget, Hugh. n.d. The free village system in Jamaica. In *Apprenticeship and emancipation*, 45–58. Mona: Department of Extra-Mural Studies, Univ. of the West Indies.

Parrinder, Geoffrey. 1961. *West African religion: A study of beliefs and practices of Akan, Ewe, Yoruba, Ibo and kindred peoples*. London: Epworth Press.

Parsons, Talcott, Edward Shils, Gordon W. Allport, Clyde Kluckhohn, et al. 1962. Some fundamental categories of the theory of action: A general statement. In *Towards a general theory of action: Theoretical foundations for the social sciences*, ed. Talcott Parsons and Edward Shils, 3–27. New York: Harper and Row.

Passmore, John. 1970. *The perfectibility of man*. New York: Charles Scribner's Sons.

Patterson, Orlando. 1967. *The sociology of slavery*. London: MacGibbon and Key.

———. 1983. *Slavery and social death: A comparative study*. Cambridge and London: Harvard Univ. Press.

Patton, Paul. 1989. Taylor and Foucault on power and freedom. *Political Studies* 37: 260–76.

———. 1993. Politics and the concept of power in Hobbes and Nietzsche. In *Nietzsche, feminism and political theory*, 144–61. London: Routledge; St. Leonards: Allen and Unwin.

Payne, Anthony J. 1988. *Politics in Jamaica*. London: C. Hurst.

Payne, Ernest A. 1933. *Freedom in Jamaica: Some chapters in the story of the Baptist Missionary Society*. London: Carey Press.

Pelton, Robert D. 1980. *The trickster in West Africa: A study of mythic irony and sacred delight*. Berkeley, Los Angeles, London: Univ. of California Press.

Peshkin, Alan. 1986. *God's choice: The total world of a fundamentalist Christian school*. Chicago and London: Univ. of Chicago Press.

Peters, John. 1956. *Christian perfection and American Methodism*. New York: Abingdon Press.

Phelps, Owen. W. 1960. The rise of the labour movement in Jamaica. *Social and Economic Studies* 9: 427–68.

Phillippo, James M. 1970 [1843]. *Jamaica: Its past and present state*. Westport: Negro Universities Press. Originally published by John Snow, London.

Phillips, Wade H. 1986. The latter rain and the latter house. In *White Winged Messenger*. May 31: 5–14, 31.

Pollard, Velma. 1980. Dread talk: The speech of the Rastafarian in Jamaica. *Caribbean Quarterly* 26: 32–41.

Poole, Ross. 1991. *Morality and modernity*. London: Routledge.

Pope, Liston. 1942. *Millhands and preachers*. New Haven and London: Yale Univ. Press.

Post, Ken. 1969. The politics of protest in Jamaica, 1938: Some problems of analysis and conceptualization. *Social and Economic Studies* 18:138–51.

———. 1978. *Arise ye starvelings: The Jamaican labour rebellion of 1838 and its aftermath*. The Hague: Martinus Nijhoff.

Potts, Eli Daniel. 1967. *British Baptist missionaries in India, 1793–1837: The history of Serampore and its missions*. London: Cambridge Univ. Press.

Povinelli, Elizabeth A. 1993. *Labor's lot: The power, history and culture of aboriginal action*. Chicago and London: Univ. of Chicago Press.

Price, Rev. E. P. 1930. *Bananaland*. London: Carey Press.

Price, Richard. 1983. *First time: The historical vision of an Afro-American people*. Baltimore and London: Johns Hopkins Univ. Press.

———. 1990. *Alabi's world*. Baltimore and London: Johns Hopkins Univ. Press.

Raboteau, Albert J. 1980. *Slave religion*. New York: Oxford Univ. Press.

Ranger, Terence O. 1986. Religious movements and politics in sub-Saharan Africa. *African Studies Review* 29:1–69.

Rattray, Robert S. 1923. *Ashanti*. Oxford: Clarendon Press.

———. 1927. *Religion and art in the Ashanti*. Oxford: Clarendon Press.

———. 1969 [1930]. *Akan-Ashanti folk tales*. Oxford: Clarendon Press.

Reid, Victor Stafford. 1985. *The horses of the morning*. Kingston: Authors Publishing.

Religious Tract Society. 1842. *Jamaica: Enslaved and free*. London: Religious Tract Society.

Reynolds, Ralph V. n.d. *History of Pentecost*. Hazelwood, Miss.: Overseas Ministries.

Richards, Audrey. 1970. A modern movement of witch-finders. In *Witchcraft and sorcery*, ed. M. Marwick, 164–77. Harmondsworth: Penguin Books.

Rice, C. Duncan. 1975. *The rise and fall of black slavery*. London and Basingstoke: Macmillan.

Ricoeur, Paul. 1967. *The symbolism of Evil*. Boston: Beacon Press.

———. 1986a. *Fallible man*. Trans. C. A. Kalbley. New York: Fordham Univ. Press.

———. 1986b. *Lectures on ideology and utopia*, ed. G. H. Taylor. New York: Columbia Univ. Press.

Roberts, George W. 1957. *The population of Jamaica*. Cambridge: Cambridge Univ. Press.

Robotham, Donald. 1981. *"The notorious riot": The socio-economic and political bases of Paul Bogle's revolt*. Working Paper No. 28. Mona: Institute of Social and Economic Research, Univ. of the West Indies.

Robotham, Hugh. 1969. Jamaica Agricultural Society North Clarendon rural development (self-help) project survey. Typescript.

Rosaldo, Renato. 1989. *Culture and truth: The remaking of social analysis*. Boston: Beacon Press.

Rose, Susan D. 1987. Women warriors: The negotiation of gender in a charismatic community. *Sociological Analysis*. 48, no. 3:245–58.

Rowe, Maureen. 1980. The women in Rastafari. *Caribbean Quarterly* 26:13–21.

Russell, Horace O. 1983. The emergence of the Christian black: The making of a stereotype. *Jamaica Journal* 16:51–58.

Russell, J. C. 1986. A brief history of Pentecostal work in Jamaica. *The Evening Light* (United Pentecostal Church in Jamaica). August 16:9–10.

Ryman, Cheryl. 1984. Jonkonnu: A Neo-African form. *Jamaica Journal* 17:18–24.

Sahlins, Marshall. 1985. *Islands of history.* Chicago: Univ. of Chicago Press.

———. 1995. *How "natives" think: About Captain Cook, for example.* Chicago: Univ. of Chicago Press.

Samarin, William J. 1972. Sociolinguistic vs. neurophysiological explanations for glossolalia: A comment on Goodman's paper. *Journal for the Scientific Study of Religion* 11:293–96.

———. 1973. Glossolalia as regressive speech. *Language and Speech* 16:77–89.

Samuel, Peter. 1850. *The Wesleyan-Methodist missions in Jamaica and Honduras.* London: Partridge and Oakley.

Sandeen, Ernest R. 1970. *The roots of fundamentalism: British and American Millenarianism, 1800–1930.* Chicago: Univ. of Chicago Press.

Sceats, D. D. 1988. Perfectionism. In *New dictionary of theology,* ed. Sinclair B. Ferguson, David F Wright, and J. I. Packer, 505–6. Leicester, England, and Downers Grove, Ill.: Inter-Varsity Press.

Schuler, Monica. 1980. *"Alas, alas, Kongo": A social history of indentured African immigration into Jamaica, 1841–1865.* Baltimore: Johns Hopkins Univ. Press.

Schutz, Alfred. 1962–66. *Collected papers.* Ed.Maurice Natanson. The Hague and Boston: Nijhoff.

Scott, Shaunna L. 1994. "They don't have to live by the old traditions": Saintly men, sinner women, and an Appalachian Pentecostal revival. *American Ethnologist* 21: 227–44.

Seaga, Edward. 1969 [rept. 1982]. Revival cults in Jamaica: Notes toward a sociology of religion. *Jamaica Journal* 3:3–13.

Semaj, Leachcim Tufani. 1980. Rastafari: From religion to social theory. *Caribbean Quarterly* 26:22–31.

Senior, Olive. 1978. The Colon people. *Jamaica Journal* 11:62–71 (March); 87–103 (Sept.).

Sider, Gerald. 1993. *Lumbee Indian histories: Race, ethnicity and Indian identity in the southern United States.* Cambridge and Melbourne: Cambridge Univ. Press.

Simey, Thomas S. 1946. *Welfare and planning in the West Indies.* Oxford: Clarendon Press.

Simpson, George Eaton. 1956. Jamaican Revivalist cults. *Social and Economic Studies* 5: 321–403.

———. 1978. *Black religions in the New World.* New York: Columbia Univ. Press.

Smith, Rev. Ashley. 1978. Pentecostalism in Jamaica. *Jamaica Journal* 42:3–13.

Smith, Edwin W. 1950. *African ideas of God, a symposium.* London: Edinburgh House Press.

Smith, Michael G. 1962. *Kinship and community in Carriacou.* New Haven: Yale Univ. Press.

———. 1965a. The plural framework of Jamaican society. In *The plural society in the British West Indies,* 162–75. Berkeley and Los Angeles: Univ. of California Press.

———. 1965b. Some aspects of the social structure of the British Caribbean about 1820. In *The plural society in the British West Indies,* 92–115. Berkeley and Los Angeles: Univ. of California Press.

———. 1966. Introduction. In *My mother who fathered me*, Edith Clarke. London: George Allen and Unwin.

———. 1984. *Culture, race and class in the Commonwealth Caribbean*. Mona: Department of Extra-Mural Studies, Univ. of the West Indies.

Smith, Michael G., R. Augier, and R. Nettleford. 1960. *The Rastafarian movement in Kingston, Jamaica*. Mona: Institute of Social and Economic Research, Univ. of the West Indies.

Smith, Raymond, T. 1967. Social stratification, cultural pluralism and integration in West Indian societies. In *Caribbean integration: Papers on social, political and economic integration,* ed. S. Lewis and T. G. Mathews, 226–58. Rio Pedras: Institute of Caribbean Studies, Univ. of Puerto Rico.

———. 1976. Religion in the formation of West Indian society: Guyana and Jamaica. In *The African diaspora: Interpretive essays,* ed. M. L. Kilson and R. I. Rotberg, 312–41. Cambridge: Harvard Univ. Press.

——— 1982. Race and class in the post-emancipation Caribbean. In *Racism and colonialism,* ed. R. Ross, 93–119. The Hague: Martinus Nijhoff.

———, ed. 1984. *Kinship ideology and practice in Latin America*. Chapel Hill and London: Univ. of North Carolina Press.

———. 1987. Hierarchy and the dual marriage system in West Indian society. In *Gender and kinship: Essays toward a unified analysis,* ed. J. F. Collier and S. J. Yanagisako, 163–96, 353–56. Stanford: Stanford Univ.Press.

———. 1988. *Kinship and class in the West Indies*. Cambridge: Cambridge Univ. Press.

———. 1995. "Living in the gun mouth": Race, class and political violence in Guyana. *Nieuwe West Indische Gids* 69 : 223–53.

Smith, Timothy L. 1957. *Revivalism and social reform in mid-nineteenth century America*. New York: Abingdon.

Smith, William Robertson. 1959. *Religion of the Semites: The fundamental institutions*. New York: Meridian Books.

Sobel, Mechal. 1988. *Trablin' on: The slave journey to an Afro-Baptist faith*. Princeton: Princeton Univ. Press.

Sobo, Elisa Janine. 1993. *One blood: The Jamaican body*. Albany: State Univ. of New York Press.

Sombart, Werner. 1906. *Das Proletariat*. Frankfurt: Rutten und Loening.

Spinner, Alice. 1896. *A reluctant evangelist and other stories*. London: Edward Arnold.

Sternberg, Meir. 1987. *The poetics of biblical narrative: Ideological literature and the drama of reading*. Bloomington: Indiana Univ.Press.

Stewart, John. 1969 [1823]. *A view of the past and present state of the island of Jamaica*. Westport: Negro Universities Press.

Stewart, Robert J. 1983. Religion and society in Jamaica, 1831–1880. Ph.D. dissertation. Department of History, Univ. of the West Indies.

———. 1992. *Religion and society in post-emancipation Jamaica*. Knoxville: Univ. of Tennessee Press.

Stone, Carl. 1991. Rethinking development: The role of the state in Third World development. in *Rethinking development,* ed. J. Wedderburn, 87–100. Kingston: Consortium Graduate School of Social Science.

Stone, James. 1977. *The Church of God of Prophecy: History and polity*. Cleveland, Tenn.: White Wing Publishing.

Sundkler, Bengt G. M. 1961. *Bantu prophets in South Africa*, 2nd ed. London: Oxford Univ. Press.

Sutton, Constance R., and E. M. Chaney, eds. 1987. *Caribbean life in New York City*. New York: Center for Migration Studies.

Sweet, William W. 1944. *Revivalism in America*. New York: Charles Scribner's Sons.

Synan, Vinson. 1971. *The Holiness-Pentecostal movement in the United States*. Grand Rapids, Mich.: Eerdmans.

———. 1973. *The old-time religion: A history of the Pentecostal Holiness Church*. Franklin Springs, Ga.: Advocate Press.

Tait, David. 1967. Konkomba sorcery. In *Magic, witchcraft and curing*, ed. J. Middleton, 155–70. Garden City, N.Y.: Natural History Press.

Tanna, Laura. 1984. *Jamaican folk tales and oral history*. Kingston: Institute of Jamaica Publications.

Taussig, Michael. 1984. History as sorcery. *Representations*. Summer:87–108.

———. 1987a. *Shamanism, colonialism and the wild man: A study in terror and healing*. Chicago: Univ. of Chicago Press.

———. 1987b. History as commodity in some recent (anthropological) literature. *Food and Foodways* 2:151–69.

Tawney, Richard H. 1926. *Religion and the rise of capitalism*. London: J. Murray.

Taylor, Charles. 1985. The person. In *The category of the person: Anthropology, philosophy, history*, ed. M. Carrithers, S. Collins, and S. Lukes, 257–81. Cambridge: Cambridge Univ. Press.

———. 1986. Foucault on freedom and truth. In *Foucault: A critical reader*, ed. D. C. Hoy, 69–102. Oxford and New York: Basil Blackwell.

———. 1989. *Sources of the self: The making of the modern identity*. Cambridge: Harvard Univ. Press.

———. 1991. *The ethics of authenticity*. Cambridge and London: Harvard Univ. Press.

———. 1994. *Multiculturalism: Examining the politics of recognition*. Princeton: Princeton Univ. Press.

Taylor, S. A. G. 1976. *A short history of Clarendon*. Jamaica: Ministry of Education, Publications Branch.

Thompson, Edward P. 1963. *The making of the English working class*. London: Gollancz.

Thomas, Keith. 1973. *Religion and the decline of magic*. Harmondsworth: Penguin.

Thornton, Robert J. 1992. The rhetoric of ethnographic holism. In *Rereading cultural anthropology*, ed. George Marcus, 15–33. Durham and London: Duke Univ. Press.

Timpson, George F. 1938. *Jamaican interlude*. London: Ed. J. Burrow.

Titon, Jeff T. 1988. *Powerhouse of God: Speech, chant and song in an Appalachian Baptist church*. Austin: Univ. of Texas Press.

Tocqueville, Alexis de. 1945 [1835, 1840]. *Democracy in America*, Vols. 1 and 2. New York: Vintage Books.

Torbet, Robert G. 1950. *A history of the Baptists*. Philadelphia: Judsen Press.

Troeltsch, Ernst. 1912. *Protestantism and progress*. Trans. W. Montgomery. New York: G. P. Putnam's Sons.

———. 1949. *The social teachings of the Christian churches and groups,* Vol. 2. Trans. W. Montgomery. New York: G. P. Putnam's Sons.

Trouillot, Michel-Rolph. 1988. *Peasants and capital: Dominica in the world economy.* Baltimore: Johns Hopkins Univ. Press.

———. 1990. *Haiti: State against nation: The origins and legacy of Duvalierism.* New York: Monthly Review Press.

———. 1992. The Caribbean region: An open frontier in anthropological theory. *Annual Reviews in Anthropology* 21:19–42.

Turner, Mary. 1982. *Slaves and missionaries: The disintegration of Jamaican slave society, 1787–1834.* Urbana: Univ. of Illinois Press.

Turner, Terence. 1988. Ethno-ethnohistory: Myth and history in Native South American representations of contact with Western society. In *Rethinking history and myth: Indigenous South American perspectives on the past,* ed. J. Hill, 235–81. Urbana and Chicago: Univ. of Illinois Press.

———. 1994. Anthropology and multiculturalism. *Cultural Anthropology* 8:411–29.

Turner, Victor. 1967. *The forest of symbols: Aspects of Ndembu ritual.* Ithaca: Cornell Univ. Press.

———. 1968. *The drums of affliction.* Oxford: Clarendon Press and International African Institute.

———. 1969. *The ritual process.* Chicago: Aldine.

Underhill, Edward B. 1862. *The West Indies: Their social and religious condition.* London: Jackson, Walford and Hodder.

———. 1867. *Dr. Underhill's letter.* London: Arthur Miall.

———. 1879. *The Jamaica mission in its relations with the Baptist Missionary Society, from 1838–1879.* London: Western Sub-Committee of the Baptist Missionary Society.

———. 1881. *Life of James Mursell Phillippo, missionary in Jamaica.* London: Yates and Alexander; E. Marlborough.

Van Gennep, Arnold. 1960 [1909]. *The rites of passage.* Chicago: Univ. of Chicago Press.

Waddell, Rev. Hope M. 1970 [1863]. *Twenty-nine years in the West Indies and Central Africa: A review of missionary work and adventure, 1829–1858.* London: Frank Cass.

Walcott, Derek. 1974. The muse of history. In *Is Massa Day dead?* ed. O. Coombs, 1–27. Garden City, N.Y.: Anchor Press, Doubleday.

Ward, Colleen. 1979–80. Therapeutic aspects of ritual trance: The Shango cult of Trinidad. *Journal of Altered States of Consciousness* 5, no. 1:19–29.

Ward, Colleen, and Michael H. Beaubrun. 1980. The psychodynamics of demon possession. *Journal for the Scientific Study of Religion* 19, no. 2:201–7.

Weber, Max. 1958. *The Protestant ethic and the spirit of capitalism.* Trans. T. Parsons. New York: Scribner's.

———. 1964. *The sociology of religion.* Trans. E. Fischoff. Boston: Beacon Press.

———. 1968. *Economy and society.* New York: Bedminster Press.

Wedenoja, William. 1978. *Religion and adaptation in rural Jamaica.* Unpublished Ph.D. dissertation. Univ. of California, San Diego.

———. 1980. Modernization and the Pentecostal movement. In *Perspectives on Pentecostalism,* 27–48. Washington: Univ. Press of America.

Whiteley, William T. 1932. *A history of British Baptists*, 2nd ed. London: Chas. Griffin.

Williams, Brackette F. 1991. *Stains on my name, war in my veins*. Durham and London: Duke Univ. Press.

Williams, Charles G. 1975. Glossolalia as a religious phenomenon: "Tongues" at Corinth and Pentecost. *Religion* 5, no. 1: 16–32.

Williams, Eric. 1944. *Capitalism and slavery*. Chapel Hill: Univ. of North Carolina Press.

Williams, Joseph J. 1934. *Psychic phenomena in Jamaica*. New York: Dial Press.

Williams, Melvin.D. 1974. *Community in a black Pentecostal church: An anthropological study*. Pittsburgh: Univ. of Pittsburgh Press.

Wilmott, Swithin. 1985. From Falmouth to Morant Bay: Religion and politics in Jamaica, 1838–1865. In *Religion and society*, ed. B. Higman, 1–18. Mona: Department of History, Univ. of the West Indies.

Wilmott, Swithin. 1986. Baptist missionaries and Jamaican politics, 1838–1854. In *A selection of papers, twelfth conference of the Association of Caribbean Historians*, ed. K. O. Laurence, 45–62. St. Augustine: Association of Caribbean Historians.

Wilson, Bryan R. 1961. *Sects and society*. London and Berkeley: Heinemann and Univ. of California Press.

———. 1975. *Magic and the millennium*. Frogmore: Paladin.

Wilson, Monica H. 1970. Witch-beliefs and social structure. In *Witchcraft and sorcery*, ed. M. Marwick, 252–63. Harmondsworth: Penguin Books.

Wilson, Peter. 1973. *Crab antics: A social anthropology of English-speaking Negro societies in the Caribbean*. New Haven: Yale Univ. Press.

Winkler, Anthony C. 1995. *Going home to teach*. Kingston: Kingston Publishers.

Wittgenstein, Ludwig. 1968. *Philosophical investigations*. Trans. Elizabeth Anscombe. Oxford: Blackwell.

Wright, Philip, ed. 1966. *Lady Nugent's journal of her residence in Jamaica from 1801–1805*. Kingston: Institute of Jamaica.

Wright, Philip. 1973. *Knibb "the Notorious": Slaves' missionary 1803–1845*. London: Sidgwick and Jackson.

Yinger, John M. 1946. *Religion and the struggle for power*. Durham: Duke Univ. Press.

INDEX

297